HUMAN RIGHTS, STATE COMPLIANCE, AND SOCIAL CHANGE

National human rights institutions (NHRIs) – human rights commissions and ombudsmen – have gained recognition as a possible missing link in the transmission and implementation of international human rights norms at the domestic level. They are also increasingly accepted as important participants in global and regional forums where international norms are produced.

By collecting innovative work from experts spanning international law, political science, sociology, and human rights practice, this book critically examines the significance of this relatively new class of organizations. It focuses, in particular, on the prospects of these institutions to effectuate state compliance and social change. Consideration is given to the role of NHRIs in delegitimizing – though sometimes legitimizing – governments' poor human rights records and in mobilizing – though sometimes demobilizing – civil society actors. The volume underscores the broader implications of such crosscutting research for scholarship and practice in the fields of human rights and global affairs in general.

Ryan Goodman is the Anne and Joel Ehrenkranz Professor of Law and chair of the Center for Human Rights and Global Justice at New York University Law School, and professor of politics and sociology at New York University. He was previously the Rita E. Hauser Professor of Human Rights and Humanitarian Law and director of the Human Rights Program at Harvard Law School. His publications include *International Human Rights in Context* (with Henry Steiner and Philip Alston), *Socializing States: Promoting Human Rights through International Law* (with Derek Jinks), and *Understanding Social Action, Promoting Human Rights* (with Derek Jinks and Andrew Woods).

Thomas Pegram is Assistant Professor in Political Science (International Relations) at the Department of Political Science, Trinity College Dublin. Previously, he was a Research Fellow at New York University School of Law with a focus on the interdisciplinary study of national human rights institutions (NHRIs) and international law, including human rights and humanitarian law. He was the NHRI Fellow of Harvard Law School's Human Rights Program from 2008 to 2009. His recent publications have appeared in *Human Rights Quarterly, Oxford Development Studies*, and the *Cambridge Journal of Latin American Studies*.

Human Rights, State Compliance, and Social Change

ASSESSING NATIONAL HUMAN RIGHTS INSTITUTIONS

Editors

RYAN GOODMAN

New York University School of Law

THOMAS PEGRAM

Trinity College, Dublin

CAMBRIDGE
UNIVERSITY PRESS

CAMBRIDGE UNIVERSITY PRESS
Cambridge, New York, Melbourne, Madrid, Cape Town,
Singapore, São Paulo, Delhi, Tokyo, Mexico City

Cambridge University Press
32 Avenue of the Americas, New York, NY 10013-2473, USA

www.cambridge.org
Information on this title: www.cambridge.org/9780521150170

© Cambridge University Press 2012

First published 2012

Printed in the United States of America

A catalog record for this publication is available from the British Library.

Library of Congress Cataloging in Publication data
Human rights, state compliance, and social change : assessing national human rights
institutions / [edited by] Ryan Goodman, Thomas Pegram.
    p.   cm.
Includes bibliographical references and index.
ISBN 978-0-521-76175-8 (hardback) – ISBN 978-0-521-15017-0 (paperback)
1. National human rights institutions.   2. Human rights.   3. International law.
I. Goodman, Ryan.   II. Pegram, Thomas Innes, 1980–
K3240.H8588   2011
341.4'8–dc23   2011025632

ISBN 978-0-521-76175-8 Hardback
ISBN 978-0-521-15017-0 Paperback

Contents

Contributors

Sonia Cardenas is associate professor of political science and director of the Human Rights Program at Trinity College in Hartford, Connecticut. She is the author of *Conflict and Compliance: State Responses to International Human Rights Pressure* (University of Pennsylvania Press, 2007); and *Chains of Justice: The Global Rise of State Institutions for Human Rights* (University of Pennsylvania Press, 2011). Her research in this area has appeared in edited volumes and journals, including *Global Governance, Human Rights Quarterly, Human Rights Review, International Political Science Review*, and *Middle East Journal*.

Richard Carver is associate lecturer, Centre for Development and Emergency Practice, Oxford Brookes University and a long-time British human rights activist, formerly of Amnesty International and the freedom of expression NGO, Article 19. He is the author of various books and articles on the work of NHRIs including *Performance and Legitimacy: National Human Rights Institutions* (International Council on Human Rights Policy, 2000); *Assessing the Effectiveness of National Human Rights Institutions* (International Council on Human Rights Policy, 2005); and (with Paul Hunt) "National Human Rights Institutions in Africa," in Kamal Hossain (ed.), *Human Rights Commissions and Ombudsman Offices: National Experiences throughout the World* (Brill, 2000).

Kieren Fitzpatrick has been the director of the Asia Pacific Form Secretariat since its inception in 1996. The APF is one of the most developed of the four regional networks of NHRIs operating in the world. Currently, the APF is made up of fourteen full-member institutions and three associate members stretching from Palestine in the west, across Asia, and down to the Pacific. His publications include "The Asia Pacific Forum: A Partnership for Regional Human Rights Cooperation," in B. Lindsnaes et al. (eds.), *National Human Rights Institutions: Articles and Working Papers* (Danish Centre for Human Rights, 2001).

Ryan Goodman is Anne and Joel Ehrenkranz Professor of Law and cochair of the Center for Human Rights and Global Justice at New York University School of Law. He is also professor of politics and professor of sociology at NYU. Previously, he was the inaugural Rita E. Hauser Professor of Human Rights and Humanitarian Law, and the director of the Human Rights Program at Harvard Law School. His publications include (with Philip Alston and Henry Steiner) *International Human Rights in Context: Law, Politics, Morals*, 3rd ed. (Oxford University Press, 2007); (with Derek Jinks) *Socializing States: Promoting Human Rights through International Law* (Oxford University Press: forthcoming 2011); and (with Derek Jinks and Andrew K. Woods), *Understanding Social Action, Promoting Human Rights* (Oxford University Press: forthcoming 2011).

Julie Mertus is associate professor and codirector of the MA program in Ethics, Peace, and Global Affairs at American University. Her seven books include *Bait and Switch: Human Rights and U.S. Foreign Policy* (Routledge Press, 2004); and *Human Rights Matters: Local Politics and National Human Rights Institutions* (Stanford University Press, 2009). The former was named Human Rights Book of the Year by the American Political Science Association Human Rights Section.

David S. Meyer is professor of sociology, political science, and planning, policy, and design at UC Irvine. His general areas of interest include social movements, political sociology, and public policy, and he is most directly concerned with the relationships between social movements and the political contexts in which they emerge. Recent publications include *The Politics of Protest: Social Movements in America* (Oxford University Press, 2007); and (with V. Jenness, and H. Ingram, eds.) *Routing the Opposition: Social Movements, Public Policy, and Democracy in America* (University of Minnesota Press, 2005).

Obiora Chinedu Okafor is a professor at Osgoode Hall Law School and has held faculty positions at the University of Nigeria and Carleton University. He has served as an SSRC MacArthur Foundation Visiting Scholar at Harvard Law School's Human Rights Program and was recently named a Canada-US Fulbright Scholar at MIT. He has published extensively in the fields of international human rights law and refugee law, as well as general public international law. His publications include *The African Human Rights System: Activist Forces and International Institutions* (Cambridge University Press, 2007); and *Legitimizing Human Rights NGOs: Lessons from Nigeria* (Africa World Press, 2006).

Thomas Pegram is Assistant Professor in Political Science (International Relations) at the Department of Political Science, Trinity College Dublin. He has held research fellowships at New York University School of Law and Harvard Law School's Human Rights Program. He holds a D.Phil. in political science from Nuffield College,

University of Oxford. His most recent publications include "Weak Institutions, Rights Claims and Pathways to Compliance: The Transformative Role of the Peruvian Human Rights Ombudsman," *Oxford Development Studies* vol. 39, 2011; "Diffusion across Political Systems: The Global Spread of National Human Rights Institutions," *Human Rights Quarterly*, vol. 32, 2010; and "Accountability in Hostile Times: The Case of the Peruvian Human Rights Ombudsman 1996–2001," *Journal of Latin American Studies*, vol. 40, 2008.

Enrique Peruzzotti is associate professor of political science and international relations at Torcuato Di Tella University in Buenos Aires. He has taught courses on political science, sociology, and Latin American Studies at universities around the world, including the University of Buenos Aires, of Minas Gerais, FLACSO Ecuador, Cornell University, and the American University in Paris. His publications include (with Catalina Smulovitz, eds.), *Enforcing the Rule of Law: Social Accountability in the New Latin American Democracies* (University of Pittsburgh, 2006); and (with Jean Grugel), "Grounding Global Norms in Domestic Politics: Advocacy Coalitions and the Convention on the Rights of the Child in Argentina," *Journal of Latin American Studies*, vol. 42, 2010. He was a Reagan-Fascell Fellow at the National Endowment for Democracy in Washington DC through 2009 and 2010.

Linda C. Reif, University of Windsor (LL.B., 1982), University of Cambridge (LL.M., 1985) is associate dean (Graduate Studies) and faculty of law at the University of Alberta, Canada. She has published widely on national human rights institutions (NHRIs), including *The Ombudsman, Good Governance and the International Human Rights System* (Martinus Nijhoff Publishers, 2004); and "Building Democratic Institutions: The Role of National Human Rights Institutions in Good Governance and Human Rights Protection," *Harvard Human Rights Journal*, vol. 13, 2000. Professor Reif was editor of publications, International Ombudsman Institute, from 1989 to 2009, editing *The International Ombudsman Yearbook*.

Catherine Renshaw is a research fellow at the Australian Human Rights Centre, faculty of law, University of New South Wales, and director of the Centre's project on National Human Rights Institutions in the Asia Pacific. Recent publications include (with Andrew Byrnes and Andrea Durbach), "Joining the club: the Asia Pacific Forum of National Human Rights Institutions, the Paris Principles, and the advancement of human rights protection in the region," *Australian Journal of Human Rights*, vol. 14, 2009; and (with Andrew Byrnes and Andrea Durbach), "A Tongue But no Teeth? The Emergence of a New Human Rights Mechanism in the Asia Pacific Region," *Sydney Law Review*, vol. 31, 2009.

Peter Rosenblum is the Lieff, Cabraser, Heimann & Bernstein Clinical Professor of Human Rights Law at Columbia University Law School. Previously, he served as associate and clinical director of the Human Rights Program at Harvard. He has also worked within the Office of the UN High Commissioner for Human Rights and as a researcher for Human Rights Watch and the Lawyers' Committee for Human Rights. He has engaged in human rights research and field missions in Africa, Eastern Europe, and Asia. His recent writing addresses human rights topics affecting Africa and human rights pedagogy in the United States. His publications include *Human Rights Watch, Protectors or Pretenders? Government Human Rights Commissions in Africa* (Human Rights Watch, 2001).

Chris Sidoti is an adjunct professor at the University of Western Sydney, Sydney, Australia. He is a human rights lawyer, activist, and teacher. He currently works from Sydney, Australia, as an international human rights consultant, specializing in the international human rights system and in national human rights institutions. He was director of the International Service for Human Rights, based in Geneva, Switzerland, from 2003 to 2007. He has been Australian Human Rights Commissioner (1995–2000), Australian Law Reform Commissioner (1992–1995), and Foundation Director of the Australian Human Rights and Equal Opportunity Commission (1987–1992). In 2007–08 he was the independent chair of the United Kingdom Government's Northern Ireland Bill of Rights Forum.

Fredrik Uggla is currently associate researcher at Department of Government, Uppsala University, Sweden. He holds a Ph.D. in political science and is a former senior associate member at St. Antony's College, University of Oxford. His publications include "The Ombudsman in Latin America," *Journal of Latin American Studies*, vol. 36, 2004.

Preface

National human rights institutions (NHRIs) are no longer the institutional oddity they were only ten or fifteen years ago. The speed with which they have moved from the periphery to the central arena of human rights politics – international and domestic – is largely unprecedented. This book is an attempt to take stock of the extraordinary proliferation and growing significance of NHRIs, as the first phase of international promotion and proliferation gives way to a second one of organizational consolidation and outward projection in shaping new human rights norms. The book also uses NHRIs as a lens to examine broader questions about human rights and the diffusion of international norms. With a diverse array of contributors, we explore these subjects from multiple disciplinary perspectives, professional experiences, and geographical areas of expertise.

The idea for this volume emerged out of a series of conferences, lectures, and fellowships convened by the Human Rights Program, Harvard Law School, during the period that Ryan Goodman served as director of the program. A goal of those initiatives was to enhance the study and practice of these novel institutions and develop linkages between legal and social science scholars, policy makers, and practitioners. Conferences held in June 2007 and May 2008 convened an array of scholars and practitioners from around the world to share their insights and experiences working from within and outside NHRIs. Crucial input was received from many people at these various conferences, meetings, and related lecture series. In particular, we wish to thank Emilio Álvarez Icaza Longoria, Raymond Atuguba, William Binchy, Brian Burdekin, Andrew Byrnes, James Cavallaro, Hyo-Je Cho, Andrew Clapham, Jorge Contesse, Brice Dickson, Raquel Dodge, Martin Flaherty, Diego García Sayán, Tyler Giannini, Mario Gomez, Niels Erik Hansen, Maina Kiai, Ifdahl Kasim, Morten Kjærum, C. Raj Kumar, Katerina Linos, Jennifer Lynch, Gianni Magazzeni, Mohamed Mahmoud Mohamedou, Rashida Manjoo, Maurice Manning, Ravi Nair, Binaifer Nowrojee, Michael O'Flaherty, Sharanjeet Parmar, Gerard Quinn, Mindy Roseman, Eric Rosenthal, Sima Samar, Miguel Sarre,

Margaret Sekaggya, Emile Short, Sébastien Sigouin, Vijayashri Sripati, Michael Stein, Chris Stone, Tseliso Thipanyane, Sergiu Troie, Andrew Woods, and David Zionts, in addition to the contributors to the present volume.

These early conferences, lectures, and research laid the groundwork for the book project. Those initiatives helped to identify gaps in the literature and the most important questions for the study of NHRIs. At the time, the Harvard program recruited Thomas Pegram, in November 2008, tasked with the development of a broader project related to a more general examination of NHRIs, their successes, and ongoing challenges in different political contexts. Pegram, a political scientist with a position inside a law school, brought a social science expertise on institutional analysis and a particular interest in the political accountability functions of NHRIs in the democratizing political systems of Latin America. The project also included the development of linkages with the International Coordinating Committee of National Institutions for the Promotion and Protection of Human Rights (ICC), and participation at ICC meetings held in Geneva, Nairobi, and Rabat. We owe a debt of gratitude to Gianni Magazzeni, then head of the National Institutions and Regional Mechanisms Section of the Office of the UN High Commissioner for Human Rights, for facilitating our work and participation at those events.

The volume chapters, in particular, are the culmination of a conference convened jointly by Harvard Law School's Human Rights Program and New York University School of Law's Center for Human Rights and Global Justice in September 2009. Development of our own conceptual and theoretical ideas about NHRIs was greatly informed by the insights generated at this workshop where initial drafts of the chapters were presented. We accordingly thank participants Sonia Cardenas, Richard Carver, Jim Cavallero, Chris Elmendorf, Kieren Fitzpatrick, Julie Mertus, David S. Meyer, Obiora C. Okafor, Enrique Peruzzotti, Linda C. Reif, Catherine Renshaw, Mindy Roseman, Peter Rosenblum, Chris Sidoti, and Mark Ungar. In addition, exceptionally useful suggestions were received from Laurence Whitehead in the process of steering Thomas toward the successful completion of his Ph.D. We thank the anonymous reviewers from Cambridge University Press for constructive suggestions. We are also deeply grateful to John Berger at Cambridge for his assistance throughout the production process.

Introduction

National Human Rights Institutions, State Conformity, and Social Change

Ryan Goodman and Thomas Pegram

1.1. INTRODUCTION

Over the past twenty years national human rights commissions and human rights ombudsmen have emerged in every continent and subregion of the world, and in dozens of democratic and dozens of undemocratic states alike. This institutional innovation – a "national human rights institution" (NHRI) in UN parlance – is broadly defined as "a body which is established by a government under the constitution, or by law or decree, the functions of which are specifically designed in terms of the promotion and protection of human rights."[1] Accounts of the number of NHRIs now in existence vary from around 120 to 178, established in approximately 130 countries.[2] By conservative measures, since 1990 the population of NHRIs has witnessed a staggering fifteen-fold increase (at the rate of over five new institutions established per year).[3]

The proliferation of NHRIs is part of a broader trend driven by international actors that promote the diffusion of legal and institutional innovations across national boundaries.[4] Beyond the question of why governments create NHRIs, this

[1] United Nations, *National Human Rights Institutions: A Handbook on the Establishment and Strengthening of National Institutions for the Promotion and Protection of Human Rights* (New York: United Nations, 1995), 6; see also R. Carver, *Performance and Legitimacy: National Human Rights Institutions* (Versoix: International Council for Human Rights Policy [hereafter ICHRP], 2000), 3 (defining an NHRI as "a quasi-governmental or statutory institution with human rights in its mandate").

[2] For NHRI population data, see International Coordinating Committee of National Institutions for the Promotion and Protection of Human Rights: http://www.nhri.net/; Jeong-Woo Koo and Francisco O. Ramirez, "National Incorporation of Global Human Rights: Worldwide Expansion of National Human Rights Institutions, 1966–2004," *Social Forces* 87 (2009), 1326.

[3] M. Kjaerum, *National Human Rights Institutions: Implementing Human Rights* (Copenhagen: Danish Institute for Human Rights, 2003), 5.

[4] See, for example, B. Simmons, F. Dobbin, and G. Garrett, *The Global Diffusion of Markets and Democracy* (Cambridge: Cambridge University Press, 2008); Ryan Goodman and Derek Jinks, "How

volume builds on existing scholarship by inquiring into why NHRIs matter, how they operate in practice, and, crucially, under what conditions they can effectuate compliance with human rights standards and bring about social change.

The relationship between NHRIs and the global order is multidimensional. NHRIs first gained recognition as potentially important links in the transmission of human rights norms from the international to the domestic level.[5] And the activities of NHRIs along that track have accelerated in recent years. The Universal Periodic Review of state practices by the UN Human Rights Council routinely involves governments' encouraging other governments to establish an NHRI if such an institution does not yet exist in the country. Two of the twenty-first century's first human rights treaties – the Optional Protocol to the Torture Convention and the Convention on the Rights of Persons with Disabilities – create an unprecedented role for NHRIs in monitoring and implementing multilateral treaty obligations.[6] In addition, the UN human rights treaty bodies have begun to rely increasingly on the work of NHRIs in reviewing state reports of compliance, and UN officials increasingly call on NHRIs to address specific subject matters such as multinational corporations and economic and social rights. In short, NHRIs are becoming instrumental in the transmission of human rights norms into domestic systems and ensuring national compliance with global standards.

NHRIs have also emerged as important actors in shaping human rights norms at the international level – both global and regional. Organized as a unified coalition in treaty negotiations, NHRIs from across the world played a significant role in drafting the Disability Rights Convention. They were also directly involved in the negotiations of the UN Declaration on the Rights of Indigenous People (Sidoti,

---

to Influence States: Socialization and International Law," *Duke Law Journal* 54 (2004), 621–703; R. Goodman and D. Jinks, *Socializing States: Promoting Human Rights Through International Law* (Oxford University Press: forthcoming); Daniel W. Drezner, "Globalization and Policy Convergence," *International Studies Review* 3 (2001), 53–78.

5   For recent UN recognition, see Report of the Secretary-General to the General Assembly, "National Institutions for the Promotion and Protection of Human Rights," UN Doc. No.: A/64/320, 24 August 2009; also UN General Assembly, "The Role of the Ombudsman, Mediator and Other National Human Rights Institutions in the Promotion and Protection of Human Rights," UNGA Res.A/RES/63/169, 20 March 2009; UN General Assembly, "National Institutions for the Promotion and Protection of Human Rights," UNGA Res.: A/RES/63/172, 20 March 2009. For practitioner and legal analysis of NHRIs see, for example, K. Hossain (ed.), *Human Rights Commissions and Ombudsman Offices: National Experiences throughout the World* (Boston: Brill, 2000); R. Gregory and P. Giddings (eds.), *Righting Wrongs: The Ombudsman in Six Continents* (Oxford: IOS Press, 2000); and L. Reif, *The Ombudsman, Good Governance and the International Human Rights System* (Leiden: Martinus Nijhoff, 2004).

6   For a recent discussion of these developments and their prospects for closing the compliance gap, see Richard Carver, "A New Answer to an Old Question: National Human Rights Institutions and the Domestication of International Law," *Human Rights Law Review* 10 (2010), 1–32.

this volume). NHRIs have a formal seat at the table of the UN Human Rights Council, providing them with an opportunity to contribute to standard setting and the development of human rights norms at the global level. And NHRIs, organized in regional associations, have also begun to shape international standards. Consider, for example, pathbreaking work on sexual orientation and gender identity by the Asia Pacific Forum of National Human Rights Institutions. Indeed, acting as a group, these institutions may be more willing to push the frontiers of human rights norms than acting separately or alone.

Despite the growing profile of NHRIs in world politics, cross-fertilization of NHRI research across academic disciplines has only just begun.[7] Situating the work of NHRIs within the framework of state compliance and social change, our volume responds to a number of converging developments. The disjuncture between human rights ideals and political reality on the ground presents a direct challenge to the aspirational claim of universal human rights.[8] In response to this compliance gap, institutional mechanisms dedicated to the promotion of human rights norms at the national level have begun to move from the periphery to the center of discussion. By bridging legal scholarship with social science concerns of political contestation and norm diffusion, this book provides a platform for generating new insights and rendering this interdisciplinary knowledge available to a wider community of academics, policy makers, and practitioners.

If the presence of NHRIs in the international human rights regime is becoming a settled fact, the significance of this new class of formal organizations is still undertheorized and not well understood. This lacuna is due, in part, to the recent nature of the NHRI surge. Early debate on the merits of NHRI formation commonly veered between dismissive critique and unmitigated support. Neither position was strongly established in evidence.[9] And the early literature focused on very general trends of diffusion and exceedingly formal features in the design of institutions. Notwithstanding these limitations, a first generation of NHRI scholarship has produced some valuable insights into why and under what conditions human rights institutions are created by states.[10]

---

[7] See J. Mertus, *Human Rights Matters: Local Politics and National Human Rights Institutions* (Stanford: Stanford University Press, 2009); S. Cardenas, *Conflict and Compliance: State Responses to International Human Rights Pressure* (Philadelphia: University of Pennsylvania Press, 2007).

[8] See Oona Hathaway, "Do Human Rights Treaties Make a Difference?" *Yale Law Journal* 111 (2002), 1935–2042.

[9] Ian Scott, "The Functions of the Ombudsman in Underdeveloped Countries," *International Review of Administrative Sciences* 50 (1984), 212–20.

[10] See Sonia Cardenas, "Emerging Global Actors: The United Nations and National Human Rights Institutions," *Global Governance* 9 (2003), 23–42; Jeong-Woo Koo and Francisco O. Ramirez, "National Incorporation of Global Human Rights: Worldwide Expansion of National Human Rights Institutions, 1966–2004," *Social Forces* 87 (2009), 1321–54.

Less attention, however, has been given to important areas of variation, such as divergent outcomes at the regional and subregional level, and unanticipated consequences of NHRI creation in particular domestic settings. For instance, the creation of an NHRI may have perverse effects – in some cases, actively undermining domestic rights frameworks and risking cooptation by a liberal state. Even the well-motivated establishment of an NHRI can unintentionally crowd out other domestic actors, draining them of political and economic resources (in this volume, Pegram, Chapter 9; Meyer, Chapter 13; Rosenblum, Chapter 12). It is important to consider such effects to gain an understanding of the power and potential of NHRIs in different domestic contexts.

This volume is accordingly in conversation with an emergent "second generation" of interdisciplinary NHRI research.[11] We focus, in particular, on the role of these institutions in state compliance with international human rights norms as well as their role in socialization of domestic actors and institutions. Three principal objectives motivate this study: (1) to contribute to the general literature concerning the transmission of human rights norms between the international and domestic levels; (2) to provide a forum in which interdisciplinary scholars and reflective practitioners can analyze new theoretical and empirical insights related to NHRIs; and (3) to reach some conclusions about the performance and effects of NHRIs within different regional and national settings. Our objective is *not* to reify "a theory of NHRIs" that aspires to a definitive account of their impact upon international and domestic politics. Notwithstanding the challenges inherent in such a task, the nascent state of the academic literature and the rapid proliferation and complexity of NHRIs in real time cautions against imposing too ambitious an agenda. Rather, this book encourages direct engagement with some of the assumptions, claims, and counterclaims that underlie current thinking on NHRIs. It also provides greater insight into the conditions under which NHRIs are more or less effective in promoting human rights.

Under this broad heading, several topics are addressed by the various authors contributing to the book. Broadly conceived, these topics include the definition of NHRIs (Mertus, Reif, and Sidoti), pathways of NHRI diffusion (Cardenas), the conditions for generating NHRI effectiveness (Cardenas, Carver, Reif, and Mertus),[12]

---

[11] See Mertus, *Human Rights Matters*; Cardenas, *Conflict and Compliance*; Obiora C. Okafor and Shedrack C. Agbakwa, "On Legalism, Popular Agency and 'Voices of Suffering': The Nigerian National Human Rights Commission in Context," *Human Rights Quarterly* 24 (2002), 662–720; Thomas Pegram, "Accountability in Hostile Times: The Case of the Peruvian Human Rights Ombudsman 1996–2001," *Journal of Latin American Studies* 40 (2008), 51–82; Fredrik Uggla, "The Ombudsman in Latin America," *Journal of Latin American Studies* 36 (2004), 423–50.

[12] Discussion on NHRI effectiveness has received sustained attention within both academic and policy circles. This discussion marks a departure from earlier contributions, which focused more narrowly on the legal form of NHRIs. Important initial advances in descriptive accounts can be found in

and the embeddedness of NHRIs within the United Nations and other global institutions (Carver and Sidoti). Further contributions reflect on political accountability and informal powers of NHRIs (Pegram, Peruzzotti, and Uggla) as well as relationships between NHRIs and social movements and advocacy networks (Okafor, Meyer, and Rosenblum). The volume also addresses important variation at the regional and domestic level. The contributions include analysis of the growing importance of regional networks of state and nonstate actors in the Asia Pacific region (Renshaw and Fitzpatrick), and features of NHRIs in Central and Eastern Europe (Carver), Latin America (Pegram), and Africa (Okafor).

1.2. SETTING THE AGENDA

In the following discussion, we reflect on three themes that run throughout the volume. We elaborate upon their significance for the study of NHRIs and human rights more generally. Each of these themes recurs in separate chapters. A consensus among the contributors emerges with respect to some issues. Productive disagreement characterizes the rest. We explain the significance of major points of agreement and disagreement with respect to the three themes.

1.2.1. *Refining the Concept of NHRIs*

Debate surrounding the definitional boundaries of NHRIs is addressed, explicitly and implicitly, by a number of contributions in this volume. Despite a growing body of academic interest and empirical research on NHRIs, these organizations remain underconceptualized and ill-defined. This volume does not attempt to close those gaps authoritatively. We, however, seek to refine the terms of debate and to forge greater understanding of the underlying points of disagreement over defining, more or less broadly, what has become something of a term of art.

The current departure point for discussion of NHRIs is the Paris Principles, devised in 1991 and adopted by the UN General Assembly in 1993.[13] The Principles reflect the codification of decades of intermittent attention to analogous entities, and they ultimately provide an internationally recognized standard for such institutions. However, as Linda Reif notes in this volume, the Paris Principles do not

R. Carver, *Performance and Legitimacy: National Human Rights Institutions* (Versoix: ICHRP, 2000); L. Reif, *The Ombudsman, Good Governance and the International Human Rights System* (Leiden: Martinus Nijhoff, 2004); R. Carver, *Assessing the Effectiveness of National Human Rights Institutions* (Geneva: UNHCR ICHRP, 2005); Rachel Murray, "National Human Rights Institutions: Criteria and Factors for Assessing Their Effectiveness," *Netherlands Quarterly of Human Rights* 25 (2007), 189–220.

[13] "Principles Relating to the Status of National Institutions," UNGA Res. 48/134, UN Doc.A/RES/48/134 (1993), art. 1.

contain a definition of an NHRI, and only refer to the basic functional principle that "[a] national institution shall be vested with competence to promote and protect human rights."[14] Reif proceeds to map different models of NHRIs. Through her contribution and others, the volume enhances the conceptual and terminological precision concerning two types of NHRIs – (1) multimember commissions and (2) ombudsmen – while also highlighting the increasingly blurred lines between these models. Importantly, the book also explores the "politics of re-defining NHRIs." That is, the volume examines the benefits and hazards in refining the concept of NHRIs through formal or informal modifications of the Paris Principles.

Indeed, considerable attention has focused on the limitations of the Paris Principles as a formal marker of the standards that an NHRI ought to meet. In a pioneering study, Richard Carver characterizes the Principles as a "vital reference point," but nevertheless notes that "they are curiously inadequate in a somewhat paradoxical way."[15] That is, the Principles demand too much and too little. Carver observes:

> On the one hand [the Paris Principles] lay down a maximum programme that is met by hardly any national institution in the world…. On the other hand, the Paris Principles do not even take it as given that a national institution will deal with individual complaints, which most observers and practitioners in this field would probably regard as an essential characteristic.[16]

Carver's observation is recast and developed in his own contribution to this book, among others.

Dissatisfaction with the Paris Principles is not confined to academics and outside observers. Certainly the most explicit criticisms of the Paris Principles have emerged from human rights nongovernmental organizations (NGOs) and activists. However, dissatisfaction with the original framework set forth in the early 1990s is also revealed in the practice of the International Coordinating Committee of National Institutions for the Promotion and Protection of Human Rights (ICC),[17] and in the orientation of many NHRI officials. The ICC has not discarded the Principles, but it has seen the need to elaborate and expand upon the original framework through dynamic interpretations of the Principles in the process of reviewing NHRIs for accreditation (discussed further later in this chapter). And a concern among many NHRI officials is whether particular national institutions – for example, those that are primarily dedicated to research and consultancy – should enjoy equal membership in their club, if included at all.

---

[14]   See Linda Reif, Chapter 3 in this volume.
[15]   See Carver, *Performance and Legitimacy*, 2.
[16]   Ibid.
[17]   The ICC was created in 1993; it is the coordinating body for NHRIs globally and represents these institutions at the UN.

As we have tackled these definitional issues, one lesson that has emerged from the contributions in this volume is the importance of *legitimacy*. First, consider the legitimacy of the Paris Principles in setting the recognition rules for NHRIs. That is, the Principles serve as a normative template establishing the criteria for international acceptance of an NHRI. Indeed, various states have apparently revised their domestic institutions to meet prevailing interpretations of the Principles – whether to obtain membership in the club of internationally recognized NHRIs (e.g., the United Kingdom) or to avoid ouster from it (e.g., France, Malaysia).

Second, consider the significance attached to the fact that NHRIs have been directly involved in the creation of the Principles, the subsequent elaboration of those Principles and related global standards, and the monitoring of compliance with these standards. In particular, the Principles enjoy special legitimacy because they were originally drafted by a group of NHRI representatives – rather than by states per se or foreign diplomats. Indeed, the "founding moment" of the meeting of NHRIs in Paris has amplified the attraction of the Principles for many stakeholders. According to a leading expert writing in this volume (Sidoti), the legitimizing effects associated with the NHRIs' authorship of the Principles provide strong reasons against reopening the Principles to revision in international fora that are vulnerable to capture by states.

The Principles accordingly constitute a highly political agreement – the product of a particular, historically contingent process of creation. Indeed, the location of the meeting in Paris is said to have influenced the outcome document such that European national institutions (and the French in particular) were sure to be covered by the Principles.[18] The standards embodied in the Principles were thus diluted, according to this line of criticism, to accommodate (read: legitimate) weaker institutional forms. Thus, direct NHRI involvement in the creation of the Principles has potentially expanded their influence and reach, but has also compromised the strength of their criteria.

That said, NHRIs have become directly involved in elaborating the Paris Principles through dynamic interpretations (Sidoti, this volume) and in developing more rigorous standards for evaluating NHRIs. The ICC is a self-governing body composed of NHRIs from around the world. Through the work of its Sub-Committee on Accreditation and the issuance of General Observations, the ICC has produced interpretations and elaborations of the Principles gradually over time. These interpretive practices have overcome some of the limitations of the original text. They have also been supplemented by the development of "soft law" on specific subject areas. Consider, for example, the Nairobi Declaration on National Human

---

[18] B. Burdekin with J. Naum, *National Human Rights Institutions in the Asia-Pacific Region* (Leiden: Nijhoff, 2007), 23.

Rights Institutions and the Administration of Justice, issued at a world conference of NHRIs organized by the ICC.[19] The power and effects of these actions depends on the legitimacy of the ICC. And the source of legitimacy for the ICC derives in large part from its working methods and the participation of leading national institutions from different parts of the globe.

The ICC also functions as a gatekeeper (Sidoti, this volume) in reviewing NHRIs and determining their accreditation status. And NHRIs guard their ability to "define their own" through this multilateral process. The ICC's Sub-Committee on Accreditation reviews the applications of candidate and current members in accordance with the Páris Principles and ICC guidelines. Success of an NHRI in the accreditation process is not only formally required for an institution to participate in particular UN meetings; success (or failure) also implicates the legitimacy of the NHRI more generally. For example, the ICC's demotion of the Sri Lankan commission helped to delegitimize the Sri Lankan state's interference with the independence of that institution. And the ICC's demotion of the Fiji commission helped expose the dereliction of core responsibilities on the part of the commission's chairperson. At least one regional organization – the Asia Pacific Forum of National Human Rights Institutions – has exercised a similar gatekeeping function and with similar results (Renshaw and Fitzpatrick, this volume).

The significance of setting criteria for evaluation and determining the international standing of NHRIs is certain to appreciate in the future. As NHRIs become further enmeshed in the human rights system, formal accreditation – and international validation more generally – will become increasingly important. The costs of exclusion are also likely to rise. NHRIs have now begun to collaborate as a unified group in international negotiations. As they work together in such coalitions, the definition and composition of their membership will become more important. In those contexts, debates among NHRIs over the legitimacy and status of a research institute or an NHRI under the control of its government will likely become more heated. Finally, the ICC accreditation process is sure to draw heat as well. University centers (e.g., Columbia Law School) and transnational advocacy organizations are increasingly reviewing the establishment and performance of NHRIs. The ICC accreditation process may appear conservative from their perspectives, as it may seem ambitious from the perspective of some states. The degree to which the ICC demonstrates outward transparency and reasoned decision making may be the key to insulating it from criticism. Otherwise the ICC could become a site of political contestation. Whichever path it follows, the ICC is sure to become a subject of

---

[19] The Nairobi Declaration, "National Human Rights Institutions and the Administration of Justice," The 9th International Conference for National Human Rights Institutions, Nairobi, Kenya, 24 October 2008.

academic intrigue – it is undoubtedly an important case of global administration and networked governance more generally.[20]

As this volume clearly shows, these topics do not simply concern "academic" disputes over definitions. Rather, the debate about the Paris Principles and the classification of NHRIs involves a fundamental disagreement over three key issues: (1) the status of various institutions; (2) the standards for evaluating them; and (3) the most appropriate institutions for interpreting and applying those standards. These controversies have significant implications for human rights politics and practice.[21] And an interdisciplinary lens is, in our view, critically needed to take stock of the debate and to inform contemporary commentary and practice.

1.2.2. *Norm Diffusion and State Compliance*

A significant body of interdisciplinary scholarship focuses on how human rights norms spread across the world.[22] This volume engages that literature by exploring the mechanisms and conditions that have fostered the transnational spread of NHRIs.[23] The volume also explores how NHRIs, in turn, function as vehicles

---

[20] For texts in the field of global administration and networked governance, see B. Kingsbury et al., "The Emergence of Global Administrative Law," *Law and Contemporary Problems* 68 (2005), 15–61; A. Slaughter, *A New World Order: Government Networks and the Disaggregated State* (Princeton: Princeton University Press, 2004); A. Chayes and A. H. Chayes, *The New Sovereignty: Compliance with International Regulatory Agreements* (Cambridge: Harvard University Press, 1996); A. Hurrell, *On Global Order: Power, Values and the Constitution of International Society* (Oxford: Oxford University Press, 2007); see also Emilie M. Hafner-Burton, Miles Kahler, and Alexander H. Montgomery, "Network Analysis for International Relations," *International Organization* 63 (2009), 559–92.

[21] The implications of some of these questions of institutional design – for example, whether to create multiple NHRIs within a country, the capacity of classical ombudsmen to serve particular human rights victims – are also usefully discussed in Richard Carver, "One NHRI or Many? How Many Institutions Does It Take to Protect Human Rights? – Lessons from the European Experience," *Journal of Human Rights Practice* 3 (2011), 1–24; Linda Reif, "The Ombudsman and the Protection of Children's Rights," *Asia Pacific Law Review* 17 (2009), 27–52; Christopher P. M. Waters, "Nationalising Kosovo's Ombudsperson: Implications for Kosovo and Peacekeeping," *Journal of Conflict and Security Law* 12 (2007), 139–48; and Amanda Wetzel, "Post-Conflict National Human Rights Institutions: Emerging Models from Northern Ireland and Bosnia and Herzegovina," *Colombia Journal of European Law* 13 (2007), 427–70.

[22] See, for example, Harold H. Koh, "Why Do Nations Obey International Law?"*Yale Law Journal* 106 (1997), 2599–659; Ryan Goodman and Derek Jinks, "How to Influence States: Socialization and International Law," *Duke Law Journal* 54 (2004), 621–703; R. Goodman and D. Jinks, *Socializing States: Promoting Human Rights through International Law* (New York: Oxford University Press, forthcoming); T. Risse et al., *The Power of Human Rights: International Norms and Domestic Change* (New York: Cambridge University Press, 1999); M. Keck and K. Sikkink, *Activists beyond Borders: Advocacy Networks in International Politics* (Ithaca: Cornell University Press, 1998); B. Simmons, *Mobilizing for Human Rights: International Law in Domestic Politics* (Cambridge: Cambridge University Press, 2009).

[23] Sonia Cardenas, "Emerging Global Actors: The United Nations and National Human Rights Institutions," *Global Governance* 9 (2003), 23–42.

for promoting the diffusion of international human rights norms into domestic political systems.

Important questions concern how international institutions promote the spread of NHRIs and the – intended and unintended – consequences of that support. It is valuable in this regard to study how various international forces have affected the specific types and timing of NHRIs. By way of analogy, consider a leading study by political scientist Martha Finnemore examining the role of the United National Educational, Scientific, and Cultural Organization (UNESCO) in promoting the worldwide adoption of national science bureaucracy boards, including in states where such organizational structures met little or no functional need. Finnemore explains that UNESCO convinced national-level actors that such commitments to the promotion of science constituted an important feature of modern statehood.[24]

The rapid spread of NHRIs may have followed a similar path.[25] As reflected in this volume, close observers credit the Office of the UN High Commissioner for Human Rights for helping to convince national-level actors to establish NHRIs in all regions of the world. Sidoti, in Chapter 5, discusses the Office of High Commissioner and how its leadership has been succeeded by UN treaty bodies promoting the establishment of NHRIs in all member states. Meyer, in Chapter 13, identifies "mimetic pressures" that lead to the construction of similar NHRI structures and missions, in part, because "each new NHRI comes into existence nested in a set of supranational bodies pursuing human rights." In a critical vein, Reif, in her chapter, contends that the High Commissioner's Office has promoted a narrowly conceived model of NHRIs for global production and bestowed legitimacy on this particular form regardless of regional and subregional variations in political and institutional demands. Rosenblum contends that the Office of the High Commissioner, and the resolve of leading norm entrepreneurs in that office, have promoted a "one-size-fits all" template that considers NHRIs valuable in almost every country. He contends that some countries would benefit from different organizational formations, which are crowded out by the establishment of an NHRI. In short, none of the contributors doubt the importance of the UN human rights machinery in the rapid establishment of NHRIs across the globe. They do, however, draw different conclusions and highlight different second-order effects of that promotion campaign.

NHRIs have also helped to replicate themselves – by way of global and regional networks. At the global level, the International Coordinating Committee of NHRIs, as discussed previously, serves as a gatekeeper. Through accreditation procedures,

---

[24] M. Finnemore, *National Interests in International Society* (Ithaca: Cornell University Press, 1996).
[25] For extended analysis of NHRI diffusion, including organizational emulation, see Sonia Cardenas, "Emerging Global Actors: The United Nations and National Human Rights Institutions," *Global Governance* 23 (2003), 23–42; Thomas Pegram, "Diffusion across Political Systems: The Global Spread of National Human Rights Institutions," *Human Rights Quarterly* 32 (2010), 729–60.

the ICC helps ensure the emergence of national bodies with characteristics that resemble a similar set of structural features and formal commitments. That is, this international organization – an association of NHRIs – helps determine what forms of NHRIs are sufficient to attain international recognition. The result is a fairly homogenous population, with some regional variations.

Those regional variations deserve special attention. Indeed, this volume provides a corrective to a broader literature that has often underspecified or overlooked the significance of regional dimensions of norm diffusion. A growing body of political science and sociological research now suggests that regional networks may provide a powerful account of the structure of transnational social influence across several domains,[26] and human rights in particular.[27] It is not just transnational networks or global culture that counts. Regional context also matters.

Regional associations and networks constitute a significant factor in the formation of NHRIs. Several authors in this volume describe region-level emulation in the adoption of NHRIs. Linda Reif, for example, discusses particular structural features that cluster by region (e.g., Ombudsmen in Latin America, and multimember commissions in the Asia Pacific). Richard Carver, in his contribution, suggests an emulation model whereby the Polish institution served as template that other states in the region copied. More broadly, Catherine Renshaw and Kieren Fitzpatrick's contribution to this volume, in particular, demonstrates the importance of regional NHRI networks in the creation and development of NHRIs. One outcome of these regional practices, as identified in multiple contributions to the book, is a population of NHRIs composed of similar organizational structures and formal agendas.

It is difficult to weigh the positive and negative implications of these forms of influence, especially because they have differential effects on countries at varied stages of human rights protection. One perverse effect of the spread of a uniform model may be a "race to the middle."[28] Under certain conditions, countries that would otherwise aspire to higher levels of human rights protection may gravitate to lowered expectations and average measures of success. Indeed, the chapters by Cardenas and Mertus elaborate on such a phenomenon whereby states that display a high degree of human rights observance face low incentives to exceed the basic NHRI model. The race to the middle may also negatively affect states emerging from dismal human rights conditions. For instance, a highly mobilized reform movement

---

[26] Jason Beckfield, "The Social Structure of the World Polity," *American Journal of Sociology* 115 (2010), 1018–68; J. C. Pevehouse, *Democracy from Above: Regional Organizations and Democratization* (Wisconsin: University of Wisconsin, 2005).

[27] B. Simmons, *Mobilizing for Human Rights*, 90–6; also Francisco O. Ramirez et al., "The Changing Logic of Political Citizenship: Cross-national Acquisition of Women's Suffrage Rights, 1890 to 1990," *American Sociological Review* 62 (1997), 735–45.

[28] Goodman and Jinks, *Socializing States*.

may call on the state to construct powerful human rights institutions. However, the presence of a globally legitimated model of an NHRI – a weak but standardized form – may reduce their expectations and the extent of political change.

On the positive side, the identified processes of international influence may inspire a more rapid adoption of NHRIs. They may also compel even rights violating states to commit to the institutionalization of fundamental human rights at an earlier stage than anticipated. Indeed, one quandary – not fully answered in these pages – is whether the creation of NHRIs that do not meet local "functional" task demands is, on balance, desirable or undesirable in particular settings. Consider the empirical finding that national-level actors can be convinced to adopt administrative bodies (such as UNESCO's science policy boards) that are costly to the state and do not serve state purposes.[29] On the basis of those empirical insights, state actors can potentially be convinced to adopt a human rights–oriented institution even though human rights protection is not in their material self-interest (e.g., tyrannical regimes and other rights violating states). Suharto's decision to create Komnas HAM is one example of an NHRI forged in such unexpected and inhospitable conditions. And Komnas HAM developed an independent and effective agenda that helped pave the way for Suharto's ouster – a result that certainly did not fit the functional interests of the regime. Less extreme cases might include India's National Human Rights Commission which was set up, in significant part, to stave off international pressure to improve human rights. The Indian commission, under bold leadership at least in its initial phase of life, went on to challenge directly the rights violations of state authorities. Later we discuss factors that enable NHRIs to transcend such origins, that is, their ability to make important contributions to human rights protection despite inhospitable domestic political settings at the time of their creation. The important point for present purposes is that the international influences may encourage even recalcitrant states to adopt an NHRI that does not serve their interests in violating human rights.

More generally, the construction of NHRIs through international associations and social processes can amplify the effectiveness of these institutions domestically. That is, as products, in significant part, of institutionalization at the international level, NHRIs are often uniquely positioned at the intersection of international and domestic domains. NHRIs may accordingly function as special vehicles for fostering the diffusion of international human rights norms within local settings.

There are two important ways this function can be conceptualized. First, scholarship on transnational socialization suggests that particular national institutions can deepen the diffusion of global norms by providing "domestic receptor sites" for the

---

[29] Young S. Kim, Yong Suk Jang, and Hokyu Hwang, "Structural Expansion and the Cost of Global Isomorphism: A Cross-national Study of Ministerial Structure, 1950–1990," *International Sociology* 17 (2002), 481; Finnemore, *National Interests in International Society*.

transmission to occur.[30] For instance, a set of studies shows that receptor sites such as natural science associations and environmental institutes have facilitated the local transmission of global models of environmentalism.[31] In the context of international human rights, national human rights commissions and ombudsmen are a close analogue and can potentially serve similar ends.[32]

Second, drawing on legal anthropologist Sally Engle Merry's work, the question arises as to the extent to which NHRIs can serve as intermediaries in the translation of global norms into a local "vernacular."[33] Notably, actors within the system recognize aspects of these relationships. UN Secretary-General Ban Ki-moon, for example, acknowledges the role of NHRIs "in the effective implementation of international human rights standards at the national level" due to their capacity to "translat[e] international human rights norms in a way that reflects national contexts and specificities."[34] Merry's research, however, brings more fundamental questions to the fore. In particular, NHRIs may be more successful in producing meaningful social change by relying upon domestic frames – for example, local discourse on equality or constitutional norms – and appropriating relevant international human rights norms either partially or only as an implicit inspiration. The mandate of some NHRIs – such as Canada's, Zambia's, and the Philippines' – does not include jurisdiction over international human rights treaties or other international human rights law. Even those NHRIs with express jurisdiction to apply international human rights law frequently rely on domestic norms to the exclusion of international sources in their published decisions. And, as Enrique Peruzzotti (Chapter 10) demonstrates, NHRIs may tap into a domestic discourse – "citizen politics" in Argentina – rather than explicit international human rights frames when engaging in local community initiatives. That said, counterexamples are certain to arise. In the context of Eastern and Central Europe, for instance, NHRIs are increasingly invoking international law to the exclusion of constitutional norms. That practice corresponds with their communities' desire for (West) Europeanization and acceptance in the international community (Carver, Chapter 8).

[30] David John Frank et al., "The Nation-State and the Natural Environment over the Twentieth Century," *American Sociological Review* 65 (2000), 96, note 1 ("Receptor sites are social structures (e.g., scientific institutes) with the capacity to receive, decode, and transmit signals from the world society to national actors"); see also Frank et al., "Environmentalism as a Global Institution," *American Sociological Review* 65 (2000), 123–24 (discussing the diffusion of international environmental norms through "scientific receptor sites").

[31] Frank et al., ibid.; see also Evan Schofer and John W. Meyer, "The Worldwide Expansion of Higher Education in the Twentieth Century," *American Sociological Review* 70 (2005), 898.

[32] See generally K. Hossain (ed.), *Human Rights Commissions and Ombudsman Offices: National Experiences throughout the World* (Boston: Brill, 2000).

[33] See S. Engle Merry, *Human Rights and Gender Violence: Translating International Law into Local Justice* (Chicago: University of Chicago Press, 2006).

[34] Report of the Secretary-General to the General Assembly, "National Institutions for the Promotion and Protection of Human Rights," UN Doc. No.: A/64/320, 24 August 2009, 4.

Merry's research and the related NHRI practice provide evidence for more general discussions about socialization and norm compliance. In international practice and academic commentary, debate currently rages over the value of addressing rights complaints at the national level through express reference to international human rights standards. For example, one view holds that reference to local legal norms – that cover the same substantive ground as their international analogues – should suffice.[35] Others contend that the strength of global standards will deteriorate if domestic institutions do not formally invoke international legal norms in rendering decisions. These debates implicate rules governing the exhaustion of local remedies before appealing to an international body, the principle of subsidiarity within supranational systems, and the application of complementarity in international criminal tribunals (when the definitions of national offenses and international offenses are semantically different). Merry's research and the related NHRI practice suggest that there is a broad range of cases in which the vernacularization of global norms into local discourses may serve the normative objectives of the human rights regime.

1.2.3. *The Domestic Impact of NHRIs*

The previous discussion ended with a consideration of effects of particular modes of international promotion on the domestic work of NHRIs. That line of inquiry also leads to a broader set of questions concerning the determinants of the impact of NHRIs. In this section, we turn to that range of concerns. We first discuss benchmarks and baselines for assessing the impact of an NHRI on social and political conditions. We then discuss a range of issues including structural determinants of NHRI success (and failure) in promoting human rights; mechanisms that NHRIs might employ for obtaining state compliance beyond coercive, enforcement measures; and potential perverse consequences of the creation and operation of an NHRI in certain circumstances.

A. Benchmarks and Baselines

What is the proper standard for measuring the impact of an NHRI on human rights conditions within a state? The answer to that question depends on two important

---

[35] See, for example, *Young v. Australia*, Human Rights Committee, Communication No 941/2000, UN Doc. CCPR/C/78/D/941/2000, 18 September 2003, Individual Opinion by Ruth Wedgwood and Franco DePasquale ("Nor can the Committee demand that rights must be incorporated by open citation of the Covenant. It is the substance, rather than the nomenclature that counts, and some national court systems may prefer to explain their choices in light of constitutional, common law, or civil law norms, even while protecting the substance of Covenant rights"): http://www.unhchr.ch/tbs/doc.nsf/0/3c839cb2ae3bef6fc1256dac002b3034?OpenDocument.

methodological issues. The first concerns setting an appropriate benchmark, or expectation, for NHRI performance. That is, one should recognize that the role and responsibility of an NHRI is limited to its sphere of influence and activities – and one should try to specify where those boundaries lie. An NHRI may successfully carry out its particular role and functions, but the ultimate impact on human rights depends on the behavior of other actors and institutions in their own areas of influence and responsibility. An NHRI might, for example, perform well in monitoring human rights abuses, but other institutions – the media and human rights advocacy organizations – may fail to build on that work. How far should an NHRI be expected to be engaged in media promotion and in building its legitimacy with the public, and how much of that responsibility should be assigned to these other institutions? Similarly, an NHRI may very effectively decide upon individual cases that merit referral to public prosecutors, and the judicial system then acquires the greater responsibility for seeing that justice is done. How far should the responsibility of the NHRI extend in such situations, and how should we measure its performance when ultimate changes in state human rights practices are lacking? Framed in this manner, a lack of compliance with NHRI recommendations may reflect the failure of complementary actors to fulfill their democratic or accountability function rather than the failure of an NHRI. A conscious regard for such considerations should inform academic researchers' and practitioners' assessment of the potential effectiveness of an NHRI. Accordingly, one of the recurring issues in this book is defining the proper scope and expectation for NHRI performance (see Meyer, Chapter 13, for an assessment of this theme).

Delving into these sorts of methodological points also opens up other considerations of benchmarks that deserve mention. First, descriptive and empirical analyses of benchmarks might generate insights for institutional design. For example, regime architects could try to assess whether an NHRI will have a larger overall impact if confined to a modest set of responsibilities or handed a more ambitious agenda. Should an NHRI, for instance, be empowered to undertake additional functions when other institutions fail in their respective responsibilities or will such a residual power create a moral hazard and overextend the NHRI? Second, a focus on benchmarks should draw attention to whether some human rights should receive greater weight when the effectiveness of an NHRI is measured. Most clearly, the benchmark for effective performance should not be restricted only to the subjects and cases in which an NHRI actively works (e.g., measuring compliance with NHRI recommendations). Chapters in this volume, for example, argue that the appropriate benchmark should be set by reference to the top national priorities within a country, that is, the most urgent and important human rights concerns (Rosenblum, Chapter 12), and the interests of the most vulnerable voices in society (Okafor, Chapter 6).

An independent methodological point concerns baselines for gauging the impact – intended and unintended – of an NHRI on political and social conditions within a country. A key question is what the human rights conditions would have been within a given country without the creation or operation of an NHRI. Absent that information, one might underestimate or overestimate the impact of such an institution. In a country with an NHRI and deteriorating human rights conditions, observers may conclude that an NHRI has proven ineffective. The appropriate question, however, is whether conditions would have been worse (and they can almost always have been worse) without the NHRI. In other situations, an NHRI may be lauded for promoting human rights NGOs, providing legal expertise (Pegram, Chapter 9), or substituting for the failures of other governmental institutions (e.g., an electoral commission). However, consider that (1) without the NHRI, the local NGOs might have received greater resources from domestic and external sources; (2) the legal expertise provided by an NHRI might crowd out more socially productive political activism; and (3) without the residual power of the NHRI to fill the void left by the weaknesses in other governmental institutions, the state might have been pressed to support those other institutions to a greater degree. Accordingly, even if the creation and operation of an NHRI correlates with improvements in human rights conditions, the question is whether there would have been more improvements absent the NHRI. Admittedly, such assessments often involve counterfactual analyses and difficult evaluations of opportunity costs. An awareness of the possible baseline should nevertheless temper both overly enthusiastic and excessively pessimistic accounts of NHRIs. And the consideration of both benchmarks and baselines can lead to more rigorous analyses and more measured assessments of the impact of NHRIs.

B. Beyond Enforcement Measures and Material Inducements

This volume embraces a broad conception of the powers that NHRIs might employ to effectuate compliance with human rights standards. In existing international relations scholarship on compliance, changes in state behavior are often predicated (ultimately) on enforcement by formal institutions or material inducements such as threats to the tenure of public authorities. Several contributors to this volume, however, adopt a more nuanced conceptualization of the institution of an NHRI and its ability to foster social change and compliance. They focus instead on channels of influence that exist outside formal enforcement authority and material inducements.

Perhaps most notable in this regard are the chapters by Peruzzotti and Uggla. Building on new scholarship in the social sciences on opportunity structures and accountability theory,[36] Peruzzotti contends that the involvement of the Argentinean NHRI in a dispute involving massive environmental contamination constituted a "turning point" in the social struggle. The NHRI, according to this case study, helped to legitimate the claims of social actors and helped to forge accountability across public authorities.[37] In his study of Bolivia, Uggla argues that the NHRI effectuated compliance not by building relationships with external civil society actors but by building relationships of trust with state authorities and mobilizing other mechanisms of influence such as peer pressure. Regardless of whether Peruzzoti's or Uggla's findings are generalizable or replicated elsewhere, the important point is for analysts to consider such diverse mechanisms of influence in encouraging states to align their behavior with existing human rights standards.

C. Social Mobilization and Activism

National human rights institutions may exert their most powerful influence in fostering – or hindering – social mobilization. This volume gives special attention to such effects. David Meyer, for example, draws directly on social science scholarship that studies the conditions under which civil society actors mobilize to secure rights guarantees. A strong determinant of social mobilization, according to this area of research, is whether political institutions signal to social actors that new structural opportunities exist. Meyer accordingly examines how NHRIs, which sit uniquely at the intersection of the state and civil society, can create and signal such political openings.

Other contributions complement Meyer's account. For example, Obiora Okafor shows how African NHRIs may achieve their greatest effects by creating platforms for NGOs to engage the state system. And Thomas Pegram's research on Latin America suggests that a virtuous circle can unfold: while NHRIs further the prospect and legitimacy of social mobilization, the mobilizing forces can, in turn, provide NHRIs a "crucial ballast against hostile state actors." Indeed, as Okafor's and Pegram's work demonstrates, in some circumstances social actors may consider NHRIs allies within the corridors of power. And the existence of such allies is another important variable in the political structure that can induce social actors to mobilize.[38]

---

[36] See J. Fox, *Accountability Politics: Power and Voice in Rural Mexico* (New York: University Oxford Press, 2008); Guillermo O'Donnell, "Horizontal Accountability in New Democracies," *Journal of Democracy* 9 (1998), 112–26; S. Mainwaring and C. Welna (eds.), *Democratic Accountability in Latin America* (New York: Oxford University Press, 2003).

[37] See more generally, E. Peruzzotti and C. Smulovitz (eds.), *Enforcing the Rule of Law: Social Accountability in the New Latin American Democracies* (Pittsburgh: University of Pittsburgh, 2006).

[38] Doug McAdam, "Conceptual Origins, Current Problems, Future Directions," in D. McAdam, J. D. McCarthy, and M. N. Zald (eds.), *Comparative Perspectives on Social Movements: Political*

The creation and operation of an NHRI may also have a demobilizing effect in some circumstances. Indeed, this book sheds light on potential perverse effects of inserting an NHRI into existing institutional arrangements within government and civil society. That is, NHRIs occupy an institutional space that can discourage or displace other actors who would otherwise help to advance human rights. Reflecting on various contributions in this volume, Meyer asks the key question: "Is the creation of NHRIs a step toward protecting and promoting human rights or a way of containing and insulating the pressure to do so?" Indeed, some of these effects may be intentional: states may deliberately use an NHRI to ward off international pressure to comply with human rights. And other consequences may be unintentional. The professionalization of human rights work through the offices of the NHRI, for instance, may help convince members of society that mobilization is unnecessary (Meyer, Chapter 13). Rosenblum, in his survey of the volume's contributions, also raises concerns that the insertion of NHRIs may redirect resources (including donor support) from other human rights organizations. Pegram suggests that "crowding out of social actors is a concern, with Defensorías ('human rights ombudsmen') potentially diverting international funding away from civil society actors as well as enticing highly qualified personnel away from the human rights sector." A systematic study of the prevalence of these effects and the success of efforts to overcome them does not appear in this volume. The contributions to the volume, however, identify the potential casual mechanisms and significance of these interactions. The research presented here thus provides strong reason for future studies to document such countervailing effects and to develop institutional designs to mitigate them.

D. Origin Matters

Finally, an empirical puzzle in the study of NHRIs is how specific institutions might escape their past or, more specifically, their origins. Most striking are cases of NHRIs born in inhospitable political conditions – brought to life, for example, by an autocratic or illiberal government – yet able to develop into an independent force that ultimately challenges the state's human rights practices. Such a path was followed by prototype NHRIs such as the Indonesian Commission on Human Rights, which subverted the intentions of its designers and helped legitimate the democracy movement that toppled Suharto.[39] On a more general level, other institutions have also transcended the constraints of their original political and institutional settings. Consider, for example, the early successes of the Indian National Human Rights

---

Opportunities, Mobilizing Structures, and Cultural Framings (Cambridge: Cambridge University Press, 1996); S. Tarrow, *Power in Movement: Social Movements and Contentious Politics*, 2nd ed. (Cambridge: Cambridge University Press, 1998).

[39] See Carver, *Performance and Legitimacy*, 21–36.

Commission discussed earlier. Related histories of transformation include institutions that develop informal powers and practices to a degree that fundamentally transcends the original framework of the institution (Pegram, Chapter 9). In the words of Sonia Cardenas in this volume, how are NHRIs seemingly hobbled by adverse beginnings able to "take on a life of their own"?

This book provides some valuable insights that at least partially explain the conditions under which NHRIs can develop an independent path despite adverse beginnings. Some contributors, for example, suggest that increased autonomy and influence of an NHRI over time may be a result of external factors such as shifts in democratic structures or political openings more generally (Carver, Chapter 8; Meyer, Chapter 13). Other contributors point to internal factors in the organization and practice of the institution such as scaling up the legitimacy of the NHRI by building connections to civil society (Okafor, Chapter 6; Pegram, Chapter 9). Additionally, other chapters demonstrate that although NHRIs may escape their fate, the durability of this outcome is far from assured, and deteriorating political conditions and lapses in individual judgment within the organization can result in significant backsliding (Renshaw and Fitzpatrick, Chapter 7).

Two final points deserve mention. First, if we are concerned about the birth of NHRIs, we should also be concerned about their "rebirth." That is, once researchers incorporate temporal dimensions into their analysis, it is important also that they take account of the potential reconfiguration of an NHRI – for example, through legislative amendment and reform. Those moments can, of course, represent new opportunities as well as new threats to the long-term success of the institution.

Finally, the well-grounded, conventional wisdom is that NHRIs will generally be constrained by their origins. Such legacy effects may result from various causal processes including relationships of power with the governing regime and path dependency. Although we focus here on a puzzle – explaining variation and divergence from that norm – it is also important to consider the standard legacy effects as well. Indeed, institutional design can exploit positive legacy effects and potentially forestall negative ones at the outset. For instance, the procedures adopted in creating an NHRI at the design stage – for example, whether public consultation occurred – can shape the public perception of the institution over time (Pegram, Chapter 9, contrasting Nicaragua's and Bolivia's experiences). Social science research more generally suggests that individuals are more likely to comply with legal institutions – including outcomes that are adverse to their interests – if they perceive that they were represented in the process of making that decision.[40] These

---

[40] See, for example, T. R. Tyler, *Why People Obey the Law* (Princeton: Princeton University Press, 2006); Margaret Levi, Tom Tyler, and Audrey Sacks, "The Reasons for Compliance with Law," in R. Goodman, D. Jinks, and A. Woods (eds.), *Understanding Social Action, Promoting Human Rights* (New York: Oxford University Press, forthcoming, 2012).

factors bear on the question of legitimacy, and policy makers would do well to take these lessons into account at the original design stage and during subsequent reforms of an NHRI.

1.3. THE BOOK AHEAD

The book is divided into three parts. In Part I, the authors discuss central theoretical and analytical questions concerning the definition, design, and effectiveness of NHRIs (Chapters 2–4). In Part II, the authors discuss the practices of NHRIs in engaging international institutions at the global and regional level, and the practices of NHRIs in domestic politics and society (Chapters 5–11). In Part III, two concluding chapters, reflecting on the earlier components of the book, consider the significance of NHRIs for political mobilization and human rights advocacy (Chapters 12–13).

In Chapter 2, Sonia Cardenas, drawing on social science research on compliance with international norms, explores relationships between NHRIs and state behavior. Cardenas suggests that empirical and theoretical assumptions about what state compliance means, why states comply, and why compliance matters are often implicit in current thinking on NHRIs. She examines domestic and international forces that motivate states to establish an NHRI. In Cardenas's theoretical model, she includes pressure exerted by the international community upon states that are human rights leaders to establish a national institution. That is, leading states not only exert pressure on others but are also targets of heightened international expectations; and Cardenas includes the burdens that result from these expectations. Cardenas then examines types of NHRIs created under different international and domestic political conditions, and the prospect for an NHRI to change – to gain or lose strength and independence – over time. Among a number of intriguing claims, Cardenas suggests that the most powerful and enduring effects of an NHRI on governmental behavior may be indirect – when an NHRI shapes wider social forces outside the state.

In Chapter 3, Linda Reif examines foundational questions about the definition and scope of institutions formed as NHRIs, and how well normative assumptions of the Paris Principles match the range of existing organizations that claim the title of an NHRI. Reif maps different categories of NHRIs and their placement along a spectrum of increasing levels of engagement with human rights protection. She embarks on a critical recentering of the NHRI concept in light of contemporary developments in NHRI practice. She contends that the boundaries between NHRI models are becoming increasingly blurred as domestic human rights institutions proliferate, presenting a challenge to conventional templates such as the Paris Principles. Without discounting the importance of conceptual clarity, Reif argues that a restrictive approach risks overlooking, even potentially undermining, other relevant actors in the domestic implementation of human rights.

In Chapter 4, Julie Mertus critiques conventional analytical frameworks for evaluating NHRI performance. Mertus argues for a partial decoupling of the Paris Principles from the task of NHRI evaluation – moving the focus away from assessing structural features and toward assessing whether the organization effectuates different forms of social change on the ground. Mertus proposes this realignment as a corrective to a literature that has underestimated the significance of "localization" and political and social processes required for enduring human rights change. In turn, she highlights a central challenge that NHRIs will confront as they move to the center of debate on human rights implementation, namely, to prove their own effectiveness. She outlines an array of measures that might be deployed to track positive and negative changes in societal attitudes and policies affecting human rights. These measures include analyzing the content of media coverage; the frequency of complaints submitted to grievance bodies that are framed in rights-based language; the level of membership in human rights–oriented political parties and civic organizations; and public opinion and human rights awareness. Prefacing subsequent contributions, Mertus concludes by speculating on the importance of contextual factors, in particular how power relations between NHRIs and other domestic actors affect the ability of NHRIs to produce durable social change.

In Chapter 5, Chris Sidoti studies NHRI engagement with the international human rights system over the past two decades. Sidoti describes a rebalancing of the relationship between NHRIs and the international human rights system. Engagement has previously emphasized a top-down relationship. Many NHRIs owed their very existence, in significant part, to international institutions, and many NHRIs were originally conceived as vehicles for fostering the transmission of international norms into domestic social and political systems. Sidoti highlights the emergence of relationships that are bottom-up. As demonstrated most clearly in the negotiations of the Convention on the Rights of Persons with Disabilities, Sidoti states that NHRIs have "come of age" – they are now accepted as important actors that can contribute meaningfully to the development of international instruments and standard setting at the global level. He also analyzes horizontal relationships, in which NHRIs can (1) act as gatekeepers for others to access the global system, (2) collaborate with UN human rights experts, and (3) help to shape international discourse on controversial human rights topics (such as blasphemy and freedom of speech). Sidoti's chapter analyzes several missed (and some taken) opportunities for NHRIs to engage the international human rights system. He argues that a virtuous circle could exist – NHRIs could benefit international actors which would, in turn, strengthen NHRIs. This is not inevitable, however, and Sidoti also identifies trade-offs and reasons for skepticism.

The volume then turns to the experience of NHRIs operating within diverse regions and often adverse institutional settings. In Chapter 6, Obiora Okafor points to the achievements and setbacks experienced by three of the NHRIs that operate in "Anglophone Africa": Nigeria, South Africa and Uganda. In explaining the significance of NHRI formation in these three cases, Okafor highlights the important influence of what he terms "popular legitimization factors," which include procedural accessibility, the absence of excessive legalism, sufficient attention to popular agency, and connections to "voices of the suffering." Okafor contends that the power of an NHRI to effectuate change depends significantly on its ability to resonate with constituencies outside the state and to respond to wider societal demands. In turn, Okafor emphasizes the importance of NHRI engagement with civil society as a way to confront different configurations of political power and, ultimately, to compel a reluctant government to act.

In Chapter 7, Catherine Renshaw and Kieren Fitzpatrick study the experience of NHRIs in the Asia Pacific region. The Asia Pacific is infamous for the lack of an intergovernmental regional human rights mechanism and the low-level ratifications of human rights treaties. This chapter discusses a significant exception to those patterns: the creation of NHRIs and their formal, highly institutionalized network, the Asia Pacific Forum for National Human Rights Institutions (APF). With a steady rise in the numbers of NHRIs and a relatively ambitious agenda on the part of the APF, what causal mechanisms explain these surprising developments? The authors identify material calculations by state actors to create particular images for foreign donors. They also emphasize the desire to emulate leading nations within the region and subregion that have established an NHRI as well as the status gained in international affairs by having such an institution to interface with the region and world. Paradoxically, the strength of the Asia Pacific NHRIs is due in part to the absence of a regional human rights regime. Renshaw and Fitzpatrick also discuss domestic determinants for the creation of NHRIs, as well as domestic challenges to the legitimacy of NHRIs due to politicization and resistance by powerful groups – in both government and civil society. The chapter documents the APF response to domestic threats to the independence and integrity of NHRIs from actors outside the institution (South Korea, Sri Lanka) and from within the institution themselves (Fiji). The authors also study other important initiatives of the APF including helping to create a human rights monitoring body for the Association of Southeast Asian Nations (ASEAN), and helping to achieve joint gains on international problems that require trust and transnational coordination such as human trafficking. The authors end with cautious optimism about the future of NHRIs in the region.

In Chapter 8, Richard Carver discusses the advent of NHRIs, now totaling twenty-eight, that have proliferated across the former communist states of Central and Eastern Europe. In Carver's analysis, NHRI formation and practice emerge in association with domestic processes of constitutional reform, but with a distinctly international orientation that reflects a regional turn toward transnational legal norms. Expanding on this theme, the chapter explores the potential of various NHRIs in the region to constitute agents of change. In particular, Carver exposes a critical tension in the mandate of these offices: (1) balancing a broad and systemic approach to human rights while (2) being drawn to respond to individual grievances across a broad spectrum of rights expectations on the part of the citizenry (see also Meyer, Chapter 13). Carver's chapter is an important reminder of the distinct challenges presented in new democracies when an NHRI is subject to a significant range of societal demands. The author concludes that the most efficacious institutions are those that have succeeded in managing a creative tension between responsibly handling individual complaints and ambitiously addressing systemic human rights problems.

In Chapter 9, Thomas Pegram surveys the experience of NHRIs in Latin America. Drawing on political accountability theory, he discusses the transformative potential of NHRIs in their relationships with other institutions along three dimensions: vertical (intra-executive branch), horizontal (state checks and balances) and social (nongovernmental, civil society). The chapter finds that although some NHRIs have emerged as credible and authoritative rights defenders – even in countries where democratic institutions have proven difficult to establish and sustain – other NHRIs have succumbed to politicization or obsolescence. Pegram argues that although formal design is important, the success of an NHRI is shaped decisively by the influence of informal rules, norms, and practices. These informal factors arise even in cases in which formal rules would otherwise suggest little flexibility (e.g., well-specified appointment procedures; formal independence from presidential control). The chapter accordingly examines gaps between formal rules and widely accepted informal practices common to contemporary Latin American democracies, and the conditions under which NHRIs operating in such circumstances can effectuate meaningful social change.

Closely examining the Argentinean NHRI – Defensor del Pueblo de la Nación – Enrique Peruzzotti in Chapter 10 focuses attention on the accountability role of the organization within a political context scarred by a recent authoritarian government and systematic human rights violations. The author describes a recent wave of research on civic action and political accountability. He then situates the Argentine NHRI within a new "civic politics" that reflects a relatively sophisticated and demanding citizenry determined to hold their elected officials to account. Peruzzotti conducts a case study of extreme environmental degradation and associated social justice issues involving contamination of a river running through the industrial belt of Buenos Aires. The case allows Peruzzotti to unpack the mechanisms and effects of a novel form of collaboration among the NHRI, state agencies, and civil society. The significance of this mode of interaction and associated accountability structures is especially important in a political culture traditionally defined by a confrontational model of "state versus civil society." Indeed, the case shows how civil society actors not only pressured state agencies from "outside," but also positioned themselves as an integral part of the controlling mechanism to monitor and regulate the environmental problem. Peruzzotti traces a chain of interactions as different horizontal relationships between state and nonstate institutions developed in the struggle to produce results for victims of social injustice.

In Chapter 11, Fredrik Uggla evaluates the Bolivian NHRI – Defensor del Pueblo – created in 1998. The author identifies an empirical puzzle: despite the lack of formal enforcement authority and a reluctance to enlist support from sympathetic forces in the state and society, the NHRI reports relatively high levels of compliance with its decisions. Uggla argues that the experience of the Bolivian office points to the primary importance of bureaucratic culture, self-image, and reputation in shaping the responsiveness of state agents. He accordingly emphasizes the use of "peer pressure" and persuasion as effective tools employed by the Bolivian NHRI to obtain compliance. On this account, compliance does not always require material sanctions to succeed. And, in sharp contrast to Okafor's and Peruzzotti's contributions to this volume, Uggla shows that the role of societal constituencies is a contributing, but not determining, factor in explaining the achievements of the Bolivian NHRI. Uggla also addresses the potential pitfalls – not just the potential gains – of pursuing such bureaucratic channels of accountability.

The final section of the volume presents two sets of reflections that will appeal to legal, human rights, and social science scholars interested in the themes discussed in the book and avenues for future research.

The section begins with Chapter 12, in which Peter Rosenblum offers a critique of the NHRI promotional project that has taken hold over the past two decades. Rosenblum, drawing on other contributions to the volume, investigates the current state of knowledge on NHRIs and the legacy of the actors and institutions that have been instrumental in the global proliferation of NHRIs. In particular, Rosenblum focuses on the gaps between the aspirational vision of NHRIs and the often sobering reality of NHRI effectiveness on the ground. He also seeks to identify missed opportunities and the diversion of resources that may accompany the choice to create an NHRI. Rosenblum discusses the significant role that NHRIs have played in advancing human rights in various contexts. The chapter, however, focuses more attention on challenges that NHRIs face over time in sustaining a positive rights impact, including having to contend with backlash from powerful adversaries and ensuring that the institution's activities are relevant to the chief human rights problems within a country. The chapter ends with a call for a skeptical approach to evaluating the impact of NHRIs, one that brings scholars and practitioners closer to the dimensions of when and why NHRIs matter.

Finally, in Chapter 13, David Meyer locates NHRIs within the social science frameworks of political opportunity structure and social mobilization. Tying diverse strands of the book together, Meyer surveys some of the key analytical problems that emerge from the empirical contributions. He analyzes how NHRIs operate as both agents and venues for action. Meyer suggests that more attention be paid to understanding NHRIs as a means of calibrating often inflated social demands and expectations. He explores the potential of NHRIs to change the perception of the institutional environment for social actors – a key variable in stimulating social movements. NHRIs may, for example, signal an opening in the political structure for new human rights agendas and new routes of influence. On the other hand, Meyer explains, an NHRI can also suggest to activists that mobilization is unnecessary. Finally, Meyer explores a paradox. NHRIs often generate unrealistically high expectations and fail to close that gap. Such a condition can have an unintended, beneficial consequence: it can mobilize advocates and compel authorities over time to reduce the dissonance between lofty formal commitments and continued human rights abuse.

PART I

NHRIs in Theory and Reality

2

National Human Rights Institutions
and State Compliance

Sonia Cardenas

2.1. INTRODUCTION

One of the purposes of any institution is to routinize compliance with a given set of rules, making it more likely that the rules will be followed regardless of changing circumstances or turnover in leadership.[1] National human rights institutions (NHRIs), most often depicted as a bridge between international norms and local implementation are, in principle, designed to assure the state's compliance with its international legal obligations.[2] Obviously diverse, NHRIs are charged most often with promoting and protecting international human rights norms domestically. Even if an NHRI does not always advance the state's compliance, NHRIs – whether through independent activism, cooperation or collusion with the state, or seemingly innocuous promotive work – can alter the human rights landscape domestically. For good or ill, incrementally or dramatically, their incorporation into national human rights struggles cannot be ignored.

NHRIs, then, are not a passing fad. Even when they reflect simple window dressing, or attempts to appease international critics, their existence is still consequential. NHRIs signal the entry of the modern-bureaucratic state into the domestic human rights arena – institutionalizing practices designed to regulate human rights locally. This development is far more crucial than it may seem. Human rights as a field

---

[1] James G. March and Johan P. Olson, "Elaborating the "New Institutionalism," in R. A. W. Rhodes et al. (eds.), *The Oxford Handbook of Political Institutions* (Oxford: Oxford University Press, 2006), pp. 3–20.

[2] See especially Anne Gallagher, "Making Human Rights Treaty Obligations a Reality: Working with New Actors Monitoring and Partners," in P. Alston and J. Crawford (eds.), *The Future of UN Human Rights Treaty Monitoring* (Cambridge: Cambridge University Press, 2000); M. Kjaerum, *National Human Rights Institutions: Implementing Human Rights* (Copenhagen: Danish Institute for Human Rights, 2003); and Sonia Cardenas, "Adaptive States: The Proliferation of National Human Rights Institutions," Carr Center for Human Rights Policy, Kennedy School of Government, Harvard University, Working Paper Series T-01–04 (2001).

has generally been dominated by nonstate actors, often by activists challenging state practices. States' actual role vis-à-vis human rights has of course varied widely, including from protector to violator to hypocrite to mediator. Indeed, even the same state can have a highly ambiguous human rights record, respecting some rights but not others or extending rights selectively to certain groups. And while some states have institutionalized human rights in their foreign policies, the state in general has not tended to regulate human rights practices at home. The "regulatory state" has been active in other arenas of governance, but it is a relative newcomer to the business of regulating human rights domestically.[3]

Despite the historic rise of NHRIs, the creation and influence of these new institutional actors remains puzzling. It is not self-evident, for example, why so many states have created these institutions. States already compliant with international human rights norms would have little incentive to do so, while it is unclear why states with relatively poor human rights records would risk creating potentially destabilizing institutions. Nor is it apparent why states create the particular NHRIs they do. What factors explain the form and function of an NHRI, and what accounts for cross-national variation? Likewise, once created, what is the impact of NHRIs on human rights practices? How, for instance, do these institutions relate to other domestic actors, both nongovernmental and state agencies? These are some of the crucial questions raised by the emergence of NHRIs, whose insertion into global and local human rights discourses merits close attention.

To begin addressing some of these questions, this chapter draws on theories of state compliance. The objective is to identify potential insights rather than offer a definitive analytical account. While the concept of compliance has not always taken center stage in the research on NHRIs, assumptions about why states comply, what constitutes compliance, or why compliance matters always lurk in the background. The study of compliance itself has been approached from virtually every social science discipline and the field of law, and research on *state* compliance is of obvious relevance for NHRIs given its central preoccupation with the state as political actor.[4]

---

[3] John Braithwaite, "The Regulatory State?" in R. A. W. Rhodes et al. (eds.), *The Oxford Handbook of Political Institutions* (Oxford: Oxford University Press, 2006), pp. 407–30.

[4] For dominant texts in international politics and law, T. R. Tyler, *Why People Obey the Law* (New Haven: Princeton University Press, 1990); M. W. Doyle, *International Law and Organization: Closing the Compliance Gap* (Rowman & Littlefield, 2004); A. Chayes and A. H. Chayes, *The New Sovereignty: Compliance with International Regulatory Agreements* (Cambridge: Cambridge University Press, 1998); R. D. Fisher, *Improving Compliance with International Law* (Charlottesville: University Press of Virginia, 1981); Beth Simmons, "Compliance with International Agreements," *Annual Review of Political Science* 1 (1998), 75–93; O. R. Young, *Compliance and Public Authority: A Theory with International Application* (Baltimore: Johns Hopkins University Press, 1979); and Anne-Marie Slaughter and Kal Raustiala, "Considering Compliance," in W. Carlnaes et al. (eds.), *Handbook of International Relations* (Thousand Oaks: Sage, 2002).

National human rights institutions intersect with state compliance in very specific ways. When a state creates an NHRI, it is already complying with a host of international standards calling for the establishment of NHRIs. Arguably, since the post-1993 Vienna World Conference on Human Rights, the expectation has been that states should create NHRIs to implement international norms domestically and that NHRIs should conform minimally to international criteria, elaborated above all in the Paris Principles. NHRIs, moreover, can play an independent role in eliciting broader state compliance. Becoming domestic actors in their own right, NHRIs can influence state compliance by challenging the state and mobilizing society. State compliance in the context of NHRIs can therefore refer to the creation and influence of these human rights institutions: the extent to which the institution complies with international expectations of an independent and effectively functioning NHRI and the degree to which the NHRI itself enhances the likelihood of greater state compliance.

The chapter proceeds as follows. The first section addresses briefly the value of the social sciences for studying NHRIs, so often approached from the perspectives of law and policy. The next section examines the question of institutional creation, reviewing general approaches to state compliance and the research on why states create NHRIs. This is followed by a discussion of NHRI strength, including issues of measurement and an analytical framework for explaining structural variance across NHRIs. The chapter then turns to consider how scholars might assess NHRI effects over time. A concluding section highlights ongoing gaps and substantive questions that might yield productive research on NHRIs: theoretically informed, methodologically rigorous, and pragmatic in its implications for improving institutional design and effectiveness.

2.2. SOCIAL SCIENCE PERSPECTIVES

Just as NHRIs have proliferated impressively in recent decades, the scholarship on these human rights institutions has proceeded apace.[5] Much of this work has

---

[5] For broad overviews and comparative studies, see Linda Reif, "Building Democratic Institutions: The Role of National Human Rights Institutions in Good Governance and Human Rights Protection," *Harvard Human Rights Journal* 13 (2000), 1–69; S. Cardenas, *Chains of Justice: The Global Rise of National Human Rights Institutions* (Philadelphia: University of Pennsylvania Press, forthcoming); J. Mertus, *Human Rights Matters: Local Politics and National Human Rights Institution* (Stanford: Stanford University Press, 2009); K. Hossain (ed.), *Human Rights Commissions and Ombudsman Offices: National Experiences throughout the World* (Boston: Brill, 2000); R. Murray, *The Role of National Human Rights Institutions at the Regional and International Levels: The Experience of Africa* (Oxford: Hart, 2007); B. Burdekin with J. Naum, *National Human Rights Institutions in the Asia-Pacific Region* (Leiden: Nijhoff, 2007); B. Lindsnaes et al. (eds.), *National Human Rights Institutions: Articles and Working Papers* (Copenhagen: Danish Institute for Human Rights, 2000); V. Ayeni et al. (eds.), *Strengthening Ombudsman and Human Rights Institutions in Commonwealth*

been legalistic or policy-driven, oriented toward describing and improving an institution's design and effectiveness. The result has been a wealth of comparative data and analysis on NHRIs, generating valuable insight into how these institutions operate across diverse national and regional contexts.[6] Relatively less work on NHRIs, however, has been done from the perspective of the social sciences, providing a more systematic understanding of why NHRIs vary in the ways and to the extent they do.

Though imperfect, social science approaches can help clarify answers to real-world empirical questions, including those raised in the study of NHRIs. Drawing on diverse methodologies and theories, social scientists often rely on structured comparisons (small or large in number) and they attempt to rule out alternative explanations systematically. The goal is to reach relatively reliable (i.e., replicable) conclusions while offering more compelling accounts of a phenomenon. Skepticism of such approaches abounds, including claims that social complexity is not amenable to scientific inquiry or generalization, presumptions of objectivity are false, causality is impossible to establish, theory is often divorced from practice, and findings can fail to provide pragmatic solutions to concrete problems. Some social science research of course falls into these traps, but much of it is also sufficiently nuanced and self-conscious of its inherent limitations to accommodate criticism. The bottom line is that social science approaches can be deployed productively alongside legal and policy analysis, even for the study of human rights – where ethics, social contestation, and humanism figure prominently.

Adopting a social science perspective toward the study of NHRIs makes sense. First, an extensive literature on compliance and institutions already exists, readily applicable to NHRIs. Second, methodologically, the large and diverse number of NHRIs lends itself to systematic analysis, drawing on a growing body of descriptive data. Third, despite extensive research on NHRIs, ongoing questions of institutional design and effectiveness remain, making a broader use of analytical tools all the more desirable. While the answers may prove elusive and knowledge of NHRIs may remain incomplete, the potential policy payoffs would seem worthwhile. Last, and from the perspective of the social sciences, NHRIs have fallen largely by the wayside, with few systematic attempts made to incorporate them into broader analyses. Yet as relatively new institutional actors situated uniquely between state and society, and concerned with the domestic implementation of international norms, NHRIs

Small and Island States: The Caribbean Experience (London: Commonwealth Secretariat, 2000); and R. B. Howe and D. Johnson (eds.), *Restraining Equality: Human Rights Commissions in Canada* (Toronto: University of Toronto Press, 2000).

6 In addition to work cited in note 5 supra, see Commonwealth Secretariat, *Comparative Study on Mandates of National Human Rights Institutions in the Commonwealth* (London: Commonwealth Secretariat, 2007).

themselves could contribute to the broader study of institutions, compliance, and human rights change.

2.3. WHY STATES ESTABLISH NHRIS

The question of why compliance varies and fluctuates, occurring only sometimes, can be approached from various angles. In general, however, existing explanations have emphasized two basic sources of compliance: strategic calculations (via enforcement or inducement) and normative commitment (via socialization and learning). These are not necessarily mutually exclusive accounts of compliance, since states may be subject to concurrent and multiple sources of compliance.[7] In this sense, normative commitments and strategic calculations can interact to produce complex outcomes or they may work more or less independently of one another to explain different aspects of compliance, such as timing or content. In another scenario, strategic calculations and normative commitments clash, pulling a state's interests in opposing directions; in such instances, social and political struggles over compliance are likely, and longer term dramatic change becomes possible. While abstract, these conceptual building blocks point to a framework for understanding the origins of NHRIs, which may be essential in turn for devising more effective policies.

2.3.1. *Strategic Calculation*

Material incentives can alter the calculations of state actors, mainly via enforcement and inducement.[8] Responding to coercion or the threat of coercion, state agents often comply because they fear the consequences of violating international norms.[9] For enforcement to be effective, however, the costs of norm violations must be sufficiently high. Yet enforcement need not entail a third-party police figure; it can consist of a range of diffuse pressures, including the threat of punishment. Punishment itself can take various forms, whether indirect linkages to broader diplomatic, economic, and political relations, or direct accountability targeting norm violators. Even when punishment is uncertain, state actors may be deterred from violating international norms to avoid indirect threats or the possibility of punishment.

---

[7] For example, Arild Underdal, "Explaining Compliance and Defection: Three Models," *European Journal of International Relations* 4 (1998), 5–30; M. Levi, *Of Rule and Revenue* (Berkeley: University of California Press, 1989).

[8] A similar approach is found in A. T. Guzman, *How International Law Works: A Rational Choice Theory* (Oxford: Oxford University Press, 2008).

[9] See Jonas Tallberg, "Paths to Compliance: Enforcement, Management, and the European Union," *International Organization* 56 (2002), 609–43.

On the inducement side, formal institutions are often viewed as purveyors of benefits rewarding states for compliance. For example, institutions can lower the costs of transactions; increase the certainty that compliance will yield payoffs to an actor's reputation; assure ongoing monitoring and transparency to discourage non-compliance; and in potentially volatile situations, reduce risk by binding the state to future compliance.[10] Likewise, domestic constituencies – depending on their electoral influence and access to information – can help elicit state accountability and compliance.[11] Those who assume that enforcement and inducement are the principal means of assuring state compliance generally view state agents as rational actors who calculate strategically the shifting costs and benefits of complying.

The empirical evidence strongly suggests that numerous states, especially those subject to human rights pressures or poor human rights records, have created NHRIs largely to appease powerful critics. Case studies of NHRIs across the Asia Pacific, Africa, and Middle East support this view.[12] In general, human rights pressures present states with a problem for which NHRIs can provide a solution.[13] Though the most powerful international critics (including major trading partners, the U.S. State Department, or international financial institutions) rarely demand that an NHRI be created, states may deem an NHRI a relatively low-cost strategy for assuaging critics. And where coercion and pressure are the primary motives, a state will in all likelihood create a relatively powerless NHRI, since the goal is to quell powerful human rights critics.

Yet even if states are pressured to create an NHRI, this still does not explain why they would actually do so. Powerful states rarely call explicitly for an NHRI per se to be created. And establishing an NHRI, even a relatively toothless one, still can entail substantial set-up costs, including the provision of facilities, professional staff, and ongoing resources.[14] Nor is it clear why states with relatively strong human rights

---

[10]   In the case of international institutions, see Beth Simmons and Lisa Martin, "International Organizations and Institutions," in W. Carlsnaes et al. (eds.), *Handbook of International Relations*, 192–211. On reputation, see Guzman, *How International Law Works*.

[11]   Xinyuan Dai, "Why Comply? The Domestic Constituency Mechanism," *International Organization* 59 (2005), 363–98; and X. Dai, *International Institutions and National Policies* (Cambridge: Cambridge University Press, 2007).

[12]   Examples include Human Rights Watch (hereafter HRW), *Protectors or Pretenders? Government Human Rights Commissions in Africa* (New York: HRW, 2001); Sonia Cardenas and Andrew Flibbert, "National Human Rights Institutions in the Middle East," *Middle East Journal* 59 (2005), 411–36; Sonia Cardenas, "National Human Rights Commissions in Asia," in J. D. Montgomery and N. Glazer (eds.), *Sovereignty under Challenge: How Governments Respond* (New Brunswick: Transaction, 2002), 55–82, and Cardenas "Adaptive States."

[13]   Sonia Cardenas, "Emerging Global Actors: The United Nations and National Human Rights Institutions," *Global Governance* 9 (2003), 23–42, following Martha Finnemore, *National Interests in International Society* (Ithaca: Cornell University Press, 1996).

[14]   See United Nations, *National Human Rights Institutions: A Handbook on the Establishment and Strengthening of National Institutions for the Promotion and Protection of Human Rights* (New York: UN, 1995).

records, whose broader domestic institutions already facilitate human rights implementation, would bother erecting an NHRI. Indeed, both democratic and nondemocratic states, economically wealthy and poor countries, have created NHRIs. The fact that a wide range of states in world politics has established NHRIs suggests that a more basic normative impetus may also be at work.

2.3.2. *Normative Commitment*

Another set of factors highlights actors' shared interests, identities, and values. Rather than assume that compliance is merely a rational decision, motivated by a universal desire to avoid costs and accrue benefits, the view is that compliance reflects an actor's own standards and prior normative commitments.[15] Under this account, an actor's preferences are socially constructed and historically contingent; while they can be deeply embedded and resistant to change, reform is possible and new norms can be internalized.

Normative commitments can be transformed through socialization, as state agents interact with civil society and counterparts elsewhere.[16] Exchanging information and communicating with others, especially through regularized networks and other institutional forums and channels, is deemed essential.[17] As norms are transmitted, actors have an opportunity to persuade others of the appropriateness of compliance and common identities can be forged. The normative commitments that underlie compliance also are reflected in state bureaucracies and their organizational routines and templates, which can reinforce expectations about compliance and encourage sustainable habits. Technical assistance that conveys expertise and know-how and facilitates training can accordingly be far more significant for complying with international norms than financial incentives – the difference between teaching a recurring skill and offering a one-time handout.[18] At the global level, a focus

---

[15] Examples include Andrew P. Cortell and James W. Davis, Jr., "How Do International Institutions Matter? The Domestic Impact of International Rules and Norms," *International Studies Quarterly* 40 (1996), 451–78; P. J. Katzenstein (ed.), *The Culture of National Security: Norms and Identity in World Politics* (New York: Columbia University Press, 1996); Jeffrey Checkel, "Why Comply? Social Learning and European Identity Change," *International Organization* 55 (2001), 553–88.

[16] Ryan Goodman and Derek Jinks, "How to Influence States: Socialization and International Law," *Duke Law Journal* 54 (2004), 621–703.

[17] M. Keck and K. Sikkink, *Activists beyond Borders: Advocacy Networks in International Politics* (Ithaca: Cornell University Press, 1998); A. Slaughter, *A New World Order: Government Networks and the Disaggregated State* (Princeton: Princeton University Press, 2004); and Emilie M. Hafner-Burton, Miles Kahler, and Alexander H. Montgomery, "Network Analysis for International Relations," *International Organization* 63 (2009), 559–92.

[18] This has been documented most extensively in the case of regulatory regimes that include a scientific component or epistemic communities. E. B. Weiss and H. K. Jacobson (eds.), *Engaging Countries: Strengthening Compliance with International Environmental Accords* (Cambridge: MIT

on "world society" suggests that states learn from repertoires of state action deemed most acceptable by the global community, complying when doing so is the socially appropriate course of action for the majority.[19] Within states, normative commitments are embedded in domestic structures (state and nonstate), institutionalizing particular notions of what constitutes state interests while privileging certain goals and approaches over others.

International standards and support have indeed defined the creation of NHRIs as appropriate and desirable goals for modern states. Even when states create an NHRI to appease critics, normative dynamics arguably are at work. Absent a broader pattern of socialization legitimizing the creation of NHRIs, it would be difficult to account for the *global proliferation* of these institutions.[20] This also helps to explain why NHRI diffusion has followed regional patterns of convergence, as similarly situated states with overlapping identities have joined the NHRI bandwagon.[21] While strategic calculations may help explain the decision of individual states to create an NHRI, normative factors underlie the worldwide diffusion of NHRIs.

2.3.3. *Complex State Preferences*

If social change is complex and dynamic, the full range of pressures a state faces to create an NHRI must be examined, just as it is important to consider distinct pressures for violating international norms.[22] State preferences for creating NHRIs most often reflect incentive structures and prevailing notions of appropriateness. These factors together help explain why states opt to create (or not create) an NHRI, including why noncompliant states may create an NHRI to implement norms they routinely violate or why, ironically, a state already implementing human rights norms

Press, 2000); Chayes and Chayes, *The New Sovereignty*; and R. B. Mitchell, *Intentional Oil Pollution at Sea: Environmental Policy and Treaty Compliance* (Cambridge: MIT Press, 1994); Peter Haas, "Introduction: Epistemic Communities and International Policy Coordination," *International Organization*, 46 (1992), 1–35.

[19] John Meyer et al., "World Society and the Nation-State," *American Journal of Sociology* 103 (1997), 144–81; Jeong-Woo Koo and Francisco O. Ramirez, "National Incorporation of Global Human Rights: Worldwide Expansion of National Human Rights Institutions, 1966–2004," *Social Forces* 87 (2009), 1321–54.

[20] Cardenas, "Emerging Global Actors"; Cardenas, "Adaptive States"; Koo and Ramirez, "National Incorporation of Global Human Rights"; and A. Pohjolainen, *The Evolution of National Human Rights Institutions: The Role of the United Nations* (Copenhagen: Danish Institute for Human Rights, 2006).

[21] Andrew Byrnes, Andrea Durbach, and Catherine Renshaw, "Joining the Club: The Asia Pacific Forum of National Human Rights Institutions, the Paris Principles, and the Advancement of Human Rights Protection in the Region," *University of New South Wales Faculty of Law Research Series* 39 (2008).

[22] Calls for synthesis include Jeffrey T. Checkel, "The Constructivist Turn in International Relations Theory," *World Politics* 50 (1998), 324–48; and Tallberg, "Paths to Compliance."

may face few pressures to establish an NHRI. Yet mounting pressure potentially can shift the structure of incentives and, in a context of global appropriateness, lead even states that previously resisted creating an NHRI to adapt and conform.

Transnational advocacy networks (TANs), for example, illustrate how various compliance mechanisms work in tandem. These networks consist of a cross-segment of actors allied across international and domestic lines to promote social change. Led by advocacy organizations, TANs can lobby powerful international actors to apply pressure on states and thereby alter their strategic calculations. Yet TANs can also serve as vehicles for forging relationships, transmitting international standards, exchanging best practices, and replicating identities. In this sense, TANs can shape state compliance by helping to reconstitute both states' strategic calculations and their normative commitments.[23]

Transnational networks promote the creation and strengthening of NHRIs. In particular, international and regional organizations (governmental and nongovernmental) provide technical assistance, essential for states otherwise lacking requisite domestic capacities, and exchange forums where learning can occur.[24] Technical assistance can be invaluable in transferring expertise, sharing staff, and designing feasible programs. In contrast to states' relative willingness to ratify human rights treaties, norm implementation and the creation of domestic institutions may thus require external assistance and capacity building.

The broader literature on norm violations nonetheless raises a cautionary note about state compliance. If states face pressures to comply, they also can face countervailing forces pushing them to violate international norms.[25] In the human rights arena, countervailing forces can include armed threats, domestic instability, or exclusionary ideologies – factors not typically responsive to compliance pressures. State resistance should not be surprising: many of the practices that today constitute state violations have been around for centuries, long before they were labeled illegal; no amount of incentives or persuasion should ipso facto overturn these powerful sources of norm violation.[26] Human rights change certainly remains possible through consistent and comprehensive approaches, but it is also bound to be highly contingent and uncertain.

---

[23] See especially M. Keck and K. Sikkink, *Activists beyond Borders*.

[24] Sonia Cardenas, "Emerging Global Actors"; Sonia Cardenas, "Constructing Rights? Human Rights Education and the State," *International Political Science Review* 26 (2005), 363–79; and Sonia Cardenas, "Transgovernmental Activism: Canada's Role in Promoting National Human Rights Commissions," *Human Rights Quarterly* 25 (2003), 775–90. See Chapter 7 of this volume for an analysis of these network dynamics in the Asia Pacific region.

[25] Thomas Franck describes similar dynamics in T. Franck, *The Power of Legitimacy among Nations* (New York: Oxford University Press, 1990).

[26] S. Cardenas, *Conflict and Compliance State Responses to International Human Rights Pressure* (Philadelphia: University of Pennsylvania Press, 2007).

2.4. INSTITUTIONAL EFFECTS

If the first generation of academic research on NHRIs focused on issues of institutional creation, more recent analyses of NHRIs have sought to assess an NHRI's effectiveness. The creation of an NHRI, after all, is one step in complying with international human rights norms, but international standards also call on states to create strong and effective NHRIs. The particular NHRIs that states create will of course vary widely in their effects, as Julie Mertus's chapter explores in this volume. This section addresses the question of how to measure the range of an NHRI's strength, before turning to an explanatory framework for why states create NHRIs of varying effectiveness. A more solid grasp of these institutional issues, including the range of NHRI effects and the reasons that NHRIs vary in these effects, may lead to an improved understanding of how to strengthen NHRIs across various contexts.

2.4.1. *Measuring NHRI Strength*

Assessing an NHRI's strength can prove challenging. These institutions are intended to perform a range of tasks; and like state compliance more generally, states often want to appear compliant with norms while simultaneously deviating from these norms. In such cases, partial glimpses at an NHRI can yield an incomplete and misleading picture of the institution's actual effects. The literature on compliance nonetheless offers some insight into how to measure an NHRI's strength.

State compliance is any action by the state that conforms to international norms. International norms, in turn, are socially shared standards of behavior taking the form of rules, laws, procedures, or informal expectations.[27] Compliance seems to be sufficiently straightforward: when state actions conform to international norms, compliance is present; when state actions deviate from international norms, noncompliance occurs. The problem is that international norms tend to stipulate a bundle of obligations, which gives states leeway in the extent to which and manner with which they comply.[28] Take, for example, international norms prohibiting torture. On the one hand, a state is clearly complying with international standards to the extent that it does not practice torture. Compliance can consequently be a matter of degree, insofar as a state complies partially with its international obligations. On the other hand, international norms are themselves complex sets of requirements, consisting

---

[27] See Martha Finnemore and Kathryn Sikkink, "International Norm Dynamics and Political Change," *International Organization* 52 (1998), 887–917; Gary Goertz and Paul F. Diehl, "Toward a Theory of International Norms: Some Conceptual and Measurement Issues," *Journal of Conflict Resolution* 36 (1992), 634–64; and T. Risse et al. (eds.), *The Power of Human Rights: International Norms and Domestic Change* (New York: Cambridge University Press, 1999).

[28] Cardenas, *Conflict and Compliance*, 7–8.

of both primary and secondary rules: primary rules stipulate the core action to be satisfied (i.e., desist from torture), whereas secondary rules refer to subsidiary obligations that a state must satisfy to fulfill compliance with primary rules (e.g., ratify treaties, monitor state practices, change domestic laws, train state agents).[29] Full compliance with primary rules thus captures only one aspect of international demands. Partial compliance, including compliance with secondary rules, cannot be overlooked when assessing a state's conformance to international standards.

Partial compliance, moreover, can be significant over the long term. Any amount of state compliance, however symbolic, can set in motion a potential chain of events, reminiscent of what scholars have dubbed the "spiral" model of human rights change: a state acts to convey an image of compliance. Nonstate and international actors, using direct or indirect threats, can treat this as a political opportunity for demanding greater consistency of action. The state may respond with a partial gesture, potentially opening the way for rising compliance. Full compliance is not guaranteed, certainly not if others desist from pressuring the state or ease off on their demands. However, precisely because state compliance is often part of a much broader dynamic process, even partial gestures and half-measures can potentially contribute to deeper social change.[30]

State compliance is accordingly a complex phenomenon that can occur to varying degrees and consist of diverse actions. Treating compliance simplistically as an all-or-nothing outcome carries the risk of misinterpreting state actions or overlooking potential pathways of influence. Where norm violations exist, political change is bound to be gradual, occurring in fits and starts more than in neat linear fashion. The implications for studying NHRIs are significant, alerting us to a range of institutional influences.

NHRIs should indeed be seen as having a range of effects, across a spectrum of human rights issues.[31] An NHRI might excel in promoting economic and social rights or disability rights but fail to advance gender equality or address human rights concerns that intersect with national security issues.[32] Cross-issue variance aside,

---

[29] On the classic distinction between primary and secondary rules, see H. L. A. Hart, *The Concept of Law* (Oxford: Oxford University Press, 1976). A somewhat similar distinction is made in the Responsibility-to-Protect doctrine between protection and prevention.

[30] See Risse et al., *The Power of Human Rights* (Cambridge: Cambridge University Press, 1990); Finnemore and Sikkink, "International Norm Dynamics and Political Change;" and Cardenas, *Conflict and Compliance*.

[31] In international relations, the distinction between regulative and constitutive norms is borrowed from David Dessler, "What's at Stake in the Agent-Structure Debate?" *International Organization* 43 (1989), 454–8; F. Kratochwil, *Rules, Norms and Decisions: On the Conditions of Practical and Legal Reasoning in International Relations and Domestic Affairs* (Cambridge: Cambridge University Press, 1989).

[32] The intersection of NHRIs and economic-social rights is explored in Mario Gomez, "Social Economic Rights and Human Rights Commissions," *Human Rights Quarterly* 17 (1995), 155–69;

an NHRI's effects can be described generally in terms of *protection* and *promotion*, two goals emphasized explicitly and repeatedly in international documents since the inception of human rights institutions.[33] Protection and promotion, moreover, correspond respectively to an institution's regulative and constitutive effects.[34] Like all analytical categories, an NHRI's protective and promotive functions may in fact overlap or omit specific practices; but the distinction as outlined below can be useful in mapping the broad range of an NHRI's domestic activities. As Chris Sidoti's chapter in this volume shows, an NHRI's effects can also extend to the international system, as NHRIs increasingly participate in recognized forums.

Regulative effects, often intertwined with a legalistic approach, point to an NHRI's capacity to protect human rights through multiple means (e.g., processing complaints, investigating instances of abuse, holding violators accountable). The overarching goal is to remedy wrongdoing, including by confronting the state's failure to protect human rights. Though the NHRI still may remain impotent vis-à-vis the powerful state, its role in demanding human rights protection should not be discounted. Since most NHRIs (like international human rights mechanisms) lack enforcement measures, it is crucial that institutional efforts to protect human rights be assessed beyond improvements in abuse. Human rights abuses offer only a partial and vastly incomplete picture of an NHRI's effects.

Constitutive effects revolve around the promotion of human rights norms, including human rights education.[35] The principal objective in promotion is to increase awareness of human rights norms. Promotive activities should certainly be considered in any assessment of an NHRI's effectiveness, even if the longer term influence of this work remains exceedingly difficult if not impossible to gauge and isolate over time. Assessment efforts are especially complicated when an NHRI's promotive and protective efforts seem to be at odds. For instance, a rise in human rights complaints might signal an advance in the NHRI's promotive but not protective efforts. Whether or not rising awareness of human rights issues leads to

Raj C. Kumar, "National Human Rights Institutions (NHRIs) and Economic, Social and Cultural Rights: Toward the Institutionalization and Developmentalization of Human Rights," *Human Rights Quarterly* 28 (2006), 755–79; and Office of the United Nations High Commissioner for Human Rights, *Economic, Social and Cultural Rights: Handbook for National Human Rights Institutions* (New York: UN, 2005).

[33] Note that the earliest statements by the United Nations on NHRIs, pre-1960, tended to emphasize the role of these institutions purely in supplementing the work of the UN Human Rights Commission itself created to protect and promote human rights. Cardenas, "Emerging Global Actors," 28–9.

[34] On the protection role of NHRIs, see B. G. Ramcharan, *The Protection Role of National Human Rights Institutions* (Leiden: Brill, 2005); Reif, "Building Democratic Institutions;" and Brice Dickson, "The Contribution of Human Rights Commissions to the Protection of Human Rights," *Public Law* 272 (2003), 272–85.

[35] Cardenas discusses the promotive work of the South African Human Rights Commission in "Constructing Rights?"

longer term improvements will vary by context, as discussed below, but social effects that occur alongside ongoing violations can be significant in their own right. Promotion by NHRIs is actually consistent with the domestic cultural change identified by Julie Mertus in her chapter or Obiora Okafor's emphasis in this volume on a holistic approach.

For the purposes of assessing an NHRI's strength, institutional effects can be viewed multidimensionally through the lens of both protection and promotion, even while recognizing that variance by issue or even jurisdiction (e.g., national versus local NHRIs in federal systems like India's or Mexico's) is possible. The assumption is that the strongest institutions will be those that both protect and promote human rights, as Richard Carver's chapter on Central and Eastern Europe shows, followed by those NHRIs that emphasize protection (remedies) over promotion (awareness).[36] While promotion can be fundamental in the long term, protection by an NHRI implies a certain level of assertiveness in interacting with powerful state actors and norm violators; it represents a more direct, if circumscribed, effect on state behavior. An NHRI's profile as a protective-promotive institution provides a typology of an NHRIs overall strength, or degree of effectiveness, a tool for comparing institutions rather than a metric for classifying NHRIs. As a simplifying device, the typology offers a reasonable vantage point from which to study NHRI influence.

2.4.2. *Beyond Form and Function*

Two key assumptions animate the research on the strength and effectiveness of NHRIs. First, analysts most often trace an NHRI's effectiveness to its formal structural characteristics. Second, broad agreement exists that an NHRI's effectiveness cannot be understood adequately without examining the local context, or the domestic environment in which the institution operates.

Structural criteria for NHRIs are delineated in international documents and are the cornerstone of the Paris Principles. Widespread agreement exists, for example, that NHRIs require formal independence from the executive power, sufficient resources, and close relations with civil society to function effectively. The assumption is that these criteria are essential both for defining an NHRI and accounting for its overall influence. These criteria are deemed so fundamental that, where these structural characteristics are severely compromised – as they were for Fiji in 2007, for example – the International Coordinating Committee can withdraw an NHRI's international accreditation.

In addition to formal structural characteristics, the literature on NHRIs has emphasized the importance of local context, which inevitably mediates an NHRI's

---

[36] See Chapter 8, this volume.

strength and effectiveness. Researchers have identified a broad range of potentially significant domestic factors, including the role of post-conflict societies, regime type, level and type of violations, democratic transitions, and even the economic climate.[37] Yet in the final analysis, the literature seems to be at a standstill in terms of which domestic factors matter and how exactly they are significant.

While an NHRI's structural characteristics – forms and functions – as well as its domestic context clearly are significant, two questions remain unanswered: Why do state leaders create the particular NHRIs they do, with varying structural characteristics that inevitably shape and constrain an institution? And which features of the domestic political context are most important in influencing an NHRI's effectiveness? These questions are probed later, again drawing on basic insights from the research on state compliance.

2.4.3. *Toward a Theory of NHRI Influence*

In creating and designing an NHRI, states can be subject to international and domestic pressures. These pressures can take various forms, as outlined later, reflecting the influence of both strategic calculation and normative commitment. On balance, the literature on compliance suggests two key propositions: the strongest NHRIs (i.e., those highly protective and promotive) will be found in (1) states that both face incentives to build a strong NHRI and deem it normatively appropriate to do so; and (2) states subject to international and domestic, or two-level, pressures. Domestic pressures should also be more closely associated with the protective aspect of an NHRI, with international pressures accounting more closely for an NHRI's promotive role.[38] Absent domestic pressures, the perceived costs of a strong NHRI may simply seem too high for a state, while a promotive NHRI could appear optimal.

Identifying domestic pressures can be challenging, but the broader human rights literature suggests that democratization is a useful indicator. Leaders of democratizing states may be more inclined to permit independent NHRIs as a means of binding the state to future compliance.[39] The appeal of doing so may be greatest

---

[37] See Mertus, *Human Rights Matters*; and M. Parlevliet, *National Human Rights Institutions and Peace Agreements: Establishing National Institutions in Divided Societies* (Versoix: International Council on Human Rights Policy (hereafter cited as ICHRP), 2006).

[38] This is consistent with the claim that compliance with international norms will be higher in states where these norms are already embedded in domestic structures. These include Risse et al., *The Power of Human Rights*; Cortell and Davis, "How Do International Institutions Matter?" Finnemore and Sikkink, "International Norm Dynamics and Political Change"; Checkel, "Why Comply?" and Katzenstein, *The Culture of National Security*.

[39] Andy Moravcsik applies this explanation to human rights treaty commitments in Moravcsik, "The Origins of Human Rights Regimes: Democratic Delegation in Postwar Europe," *International Organization* 54 (2000), 217–52.

in the context of domestic constitutional reform, itself signaling an interest in self-regulation. For democratizing states, a stronger NHRI will serve as a useful binding device and be normatively appropriate (insofar as democracies are substantively associated with higher degrees of human rights commitment and protection).[40] The claim is not that all democratizing states will create highly protective NHRIs, only that democratizing states are most likely to face domestic pressures for creating a relatively strong NHRI. And while long-standing democracies – in all of their variants – generally respect human rights to a higher degree than other types of regimes, incentives to create a strong NHRI are relatively low for long-standing democracies, precisely because human rights compliance and norm implementation are already high. In general, then, democratizing states (compared to long-standing democracies and nondemocracies) will face the most pressures for building a protective NHRI.

International pressures can raise the costs of noncompliance for a state and define the criteria by which a strong NHRI should be created. While international pressure is not always applied in direct proportion to human rights abuses, to some extent it is a response to existing violations – so the level of abuse can serve as a proxy for international pressure. Human rights is more likely to be on the agenda of states violating international norms, making the promotion (versus protection) of human rights seem a relatively innocuous task to placate human rights critics. Past abuses will instead fall under the purview of temporary, ad hoc truth commissions, not permanent NHRIs. International pressures may also be relevant for states that have already committed to human rights in their foreign policies, since such states may have an international incentive to maintain their status as international human rights leaders. Likewise, international pressures are likely to be strong for states entering an internationally brokered peace agreement, as these agreements often call for the creation of an NHRI and can lead to extensive international assistance.[41]

These dynamics trace the strength of an NHRI to a particular mix of domestic and international factors. As Table 2.1 shows, the most protective and promotive NHRIs should be found in states subject to both international and domestic pressures. Second, states facing high domestic pressures but few international ones may devise, somewhat paradoxically, NHRIs that are mostly protective, though this outcome

---

[40] For empirical evidence, see Christian Davenport and David A. Armstrong, "Democracy and the Violation of Human Rights: A Statistical Analysis from 1976 to 1996," *American Journal of Political Science* 48 (2003), 538–54; Bruce Bueno de Mesquita et al., "Thinking Inside the Box: A Closer Look at Democracy and Human Rights," *International Studies Quarterly* 49 (2005), 741–3; Stephen Poe et al., "Repression of Human Rights to Personal Integrity in the 1980s: A Global Analysis," *American Political Science Review* 88 (1994), 853–72; and Stephen Poe et al., "Repression of the Human Right to Personal Integrity Revisited: A Global Cross-National Study Covering the Years 1976–1993," *International Studies Quarterly* 43 (1999), 291–313.

[41] See A. Brysk, *Global Good Samaritans: Human Rights as Foreign Policy* (Oxford: Oxford University Press, 2009); Parlevliet, *National Human Rights Institutions and Peace Agreements*.

TABLE 2.1. *Two-level sources of NHRI strength*

		International pressures	
		Lower	*Higher*
Domestic Pressures	*Higher*	II Mostly Protective	I Most Protective and Promotive
	Lower	IV Least Protective and Promotive	III Mostly Promotive

may be the least frequent in practice. In contrast, where international pressures are strong but domestic pressures are relatively low, an NHRI may tend to be fairly promotive. This common situation reveals how long-standing democracies with relatively strong human rights records still may opt for a weakly promotive NHRI or, alternatively, why an abusive regime will attempt to establish an NHRI. The weakest NHRIs, however, will be associated with low domestic and international pressures.

In simplifying a complex set of interactions, this analysis does not deny the influence of other factors. On the contrary, civil society groups can be essential in applying international pressure and in supporting processes of democratization and constitutional reform.[42] Likewise, the role of individual leadership should not be overlooked, since many NHRIs – like any organization – thrive under the independent-mindedness or perseverance of particular commissioners or, alternatively, flounder in the face of passive leadership. Nor should the interests of powerful state actors who might oppose an NHRI, such as security forces, be discounted. All of these interests are accounted for in this framework by the level of ongoing abuse and the extent of democratization. Empirical studies, certainly, should incorporate these various actors into a close analysis of NHRI influence.

The fact that NHRIs are designed to implement international human rights norms domestically does curtail their strength from the outset and presents these institutions with a particular set of challenges vis-à-vis state compliance. First, NHRIs are most needed where state compliance is weakest. The same sources that propel norm violations will therefore constrain an NHRI's effectiveness. Second, human rights compliance requires norm implementation. Human rights compliance, after all, entails not just desisting from prohibited actions. It requires that state agents learn alternative strategies and rights-protective procedures for interacting with civil society and, should norm violations occur, that societal actors know how

---

[42] See, for instance, A. Florini et al. (eds.), *The Third Force: The Rise of Transnational Civil Society* (Washington, DC: Carnegie Endowment for International Peace, 2000); and S. Burgerman, *Moral Victories: How Activists Provoke Multilateral Action* (Ithaca: Cornell University Press, 2001).

to make claims against the state for restitution and accountability. Implementation is thus part and parcel of human rights compliance. Third, human rights compliance entails *self-regulation*. This engages a very different set of incentives from other forms of compliance where strategic interaction with other actors (including fears of cheating) may prevail. Unlike other types of state compliance, for which trust and third-party external intervention may be more relevant, self-regulation necessitates that compliance be rooted in a state's normative commitments.[43] All told, NHRIs face substantial challenges: they are most constrained where they are most needed, they are essential in the long term, and they must ultimately change normative commitments to succeed.

2.5. INSTITUTIONAL TRAJECTORIES AND HUMAN RIGHTS CHANGE

Human rights change is inherently dynamic, so static snapshots of an institution's effects can be incomplete and even misleading. While an NHRI's effectiveness at any given moment may be constrained by its origins, institutions can also take on a life of their own as this section elaborates. Institutions, that is, can come to have effects over time that are quite independent of their original capabilities and performance.[44] This can help to explain why an NHRI that is mostly promotive can become rather influential and even more protective, or how emerging normative commitments may help transform strategic calculations. In this regard, the broader domestic environment can play a crucial role.

An NHRI's impact on state compliance varies depending on whether it is "protective" or "promotive" or both. National human rights institutions that are "protective" are relatively more capable of challenging the state to comply with its international legal obligations. Though rarely in a position to punish the state directly, NHRIs threaten to raise the costs of noncompliance; and in some cases, NHRIs have powerful international allies that can apply pressure on a recalcitrant state. Even if reform does not occur instantly, in the give-and-take of communication states may relent and at least offer gestures or concessions.[45] Concurrent international human rights pressure certainly may contribute to greater state compliance, since NHRIs never operate in isolation; but calling on states consistently and forcefully to comply with international human rights norms is one of the most effective actions an NHRI can take to protect human rights in the long run.

---

[43] For a relevant discussion of self-regulation, see D. Brown and N. Woods, *Making Global Self-Regulation Effective in Developing Countries* (Oxford: Oxford University Press, 2007).

[44] See generally Rhodes et al., *The Oxford Handbook of Political Institutions*, Parts I and II.

[45] Thomas Risse, "'Let's Argue': Communicative Action in World Politics," *International Organization* 54 (2000), 1–39. See also Rodger A. Payne, "Persuasion, Frames, and Norm Construction," *European Journal of International Relations* 7 (2001), 37–61.

Even a largely promotive NHRI can prove significant by mobilizing societal actors, as Enrique Peruzzotti traces in his chapter on the ombudsman office in Argentina. In promoting human rights norms, NHRIs engage in socializing activities that are essential for compliance, including agenda-setting (as human rights issues are placed on local and national agendas) and disseminating notions of human rights within civil society and the state apparatus. These activities serve to raise public awareness, legitimating the concept of human rights and potentially shifting expectations about appropriate state behavior. NHRIs can socialize state actors (principals and agents) to the understanding that human rights compliance is appropriate, in the process delegitimizing norm violations. Human rights training of state professionals also can contribute to compliance incrementally, as the state's representatives perhaps learn to change their practices and operating procedures. At the level of civil society, NHRIs can tap into the mobilizing role of the media, while human rights awareness can lead to rising demands and claims for human rights protection. Though social demands and claims need not translate into actual protection, they make reform possible, both by reinforcing the place of human rights on a state's agenda and enhancing the likelihood of transnational pressure. In a subsequent "boomerang" effect, a state that initially neglected its domestic opposition could be forced to respond to more intense transnational pressures.[46]

States violating human rights will not tend to respond to domestic pressures for social change instantly or fully, but the gestures and concessions they make to appease critics often constitute partial compliance or steps on the way to fuller compliance.[47] In some cases, states will respond so as to further implement human rights norms, even strengthening or reforming NHRIs. And as the domestic political climate shifts, even partial forms of state compliance (themselves reflecting a broad configuration of factors, beyond NHRIs) can feed back to strengthen an NHRI still further. Just as a human rights treaty's most significant effects may be indirect, energizing domestic constituencies, the mobilizing potential of NHRIs should be duly recognized.[48]

That said, NHRIs can also affect state compliance more directly, as Figure 2.1 illustrates. Insofar as state elites can be deterred from violating human rights due to the certainty of punishment (and this is debatable), a strong NHRI that enhances the likelihood of state accountability and punishment for human rights crimes may contribute to state compliance directly. This mechanism, however, may be relevant for states that are already relatively compliant. In democratizing and transitional contexts where the state has aligned its normative commitments with human rights

---

[46] On the boomerang effect, see Keck and Sikkink, *Activists beyond Borders*.
[47] See Jonas Tallberg, "Paths to Compliance."
[48] B. Simmons, *Mobilizing for Human Rights* (Cambridge: Cambridge University Press, 2009).

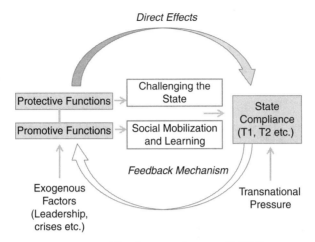

FIGURE 2.1. The domestic impact of NHRIs.

norms and state leaders may seek to lock in the state's future compliance, the reports and information generated by NHRIs about norm violations may be valuable in increasing transparency and assuring that individual state agents do not deviate from public commitments to human rights. In these settings, human rights education can also play a crucial role in socializing state agents and stabilizing domestic expectations about appropriate modes of state-society interaction.[49]

This analytic framework, summarized in Figure 2.1, suggests that the influence of NHRIs is only partially driven by a path-dependent logic. To be sure, institutional origins leave an indelible imprint on an NHRI's development. International and domestic pressures, reflecting both strategic calculation and normative commitment, go a long way toward explaining when an NHRI is created and the particular form it takes. Structural design in turn plays a key role in shaping an institution's capacities and interests, as Linda Reif suggests in her chapter. Institutional origins thus can account partly for the effectiveness of NHRIs in protecting and promoting human rights. An NHRI's broader impact on state compliance, however, is not predetermined. Even an institution's direct effects on state compliance are mediated by domestic incentives and norms, while exogenous factors (including individual leaders or national crises) can intervene to alter outcomes.

Perhaps more important, NHRIs can shape state compliance indirectly and over the long term, by challenging the state to comply and by mobilizing social actors on behalf of human rights. Sometimes the state will respond in ways that feed back to

---

[49] Beth Simmons suggests that the potential for human rights treaties to mobilize society and elicit change is lowest in stable democracies or stable autocracies. See Simmons, *Mobilizing Human Rights*.

reinforce and strengthen an NHRI, especially when faced with consistent or intense transnational pressure. NHRIs can contribute to state compliance in the long term, therefore, both directly and indirectly. Where egregious and systemically embedded human rights violations have occurred in the recent past, state compliance is bound to be a dynamic and protracted process. NHRI's can shape, but not overcome, this reality.

2.6. COMPLIANCE AND NHRIS THROUGH A CRITICAL LENS

State compliance and NHRIs are often treated as unproblematic policy goals and outcomes, though both can be viewed critically. Critics may warn of the unintended consequences of promoting NHRIs aggressively. Observers like Obiora Okafor, among others in this volume, have noted for example that an overreliance on the Paris Principles has led to minimalist appraisal of NHRI effectiveness. Too much emphasis on institutional creation can lead states to establish NHRIs that conform to the basic parameters of an NHRI but are not optimally tailored to local conditions or that remain inaccessible to those members of society who most need them.

Under some circumstances, NHRIs may even have destabilizing effects. Although NHRIs have become staples advocated by the world community for post-conflict societies, the optimum circumstances for their creation in these volatile contexts are far from clear.[50] They may carry the risk of being imposed prematurely on an institutional landscape ripe with unresolved questions of transitional justice. Even under far more stable conditions, NHRIs that represent a large gap between institutional promises and capacities can serve to heighten expectations that cannot be met.[51] This in turn can undermine the broader legitimacy of human rights institutions, perpetuating the view that human rights belong purely to the realm of rhetoric. NHRIs can therefore lead to domestic instability as heightened social demands confront a resistant state and feed into violence. Under other circumstances, an NHRI can take steps that systematically displace human rights supporters, whether in or out of the state, essentially subverting the broader human rights agenda.

Most broadly, moreover, the unquestioning promotion of NHRIs may be subject to a familiar critique of imperialism. The universal promotion of NHRIs, or the domestic implementation of international human rights, across various contexts – democratizing regimes, diverse regions and cultures, and post-conflict societies – assumes that a rights model can and should be readily exported.[52] While

---

[50] Parlevliet, *National Human Rights Institutions and Peace Agreements*; and Mertus, *Human Rights Matters.*

[51] For example, Cardenas, "Transgovernmental Activism" and "Constructing Rights?"

[52] For related critiques, see C. Douzinas, *Human Rights and Empire: The Political Philosophy of Cosmopolitanism* (New York: Routledge, 2007); and Upendra Baxi, "Politics of Reading Human

international best practices do leave room for tailoring NHRIs to local conditions, in practice the promotion of NHRIs often emphasizes the adoption of particular organizational infrastructures, blueprints that may not be entirely compatible with a domestic context.[53]

One basic danger is that states are becoming more interested in creating an NHRI per se than in the general principle of implementing human rights domestically. NHRIs may come to acquire the structural features associated with a checklist of international requirements but substantively remain shallow, or simply fail to fulfill their potential. While the alternatives may be no better, critical awareness of the domestic context and the social impact of NHRIs is essential if these institutions are to contribute to sustainable human rights reform.

2.7. RESEARCH AND POLICY IMPLICATIONS

The state has variously fallen in and out of fashion with students of international politics and law. Within the human rights field, the state has more often than not been demonized as the principal violator of international norms.[54] While the role of international actors and domestic nonstate actors has been emphasized, domestic state institutions have received remarkably little attention (with the partial exception of agents of atrocity like the police or military and agents of legal reform like the judiciary). Yet NHRIs figure uniquely in the human rights landscape, situated between the state and society and serving as a potential bridge between international norms and domestic implementation.[55] A well-functioning NHRI (assuming no redundancy with similar national bodies) can play a coordinating role domestically, serving as a focal point for the state's human rights policies.

Despite ongoing criticism, NHRIs are here to stay, certainly as long as states seek to regulate and manage discrete issues via the creation of national commissions and institutions.[56] Arguably, domestic change and reform cannot occur without embedding human rights norms within state structures. While the bureaucratization of human rights concerns within the state apparatus may sit uneasily with some,

---

Rights: Inclusion and Exclusion within the Production of Human Rights," in S. Meckled-García et al. (eds.), *The Legalization of Human Rights: Multidisciplinary Perspectives on Human Rights and Human Rights Law* (New York: Routledge, 2006).

[53] See Amnesty International, *NHRIs: Recommendations for Effective Protection and Promotion of Human Rights* (London: AI Index: IOR 40/007/2001); and Commonwealth Secretariat, *National Human Rights Institutions: Best Practice.*

[54] Sonia Cardenas, "Human Rights and the State," in K. Mills and C. Sriram (eds.), *International Studies Encyclopedia* (Oxford: Blackwell, forthcoming).

[55] Anne Smith, "The Unique Position of National Human Rights Institutions," *Human Rights Quarterly* 28 (2006), 904–46.

[56] Braithwaite, "The Regulatory State?" and Slaughter, *A New World Order.*

observers and activists should resist the temptation to dismiss these institutions. Even in contexts where NHRIs are powerless bodies – shameless attempts by a hypocritical state to appease critics – NHRIs constitute a new domestic actor; and their potential to contribute to state compliance is real if no less difficult. Like the state itself, NHRIs must be factored into human rights analysis.

National human rights institutions may well shed light on a broader set of dynamics. While studies of state compliance and commitment abound, it may be useful to examine more fully and empirically the mechanisms and impact of implementing international norms domestically. Why, for instance, do attempts at norm implementation appear to succeed only sometimes? How should we measure and assess norm implementation? How does norm implementation interact with treaty commitments to further state compliance?[57] And what role do trans-governmental networks of NHRIs, versus other actors, play in shaping an NHRI'sperformance?[58] How do the domestic legal and political realms interact in shaping an NHRI's effectiveness, and how exactly does civil society mediate an NHRI's influence?

Interested in improving the real-world effectiveness of NHRIs, the research on NHRIs is becoming increasingly concerned with devising evaluative metrics and deriving policy lessons.[59] One of the key challenges in this regard is that both an NHRI's influence and human rights change are dynamic processes: what may work at one time or in one place may not be effective in another. Theory can help model some of these complexities and delimit scope conditions, but systematic empirical analysis (including up-close analysis of conditions on the ground, as perceived by a spectrum of state and nonstate actors) is also needed.

Insights from the research on state compliance presented here advance a few propositions worth exploring further. Institutional design is rooted in a complex set of political and social circumstances, reflecting international and domestic pressures, which are not fixed but cannot be readily overcome. Institutional design not only shapes what an NHRI does; it also affects the organization's broader capacity to make a mark domestically, influencing state compliance both directly and indirectly. Even partial, ambiguous, and largely promotive actions can matter,

---

57 A. Müller and F. Seidensticker, *The Role of National Human Rights Institutions in the United Nations Treaty Body Process* (Berlin: German Institute for Human Rights, 2007); and Gallagher, "Making Human Rights Treaty Obligations a Reality."
58 Noha Shawki, "Transgovernmental Networks of National Human Rights Institutions and Their Contribution to Global Governance," in N. Shawki and M. Cox (eds.), *Rethinking Sovereignty and Human Rights after the Cold War* (Farnham: Ashgate, 2009).
59 Examples include R. Carver, *Assessing the Effectiveness of National Human Rights Institutions* (Versoix: ICHRP, 2005); R. Carver, *Performance and Legitimacy: National Human Rights Institutions* (Versoix: ICHRP, 2004); and Stephen Livingstone and Rachel Murray, "The Effectiveness of National Human Rights Institutions: The Northern Ireland Human Rights Commission with Comparisons from South Africa," in S. Halliday and Patrick Schmidt (eds.), *Human Rights Brought Home: Socio-Legal Perspectives on Human Rights in the National Context* (Oxford: Hart, 2005).

potentially altering the domestic environment. In fact, the most long-lasting and powerful effects of an NHRI may be indirect: challenging and persuading the state while mobilizing social forces.

National human rights institutions have an inordinately difficult task before them. Where they are most needed, they are virtually doomed to disappoint. Assessing these institutions therefore requires adopting a highly mediated and long-term view of human rights change and state compliance. Just as NHRIs cannot automatically be equated with the state, norm implementation remains distinct from a state's compliance. The social science research on compliance and NHRIs suggests above all that institutional origins matter but are not determinative and that institutional effects are both complex and dynamic.

Contrary to the human rights field's focus on violations, the level of human rights abuse should not be the primary touchstone for evaluating an NHRI's influence. In most cases, it is too difficult to determine the causal connections between an NHRI and changing levels of human rights abuse within a country. An NHRI's effectiveness is most evident in the intermediate actions it takes: NHRIs that challenge the state and mobilize civil society on behalf of human rights concerns may potentially contribute most to state compliance.

3

The Shifting Boundaries of NHRI Definition in the International System

Linda C. Reif

3.1. INTRODUCTION

NHRIs and related institutions for the protection and promotion of human rights are horizontal accountability state institutions that provide checks and balances on government conduct.[1] Most of them do not have the power to impose their own decisions on the government. Instead, they are given a range of soft powers, from advice and recommendation to the ability to bring actions before constitutional and other courts.[2]

A sustained focus has been placed on NHRIs for two decades, yet there are still different points of view on which domestic institutions involved in human rights protection and promotion should be identified as NHRIs. NHRI identification is increasingly important on the international level for the access it brings to the human rights machinery of the UN and other regional organizations. However, NHRI identification has been complicated over the same period by the establishment of a variety of domestic institutions that engage fully or partly in human rights activities.

Human rights commissions are universally recognized as NHRIs and hybrid human rights ombudsman institutions are increasingly accepted as such, although some still minimize the role of the latter.[3] Thematic human rights institutions (such

---

[1] United Nations, *National Human Rights Institutions: A Handbook on the Establishment and Strengthening of National Institutions for the Promotion and Protection of Human Rights* (New York: UN, 1995), p. 6 (*hereafter* NHRI Handbook); A. Schedler, L. Diamond, and M. F. Plattner (eds.), *The Self-Restraining State: Power and Accountability in New Democracies* (Boulder: Lynne Rienner, 1999).

[2] Linda Reif, "Building Democratic Institutions: The Role of National Human Rights Institutions in Good Governance and Human Rights Protection," *Harvard Human Rights Journal* 13 (2000), 7–11; Christopher Elmendorf, "Advisory Counterparts to Constitutional Courts," *Duke Law Journal* 56 (2007), 961–3.

[3] United Nations, *Office of the High Commissioner for Human Rights, Survey on National Human Rights Institutions* (Geneva: UN, 2009) (*hereafter* NHRI Survey) (includes commissions and human

My special thanks to Shannon Mather (LLB 2010) for her valuable research assistance and to the University of Alberta which provided an EFF/SAS grant to fund the research for this chapter.

as those for children's rights, equality or minority rights) are also candidates for inclusion although it is argued that they are too narrowly focused to be called NHRIs.[4] Although classical ombudsman institutions do not have an express human rights mandate, some of them engage in investigations that involve human rights and the application of human rights law.[5] However, they are often excluded from the NHRI definition.[6] Sub-national human rights institutions are also often excluded.

This chapter argues that while there are different NHRI definitions in use on the international level, the predominant definition is that implemented through the UN Office of the High Commissioner for Human Rights (OHCHR) and the International Coordinating Committee of National Institutions for the Promotion and Protection of Human Rights (ICC) accreditation process, which rely on the UN Paris Principles as fleshed out by General Observations.[7] This predominant definition includes essentially only national-level human rights commissions and human rights ombudsman institutions. While this has resulted in a recentering of the NHRI concept, it is a relatively conservative movement. In contrast, the European region has embraced a more liberal conceptualization that includes the full range of domestic institutions involved in human rights matters. These differing definitions are used to implement the organizations' gatekeeper, participation, and quality oversight functions in their relationships with NHRIs and member states. Human rights researchers need to be aware of NHRI definitional boundaries implemented in different contexts and move beyond them if necessary to explore the full range of domestic institutions involved in human rights protection and promotion that may be active in a nation.

3.2. DIVERGENT UN AND REGIONAL INTERNATIONAL ORGANIZATION ATTITUDES TO NHRI

Different approaches to NHRI definition can be found inside the UN and in regional international organizations. These differences have been exacerbated by developments on the ground in the different regions.

---

rights ombudsmen). But see B. G. Ramcharan, *The Protection Role of National Human Rights Institutions* (Leiden: Brill, 2005) (*hereafter* Protection Role of NHRIs) (includes only one hybrid, the Ghana NHRI); Gauthier de Beco, "Networks of European National Human Rights Institutions," *European Law Journal* 14 (2008), 860–77 (excludes the many human rights ombudsman institutions). "Ombudsman" means "representative."

4 M. Kjaerum, *National Human Rights Institutions: Implementing Human Rights* (Copenhagen: Danish Institute for Human Rights, 2003), 6. But see *NHRI Handbook*, 8.

5 L. Reif, *The Ombudsman, Good Governance and the International Human Rights System* (Leiden: Martinus Nijhoff, 2004) (*hereafter* Ombudsman and International Human Rights System).

6 B. Lindsnaes, L. Lindholt, and K. Yigen (eds.), *National Human Rights Institutions: Articles and Working Papers* (Copenhagen: Danish Institute for Human Rights, 2001), 2–3.

7 Principles Relating to the Status of National Institutions, U.N.G.A. Res. 48/134, UN Doc. A/RES/48/134 (1993), rep. in *NHRI Handbook*, supra note 1, 37–8 (*hereafter* the Paris Principles).

3.2.1. *UN System*

Many institutions do not fit easily within the fairly narrow NHRI conceptualization in the UN's 1991 Paris Principles. This can be attributed in part to an important institutional design development that was omitted when the Paris Principles
were drafted. The Paris Principles do not contain a definition of an NHRI and
only refer to the basic functional principle that "[a] national institution shall be
vested with competence to promote and protect human rights."[8] The Principles
also state that ombudsmen and mediators are "other bodies ... responsible for
the promotion and protection of human rights" – a contradiction that technically excludes them from the NHRI definition yet recognizes that they are human
rights institutions.[9] However, the UN Human Rights Centre recognized early on
that the Paris Principles were "standards on the status and advisory role of national
human rights commissions."[10] The focus on the advisory commission model is seen
in the emphasis on pluralism of "membership," use of "commission" language
and an optional complaints-investigation mandate.[11] Yet, by 1991, the human rights
ombudsman had spread beyond Spain and Portugal to Latin America (Guatemala,
Colombia), Central Europe (Poland, Hungary, Croatia, Slovenia, Macedonia, and
Romania) and Africa (Namibia) with many more established subsequently.[12] Today,
there are almost as many human rights ombudsman institutions as there are commissions. The Paris Principles' commission-bias is now outdated in terms of institutional structural realities.

In 1995, the UN Human Rights Centre, for the purpose of UN activities, defined
an NHRI as "a body which is established by a Government under the constitution, or by law or decree, the functions of which are specifically defined in terms
of the promotion and protection of human rights."[13] It indicated that the majority
of NHRIs at the time could be divided into the two "broad categories" of human
rights commissions or ombudsmen.[14] While the *Handbook* recognized the development of the human rights ombudsman, it was ambivalent on whether the classical ombudsman could be considered an NHRI, although the proposed definition
appeared to exclude it.

---

[8] Ibid., "Competence and responsibilities," art. 1.
[9] Ibid., "Methods of operation" (f).
[10] *NHRI Handbook*, 6.
[11] The Paris Principles, "Competence and responsibilities"; "Additional principles concerning the status
of commissions with quasi-jurisdictional competence."
[12] Reif, Ombudsman and International Human Rights System, 157–60, 188–90, 234–7; G. Kucsko-
Stadlmayer (ed.), *European Ombudsman-Institutions: A Comparative Legal Analysis Regarding the
Multi-faceted Realisation of an Idea* (Springer Wein: New York, 2008).
[13] *NHRI Handbook*, p. 6.
[14] Ibid., pp. 7–8.

Subsequently, many UN human rights bodies have referred to independent NHRIs and their importance.[15] However, in UN treaty committee General Comments and related documents this is often accomplished without definitional/design specificity beyond the independence requirement and the importance of compliance with the Paris Principles.[16] One exception is the Committee on Economic, Social and Cultural Rights' General Comments that, until 2009, have included "ombudsmen" within the NHRI concept or have listed them and human rights commissions as institutions that should be used by International Covenant on Economic, Social and Cultural Rights (ICESCR) state parties to address violations of ICESCR rights.[17] The Committee on the Rights of the Child calls for the establishment of thematic NHRIs for children that are Paris Principles-compliant, initially conceptually separating the NHRI concept from the single-office holder children's ombudsman or commissioner, but later including the latter institutions as NHRIs.[18] For states with limited resources, the Committee recognizes that a thematic NHRI may not be feasible and allows for

[15] See Chris Sidoti in this volume, "National Human Rights Institutions and the International Human Rights System."

[16] E.g., Human Rights Committee, General Comment No. 31, "The Nature of the General Legal Obligation Imposed on State Parties to the Covenant." UN Doc. CCPR/C/21/Rev.1/Add.13 (May 26, 2004), para.15 (ICCPR, art. 2(3). But see Committee on the Elimination of Racial Discrimination, General Recommendation No. 17, "Establishment of National Institutions to Facilitate Implementation of the Convention" (March 25, 1993), para.1 ("National Commissions or Other Appropriate Bodies").

[17] Committee on Economic, Social and Cultural Rights: General Comment No. 10, "The Role of National Human Rights Institutions in the Protection of Economic, Social and Cultural Rights," UN Doc. E/C.12/1998/25 (December 14, 1998) para. 2 (NHRIs include national human rights commissions, ombudsman offices, human rights advocates, and defensores del pueblo); General Comment No. 16, "The Equal Right of Men and Women to the Enjoyment of All Economic, Social and Cultural Rights" (ICESCR art. 3), UN Doc. E/C.12/2005/4 (August 11, 2005), para. 38; General Comment No. 17, "The Right of Everyone to Benefit from Any Scientific, Literary or Artistic Production of which He or She Is the Author" (ICESCR art. 15(1)(c)), UN Doc. E/C.12/GC/17 (January 12, 2006) para. 54; General Comment No. 19, "The Right to Social Security" (ICESCR art. 9), UN Doc. E/C.12/GC/19 (February 4, 2008), para. 77. But see General Comment No. 18, "The Right to Work," UN Doc. E/C.12/GC/18 (November 24, 2005), para. 48. (Trade unions and human rights commissions should play an important role in defending the right to work.) General Comment No. 20, "Non-discrimination in Economic, Social and Cultural Rights" (ICESCR art. 2(2)), UN Doc. E/C.12/GC/20 (June 20, 2009) para. 40 (institutions include "national human rights institutions and/or ombudspersons").

[18] UN Committee on the Rights of the Child: General Comment No. 2, "National Human Rights Institutions in the Promotion and Protection of the Rights of the Child," UN Doc. CRC/GC/2002/2 (November 15, 2002), paras. 1 ("NHRIs and Children's Ombudspersons/Children's Commissioners"), 4, 6; General Comment No. 5, "General Measures of Implementation of the Convention on the Rights of the Child" (CRC arts. 4, 42, 44(6)), UN Doc. CRC/GC/2003/5 (November 27, 2003), paras. 65, 73 (independent human rights institutions for children); General Comment No. 9, "The Rights of Children with Disabilities," UN Doc. CRC/C/GC/9 (February 27, 2007), para. 24 ("[NHRIs] can take many shapes or forms such as an Ombudsman or a Commissioner and may be broad-based or specific"); General Comment No. 12, "The Right of the Child to Be Heard," UN Doc. CRC/C/GC/12 (July 12, 2009), paras. 49 ("Establish independent human rights institutions such as children's ombudsmen or commissioners"), 97.

a "broad-based NHRI that includes a specific focus on children" that "include[s] within its structure either an identifiable commissioner specifically responsible for children's rights, or a specific section or division responsible for children's rights."[19] In contrast to the Paris Principles, the Committee on the Rights of the Child states that NHRIs "must" have the power to receive and investigate individual complaints.[20]

The UN General Assembly periodically passes resolutions on NHRIs. In the 2008 session, for example, the General Assembly passed two resolutions: on "national institutions for the promotion and protection of human rights" and on "the role of the Ombudsman, mediator and other national human rights institutions in the promotion and protection of human rights."[21] Resolution 63/172 on NHRIs encourages the establishment and strengthening of NHRIs, recognizes that "it is the right of each State to choose the framework for national institutions that is best suited to its particular needs at the national level in order to promote human rights" and encourages states to give their NHRIs more independence and autonomy, including an investigations role.[22] Resolution 63/169 expressly includes classical ombudsman institutions within the NHRI category and recognizes their role in the promotion and protection of human rights.[23]

Yet, over the same recent time period, elements of the UN human rights machinery have supported statements that exclude the ombudsman from the NHRI category. This is seen in a recent General Comment of the Committee on Economic, Social and Cultural Rights and in communications between the OHCHR and the International Ombudsman Institute membership, albeit the OHCHR does recognize the role of the ombudsmen in protecting human rights.[24]

The ICC, composed of NHRI representatives, is mandated to review applications for NHRI accreditation and reaccreditation. While the ICC is incorporated as a legal entity under Swiss law, its meetings are held under OHCHR auspices.[25] The ICC-accreditation system ranks institutions that apply voluntarily based on compliance with the Paris Principles, with accreditation (and increasingly only A-status accreditation) leading to NHRI access to UN human rights

[19] General Comment No. 2, ibid., para. 6.
[20] Ibid., para. 13; CRC General Comment No. 9, supra note 18, para. 24(d).
[21] "National Institutions for the Promotion and Protection of Human Rights," A/RES/63/172 (December 18, 2008, without a vote); "The Role of the Ombudsman, Mediator and Other National Human Rights Institutions in the Promotion and Protection of Human Rights," A/RES/63/169 (December 18, 2008, without a vote).
[22] UN GA Res 63/172, ibid., paras. 5, 11.
[23] UN GA Res 63/19, supra note 21.
[24] General Comment No. 20, supra note 17; Liza Sekaggya, OHCHR, "Communication to I.O.I. International Conference," Stockholm (June 2009, copy on file with author), para. 2 ("OHCHR recognizes the similarities with, and the complementarity between, NHRIs and Ombudsman Institutions ...").
[25] OHCHR: www.ohchr.org/EN/Countries/NHRI/Pages/NHRIMain.aspx.

bodies.[26] The accreditation classifications are A (compliance with the Paris Principles), B (observer status, not fully in compliance with the Principles), and C (non-compliance with the Paris Principles). The ICC has developed General Observations as interpretive tools of the Paris Principles to inter alia guide the ICC in its accreditation determinations, a form of soft law to interpret soft law.[27]

The ICC-accreditation system is geared toward the establishment and strengthening of NHRIs. Its effect is that most national-level human rights commissions and national-level human rights ombudsman institutions are considered to be Paris Principles-compliant NHRIs, with most of those applying obtaining A status. However, the system is still not comprehensive since some commissions and human rights ombudsman have not applied.[28] The General Observations give some flexibility to the Paris Principles so that human rights ombudsman can certainly meet their requirements.[29] The classical ombudsman institution is not mentioned at all, although General Observation 1.2 states that "[a]ll NHRIs should be mandated with specific functions to both protect and promote human rights, such as those listed in the Paris Principles."[30] As a result, national-level classical ombudsman institutions, which lack express human rights protection and promotion mandates, while not excluded from applying for accreditation as an NHRI, are unlikely to receive more than a C grade if they do.[31]

Sub-national and thematic institutions are considered to be "statutory institutions established also for the promotion and protection of human rights," and NHRIs are encouraged to cooperate with these institutions. The implication is that the ICC considers neither to be NHRIs and, except for the unique case of the UK, no sub-national institutions are accredited.[32] General Observation 6.6

---

[26] R. Murray, *The Role of National Human Rights Institutions at the International and Regional Levels: The Experience of Africa* (Oxford: Oxford University Press, 2007), 30–36 (*hereafter* NHRIs: The Experience of Africa); UN Human Rights Council, Information for National Human Rights Institutions, www2.ohchr.org/English/bodies/hrcouncil/nhri.htm (participation of NHRIs in HRC sessions limited to ICC A-status institutions); OHCHR National Institutions Unit, National Human Rights Institutions: Information Note Issue 14 (January 2009) (ICC Geneva representative may represent only A-status NHRIs in treaty body sessions).

[27] ICC Sub-Committee on Accreditation, "General Observations" (June 2009): www.nhri.net/2009/General percent20observations percent20June percent202009 percent20/English.pdf.

[28] ICC, "Chart of the Status of National Institutions: Accreditation Status as of June 2, 2009," (88 NHRIs). Most listed human rights commissions and human rights ombudsmen received As; three of the four accredited classical ombudsmen received Cs; and the Austrian Ombudsman Board received a B. There are five accredited thematic institutions with B or C status and no sub-national institutions.

[29] General Observation 2.1 (Ensuring pluralism), supra note 26.

[30] Ibid., General Observation 1.2 (Human rights mandate) (emphasis deleted).

[31] See supra note 27.

[32] Ibid. General Observation 1.5 (cooperation with other human rights institutions). Both the Great Britain Equality and Human Rights Commission and the Northern Ireland Human Rights Commission are accredited.

applies when there is more than one national institution in a state, encourages "one consolidated and comprehensive" NHRI in the nation and indicates that only in "very exceptional circumstances" will more than one national institution be considered for accreditation, with several precedent conditions required. This position disadvantages national human rights ombudsman institutions in nations that also have a human rights commission; in several nations, the commission is accredited but the human rights ombudsman is not.[33] For thematic institutions, the ICC position conflicts with the UN Committee on the Rights of the Child General Comment that states should establish thematic NHRIs for children. Thus, thematic national institutions are likely to find it difficult to obtain accreditation and the few that have applied have received a B or C grade. Although there is not a General Observation on point, the five accredited thematic institutions all come from states or jurisdictions where there is no national-level human rights commission or human rights ombudsman.[34]

3.2.2. *Regional Organizations and NHRI Groups*

On a regional basis, a focus on NHRI definition and participation that includes national-level commissions and human rights ombudsmen and excludes other candidate institutions can be seen in the African and Asia Pacific regions. Both regions have relatively large numbers of commissions compared to other types of human rights institutions.

In Africa, for example, the Network of African National Human Rights Institutions (NANHRI) has thirty-two members, twenty-eight of which are human rights commissions/councils and the remaining four are hybrids with human rights and administrative governance mandates in ombudsman or commission formats.[35] There are other human rights ombudsman institutions in the African region and some ombudsman institutions have other or multiple mandates including anti-corruption and environmental protection.[36] A few Commonwealth African nations have classical ombudsman institutions, some Francophone African states have mediator institutions (a classical ombudsman variant that uses the French Mediator model) and there are both commissions and mediator/ombudsman institutions in some of these countries.[37]

---

[33] E.g., Greece, Norway, Tanzania, Malawi.

[34] Supra note 27.

[35] NANHRI: www.nanhri.org. The four hybrids are Angola's Provider of Justice and Rights, Namibia's Ombudsman, Ghana's Commission on Human Rights and Administrative Justice, and Tanzania's Commission for Human Rights and Good Governance.

[36] Reif, *The Ombudsman and International Human Rights System*, 220–5. Swaziland also established a hybrid human rights and public administration commission in 2009.

[37] Reif, ibid.

As part of the African human rights system, the African Commission on Human and Peoples' Rights has developed relationships with African NHRIs and the ICC, has relied on Paris Principles compliance as the standard for NHRIs, and has used ICC-accreditation status, albeit sometimes loosely, to determine whether NHRIs can obtain affiliate status in order to attend and speak at Commission sessions.[38] The NANHRI also uses the Paris Principles and ICC-accreditation status as standards, although ICC-accreditation status does not appear to be a prerequisite for membership.[39]

The Asia Pacific region, defined broadly, has national human rights commissions throughout the region, and state-level and thematic children's commissions also exist in several countries – for example, in Australia and New Zealand.[40] The region also has a variety of types of ombudsman institutions. Most ombudsman institutions have multiple mandates: there are only a few with human rights mandates, such as East Timor's Provider for Human Rights and Justice, and most have anti-corruption and/or leadership ethics mandates.[41] Although the Asia Pacific region lacks an overarching regional human rights system that can address NHRIs, the Asia Pacific Forum of National Human Rights Institutions (Asia Pacific Forum) is a regional network of NHRIs that supports the establishment and strengthening of NHRIs in the region.[42] The Asia Pacific Forum requires that NHRIs must comply with the Paris Principles to be admitted as full members with voting rights, and a domestic institution will be classified as an NHRI by the Forum only if it is established by a national government "with the specific role of promoting and protecting human rights."[43] As a result, fourteen of the fifteen full members of the Asia Pacific Forum are national human rights commissions/centers and only one, East Timor's Provider, is a human rights ombudsman. Asia Pacific Forum associate membership is open to NHRIs that do not comply with the Paris Principles and are unlikely to do so within a reasonable time, but only one institution per UN

---

[38] Murray, *NHRIs: The Experience of Africa*, 47–55; ACHPR, *Resolution on Granting Affiliate Status to National Human Rights Institutions* (Banjul, October 31, 1998), ACHPR: www.achpr.org/english_info/directory_nhri_en.html. (Only twelve human rights commissions have affiliate status.)

[39] NANHRI (e.g., ICC accreditation status lettering for members are noted, nine members do not have any such accreditation noted.)

[40] Asia Pacific Forum of National Human Rights Institutions: www.asiapacificforum.net/members (e.g., sixteen national human rights commissions/centers at different membership levels); Brian Burdekin, *National Human Rights Institutions in the Asia-Pacific Region* (Leiden: Martinus Nijhoff, 2007). See, for example, State of Victoria (Australia) Equal Opportunity and Human Rights Commission, Children's Commissioners in Various Australian Jurisdictions, Australian Human Rights Commission, *An Australian Children's Commissioner: Discussion Paper* (October 2010); New Zealand Children's Commissioner: wwwocc.org.nz.

[41] Reif, *Ombudsman and International Human Rights System*, 242–9.

[42] Asia Pacific Forum: www.asiapacificforum.net.

[43] Asia Pacific Forum: www.asiapacificforum.net/members/what-is-an-nhri; www.asiapacificforum.net/members.

member state will be admitted as a member.[44] The Asia Pacific Forum approach, then, includes national-level human rights commissions and human rights ombudsman institutions and excludes sub-national level, thematic, and classical ombudsman institutions.

Europe is the region with the most diversity in domestic human rights institutions. Human rights ombudsmen were first established in Southern Europe in the mid-1970s, followed by large numbers in Central and Eastern Europe and an increasing number of converted human rights ombudsmen in Western Europe starting in the 1990s. Human rights commissions are not as numerous. Europe also has large numbers of classical ombudsman and thematic and sub-national institutions. The Council of Europe (COE), currently with forty-seven member states, has always treated the ombudsman as an important vehicle for domestic human rights protection.

In 1985, the COE Committee of Ministers recommended giving ombudsmen express human rights protection powers and in 1997 called on members without NHRIs to establish such institutions, in particular "human rights commissions ..., ombudsmen or comparable institutions."[45] The COE created the office of the Commissioner for Human Rights in 1999, two of whose core functions are to "facilitate the activities of national ombudsmen or similar institutions in the field of human rights" and cooperate with human rights structures in the member states.[46] The commissioner's legal structure makes no explicit mention of NHRIs. The work of the commissioner, however, has evolved to include activities involving NHRIs in member states and ombudsman offices at the sub-national level.[47] The commissioner has recently stated that "[w]hile the concept of 'national human rights institutions' (NHRIs) has been developed mainly in the UN context and with reference to the Paris Principles, the Commissioner also uses the term 'national human rights institutions' to denote ombudsmen institutions as well as human rights commissions or institutes set up with reference to the Paris Principles."[48] The commissioner has also introduced the concept of "national human rights structures" (NHRSs), and the "[p]artners of this network are national, regional, local or thematic institutions which comply with the Paris Principles and abide by the Council of Europe's

---

[44] Asia Pacific Forum: www.asiapacificforum.net/members/apf-member-categories/associate-members. The two associate members are also human rights commissions.

[45] Council of Europe, Committee of Ministers, Rec. No.R(85)13 (September 23, 1985); Committee of Ministers, Rec. 97(14) (September 30, 1997), para. a.

[46] Council of Europe, Committee of Ministers, Res. No. (99)50 (May 7, 1999), paras. 3(c)–(d); COE Commissioner for Human Rights: www.coe.int/t/commissioner/default_en.asp.

[47] Reif, *Ombudsman and International Human Rights System*, 359–60.

[48] Thomas Hammarberg, COE Commissioner for Human Rights, "Recommendation on Systematic Work for Implementing Human Rights at the National Level," CommDH (2009) 3 (February 18, 2009), fn. 10.

values."[49] Both human rights ombudsmen and classical ombudsmen are included as NHRSs.[50] Thus, the European region takes a more inclusive approach to institutions involved in human rights protection and promotion.

Many nations in the Americas have established human rights ombudsman institutions, while others have human rights commissions and/or classical ombudsmen. For some years, the Organization of American States (OAS) General Assembly made supportive references to the human rights work of ombudsmen, defenders of the people, and other human rights ombudsman institutions.[51] These resolutions have also affirmed the work, among others, of the Network of National Institutions for the Promotion and Protection of Human Rights of the Americas (Network of the Americas), comprising A-status ICC-accredited national-level human rights ombudsmen and commissions, and the Caribbean Ombudsman Association, comprising mainly classical ombudsmen.[52] The Iberoamerican Federation of Ombudsmen is also active in the region, composed of human rights ombudsmen at both the national and sub-national levels.[53] However, more recently, the OAS General Assembly has begun to use NHRI language, referring to the important contributions to human rights protection that can be made by ICC-accredited NHRIs and establishing a system for Network of the Americas members to participate in the OAS human rights machinery.[54] Thus, this region is beginning to adopt the UN OHCHR and ICC approaches to NHRIs which increasingly excludes the classical ombudsman and all types of sub-national and thematic institutions.

3.3. TREATY AND OTHER INTERNATIONAL INITIATIVES USING NHRIS TO IMPLEMENT OBLIGATIONS

Some recent human rights treaty and other international initiatives require or call on states to use domestic institutions to implement the international undertaking. Torture prevention and the regulation of corporate human rights abuses are two areas.[55] In addition to human rights commissions, human rights ombudsman,

---

[49] COE Commissioner for Human Rights, "Co-operation with National Human Rights Structures," www.coe.int/t/commissioner/Activities/NHRS/default/_en.asp.

[50] COE Commissioner for Human Rights, "National Human Rights Structures," www.coe.int/t/commissioner/links/omb_nhri_en.asp.

[51] Reif, *Ombudsman and International Human Rights System*, 92–93; OAS G.A. RES 2132, XXXV-O/05 (June 2005); OAS G.A. RES 2221, XXXVI-O/06 (June 2006); OAS G.A. RES 2345, XXXVII-O/07 (June 2007); OAS G.A. RES 2411, XXXVIII-O/08 (June 2008).

[52] Ibid.; Network of the Americas, www.rindhca.org.ve.

[53] See www.portalfio.org/inicio/ique-es-la-fio.

[54] OAS G.A. RES 2421, XXXVIII-O/08 (June 2008); OAS G.A. RES 2448, XXXIX-O/09 (June 2009); Third Summit of the Americas, Plan of Action (2001).

[55] See also UN Convention on the Rights of Persons with Disabilities, art. 33(2), www.un.org/disabilities/convention/conventionfull.shtml; "International Convention for the Protection of All Persons from

classical ombudsman, and thematic human rights institutions are being used or contemplated for the implementation of these obligations.

The Optional Protocol to the Convention against Torture and other Cruel, Inhuman or Degrading Treatment or Punishment (OPCAT) establishes a system of international and domestic oversight of facilities where persons are deprived of their liberty.[56] The OPCAT requires states parties to "maintain, designate or establish" one or more independent national preventive mechanisms (NPMs), that meet the criteria specified in the OPCAT including giving due consideration to the Paris Principles.[57] NPMs are to conduct visits to these facilities for the purpose of strengthening, if needed, the protection of persons deprived of their liberty. States parties must permit regular, unencumbered visits by the NPMs; and the NPMs must be given powers to examine detainees, make recommendations to the government for improvement of detainee treatment and conditions that take into consideration the international obligations of the state, and submit observations and proposals concerning current or draft legislation.[58] While some current and prospective OPCAT parties are creating new institutions as their NPMs, many are using existing institutions – human rights commissions, human rights ombudsmen, and occasionally, classical ombudsmen and thematic human rights institutions. As of November 2009, seven countries had designated their human rights commissions as NPMs and another four states were considering such a move.[59] Fourteen human rights ombudsmen in Europe and Latin America have been designated NPMs and seven are being considered for designation.[60] The classical ombudsman institutions

Enforced Disappearance," art. 28, www2.ohchr.org/English/law/disappearance-convention.htm (not yet in force); "EU Directives Combating Discrimination Are Being Implemented by Member States," Thematic Institutions or Human Rights Ombudsman, Equinet European Network of Equality Bodies, www.equineteurope.org.

[56] (2003) 42 I.L.M. 26 (in force June 22, 2006), art.1. On August 11, 2009, there were forty-nine contracting parties and another twenty-four signatories.

[57] Among other criteria, the NPM and its personnel must be functionally independent, experts of the NPM must have the required capabilities and professional knowledge, the organization must strive for gender balance and the adequate representation of ethnic and minority groups in the country, and the funding body must provide necessary resources for the functioning of the NPM, ibid., arts. 3–4, 17–24; Malcolm D. Evans and Claudine Haenni-Dale, "Preventing Torture? The Development of the Optional Protocol to the UN Convention against Torture," *Human Rights Law Review* 4 (2004), 50–3.

[58] OPCAT, ibid., arts. 20–21 provide for powers to be given to the NPM re conduct of visits.

[59] Mali, Mauritius, Mexico, Maldives, New Zealand, Scotland designated, and Chile (to be established), Liberia, Madagascar (to be established), and Morocco under consideration, Association for the Prevention of Torture, OPCAT Country Status: Ratification and Implementation (November 17, 2009), www.apt.ch/content/view/44/84/lang.en/.

[60] Albania, Armenia, Azerbaijan, Costa Rica, Cyprus, Czech Republic, Estonia, Georgia, Macedonia, Moldova (with Consultative Council), Poland, Slovenia (with NGOs), Spain (NPM functions delegated to Deputy Defensor), and Sweden (with Chancellor of Justice) have been designated; Croatia, Finland, Ghana, Kyrgyz Republic, Montenegro, Nicaragua, and Ukraine are under consideration,

in Denmark and New Zealand have been given NPM status, and Luxembourg's ombudsman is under consideration.[61] The Children's Commissioners in England and New Zealand have been included among their state's multiple NPMs.[62] In Europe, the use of the ombudsman as an NPM is facilitated by the fact that a substantial number of them already have strong inspection powers.

The UN has also begun to address the legal issues surrounding corporate conduct that violates or is complicit in the violation of human rights. In 2008, the UN secretary-general's special representative issued his report, Protect, Respect and Remedy: A Framework for Business and Human Rights (Ruggie Report).[63] The "remedy" element of the Report's framework states that more effective judicial and non-judicial remedies for victims of corporate human rights abuses are needed – NHRIs are included as an important non-judicial remedy and may even substitute for the judiciary in states where the courts are ineffective.[64] The Report states that where NHRIs have jurisdiction over corporate conduct they are "particularly well-positioned to provide processes – whether adjudicative or mediation-based – that are culturally appropriate, accessible and expeditious."[65] This part of the Report was supported by research on the "85 recognized" NHRIs that discovered that at least forty can take complaints concerning human rights-related corporate conduct.[66] The survey appears to have used only the ICC-accredited NHRIs and, accordingly, it is incomplete given the larger number of institutions that have not applied for accreditation but the research does include the accredited classical ombudsman institutions.[67]

The Ruggie Report approach has been endorsed by the Human Rights Council, and in 2009 the special representative issued a report on operationalizing the framework.[68] The 2009 report affirmed the potential remedial role of NHRIs, stating

---

ibid.; Jari Pirjola, "The Parliamentary Ombudsman of Finland as a National Preventive Mechanism under the Optional Protocol to the United Nations Convention against Torture and Other Cruel, Inhuman or Degrading Treatment or Punishment," *Nordic Journal of International Law* 77 (2008), 163–74.

[61] OPCAT Country Status, ibid. (New Zealand has multiple NPMs, the Human Rights Commission is the central, coordinating NPM).

[62] Ibid.

[63] Report of the Special Representative of the Secretary-General on the Issue of Human Rights and Transnational Corporations and Other Business Enterprises, "Protect, Respect and Remedy: A Framework for Business and Human Rights," UN Doc. A/HRC/8/5 (April 7, 2008).

[64] "Protect, Respect and Remedy," ibid., paras. 84–5.

[65] Ibid., para. 97.

[66] Ibid., para. 96; United Nations Office of the High Commissioner for Human Rights, Business and Human Rights: A Survey of NHRI Practices (May 2008) (surveying 43 NHRIs).

[67] Ibid.

[68] Business and human rights: toward operationalizing the "Protect, Respect and Remedy" framework. "Report of the Special Representative of the Secretary-General on the Issue of Human Rights and Transnational Corporations and Other Business Enterprises," Human Rights Council, 11th Sess., Agenda item 3, UN Doc. A/HRC/11/13 (April 22, 2009).

that "[w]hile the mandates of some NHRIs may currently preclude them from work on business and human rights, for many it has been a question of choice, tradition or capacity. The Special Representative hopes that more NHRIs will reflect on ways they can address alleged human rights abuses involving business."[69] The 2009 report also looked to Australia's banking and telecommunications industry classical ombudsman system as interesting sector-specific models for addressing human rights business-impacts.[70]

3.4. NHRI CANDIDATES

Initially, the UN took an expansive view of NHRIs but over time bodies such as courts, administrative tribunals, legislative bodies and NGOs were excluded as the organization took a narrower and functional approach to NHRI conceptualization.[71]

3.4.1. *Human Rights Commissions*

Early human rights commissions appeared after World War II in France and Commonwealth nations, and then exploded in number during the 1990s.[72] Human rights commissions are collegiate bodies, appointed by the legislature or executive, with a legal framework based in the constitution, legislation, or executive decree. They are given a variety of human rights promotion functions such as providing advice and lobbying governments to ratify human rights treaties and implement them domestically, engaging in human rights research and education, providing information to UN human rights treaty bodies, and encouraging the implementation of treaty body recommendations.

Pohjolainen distinguishes among commissions (many with investigatory powers), advisory commissions (the French model, also popular in Francophone Africa, usually without investigatory power, focusing on advice to government), and institutes (found in Western Europe, usually without investigatory power, focusing on research and education).[73] Commissions with investigatory power can investigate on receipt of a complaint or *suo motu*, make recommendations to remedy a breach (and some can refer unresolved cases to tribunals), conduct public inquiries, inspect facilities where persons are involuntarily detained, intervene or act as amicus curiae in human rights litigation, and even issue orders for compliance with

---

[69] Ibid., paras. 103, 102.
[70] Ibid., para. 105.
[71] UN, *NHRI Handbook*, p. 6.
[72] A. Pohjolainen, *The Evolution of National Human Rights Institutions: The Role of the United Nations* (Copenhagen: Danish Institute for Human Rights, 2006), 16–20.
[73] Ibid., 16–20.

their determinations. Commissions differ widely in the extent of their jurisdiction over human rights: some are essentially anti-discrimination commissions (e.g., most commissions in Canada), while others have jurisdiction over a broad range of rights. While some commissions have jurisdiction only over the public sector, others have additional jurisdiction over private sector conduct.

Human rights commissions have appeared at both national and sub-national levels in countries around the world, particularly in Western Europe, Africa, Asia Pacific, and parts of the Americas. There are about sixty national-level commissions with more at the sub-national and overseas territories levels.[74] Western Europe has a variety of commissions and institutes with divergent mandates.[75] There are many commissions in Africa, covering both the investigatory and advisory forms.[76] The Asia Pacific region has a growing number of countries with human rights commissions.[77] In the Americas, commissions are found in Canada (federal and provincial/territorial levels), Mexico (national and state levels), and Bermuda, with Uruguay establishing and Chile considering institutes.[78] Blurring the boundaries, Ghana and Tanzania have hybrid human rights/ombudsman institutions using the commission format.[79]

3.4.2. *The Ombudsman*

Instituted in the nineteenth century, the classical ombudsman spread outside Scandinavia in the early 1960s, first to Commonwealth countries and then worldwide.[80] Associated with the legislative branch as a monitor of administrative illegality and unfairness, the core powers of the ombudsman are those of impartial investigation of the administrative/executive branch on receipt of public complaints or *suo motu* backed up by statutory subpoena powers, making recommendations for reform of law and administrative practice, and making annual and special reports to the legislature and the public.[81] Ombudsman institutions are typically established

---

[74] Reif, *Ombudsman and International Human Rights System*, 83–4 (2003 statistics); "National Human Rights Institutions" (about 61 commissions after excluding human rights and classical ombudsman etc. on list), www.nhri.net/nationaldatalist.asp (October 23, 2009).

[75] Research-focused institutes, large advisory commissions/committees and commissions with investigatory power, see, Pohjolainen, *The Evolution of National Human Rights Institutions*, 16–20; J. Mertus, *Human Rights Matters: Local Politics and National Human Rights Institutions* (Stanford: Stanford University Press, 2009).

[76] Pohjolainen, ibid., 17; Ramcharan, *Protection Role of NHRIs*, 165.

[77] Burdekin, *National Human Rights Institutions in the Asia-Pacific Region*; Asia Pacific Forum, www. asiapacificforum.net/members; see Catherine Renshaw and Kieren Fitzpatrick in this volume, "NHRIs in the Asia Pacific Region" (includes Middle East).

[78] Uruguay, Ley No. 18.446, Institución Nacional de Derechos Humanos (2009).

[79] Reif, *Ombudsman and International Human Rights System*, 223–31.

[80] Ibid., 6–7.

[81] Ibid.

by constitution and/or legislation. Some ombudsmen have multiple members and some are appointed by the executive power. Some ombudsman institutions, especially those in Europe, have powers to inspect facilities where persons are involuntarily detained.[82]

The classical ombudsman does not have an express mandate to protect and promote human rights. However, since ombudsmen scrutinize administrative conduct they regularly investigate authorities that are infringing human rights such as the police, prisons, and immigration authorities. Some ombudsmen use domestic human rights law (including internalized international human rights law obligations of the state) in some cases to determine whether administrative conduct is legal and comports with the broader ombudsman fairness standards.[83] They also use international human rights law to elucidate these fairness standards. For example, European classical ombudsmen (e.g., Netherlands, Denmark, Malta) have used international human rights norms, especially the European Convention on Human Rights (ECHR).[84] Canadian provincial ombudsmen have used UN human rights treaties and guidelines in investigations concerning treatment of prisoners and prison conditions.[85] Ombudsmen in British Columbia, the Netherlands, and Bermuda have used the UN Convention on the Rights of the Child (CRC) in investigative reports and recommendations concerning children.[86] Furthermore, an evolving human right to good administration, especially in the European Union (EU) zone, places the ombudsman center stage as a mechanism to enforce this norm.[87]

However, the human rights activities engaged by classical ombudsman institutions typically represent a small percentage of their workload, and some ombudsmen do not address human rights matters at all. Further, most classical ombudsmen

[82] Linda C. Reif, "Transplantation and Adaptation: The Evolution of the Human Rights Ombudsman," *Boston College Third World Law Journal* 31 (2011) 269(in press); Kucsko-Stadlmayer, *European Ombudsman-Institutions*, 491–2.

[83] Reif, *Ombudsman and International Human Rights System*, 86–7, 142–5, 142–5, 304–5.

[84] Ibid.; A. F. M. Brenninkmeijer and Y. van der Vlugt, *Principles of Proper Conduct as Guarantee of Human Rights: The Role of the National Ombudsman in the Protection of Human Rights* (Netherlands National Ombudsman, 2009); Matthew Vela, "Ombudsman Lambastes Registrar for Violating Asylum Seekers' Right to Marry," *Media Today* (August 23, 2009), Malta. http://www.mediatoday.com/mt.

[85] Linda Reif, "The Domestic Application of International Human Rights Law in Canada: The Role of Canada's National Human Rights Institutions," in O. E. Fitzgerald (ed.), *The Globalized Rule of Law: Relationships between International and Domestic Law* (Toronto: Irwin Law, 2006), 508–10 (*hereafter* "Canada's NHRIs").

[86] Linda Reif, "The Ombudsman and the Protection of Children's Rights," *Asia Pacific Law Review* 17 (2009), 30–3.

[87] EU Charter of Fundamental Rights, art. 41 (2000); in Treaty of Lisbon (2007); South Africa Constitution, s. 33(1); J. Wakefield, *The Right to Good Administration* (Netherlands: Kluwer Law International, 2007).

undertake only complaint handling and *suo motu* investigations and do not have the broader promotional mandates usually given to human rights ombudsmen and commissions. From the UN perspective, to include classical ombudsmen as NHRIs would excessively dilute the Paris Principles requirements and enable rights-averse states to avoid substantive human rights protections by creating classical ombudsman institutions that would not have to address human rights at all. Further, many ombudsman appointees do not have human rights expertise. However, some classical ombudsmen stand at the NHRI boundary given their consistent use of human rights norms (some in Western Europe) and some may even fall inside the boundary (classical ombudsmen given OPCAT NPM status). From the European perspective, classical ombudsmen are included within the more broadly conceived NHRS system. Also, as discussed below, the current tendency of states is to establish human rights ombudsmen rather than classical ombudsman institutions. While classical ombudsmen may not disappear, their relative numbers are likely to fall.

3.4.3. *The Human Rights Ombudsman*

Human rights commission and classical ombudsman models are successful "legal transplants," adopted in many countries without material change.[88] Some nations (often Commonwealth countries) have established both a commission and an ombudsman. However, a fundamental adaptation of these two models began to occur in the mid-1970s. Various jurisdictions, often democratizing countries, selected elements from both models to create a hybrid institution, the "human rights ombudsman."[89] Portugal's Provider of Justice and Spain's Defender of the People (Defensor del Pueblo) started the trend.[90]

Human rights ombudsman institutions are usually headed by one officeholder (ombudsman, commissioner), and some have legislated requirements for deputy ombudsman positions. They are enshrined in the constitution and/or legislation and most are legislative appointments. They each have some combination of human rights protection and administrative oversight mandates, with some given additional roles. Human rights ombudsmen always have the power to investigate public complaints, and many have additional powers such as *suo motu* investigations, the right

---

[88] Michele Graziadei, "Comparative Law as the Study of Transplants and Receptions," in M. Reimann and R. Zimmermann (eds.), *The Oxford Handbook of Comparative Law* (Oxford: Oxford University Press, 2006), 441–76.

[89] "Human rights ombudsman" will be used as the generic term, although the titles for such institutions differ, for example, Defensor del Pueblo, Attorney (Procurador) for Human Rights, Commissioner for Civil Rights, Human Rights Ombudsperson, and Ombudsman.

[90] Reif, *Ombudsman and International Human Rights System*, 8–9.

to inspect closed facilities, taking cases to constitutional and other courts, prosecution of public officials, research, and education.[91] While many have jurisdiction over the public sector only, a few also have full or partial jurisdiction over private sector conduct.[92]

Numerous forces have impelled the increase in the number of human rights ombudsmen over the past three decades, either through the establishment of a new institution or by giving an express human rights mandate to an existing classical ombudsman. These include the democratization movement, comparative law influences (e.g., Spain's model was attractive to civil law states in Latin America), limited state resources given the cost-effectiveness of assigning multiple horizontal accountability mandates to one institution and, as discussed above, new human rights treaty initiatives calling on states to use domestic institutions to implement their obligations.[93]

Thus, by mid-2003, of the approximately 110 national-level ombudsman institutions around the world, about 50 percent were human rights ombudsmen, and there were additional human rights ombudsmen at the sub-national level in countries such as Spain and Argentina.[94] Most countries in Latin America and some in the Caribbean use the human rights ombudsman model.[95] Most countries in Central and Eastern Europe have human rights ombudsman institutions.[96] Hybrid institutions are also found in the African and Asia Pacific regions.[97] Growing numbers of ombudsmen in Western Europe have been established as hybrids or have been given human rights mandates.[98] Countries in other regions have also replaced their preexisting institutions with a hybrid, for example, Ghana, Tanzania, Jamaica, and Latvia.[99]

---

[91] Ibid.; Reif, "Transplantation and Adaptation: The Evolution of the Human Rights Ombudsman."
[92] Ibid.
[93] Ibid.
[94] Reif, *Ombudsman and International Human Rights System*, 11, 393.
[95] Ibid., 187–213; J. Mark, J. Payne et al., *Democracies in Development: Politics and Reform in Latin America* (Washington, DC: Inter-American Development Bank, 2007), 117–43; Fredrik Uggla, "The Ombudsman in Latin America," *Journal of Latin American Studies* 36 (2004), 423–50.
[96] Reif, ibid., 155–68; Kucsko-Stadlmayer, *European Ombudsman-Institutions*.
[97] E.g., Angola, Ethiopia, Gambia, Ghana (hybrid commission), Lesotho, Malawi, Namibia, Seychelles, Tanzania (hybrid commission), East Timor, Papua New Guinea (discrimination), Reif, ibid., 218–225; 245–52.
[98] Ibid., 137–55; Kucsko-Stadlmayer, *European Ombudsman-Institutions*, 503 (Spain, Portugal, Sweden, Greece, Cyprus, Andorra, Finland, Norway). See also France's 2008 constitutional amendment creating a Defender of Rights, with a September 2009 draft Organic Law for the Defender of Rights eliminating the Mediator (Ombudsman) and Defender of Children institutions, France, 1958 Constitution as am., art. 71–1, www.assemblee nationale.fr/english/8ab.asp; Senate Organic Bill on the Defender of Rights, No. 610 (September 9, 2009).
[99] Ibid., 209, 221–31; Latvia's National Human Rights Office was changed to a human rights ombudsman in 2006–2007, Kucsko-Stadlmayer, *European Ombudsman-Institutions*, 270.

3.4.4. *Thematic NHRIs*

Vulnerable populations with special human rights needs include children, ethnic minorities, and indigenous persons. Thematic NHRIs to protect these populations have been established in a growing number of countries, particularly in Europe. These include the children's ombudsman or commissioner,[100] commissioners for the protection of ethnic and racial minorities,[101] and different forms of equality commissions.[102] As discussed earlier, the UN Committee on the Rights of the Child calls for the establishment of thematic institutions to assist in CRC implementation.[103]

The independence and powers of thematic institutions vary markedly. The relationships between general and thematic NHRIs in one state can be complicated. These institutions may have overlapping jurisdictions which may, if not allocated efficiently through legislation or institutional agreement, result in duplication or loss of coverage. The general NHRI may resent its partial loss of jurisdiction to another body. However, the general NHRI in a multiple-NHRI state may defer to a thematic institution, as the South African Human Rights Commission has done with the Gender Equality Commission.[104] While some may see this as a failure of the general NHRI to exercise its full jurisdiction or as a lack of gender mainstreaming, the thematic NHRI focuses entirely on gender issues and raises the gender equality profile rather than having it potentially lost in a larger set of competing human rights priorities.

However, thematic NHRIs are vulnerable. The ICC supports one comprehensive NHRI in a state. The focus of thematic institutions on marginalized populations may not be popular with the majority. As a result, they may be under-resourced and/or given weak powers. Thematic NHRIs are particularly susceptible to loss of their independent status, often through incorporation into a general-service NHRI. In addition to their controversial roles, other reasons for their abolition are the resource constraints on government that make the thematic NHRIs in multiple-NHRI states inviting targets for government cutbacks and the rationalization of institutions with overlapping mandates. For example, Sweden recently abolished four specialized anti-discrimination ombudsmen and their associated statutes and replaced them with one

---

[100] Mainly found in Europe and in some other parts of the world, for example, New Zealand, with similar bodies found in some Canadian provinces, Australian states. See European Network of Ombudsmen for Children, http://crin.org/enoc/; Reif, *Ombudsman and International Human Rights System*, 313–30; New Zealand Children's Commissioner, www.occ.org.nz.

[101] Mainly found in Europe, Reif, ibid., 36–8; Elena A. Baylis, "Minority Rights, Minority Wrongs," *UCLA Journal of International Law and Foreign Affairs* 10 (2005), 66.

[102] For example, Lithuania Ombudsperson for Equal Opportunities, Sweden Equality Ombudsman.

[103] Supra note 18.

[104] See Obiora C. Okafor in this volume, "National Human Rights Institutions in Anglophone Africa."

anti-discrimination statute monitored by one Equality Ombudsman.[105] In Ireland, a government report has recommended that Ireland's Children's Ombudsman and other institutions be merged into the Ombudsman institution.[106] Also, 2009 draft legislation is aimed at eliminating France's Defender of Children, giving child protection functions to the new Defender of Rights institution.[107] Furthermore, rather than operationalize thematic institutions that have their own statutory framework by giving them their own officeholder and separate facilities, some governments have increasingly given "second hats" to existing ombudsmen so that they exercise two separate horizontal accountability functions on the same premises. For example, the New Brunswick Ombudsman was also appointed as the province's Child and Youth Advocate.[108]

3.4.5. Sub-National NHRIs

There are numerous federal and decentralized countries around the world. In these countries, legislative competence is typically divided between the national and subnational governments (e.g., states, provinces), with the result that legislative competence over human rights matters is also divided in some manner between the different levels of government. In some federal states, as a matter of constitutional law, national-level NHRIs cannot be given jurisdiction over human rights matters that fall within the competence of the sub-national units. Rather, only sub-national human rights institutions can promote and protect the human rights falling within their jurisdictions.

Various human rights institutions have been established at the sub-national levels in federal and decentralized states. For example, there are federal and provincial human rights commissions in Canada and Mexico; Spain has a national Defensor del Pueblo and human rights ombudsman in a majority of its autonomous communities; and Argentina has national and state *defensores*.

There are understandable political and logistical reasons for the exclusion of sub-national institutions from the accreditation system. For example, the numerous sub-national institutions in some states means that there would be administrative

---

[105] Act Concerning the Equality Ombudsman, SFS 2008: 568 (Sweden); Government Offices of Sweden, "New Anti-discrimination Legislation and a New Agency, the Equality Ombudsman," Fact Sheet (January 2009) (Replaces Equal Opportunities Ombudsman, Ombudsman against Ethnic Discrimination, Disability Ombudsman, Ombudsman against Discrimination because of Sexual Orientation.)

[106] Barry O'Halloran and Ruadhán MacCormaic, "Merger of State Bodies Would Save €83m," *Irish Times* online (July 17, 2009).

[107] Supra note 88; La Défenseure des Enfant, Communiqué de Presse (September 21, 2009).

[108] New Brunswick Ombudsman: www.gnb.ca/0073/index-e.asp, Child and Youth Advocate Act, S.N.B. 2007, c. C-2.7.

and political difficulties in providing for multiple institutional representation; allowing for their representation could allow the respective national governments to avoid establishing or strengthening a national-level institution; and it can be questioned whether some sub-national institutions have sufficient interests in implementing and furthering the state's global or regional human rights obligations. Also, sub-national institutions may not have the same range of powers enjoyed by their national counterparts, for example, they may not be able to give advice on treaty ratification and cannot lodge complaints with the constitutional courts. Including only the national-level NHRI in a federal state when it has exclusive jurisdiction over all human rights and levels of government is appropriate. However, the exclusion of sub-national human rights institutions in federal states where sub-national governments have exclusive jurisdiction over certain categories and fields of human rights results in an incomplete and inaccurate picture of the actual level of human rights protection and implementation of international human rights obligations in that country.

3.5. NHRI DEFINITION REVISITED

Clarity in NHRI definition assists in determining important elements of NHRI institutional design and identifying factors that lead to an effective NHRI. However, the preceding sections demonstrate that there are different definitions of NHRIs applied in different parts of the international community.

It is universally understood that national-level human rights commissions are NHRIs. Further, it is now generally accepted that the large numbers of national-level human rights ombudsman institutions are NHRIs. In this sense, a recentering of the NHRI concept has occurred. However, for many organizations, these two types of institutions comprise the entirety of NHRIs. This is illustrated through the ICC-accreditation process based on the Paris Principles that has given A-status preferences to many national commissions and human rights ombudsmen, a process that has been adopted or relied on by elements of the UN human rights system and by most regional international organizations and institutional groups. However, the boundaries set for this NHRI definition exclude classical ombudsman institutions and thematic and sub-national human rights institutions, although these institutions may be given almost equivalent names such as "statutory institutions for the protection and promotion of human rights."

Nonetheless, there are still different attitudes toward NHRI definition inside the UN system itself. The UN Committee on the Rights of the Child promotes the establishment and strengthening of thematic NHRIs for children as part of CRC state parties' treaty obligations, and the UN General Assembly has classified the classical ombudsman as an NHRI. Further, while most regional organizations and associations are coalescing around the ICC approach to NHRI definition, the sizable and diverse European region has followed a much broader NHRI (or NHRS) conceptualization that is not so reliant on a narrow reading of the Paris Principles and the ICC's General Observations and includes national and sub-national human rights ombudsman, classical ombudsman, commissions, and thematic institutions.[109]

The different NHRI definitions used by international organizations and groupings are imposed for a multiplicity of political and pragmatic reasons. They are typically used to implement the organizations' gatekeeper, participation, and oversight functions in their relationships with NHRIs and member states. Gatekeeper functions limit the number of NHRIs that can participate in the international organization's human rights machinery in terms of representation and voice (written and oral submissions). Definitional specificity used as a gatekeeper mechanism to limit access to preferential treatment enables international organizations to engage in quality control and oversight, thereby pressuring NHRIs and their governments to strengthen the institution's design and improve other effectiveness factors. The UN's OHCHR and the ICC both have a global reach and work with national governments that have considerably different attitudes toward human rights protection. For this reason, a narrow NHRI definition used to limit access and participation and to influence institutional effectiveness factors helps to ensure that the human rights institutions established by governments, especially the rights-averse, are best suited for human rights protection and promotion. In contrast, the European region, with its long history of respected ombudsman institutions, support for thematic institutional protection and strong regional human rights machinery can afford to be more liberal in its embrace of a variety of domestic human rights institutions.

The human rights researcher needs to be aware of the differing NHRI definitions used in different parts of the international community and look beyond these definitions when necessary. In order to get a full picture of a state's implementation of and compliance with its international and domestic human rights legal obligations, any and all horizontal accountability institutions in the state playing roles in human rights protection and promotion should be examined: commissions, human rights or classical ombudsmen, thematic institutions, and/or equivalent institutions at sub-national levels of government.[110]

---

[109] See B. Simmons, *Mobilizing for Human Rights: International Law in Domestic Politics* (Cambridge: Cambridge University Press, 2009), 90–6, who finds that states' location in particular regions (e.g., Europe) influences human rights treaty ratification. Regional location likely also influences NHRI form and design.

[110] See Ryan Goodman and Derek Jinks, "How to Influence States: Socialization and International Human Rights Law," *Duke Law Journal* 54 (2004), 621–703. For example, for Norway, the ICC has accredited only the Center for Human Rights (A status), while the country also has a human rights ombudsman with investigatory power and a Children's Ombudsman, supra note 33.

3.6. CONCLUSION

While there are different approaches to the conceptualization and definition of NHRIs inside the UN and among international organizations and institutional groups, the majority view is coalescing around the ICC-accreditation system which gives preferential status only to national-level human rights commissions and human rights ombudsman institutions. Much of the UN human rights system and most regional international organizations increasingly rely on the ICC-accreditation rankings. While the general acceptance of human rights ombudsman institutions as NHRIs confirms a recentering of the NHRI definition, it is only a modest shift that reflects the massive increase in the number of these national-level hybrid institutions over the past two decades around the world. The strict boundaries around the NHRI definition are imposed by these organizations and groups to fulfill gatekeeper, participation, and quality oversight functions for the institutions and their governments. However, more liberal approaches to NHRI definition remain inside the UN and in the European region.

Human rights researchers need to be aware of the different NHRI definitional boundaries used on the international level and look outside them where necessary to examine additional domestic institutions that may play roles in human rights protection and promotion. In particular, thematic human rights institutions, the classical ombudsman, and all the variants of human rights institutions at sub-national levels of government in federal states are relevant players in the domestic implementation of and compliance with the human rights obligations of the state.

4

Evaluating NHRIs

Considering Structure, Mandate, and Impact

Julie Mertus

4.1. INTRODUCTION

Scholars and practitioners of human rights have long espoused the centrality of "the local" – as opposed to "the international" for international human rights promotion and protection.[1] It is the job of national human rights institutions (NHRIs) to connect the local with the international, making immediate and concrete what appeared previously to be far away and abstract. This localization of rights is an essential, ongoing process. Progress in human rights standard setting, promotion, and enforcement is not possible without local buy-in. It is the local embrace of rights and the institutions they espouse that give them their legitimacy. The benefits of "embedding a human rights institution within the state"[2] include "the fact that the institution can work closely with government in implementing human rights, while still retaining a critical independence; the institution's awareness of the socio-cultural context into which the panoply of human rights must be translated; and, the sense of ownership by civil society of the human rights institution and the principles it embodies."[3]

Human rights treaty drafters now routinely seek to account for national level implementation by inserting specific provisions into treaty texts, seeking to confer monitoring roles on NHRIs, or, indeed, to prompt their establishment. For example, the drafters of the UN Convention on the Rights of Persons with Disabilities

---

[1] For two leading texts on the role of actors at the national level in human rights implementation, see M. Kjaerum, *National Human Rights Institutions: Implementing Human Rights* (Copenhagen: Danish Institute for Human Rights, 2003); B. Lindsnaes, et al. (eds.), *National Human Rights Institutions: Articles and Working Papers* (Copenhagen: Danish Institute of Human Rights, 2000).

[2] Catherine Renshaw, Andrew Byrnes, and Andrea Durbach, "Implementing Human Rights in the Pacific through the Work of National Human Rights Institutions: The Experience of Fiji," UNSW Law Research Paper, no. 2008–66.

[3] Ibid.

specifically incorporated a provision addressing national level monitoring and implementation and called upon states to endow an independent national human rights institution with monitoring responsibilities, as well as a far-reaching article of general application on awareness-raising.[4] While NHRIs cannot make up for a lack of workable domestic human rights institutions, they can use their investigation function to press for adequate remedies and to hold institutions accountable. By issuing reports exposing abuses, they can create public concern, and educate both government and the general public as to new courses of action.[5]

The overarching goal of localizing international human rights is supported through the day-to-day operation of NHRIs. A properly functioning NHRI serves several roles indispensable for human rights promotion, including "documenting the national human rights situation; providing expertise on the national protection systems, including key national institutions; advocating and advising the state on the scope and implementation of its human rights obligations; [and] assisting in follow-up to the recommendations of the UN bodies."[6]

While the academic bookshelf on NHRI establishment is starting to fill, the literature on evaluation of NHRIs and how effective they are in fulfilling the promise of human rights is still quite sparse. This chapter seeks to address this gap in the literature. While the focus here is on NHRIs, the discussion of approaches to evaluation may be applied to other human rights institutions, such as governmental human rights ministries and agencies or parliamentary human rights committees. The chapter outlines a typology of NHRI evaluative approaches, explaining structural, mandate, and impact methods, underscoring their potential to respond to the local context within which they operate and succeed or fail. The chapter concludes with some suggested avenues for research to deepen our understanding of NHRI evaluation in line with an agenda that seeks to understand and account for the local.

---

[4] See generally Janet E. Lord, "Disability Rights and the Human Rights Mainstream: Reluctant Gate-Crashers?" in Bob Clifford (ed.), *The International Struggle for New Human Rights* (Philadelphia: University of Pennsylvania Press, 2008).

[5] Asia Human Rights Commission, "Lesson 1: A Review of the Functions of National Human Rights Institutions for Guaranteeing Adequate Remedies for Rights Violations," http://www.hrschool.org/doc/mainfile.php/lesson17/92/.

[6] The Paris Principles state: "3. A national institution shall, inter alia, have the following responsibilities: (d) To contribute to the reports which States are required to submit to United Nations bodies and committees, and to regional institutions, pursuant to their treaty obligations and, where necessary, to express an opinion on the subject, with due respect for their independence; (e) To cooperate with the United Nations and any other organization in the United Nations system, the regional institutions and the national institutions of other countries that are competent in the areas of the promotion and protection of human rights." The Paris Principles, G.A. Res. 134, U.N. GAOR, 48th Sess., U.N. Doc. A/RES/48/134 (1993) (*hereafter* "the Paris Principles"). See www.un.org/documents/ga/res/48/a48r134.htm.

4.2. A TYPOLOGY OF NHRI EVALUATIVE APPROACHES

Evaluation approaches for NHRIs can be classified according to the selected standard for evaluation: (1) "structural" (the Paris Principles approach)[7]; (2) "mandate-focused," and (3) "impact-based." In addition, as indicated in Table 4.1, this classification scheme draws from two additional factors: their *source*, that is, whether they reflect interests and ideas originating within or outside the institution and state; and *signs of progress*, that is, how evaluators know when the institution is moving in the correct direction. These factors will inform the discussion of the three evaluative approaches, which will proceed in turn.[8]

4.2.1. *Approach 1: The Structural Approach (Applying the Paris Principles)*

In 1991, the United Nations International Workshop on National Institutions for the Promotion and Protection of Human Rights formalized the commitment of the UN assistance to NHRIs. The workshop produced guiding principles regarding the status, powers, and functioning of national human rights institutions. Thereafter, in 1993, the UN General Assembly endorsed the Principles Related to the Status of National Institutions, which has become better known as the "Paris Principles."[9] The most common approach to evaluating NHRIs today involves scrutiny using the Paris Principles as the principal means of assessment.[10] Utilizing the Paris Principles as a means of assessment focuses attention largely on structural issues. Critics and supporters alike recognize that "satisfying the Paris Principles does not necessarily mean that an NHRI will be an effective institution in ensuring the protection of human rights and bringing about change."[11] Nonetheless, "the international community has been prepared to accept that Paris Principle compliance will probably increase the likelihood that an NHRI will be responsive and effective."[12]

The Paris Principles establish standards regarding the status, powers, and functioning of national human rights institutions.[13] The work of NHRIs is advisory; they

---

[7] See CRPD, supra note 3 at art. 33. See also UN Commission for Human Rights Res. 1992/54, March 3, 1992; UN GA Res. 48/134, December 20, 1993.

[8] The author explores these issues in greater detail in J. Mertus, *Human Rights Matters: Local Politics and National Human Rights Institution* (Stanford: Stanford University Press, 2009).

[9] See http://www2.ohchr.org/English/law/parisprinciples.htm.

[10] Commission on Human Rights Res. 1992/54, Annex, U.N. ESCOR, Supp. 22, E/1992/22, ch. II, sec. A (1992), U.N. Doc.A/48/134 Annex (1993).

[11] Andrew Byrnes, Andrea Durbach, and Catherine Renshaw, "Joining the Club: The Asia Pacific Forum of National Human Rights Institutions, the Paris Principles, and the Advancement of Human Rights Protection in the Region," *Australian Journal of Human Rights* 14 (2009), 63–98.

[12] Ibid.

[13] See, for example, Amnesty International, "NHRIs: Recommendations for Effective Protection and Promotion of Human Rights" (London: AI Index: IOR 40/007/2001). The Asia Pacific Forum

TABLE 4.1. *Three evaluation approaches for NHRIs*

Evaluation	Structural (Paris Principles)	Mandate-focused	Impact-based
Source of Criteria	External	Internal	Internal and external
Sign of Progress	Change in formal rules	Efficiency/efficacy in fulfilling mandate	Socialization

do not have the authority to legislate or adjudicate, although those that set up individual complaint mechanisms have de facto quasi-adjudicative authority.[14] While complaint mechanisms are optional, monitoring is not. NHRIs are expected to monitor their own (other states optional) country conditions and report on abuses committed by state actors.[15] Equally important, the NHRIs are to advise the government on issues related to legislation and its compliance with international human rights treaties.

The Paris Principles also delineate a series of structural requirements for all NHRIs.[16] The institution must have a founding constitutional or legislative statute. Its mandate must be broad and far-reaching. The procedure for constituting the membership of the NHRI must be independent, with terms of office specified by law. The overall composition of the body must be pluralistic and representative. Its work must be regular and its function effective, with sufficient funding to achieve its mandate. Above all else, the NHRI must be independent from the executive branch.[17]

The International Coordinating Committee of National Human Rights Institutions (ICC) – a mechanism supported by the United Nations and essentially run by NHRIs – accredits NHRIs across the world by reference to their level of compliance with the Paris Principles. Having reviewed paper and oral submissions of applicants, the ICC assigns each institution to one of three categories following a formal application procedure: "A" (the institution is in compliance with the Paris Principles and thus has full membership), "B" (the institution is not fully compliant

of National Human Rights Institutions, Draft Guidelines for the Process of Establishing National Institutions in Accordance with the Paris Principles, http://www.asiapacificforum.net/training/nhris/guidelines.doc (*hereafter* "Asia Pacific NHRIs Draft Guidelines").

[14] See Brian Burdekin, "Human Rights Commissions," in K. Hossain (ed.), *Human Rights Commissions and Ombudsman Offices: National Experiences throughout the World* (Boston: Brill, 2000), 801–8; Sonia Cardenas, "Emerging Global Actors: The United Nations and National Human Rights Institutions," *Global Governance* 9 (2003), 28.

[15] See Rachel Murray, *The Role of National Human Rights Institutions at the International and Regional Levels: The Experience of Africa* (Oxford: Hart, 2007).

[16] United Nations Office of the High Commissioner for Human Rights, Fact Sheet No. 19: National Institutions for the Promotion and Protection of Human Rights, http://www.unhchr.ch/html/menu6/2/fs19.htm.

[17] Ibid.

with the Paris Principles and thus is granted the status of "observer"), or "C" (the institution is not compliant with the Paris Principles and accordingly has no status). Accreditation by the ICC has become increasingly important, as the possession of "A" status entitles an NHRI to participate in a number of ways in the proceedings of the UN Human Rights Council.[18] NHRIs may face temporary or permanent suspension of their "A" or "B" should their operations not conform to the Paris Principles (see, e.g., Nepal).[19]

One of the most important tasks the ICC undertakes is to monitor NHRI pluralism, as reflected in its composition and by the existence of procedures promoting diverse and open participation. Questions to be addressed in this area include these[20]: Does the composition of the institution reflect the social profile of the community in which it operates? What is the male/female ratio? What is the ethnic group breakdown? The criteria for appointment are to be "objectively verifiable criteria against which the actual appointment can be assessed."[21] Are the appointment criteria based on merit? Do the criteria require knowledge of human rights? The failure of the ICC to ask such questions in a consistent manner for all states has led to some odd results. For example, the struggling NHRI in Malaysia is granted "A" status based on its improvement on pluralism questions, while the NHRI in Switzerland, a comparatively human-rights friendly country, receives a "B" for its sub-optimal treatment of women.[22] Such results have led to the ICC being criticized as a highly politicized body of peers casting judgment on other peers in their role as gatekeepers.

Another downside of reliance on the Paris Principles for NHRI evaluation is that they were not created by the state to address problems within a state, but rather were created by authorities outside the state who may have different expectations and priorities based on their own situation. This problem of differing expectations is particularly acute where the NHRI is the product of a UN-sponsored peace agreement, as with the 1995 Dayton Agreement[23] for Bosnia-Herzegovina and the 1998 Good Friday Agreement for Northern Ireland.[24] The problem is also evident whenever states do not have much previous experience with independent institutions.

---

[18] The Human Rights Council was established in 2006 to replace the former UN Commission on Human Rights (2008b).

[19] "Brief for the Subcommittee to Consider the Accreditation Process of the Human Rights Commission of Nepal" (November 2008), http://www.nhri.net/.

[20] These questions are drawn in part from the American University, Center for Global Peace, "Checklist for National Human Rights Institutions" (Janet E. Lord and Katherine Guernsey, 2009), http://www1. american.edu/cgp/IHRC/pdfs/NHRIEstablish.pdf (*hereafter* "Checklist").

[21] R. Carver, *Assessing the Effectiveness of National Human Rights Institutions* (Versoix: International Council for Human Rights Policy, 2005), 14.

[22] See http://www.nhri.net/default.asp?PID=607&DID=0.

[23] See discussion of Bosnia-Herzegovina in Mertus, *Human Rights Matters*.

[24] See discussion of Northern Ireland in ibid.

A hallmark of NHRIs is their independence from both the state and civil society. This is simply unimaginable in places like Iraq where, historically, institutions have been an appendage of the state or captured by particular Iraqi political and religious groupings. Nonetheless, in the face of a huge disconnect with local attitudes, the campaign to build an Iraqi NHRI lumbers on.[25]

One of the most consistent critics of the Paris Principles, C. Raj Kumar, argues that in addition to being externally imposed, the provisions of the Paris Principles are vague and unworkable. For example, "guarantees of independence and pluralism," even though mentioned in the sub-heading of the Paris Principles, offer very little guidance to the states as to how to achieve this independence.[26] Kumar forcefully concludes that the Paris Principles are, at best, a good starting point for discussions relating to the formation of NHRIs, but that it is not in the human rights movement's best interest to give them more importance than they deserve in light of their weaknesses and limited nature.[27] In response to Kumar, one might argue that the Paris Principles were never intended as an evaluative tool. Rather, their purpose has always been to accord status to individual offices and in effect protect the gatekeeper responsibility of NHRIs to define their own role.

A handful of advocacy groups have sought either to create new criteria for NHRIs or to clarify the status of NHRIs under the criteria provided by the Paris Principles.[28] The Geneva-based International Council on Human Rights Policy (ICHRP), for example, has suggested twelve structural modifications that, if addressed, could serve to guide NHRIs in ensuring the effectiveness of their work.[29] NHRIs, in accordance with the ICHRP recommendations, should enjoy public legitimacy in part by having a formal legal status. They must be accessible to all, particularly marginalized groups. The culture of the NHRI should be open, collaborative, and self-critical. Its membership must be of a high quality; it must also be diverse, representative of the constituency it seeks to serve. Its staff should demonstrate the same diversity. NHRIs should proactively engage with civil society and be directed by a broad mandate. The NHRI must have an all-encompassing jurisdiction on human rights matters, have the power to monitor compliance with recommendations, treat human rights issues systematically, have adequate budgetary resources, and maintain effective international relations.

---

[25] Comments on Iraq are drawn from the author's own experiences working with the Center for Global Peace (of American University and the U.S. government) on the creation of an NHRI in Iraq.

[26] C. Raj Kumar, "National Human Rights Institutions: Good Governance Perspectives on Institutionalization of Human Rights," *American University Law Review* 19 (2003), 259–90.

[27] Ibid.

[28] See Human Rights Watch (*hereafter* HRW), *Protectors or Pretenders? Government Human Rights Commissions in Africa* (New York: HRW, 2001).

[29] R. Carver, *Assessing the Effectiveness of National Human Rights Institutions* (Versoix: International Council on Human Rights Policy [*hereafter* ICHRP], 2005), 7–8.

Yet this assumed relationship may not always be correct. If "effectiveness" is defined by its more common dictionary definition – ability to produce desired results – the focus on the composition and functioning of NHRIs falls short. The desired ultimate result is not independence qua independence but rather human rights promotion, as envisioned by the NHRI mandate.

An NHRI can be highly independent and cooperative and still unable to affect much in terms of social and political human rights gains. Robust institutional design is important,[30] but only to the degree to which formal rules and procedures affect outcomes.[31] "Many factors contribute to the effectiveness of an NHRI, and not all of these will be in the control of the commission (including the attitude of the government and community)."[32] A strong argument can be made that a more useful evaluation of the work of NHRIs would not only appraise the formal establishment of an NHRI but also focus on its performance in fulfilling a human rights mandate.

4.2.2. *Approach 2: Mandate-Based*

A mandate-based evaluative approach assesses the effectiveness of each NHRI according to its ability to fulfill its formal substantive mandate. States, ideally working in concert with civil society and broad constituencies within society, agree to the terms of the mandate. Given this process of local negotiation, mandates vary widely according to prevalent political expectations, which, in turn, are informed by the historical relationship between individuals and the state.[33] When a state is in a transitional period – for instance, recovering from conflict (e.g., Bosnia and Northern Ireland)[34] or changing from one form of government to another (e.g., the Czech Republic)[35] – the NHRI may be called upon to address intra-communal tensions and to (re)build social trust in the state.[36] An individual complaint mechanism may be more of a priority for a state that lacks an institution capable of playing such a rights-advancing role (e.g., the Czech Republic).[37] States with stronger national rights-promoting institutions may instead use their NHRI to draw worldwide

---

[30] See Amanda Whiting, "Situating Suhakam: Human Rights Debates and Malaysia's National Human Rights Commission," *Stanford Journal of International Law* 39 (2003), 72–4; Vijayashri Sripati, "India's National Human Rights Commission: A Shackled Commission?" *B. U. International Law Journal* 1 (2000), 4–6; Stephen Livingstone, "The Northern Ireland Human Rights Commission," *Fordham International Law Journal* 22 (1999), 1468–9.

[31] Khalil Z. Shariff, "Designing Institutions to Manage Conflict: Principles for the Problem Solving Organization," *Harvard Negotiation Law Review* 8 (2003), 139–56.

[32] Byrnes et al., "Joining the Club," p. 66.

[33] See Mertus, *Human Rights Matters*.

[34] Ibid., chapters 3 and 4.

[35] Ibid., chapter 5.

[36] Ibid.

[37] Ibid.

attention to their achievements (such as Denmark and Germany).[38] Although the *Paris Principles* encourage NHRIs to adopt broad mandates, a mandate-based evaluation considers only its achievements under its current mandate rather than under a more inclusive future agenda. States favor this approach as they need only comply with the minimal expectations associated with the NHRI mandate. For human rights advocates, however, inherent in mandate-focused evaluations are three substantial shortcomings.

First, there are certain structural baseline commitments that must be in place for an NHRI to function effectively. States may agree to mandates that are impossible to satisfy under the current country conditions, often as the result of steps taken (or not taken) by the state itself. For example, the state may agree that the NHRI's mandate includes monitoring the national human rights situation, but at the same time, the framers may severely constrain the evidence-gathering powers of the NHRI. This has been a problem in Northern Ireland, to take one illustration.[39] In other words, even as it publicly endorses the creation of an NHRI, the state may quietly clip its wings. The NHRI may not have the authority to review any law or intervene in any court case relevant to human rights. Even if an NHRI is permitted to instigate investigations, it may be denied subpoena powers and be unable to compel the release of evidence or require witnesses to appear. In addition, the NHRI may not have the authority to recommend reparations for victims or even the authority to take recommendations to court for enforcement.

A second drawback of a mandate-focused evaluation pertains to the advisory role played by NHRIs. Most NHRI mandates envision that they will analyze state commitments under international standards and provide assistance with treaty-body reporting, in particular offering specific evidence of positive or negative trends in state human rights compliance. In more contentious situations, NHRIs may submit their own "parallel report" challenging the state's own report.[40] In less contentious situations and where states have not obtained a sufficient level of competency on human rights reporting, NHRIs may find themselves providing information to the state for the official state report. The reputation of NHRIs demands that they remain active and continually share their expertise. At the same time, however, they cannot afford to be too close to the state lest they lose their credibility as independent institutions.[41] Striking the appropriate balance can be incredibly difficult. The multiple NHRIs found in Bosnia-Herzegovina, for example, have continually faced this identity crisis.

---

[38] Ibid., chapters 2 and 6.
[39] Ibid.
[40] See Chris Sidoti in this volume, "National Human Rights Institutions and the International Human Rights System."
[41] See "the Paris Principles."

A third limitation of the mandate-based evaluation approach is, paradoxically, the very reason states tend to favor it: the approach only requires that the NHRI advance its own agenda, regardless of whether in so doing it effectively promotes human rights. As long as the breadth of the NHRI mandate remains a matter of state discretion, NHRI performance can be evaluated based strictly on its compliance with a sub-standard mandate.

A handful of advocacy groups has challenged NHRIs that adopt limited mandates, in particular those that exclude economic, social, and cultural rights (ESCR). For example, representatives of twenty-four national human rights institutions met in New Delhi in 2005 for the International Round Table on National Institutions Implementing ESCR. At the conclusion, they issued a national plan of action for ESCR recommending that NHRIs create ESCR units or focal points and develop substantive policy capacity in this area so as to engage effectively on ESCR issues. They also sought to develop new and innovative strategies using community dialogue, information gathering, outreach to vulnerable groups and women and children, and the development of national plans of action to further ESCR implementation.[42] Other advocacy efforts have similarly sought to expand the parameters of NHRI mandates, including, for example, the proactive efforts to encourage NHRIs to incorporate disability rights into their mandates and work plans, as spearheaded by the International Coordinating Committee of NHRIs, along with the Harvard Law School Project on Disability.[43]

In addition to attempts to broaden the NHRI mandate, advocates engaged in mandate-based evaluations have tried to include a wider range of stakeholders with a number of expectations, some of which predate the NHRI, and some of which were created by, or at least encouraged by, the NHRI. Ideally, the first step in any mandate analysis would focus on the human rights concerns of stakeholders, asking what human rights issues matter most for local stakeholders. At a minimum, mandate-fulfillment requires that citizens know that the NHRI exists and that they see it as relevant to their lives. This would involve engagement with, among others, human rights organizations and civil society organizations more broadly, representatives of marginalized groups, government officials, members of the legislature, government ministers, members of political parties, lawyers and judges, trade union groups and other professional associations, academics, and particularly human rights experts. After the concerns of stakeholders are identified through a participatory process, the next step would be to examine the extent to which stakeholder concerns are being addressed by the NHRI. This entails moving beyond technical analysis of

---

[42] International Round Table on National Institutions Implementing ESCR, "Final Comments," December 2005, http://www.nhri.net/pdf/RT_New_Delhi_Conclusions_011205.pdf.

[43] See www.hpod.org.

state lawmaking and institution building, toward greater receptivity of social change at a local level.

4.2.3. *Approach 3: Impact-Based Approach*

While the structural evaluation examines whether an NHRI was established in line with certain structural precepts and the mandate-based evaluation asks whether an NHRI has actually achieved what it set out to do, an impact-based approach measures "whether those activities [undertaken by the NHRI] actually changed the human rights situation."[44] In the structural model of evaluation, the criteria for progress are largely generated by concerns *external* to the state and the NHRI; and in the case of the mandate-based evaluation model, the criteria for progress stem from concerns closer to home and thus may be considered *internal*. With the impact-based approach, all evidence that the NHRI has influenced (in an affirmative manner) the promotion of human rights is marshaled together to demonstrate impact. This includes usage of formal indicators of social change and compliance with human rights norms, as well as charting socialization of human rights understandings and practices as developed in the following section.

The most exhaustive list of formal indicators for assessing NHRI impact can be found in the work of the ICHRP, a well-respected, independent European research and advocacy organization. In 2005, the ICHRP, with the support of the National Institutions Unit of OHCHR, conducted a research project on how NHRIs may assess their own effectiveness. The resulting report, a follow-up to the International Council's 2000 report on NHRIs, entitled Performance and Legitimacy,[45] has wielded considerable influence, with the ICC officially including discussion of the report on its agenda.[46]

The notion of benchmarks and indicators figures prominently in the ICHRP report. Benchmarks are standards against which NHRIs can assess themselves, and indicators are specific measures according to which NHRIs can measure their performance. As the report explains,

> Benchmarks are standards that define the minimum attributes of national institutions with respect to their legal foundation, membership, mandate, funding and so on. National institutions should meet such benchmarks because, if well-defined, they will determine whether or not the institution is in a position to achieve its fundamental purpose which is to promote and protect human rights effectively, as well

[44] Carver, *Assessing the Effectiveness of National Human Rights Institutions*, 7.

[45] Ibid.

[46] Discussion on an initiative to develop measurement indicators concerning NHRIs and their compliance with the Paris Principles, para 7 (d), http://www.nhri.net/pdf/document_ICC_meeting-April_2005.pdf.

as more specific programme objectives. Indicators, by contrast, are tools that measure NHRIs' performance, in relation both to their objectives and their benchmarks, but also over time and relative to other matters achieved by the NHRI. These indicators of performance and impact are intended for an NHRI to be able to assess the human rights situation, its own performance and the impact of the institution on the enjoyment of human rights.[47]

The detailed benchmarks suggested by the ICHRP derive, in part, from the Paris Principles, which, as noted earlier in this chapter, are imperfect and certainly no guarantee of effectiveness. For example, the list of benchmarks includes such matters as

- Independence
- Establishment by law/constitution
- A fair and transparent appointments procedure
- Criteria for membership advancing pluralism
- Inclusion of members with professional skills and knowledge of human rights
- Good relations with civil society
- A broad and responsive mandate
- Public accountability

NHRIs can employ quantitative, qualitative, and participatory indicators to assess their own progress in achieving these benchmarks. In addition to this formal set of principles drawn from the Paris Principles, NHRI impact may be evaluated by the ability of the NHRI to change formal incentive structures and thus the behavior of states and institutions through several mechanisms:

- Constitutional review powers
- Legislative review powers
- Legal sanction (through referral to courts)
- Monitoring of human rights situations and implementation of law
- Critical reports that lead to change in operational norms
- Increasing responsiveness of rights redress mechanisms
- Increasing access to rights redress mechanisms
- Emulation of NHRI activities in the work of other state agencies

Identifying NHRI impact is no exact science. While it is possible to develop sets of benchmarks that will be broadly applicable to most NHRIs, indicators may only be devised and understood within their specific context. Thus, "indicators must always be developed, understood and interpreted with judgment, taking account of the political and economical context in which the NHRI operates as well as of

---

[47]   Carver, *Assessing the Effectiveness of National Human Rights Institutions*, 9.

its characteristics."[48] In the final analysis, indicators are a blunt instrument, capable of charting progress only with regard to particular measurable criteria, but they are ill-suited to account for the nuances of social change.

A. Charting Socialization

Socialization approaches to understanding behavioral change in a state and the conditions under which such change occurs emphasize the normative – as opposed to coercive – influence of the international system upon states, and the distinct mechanisms by which such influence is exerted. Two variants of this school of thought are "persuasion" and "acculturation" theory. According to these approaches, the receptiveness of state actors to international norms and ideas – such as NHRIs – is not necessarily guided by instrumental calculation levered by rewards and/or sanctions. Instead, both norms-based theories define participants in international society as *deeply social*, with identities shaped by the institutionalized norms, values, and ideas of the social environment in which they act. Notably, however, the logic and patterns of norm transmission differ considerably across these two approaches.

Persuasion involves the inculcation of norms so that one side ends up convinced of the truth, validity, or appropriateness of a norm, belief, or practice. The active nature of persuasion is a distinguishing feature. As Alastair Iain Johnston observes, persuasion "is not simply a process of manipulating exogenous incentives to elicit desired behavior from the other side," but rather "requires argument and deliberation in an effort to change the minds of others."[49] The socialization process begins when certain states (or, according to some theorists, other actors) undertake the task of "norm entrepreneurs" and attempt to persuade states to adopt a new norm. Norm entrepreneurs use several strategies to persuade, including framing the issue at hand to resonate with already accepted norms.[50] Governments promote norms abroad because they are consistent with universal ideals to which they adhere; governments accept them at home because they are convinced that doing so is "appropriate." Persuaded actors "internalize" new norms and rules of appropriate behavior and redefine their interests and identities accordingly.[51] Norm internalization occurs

---

[48] International Coordinating Committee of NHRIs, "Discussion on an initiative to develop measurement indicators concerning NHRIs and their compliance with the Paris Principles," Annual Meeting, April 1, 2005, http://www.nhri.net/pdf/document_ICC_meeting-April_2005.pdf.

[49] Alastair Iain Johnston, "The Social Effects of International Institutions on Domestic (and Foreign Policy) Actors," in D. W. Dresdner (ed.), *Locating the Proper Authorities: The Interaction of Domestic And International Institutions* (Ann Arbor: University of Michigan Press, 2002), 145, 153.

[50] See David A. Snow et al., "Frame Alignment Processes, Micro Mobilization, and Movement Participation," *American Sociological Review* 51 (1986), 467–75.

[51] See, for example, Jeffrey T. Checkel, "Norms, Institutions, and National Identity in Contemporary Europe," *International Studies Quarterly* 43 (1999), 98–9.

when the number of states accepting a norm reaches a "tipping point" triggering a "norm cascade."[52] According to the work of Risse, Ropp, and Sikkink, the process of norm socialization is helped along through three processes: "strategic bargaining, moral consciousness-raising through argumentative discourse, and institutionalization and habitualizations."[53]

A counterpart to persuasion theories of socialization are acculturation theories. Acculturation refers to "the general process by which actors adopt the beliefs and behavioral patterns of the surrounding culture."[54] Socialization occurs under this theory, not because anyone is convinced of the truth of anything, but because an actor perceives that an important reference group harbors the belief, engages in the practice, or subscribes to the norm.[55] According to the main proponents of this theory,

> Acculturation depends less on the properties of the rule than on the properties of the relationship of the actor to the community. Because the acculturation process does not involve actually agreeing with the merits of a group's position, it may result in outward conformity with a social convention without private acceptance or corresponding changes in private practices.[56]

In contrast to persuasion, acculturation need not be an active process. In fact, acculturation processes "frequently operate tacitly; it is often the very act of conforming that garners social approval and alleviates cognitive discomfort."[57] Through acculturation, international norms have great impact, not merely because they keep us from doing something that we want (coercion), nor because they persuade us to change our minds, but because they have transformed the geography where decision making occurs.

The process of social change is also difficult to chart because it is influenced by a variety of internal and external influences, and the field of human rights is no exception. In the case of human rights, the ability and willingness of a state to accept cultural change depends a great deal on the balance between peace and war within the country. When a country is at war, pressures within the country may make building or maintaining a robust human rights culture difficult. While war is a factor,

---

[52] Martha Finnemore and Kathryn Sikkink, "International Norm Dynamics and Political Change," *International Organization* 52 (1998), 887–917.

[53] See T. Risse et al., *The Power of Human Rights: International Norms and Domestic Change* (New York: Cambridge University Press, 1999).

[54] Ryan Goodman and Derek Jinks, "How to Influence States: Socialization and International Human Rights Law," *Duke Law Journal* 54 (2004), 626.

[55] See W. W. Powell and P. J. DiMaggio (eds.), *The New Institutionalism in Organizational Analysis* (Chicago: University of Chicago Press, 1991).

[56] Goodman and Jinks, "How to Influence States," 643.

[57] Ibid., 640.

other problematic factors include globalization, militarization, huge dislocation and movement of peoples, the rise in global insecurity following 9/11 and the invasion of Iraq. The role of NHRIs in a society at war or recovering from war differs dramatically from the role of an NHRI located in a country that has not experienced war for some time.[58]

Notwithstanding the challenges of assessing social change and human rights culture-building, it is, however, possible to use normative pressure/socialization mechanisms to bring about change and indeed, in some instances, even change underlying preferences.[59] Applying the insights of socialization mechanisms and normative pressure approaches to the immediate problem, namely, the ability of NHRIs to exert pressures on state agents, it is possible to articulate suggested indicators for this kind of social measure assessment. These might include (non-exhaustively) the following: (1) critical reportage and media coverage generally, (2) discernible shifts in public policy, (3) human rights education attainment by state agents (e.g., police, prison officials, prosecutors, judges, election commissions, social care institutions), (4) increase in claims to grievance bodies framed in rights-based language, (5) increase in petitions to legal bodies (e.g., courts, administrative tribunals) by the public, (6) increase in membership of human rights-oriented political parties, (7) increase in membership of human rights organizations, and (8) public opinion and human rights awareness.

It is worth exploring, in particular, the possibility of survey methods. Indeed, scholars and practitioners have begun to explore survey-based methods for evaluating public opinion of human rights protection and awareness, as well as individuals' perceptions of themselves and others as rights-bearing actors in society.[60] Perception data on rights can be found in the annual surveys conducted by a range of regional barometers.[61] Such sources of information provide a valuable picture of the human rights experience of citizens on the ground. Surveys such as the Eurobarometer provide insight into the general perception of rights conditions within those states as well as awareness relating to more specific rights-issue areas such as domestic violence against women[62] and access to justice.[63] The Afrobarometer, for example,

[58] See Mertus, *Human Rights Matters*.
[59] See Finnemore and Sikkink, "International Norm Dynamics."
[60] See Todd Landman, "Measuring Human Rights: Principle, Practice, and Policy," *Human Rights Quarterly* 26 (2004), 906–31; T. Landman and E. Carvalho, *Measuring Human Rights* (New York: Routledge, 2009), see, in particular, chapter 6.
[61] See Arab Democracy Barometer: http://www.arabbarometer.org/; The Eurobarometer, http://ec.europa.eu/public_opinion/index_en.htm; The Afrobarometer, http://www.afrobarometer.org/; and the Latinobarómetro, http://www.latinobarometro.org/.
[62] See Eurobarometer, *Domestic Violence against Women Report Special Eurobarometer 344* (Brussels: European Commission, 2010).
[63] See Eurobarometer, *European Union's Citizens and Access to Justice Special Eurobarometer 195* (Brussels: European Commission, 2004).

studies public perception of opportunities to participate in the political sphere[64] and perceptions of poverty and living standards.[65] NGOs working in the field have also utilized survey methods to expose direct experience of rights violations, especially among vulnerable populations. Physicians for Human Rights, in particular, has pioneered survey data as a tool for raising awareness around precise rights violations.[66] Other cross-national surveys, including the World Values Survey, attempt to measure broad cultural changes in a comparative perspective.[67] In sum, the limitations of surveys as a source of systematic human rights data notwithstanding,[68] they constitute a powerful additional tool for determining social changes in human rights and the development of a human rights culture within different sectors of society. And, of course, survey methods do not exhaust the potential tools for measuring levels of human rights awareness, the expression of human rights values, and rights-related practices within a society.

The listed social change assessment indicators suggest a methodology that is applied over time and within a particular historical context according to which NHRIs may undergo shifts and phases in their transformation. Thus, NHRIs may manifest social change as institutions of resistance, as institutions of political transition and as transformative institutions of norm reception. The process is not linear and is highly dependent on local context.

One sign of socialization and the spread of a human rights culture is the number of news stories mentioning human rights issues; a possible benchmark that this indicator points to would be to double the number of news stories on human rights. One source of evidence of cultural shifts is popular culture, including film, video games, television, rock music, and other similar fields. Over the past ten years, an explosion in popular culture devoted to human rights has been accompanied by a tangible increase in the number of high-profile celebrities championing human

---

[64] Afrobarometer Briefing Paper No.32, *Give Us a Chance! Uncovering Latent Political Participation among Malawians* (April 2006), http://www.afrobarometer.org/papers/AfrobriefNo32.pdf.

[65] Afrobarometer Briefing Paper No. 36, *Despite Economic Growth, Tanzanians Still Dissatisfied* (June 2006).

[66] For instance, a large-scale field survey conducted by Physicians for Human Rights (PHR) in 2004 and 2005 provided compelling evidence that gender inequity and HIV infection are linked and that upholding women's rights was paramount if rates of HIV infection were to be reduced. See Physicians for Human Rights, *Epidemic of Inequality: Women's Rights and HIV/AIDS in Botswana and Swaziland, an Evidence-based Report on the Effects of Gender Inequity, Stigma and Discrimination* (Washington, DC: Physicians for Human Rights, 2007).

[67] See generally http://www.worldvaluessurvey.org/.

[68] Landman and Carvalho point to a range of limitations of survey-based measures, "including issues surrounding low response rates, forced responses, timidity and misinformation, absence of voice in providing a human rights assessment or account, and their 'snapshot' nature." Landman and Carvalho, *Measuring Human Rights*, 93.

rights causes. Another source of evidence of the spread of human rights norms can be found in changes in political culture. NHRIs often claim a victory when the text of their speeches and reports makes its way into political speeches and government reports. Journalists also may crib ideas and even exact text from NHRI reports. That this "borrowing process" exists may not demonstrate a cataclysmic social transformation in favor of human rights, but it does provide some evidence that a shift in favor of human rights has begun.

4.3. CONCLUSION

The establishment of NHRIs now occupies a significant space on the international human rights agenda, supported by UN technical assistance programs and other multilateral and bilateral donor effort. Meaningful engagement with NHRIs assumes an increasingly important activity for human rights advocacy groups. NHRIs are not only active at the national level but are increasingly engaged in both regional and international processes, as illustrated by the extensive participation of NHRIs in the negotiation of the UN Disability Convention. While their arrival on the human rights scene has generated a triumphal applause – particularly by the UN and donor governments, but also by the international human rights community more generally – the proliferation of NHRIs alone is no measure of their impact or effectiveness. As human rights actors, whether governmental or nongovernmental, are increasingly called upon to demonstrate their legitimacy and overall success, NHRI evaluation must be an important part of the evaluative agenda.

Simply establishing NHRIs is not the magic bullet of twenty-first-century human rights realization but these institutions may help strengthen human rights promotion and protection. Gone are the days when NHRIs could set up shop and operate quickly and with great zest, following the scripture of the Paris Principles as if they alone could determine their effectiveness. Increasingly, NHRIs are being called upon to prove their effectiveness. Reopening the Paris Principles is not an option; a reopening could be co-opted by states with their own political agenda. Despite their flaws, the Paris Principles are a useful point of departure, but they do little to measure either mandate or impact.

A review of NHRI activities can provide some measure of its performance under its mandate, but only an impact analysis will provide evidence of the NHRI's role in fostering and shaping a human rights culture. NHRI scholars and practitioners alike would do well to facilitate a dialogue on how these institutions can contribute in a meaningful way to building local human rights cultures, moving beyond appeals to conformity with the Paris Principles or any other measure that provides only superficial insight into their actual impact and effectiveness. Moving forward, scholarship might advance theoretical understandings of human rights practice, explaining, for example, how power relations between NHRIs and other domestic structures work to constrain or enable NHRIs within domestic politics or assessing power differentials among NHRIs inter se within regional and international structures. A new emphasis on evaluating the effectiveness of NHRIs would be advanced by pressing on in this light.

PART II

NHRI Performance

Global, Regional, and National Domains

5

National Human Rights Institutions and the International Human Rights System

Chris Sidoti

5.1. INTRODUCTION

National human rights institutions (NHRIs or national institutions) and the international human rights system have a history of engagement but too often it has been one sided. Although national human rights institutions are the creations of their own domestic laws and processes, their existence is closely connected with the international human rights system that has nurtured and promoted them for many decades, especially since 1993. The international system now looks to the institutions to play significant roles through engagement with its mechanisms and processes. Yet, national institutions have often been slow to respond to this expectation and few make more than sporadic, ad hoc contributions. This chapter examines the relationship. It discusses the importance of international engagement by national institutions and describes the opportunities and procedures for engagement that are available if national institutions are prepared to use them. It argues that the international human rights system now needs their support and contribution and that it is in the interests of the institutions themselves to respond positively.

5.2. A TWO-WAY RELATIONSHIP

5.2.1. *National Institutions Are Products of the International System*

Although the first national institutions were established in the late 1970s and 1980s, their growth in numbers and strength can be traced directly to the strong endorsement they received from the Second World Conference on Human Rights in 1993:

> The World Conference on Human Rights reaffirms the important and construct-
> ive role played by national institutions for the promotion and protection of human
> rights, in particular in their advisory capacity to the competent authorities, their

role in remedying human rights violations, in the dissemination of human rights information, and education in human rights.

The World Conference on Human Rights encourages the establishment and strengthening of national institutions, having regard to the "Principles relating to the status of national institutions" and recognizing that it is the right of each State to choose the framework which is best suited to its particular needs at the national level.[1]

Each year following the Vienna World Conference the United Nations Commission on Human Rights passed a resolution reaffirming international support for national institutions and encouraging all states to establish them.[2] There were similar resolutions in the General Assembly.[3] However the new Human Rights Council has yet to adopt a resolution on national institutions, perhaps reflecting that this is now an uncontroversial issue and that the position and importance of national institutions are well accepted. More recently Treaty Monitoring Bodies have added their voices, often including recommendations for establishing or strengthening national institutions in their Concluding Observations.[4] And since the commencement of the Universal Periodic Review procedure in the Human Rights Council in 2008, recommendations on national institutions have featured prominently in the reports adopted by the Council on individual states. At the twelfth session of the Council in September 2009, for example, of the sixteen states under review, fourteen received recommendations concerning the establishment or strengthening of a national human rights institution in accordance with the Paris Principles.[5]

From 1995 the High Commissioner for Human Rights responded to the Vienna Declaration and Program of Action and to the resolutions of United Nations bodies by supporting these institutions. This support was especially active and effective from 1995 to 2003 when the high commissioner had a very senior special adviser

---

[1]   "Vienna Declaration and Programme of Action," part 1, para. 36, at www2.ohchr.org/english/law/vienna.htm.

[2]   The last such resolution of the Commission on Human Rights was resolution 2005/74, E/CN.4/RES/2005/74.

[3]   The most recent is General Assembly Resolution 65/207, adopted on December 21, 2010, A/RES/65/207.

[4]   The International Coordinating Committee has prepared a compilation of treaty monitoring committee recommendations concerning national institutions, arranged by treaty committee and region, at www.nhri.net/default.asp?PID=281&DID=0.

[5]   The fourteen nations receiving recommendations were the Central African Republic (document A/HRC/12/2), Monaco (document A/HRC/12/3), Belize (document A/HRC/12/4), Chad (document A/HRC/12/5), Congo (document A/HRC/12/6), Malta (A/HRC/12/7), Afghanistan (document A/HRC/12/9), Chile (document A/HRC/12/10), Uruguay (document A/HRC/12/12), Yemen (document A/HRC/12/13), Vanuatu (document A/HRC/12/14), Former Yugoslav Republic of Macedonia (document A/HRC/12/15), Comoros (document A/HRC/12/16), and Slovakia (document A/HRC/12/17). Only two states under review did not receive recommendations relating to a national human rights institution: New Zealand (document A/HRC/12/8) and Vietnam (document A/HRC/12/11).

with a wide mandate to assist in this work.[6] While the position of special adviser was not continued after 2003, the work on national institutions continued to be considered important and a specialist unit was established in the High Commissioner's Office. At the end of 2010, that unit, called the National Institutions and Regional Mechanisms Section, had more staff than at any previous time, but its staffing complement remains well below its workload in relating to around 100 developing or developed national institutions and potentially up to 190 governments.

Recognition and promotion of national institutions has moved beyond the political processes of the United Nations to international law itself, in their specific or implicit recognition in human rights treaties. The Convention on the Rights of Persons with Disabilities provides that states that have ratified the Convention must have independent monitoring mechanisms for compliance with the Convention's obligations:

> When designating or establishing such a mechanism, States Parties shall take into account the principles relating to the status and functioning of national institutions for protection and promotion of human rights.[7]

The Optional Protocol to the Convention against Torture and other Cruel, Inhuman and Degrading Treatment or Punishment (OPCAT) also requires the establishment of independent monitoring mechanisms and provides that

> When establishing national preventive mechanisms, States Parties shall give due consideration to the Principles relating to the status of national institutions for the promotion and protection of human rights.[8]

5.2.2. *The Paris Principles*

These *Principles relating to the status of national institutions for the promotion and protection of human rights* (the Paris Principles) are international minimum standards by which institutions could be established and assessed for their seriousness. They were drafted and adopted by national human rights institutions themselves. Fortunately this occurred before the Vienna World Conference instigated the rush of interest in national institutions.

In 1991 there were fewer than twenty national institutions. In that year the UN Centre for Human Rights convened a workshop of national institutions for the first time. They met in Paris from October 7–9, 1991, along with representatives

---

6 The Special Adviser was Brian Burdekin who had been Australian Human Rights Commissioner from 1986 to 1994. The engagement of an experienced practitioner in this role proved to be critical to its effectiveness. Mr. Burdekin was not replaced when he left the High Commissioner's Office in 2003.

7 Article 33.2.

8 Article 18.4.

of governments, UN agencies, nongovernmental organizations, and regional human rights mechanisms.[9] These Principles were subsequently endorsed by the Commission on Human Rights and the General Assembly.[10]

The adoption of the principles was unusual in that the United Nations system usually does not endorse standards that are not drafted through its own processes. The fact that they were drafted by national institutions themselves, however, makes them relevant to and credible among the institutions. They are certainly far from perfect. They suffer from vagueness and a lack of specificity about national institutions, reflecting the breadth of structure and function of their drafters. The institutions represented at the Paris workshop, though small in number, were the major institutions at that time. They were very diverse. Their representatives shared a common commitment to develop international minimum standards but none of them wanted her or his own institution to fall outside whatever standards were adopted. So the principles had to be drafted so widely and at times so flexibly that they would encompass and endorse each of the then major institutions and the various models they reflected.[11] They were also drafted so hurriedly that they contain errors that no one has been prepared to correct. Most notably, the final section is entitled "Additional principles concerning the status of commissions with quasi-jurisdictional competence." The correct term is quasi-judicial competence, "quasi-jurisdictional competence" being meaningless.

In spite of their shortcomings, for almost two decades the Paris Principles have played a very important role, so important that few are prepared to suggest that they be revised to be made more useful. They provided a benchmark, a set of minimum requirements, for national institutions before the numbers of these institutions began growing rapidly. They continue to be the standard by which the structure, form, and legal basis of an institution are assessed in determining whether the institution is to receive international recognition. States would reassert their central role in the UN system and insist on leading any revision of the Principles so that they would no longer be the product of the institutions themselves but the result of political negotiation among states. Each state would ensure that its own institution, however inadequate,

---

[9] Those attending the Paris meeting were the International Labor Organization, the United Nations Educational, Scientific and Cultural Organization, the Organization for Economic Cooperation and Development, the Commonwealth Secretariat for Human Rights, the European Court of Human Rights, Inter-American Court of Human Rights, and the Inter-American Commission on Human Rights. See A. Pohjolainen, *The Evolution of National Human Rights Institutions: The Role of the United Nations* (Copenhagen: Danish Institute for Human Rights, 2006), 58–60.

[10] The Paris Principles were drafted and approved at the first International Workshop on National Institutions for the Promotion and Protection of Human Rights in Paris, 7–9 October 1991. They were subsequently endorsed by Commission on Human Rights Resolution 1992/54 in 1992 and General Assembly Resolution 48/134 in 1993.

[11] For a discussion of the various models of national human rights institutions, see Linda Reif in this volume, "The Shifting Boundaries of NHRI Definition in the International System."

came within the scope of new standards. Institutions that have been denied recognition because of their limited mandate or weak basis, such as the Islamic Human Rights Commission of Iran, would therefore gain international credibility.

The Paris Principles do not ensure the effectiveness of a national human rights institution, only that it conforms in law, structure, mandate, and scope of operations with what is the minimum acceptable internationally. They are an instrument for structural evaluation, not for performance-based or impact-based evaluation.[12] They do not purport to evaluate effectiveness or impact but merely to set some benchmark by which a national institution can be assessed for its formal compliance with these minimum standards. They are the gate to international acceptance and the gatekeeper is the International Coordinating Committee of National Institutions for the Promotion and Protection of Human Rights.[13]

The gatekeeping role of the International Coordinating Committee is another experience that is unique within the United Nations system. States jealously guard UN mechanisms to ensure that only those they approve have access. Nongovernmental organizations, for example, have to run the gauntlet of the Economic and Social Council's Committee on Non-Governmental Organizations, probably the worst, most politicized, and most anti-human rights body in the United Nations system.[14]

The International Coordinating Committee was established by the national institutions themselves in 1993 and it soon received recognition in resolutions of the Commission on Human Rights. In 2000 it commenced its own process of accrediting national institutions on the basis of their compliance with the Paris Principles. At first the process was a "light touch" one that rarely resulted in accreditation being denied to an institution with long-standing participation in international forums. However, during the following years the process was tightened up, made more rigorous, and extended beyond new institutions to those already accredited by means of a compulsory review of accreditation every five years or earlier if considered

---

[12] Julie Mertus develops this analysis of evaluation of national human rights institutions in her chapter. See also Richard Carver, *Performance and Legitimacy: National Human Rights Institutions*, 2nd ed. (Versoix: International Council for Human Rights Policy, 2004).

[13] The International Coordinating Committee of National Institutions for the Promotion and Protection of Human Rights was first established as a loose, informal association. In 2008 it was incorporated under Swiss law with its own statute. See www.nrhi.net.

[14] The Committee has nineteen members. From 2007 to 2010 its members were Angola, Burundi, China, Colombia, Cuba, Dominica, Egypt, Guinea, India, Israel, Pakistan, Peru, Qatar, Romania, Russian Federation, Sudan, Turkey, United Kingdom and the United States. China, Cuba, Egypt, India, Pakistan, Russian Federation, and Sudan have been especially hostile to effective human rights nongovernmental organizations (NGOs). Sudan held the chair of the Committee in 2008 and 2009. For 2011 to 2014, Egypt has left the Committee. The other hostile members remain on the Committee and Nicaragua and Venezuela have joined it. For over fifteen years, the Committee has consistently refused to recommend accreditation for a single NGO working on issues of human rights and sexual orientation and gender identity. In recent years its recommendations against accreditation have been rejected several times by the Economic and Social Council, to which it reports.

necessary.[15] Working through a Sub-Committee on Accreditation, the International Coordinating Committee recognized sixty-five national institutions with full status in 2010.[16] It has also refused status to a number and has acted to withdraw full status on some occasions.[17] When the Commission on Human Rights extended the participation rights of national institutions, it gave those rights only to those national institutions fully accredited by the International Coordinating Committee.[18]

Importantly, in view of the deficiencies in the Paris Principles themselves, the International Coordinating Committee has also commenced making General Observations on the interpretation and application of the Paris Principles.[19] These General Observations are effectively refining and giving increased substance to the Paris Principles. They give weight to the position of the Paris Principles as the gate to international recognition and acceptance and to the role of the International Coordinating Committee as gatekeeper.

The Paris Principles are credible because they were developed by national institutions themselves and are now being further supplemented, through the General Observations, by national institutions. They were not developed by diplomats with no knowledge or experience in the actual work of human rights and with their states' interests at heart. They were not externally imposed. The significance of the accreditation process is that it is a peer review process, undertaken by practitioners. It keeps the recognition of institutions, and therefore their participation in international forums, completely separate from the politics of the UN and its member states. The engagement of national human rights institutions in the international human rights system has this unique basis, and national institutions benefit from it.

5.2.3. *The Paris Principles and International Engagement*

Having promoted the establishment of national institutions in accordance with the international minimum standards of the Paris Principles, the international system required something in return, the contribution of these institutions to the international system itself. The Paris Principles acknowledged this as part of the essential "competence and responsibilities" of national institutions, to cooperate with the United Nations and any other organization in the United Nations system,

---

[15] Statute of the International Coordinating Committee of National Institutions for the Promotion and Protection of Human Rights, Article 15.

[16] There were also sixteen with observer status on the basis of being not fully compliant and nine considered non-compliant. See www.nhri.net.

[17] The institutions of Algeria, Cameroon, Madagascar, Nigeria, and Sri Lanka have been downgraded from fully compliant status to observer status because of their partial compliance with the Paris Principles, and the institution of Fiji has been suspended. See www.nhri.net.

[18] Resolution 2005/74 operative paragraph 11(a).

[19] See www.nhri.net/?PID=253&DID=0.

the regional institutions and the national institutions of other countries that are competent in the areas of the promotion and protection of human rights.[20] This provision is being strictly applied by the Sub-Committee on Accreditation of the International Coordinating Committee of National Human Rights Institutions. The Sub-Committee has said:

> The Sub-Committee would like to highlight the importance for NHRIs to engage with the international human rights system, in particular the Human Rights Council and its mechanisms (Special Procedures Mandate Holders) and the United Nations Human Rights Treaty Bodies. This means generally NHRIs making an input to, participating in these human rights mechanisms and following up at the national level to the recommendations resulting from the international human rights system. In addition, NHRIs should also actively engage with the ICC and its Sub-Committee on Accreditation, Bureau as well as regional coordinating bodies of NHRIs.[21]

In accreditation reports, the Sub-Committee frequently comments on the international engagement of the national institution under review and draws its attention to the General Observation on the subject.[22]

5.2.4. Why Should National Institutions Engage?

There are good reasons for national institutions to be engaged in the international human rights system, quite apart from their desire to be recognized as fully compliant with the Paris Principles. The international human rights system is a highly defective and relatively ineffective system. The General Assembly has recognized "the importance of ensuring universality, objectivity and non-selectivity in the consideration of human rights issues, and the elimination of double standards and politicization."[23] However, the international human rights system as a whole fails to meet those criteria in full, and the Human Rights

[20] Paris Principles, "Competence and responsibilities," para.3(e).

[21] Sub-Committee on Accreditation General Observations 1.4, "Interaction with the International Human Rights System," accessible through the national human rights institutions website at www.nhri.net.

[22] See, for example, the comments on the Russian Office of the Commissioner for Human Rights, the People's Advocate of Albania and the Defensoría del Pueblo of Paraguay in the report and recommendations of the session of the Sub-Committee on Accreditation of November 3–6, 2000 and the comments on the Qatar National Human Rights Committee, the Commission Nationale Consultative de Promotion et de Protection des Droits de l'Homme of Algeria, the Defensoría del Pueblo de Ecuador, and the National Human Rights Commission of Malaysia in the report and recommendations of the session of the Sub-Committee on Accreditation of March 26–30, 2009. Both reports are accessible through the national human rights institutions website at www.nhri.net/default.asp?PID=607&DID=0.

[23] Resolution 60/251.

Council in particular meets none of them.[24] The system needs national institutions far more than they need it.

The international system needs national institutions to provide independent, objective information about human rights situations. States' reports to international bodies are invariably self-serving and reports from nongovernmental organizations are often criticized as being political or inaccurate. National institutions that comply with the Paris Principles are official but independent bodies able to speak authoritatively. They have responsibility and power under the law to investigate and report on situations of human rights violation. They have the information and the experience to bring a measure of honesty to international forums where it is lacking. In addition, they are able to draw from their national experiences to identify gaps in existing international protection and assist in developing international law and practice so that they are more responsive and more effective.

International engagement is important for the national institution too. It can be an effective strategy to advance the institution's principal responsibility, which is the promotion and protection of human rights at home. International engagement enables a national human rights institution to contribute to the following:

- Setting the international human rights agenda, thereby increasing the pressure on a state to address significant human rights issues at home
- Developing international law and practice, to provide a legal basis for national debates in favor of better human rights performance
- Increasing the state's international accountability for its human rights performance, which in turn can increase domestic accountability
- Reinforcing the principle of the universality of human rights, enabling it to call on international standards when confronted with domestic traditional and cultural practices that violate human rights
- Identifying human rights issues of common concern within a region or across regions and developing strategies to address them on a regional or international basis
- Fostering international and regional alliances around particular human rights issues, including nongovernmental organizations, academics and other civil

---

[24] For excellent annual critiques of the Human Rights Council, see Rachel Brett, of the Quaker United Nations Office, "Neither Mountain nor Molehill – UN Human Rights Council: One Year On," July 2007; "Digging Foundations or Trenches? UN Human Rights Council: Year 2," August 2008; and "A Curate's Egg UN Human Rights Council: Year 3, 19 June 2008 to 18 June 2009," August 2009 at www.quno.org/humanrights/UN-CHR/commissionLinks.htm#QUNOPUB. See also the analytical overview of each session of the Human Rights Council by the International Service for Human Rights at www.ishr.ch. For an example of NGO media statements on aspects of the Human Rights Council, see Human Rights Watch at www.hrw.org/en/news/2009/10/05/un-human-rights-council-traditional-values-vote-and-gaza-overshadow-progress and www.hrw.org/en/news/2009/05/01/un-racism-conference-halls-shame-and-fame.

society actors, that can be active partners of the institution in working on those issues

- Building international solidarity among national institutions so that it receives support from its peers when under pressure from its own government
- Learning best practices from other national institutions, to be adapted and applied in its own work.

In all of these ways the NHRI is working to increase its own effectiveness at home, strengthening its base in law and practice, consolidating its position, building support, and widening its partnerships.

The engagement can have many dimensions. It can be part of a bottom to top strategy, seeking to build links between international mechanisms and bodies on the one hand and local and national-level activists on the other. The Human Rights Commission of the Maldives, for example, has undertaken work on the right to housing in the Maldives. In 2007, housing issues were the basis for the third highest number of complaints to the Commission; and so in 2008 the Commission undertook a "rapid assessment" of the problem, working closely with local organizations. In November 2008 it published its report.[25] In February 2009 the UN Human Rights Council's Special Rapporteur on the Right to Adequate Housing visited the Maldives and then produced her own report on the problem.[26] The Commission has been following up on its recommendations and those of the Special Rapporteur since then. The Commission's report provided good information and analysis to inform the Special Rapporteur's visit and, in turn, the Special Rapporteur's report provided international validation of the Commission's assessment and recommendations. There was complementarity between international and national mechanisms and as a result significant pressure for better promotion and protection of the right to adequate housing.

International engagement can also be a horizontal strategy that provides a basis for joint action and mutual support. An example of joint action is the initiative undertaken by the Asia Pacific Forum of National Human Rights Institutions on migrant workers in the region.[27] This human rights issue resonates strongly within a region that has countries of origin, countries of transit, and host countries. National institutions from all three categories of states are working together to identify strategies to protect the rights of these workers, from recruitment to return. In terms of providing mutual support, mobilization in defense of the organizational integrity of individual NHRIs by large numbers of national institutions from all regions has

---

[25] Human Rights Commission of the Maldives, "Rapid Assessment of the Housing Situation in the Maldives," November 2008.

[26] The Special Rapporteur's report on her mission is UN document A/HRC/10/7/Add.4: www.ohchr.org/EN/countries/AsiaRegion/Pages/MVIndex.aspx.

[27] See www.asiapacificforum.net/news/nhris-join-forces-to-tackle-abuse-of-workers.html.

been a feature of engagement, as when the independence of the Danish institution was at risk in 2002 and that of the Nigerian institution in 2007.

5.2.5. Which National Institutions Are Engaging?

Many national institutions are already heavily engaged with the international human rights system but their number is still far too small. Some cannot see any advantage or relevance in it and so do not engage. Some simply do not know how to contribute effectively.

According to the results of a survey of national institutions published by the Office of the High Commissioner for Human Rights in July 2009, the majority of national institutions are not heavily engaged:

> While NHRI participation in the Council's UPR process was high, interaction with the treaty bodies remained moderate. Participation in the Human Rights Council and interaction with its special procedures mandate holders was low and interaction with other international mechanisms, conferences, workshops was minimal.[28]

There were significant regional variations in engagement. African and European institutions indicated a higher level of engagement with the Universal Periodic Review mechanism of the Human Rights Council but in general European institutions were by far the least engaged. Institutions in the Americas and Asia Pacific were more heavily engaged generally and especially in relation to the Human Rights Council and its Special Procedures. It is significant that these institutions had also received the most training on interaction with the international mechanisms.[29] Clearly, training led to greater engagement. Proximity to Geneva, however, seems to have had little or no effect in increasing the involvement of the European national institutions.

Little other information is available on which institutions engage. For example, it is not known whether older institutions engage more than newer ones. Attendance records of the Human Rights Council, however, indicate very little participation by classical ombudsman institutions, even though they have human rights mandates,

---

[28] United Nations, Office of the High Commissioner for Human Rights, Survey on National Human Rights Institutions (Geneva: UN, 2009), 42–3 (*hereafter* "NHRI Survey"). National institutions were invited to respond to a questionnaire on many issues about their structure and work. Sixty-one institutions did so. Unfortunately, a number of the more active, engaged institutions were not among the respondents. Non-respondents included the national institutions of Australia, Denmark, Ghana, India, Indonesia, Kenya, and Republic of Korea, all of which play very significant roles at the regional level and have been actively engaged at the international level, in most cases since the early to mid-1990s.

[29] Asia Pacific 83.3 percent, the Americas 66.6 percent, Europe 47.6 percent, and Africa 42.1 percent. Ibid., 47.

or by their international association, the International Ombudsman Institute. Only institutions with a specialized human rights mandate engage with the international human rights system.[30]

5.2.6. *Obstacles to Engagement*

National institutions encounter real obstacles to their international engagement, however. There can be political obstacles: governments do not like to be held up to criticism in international forums or from international mechanisms and so resent any work by national institutions that is thought to be contributing to that; governments and civil society will criticize institutions that seem to be giving too much priority to international engagement rather than domestic human rights issues or the leaders of institutions who are considered to travel too much rather than staying at home. There will certainly be financial and personnel obstacles: international engagement can be demanding and expensive and institutions will rightly worry about expenditure on travel to international meetings and conferences rather than on domestic work; travel can also be very time-consuming, taking key members and staff of institutions away for significant periods. Lack of or limited knowledge of the workings of the international system will also present an obstacle to involvement for many institutions, especially newer institutions. And a lack of confidence in the international system's ability to deliver improvements in human rights observance reduces the enthusiasm to engage with the system, especially when there are so many obstacles to doing so.

If international engagement is to be accepted and broadly undertaken, these obstacles have to be recognized and addressed. The Office of the High Commissioner for Human Rights, regional associations of national human rights institutions, such as the Asia Pacific Forum, and academic and other organizations, such as the Raoul Wallenberg Institute in Sweden and the International Service for Human Rights in Geneva, have been providing training for national institution members and staff in accessing and using the international human rights system. Some funding is provided from UN and other donors to assist national institutions to send representatives to important international meetings. These kinds of support are essential if the institutions are to be able to play their role in the international system.

There is a clear tension between the domestic priorities of national institutions and their international engagement. Those tensions will only be resolved satisfactorily if the international engagement is seen as a necessary and beneficial adjunct to their domestic work, providing support for that work and making it more effective.

---

[30] See Linda Reif in this volume, "The Shifting Boundaries of NHRI Definition in the International System."

Institutions understand the contribution they can make to the international human
rights system, but that reason, by itself, is insufficient grounds for engagement. It
requires justification on the basis of its usefulness in promoting and protecting
human rights at home.

5.3. ARENAS OF ENGAGEMENT

National institutions now have opportunities to contribute to and through many
international human rights mechanisms. This section of the chapter examines
the opportunities for engagement and the experiences of national institutions that
engage. It deals with both that part of the system derived from the United Nations
Charter (the Human Rights Council, its Special Procedures and the Universal
Periodic Review) and that part derived from human rights treaties (the Treaty
Monitoring Committees).

5.3.1. *Human Rights Council*

In its resolution establishing the Human Rights Council, the General Assembly:

> *Decide[d]* that the Council shall apply the rules of procedure established for
> committees of the General Assembly, as applicable, unless subsequently other-
> wise decided by the Assembly or the Council, and also decides that the partici-
> pation of and consultation with observers, including States that are not members
> of the Council, the specialized agencies, other intergovernmental organizations
> and national human rights institutions, as well as nongovernmental organizations,
> shall be based on arrangements, including Economic and Social Council reso-
> lution 1996/31 of 25 July 1996 and practices observed by the Commission on Human
> Rights, while ensuring the most effective contribution of these entities.[31]

This provision gave both reassurance and uncertainty: reassurance that the past
practices of the Commission on Human Rights would be continued; uncertainty as
the Council could still decide to change those practices by altering its rules, especially as the rules of procedure of committees of the General Assembly made no
provision whatsoever for the participation of nongovernmental organizations and
NHRIs. When the Human Rights Council came to adopt its own rules of procedure, it incorporated this paragraph into them, without change.[32]

Nongovernmental organizations have been able to argue, with good justification,
that the General Assembly resolution provided a guarantee of the basis for their
participation in the Council. Their participation in the former Commission had

[31]   Resolution 60/251, para. 11.
[32]   Human Rights Council Rules of Procedure, Rule 7.

been the subject of very specific rules of procedure, laid down by the Economic and Social Council's resolution specifically cited in the paragraph and applied in practice. That was not so for NHRIs. For them, participation in the Commission had been far more a matter of practice than of rules of procedure.

Until the late 1990s national institutions addressed the Commission from the seats of their governments, speaking only in the place of their governments. This compromised the institutions as it led to the perception that they were government spokespersons, not independent institutions, even if in fact they were speaking quite independently. From 1997 the Bureau of the Commission adopted guidelines before each session, enabling national institutions to address the Commission in their own right and from their own seats. However, their interventions were permitted only under one sub-item in the Commission's agenda, that dealing with national institutions themselves. After some years of discussion, in 2005 in its annual resolution on NHRIs, the Commission decided to permit full participation by national institutions accredited by the International Coordinating Committee as fully compliant with the Paris Principles.[33] The Commission instructed its chairperson to finalize the modalities for this, with the anticipation that it would approve those modalities at its next session, but it was abolished first.

National institutions entered the era of the new Human Rights Council, therefore, with only very limited "practice of the Commission" on which to base their participation. Fortunately, practice developed during the Council's important first "institution building" year on the basis of the Commission's unimplemented resolution. National institutions have been accorded the right to full and broad participation in all aspects of the Council's work. They succeeded in having the Rules of Procedure specifically incorporate the unimplemented resolution of the Commission on Human Rights:

> Participation of national human rights institutions shall be based on arrangements and practices agreed upon by the Commission on Human Rights, including resolution 2005/74 of 20 April 2005, while ensuring the most effective contribution of these entities.[34]

As a result, their participation in the Human Rights Council is in fact far greater than in the old Commission on Human Rights. National institutions are now able to

- Submit documents for the consideration of the Council
- Make written statements on any item on the Council's agenda
- Make oral interventions on any item on the Council's agenda

---

[33] Resolution 2005/74, para. 11.
[34] Para.11(b).

- Sponsor parallel events, for example on the role of national institutions themselves or on specific human rights themes or issues or on particular country situations

They have their own distinct seating and access to the floor of the Council during sessions. They can participate in open consultations on draft resolutions and conduct all the lobbying and advocacy work that they wish.[35] Having secured participation rights, however, few national institutions have played an especially active role in the Council. The survey by the Office of the High Commissioner for Human Rights found that about 20 percent or less had interacted with the Council.[36]

Many institutions go to Geneva annually for the meeting of the International Coordinating Committee and, since those meetings usually coincide with an ordinary session of the Council, most avail themselves of the opportunity to make an oral statement to the Council. Their statements are generally directed toward describing their own work, rather than offering comment on the human rights situation in their country of origin or advocating any particular policy or view on a matter of human rights law. They are not part of the debate on the most critical issues in international human rights discourse. They miss the opportunity to make a serious contribution, in accordance with their mandate to promote and protect human rights. Yet they have much to offer on these questions because of their practical experience and their acceptance of universal human rights standards as opposed to the political views of individual states. They can also be advocates for a strong and effective international human rights system when many states want to weaken and undermine it.

An example of the potential and the failure is the debate on "religious defamation" in recent years. Since 2005 many states, especially those in the Organization of the Islamic Conference, have pursued vigorously the issue of what they call defamation of religion. This is a concept unknown to international human rights law. The law protects the rights of human beings, not of ideas, ideologies, cultures, or religions or beliefs.[37] A human being has the right to be protected from "attacks on his honor and reputation" but ideas, ideologies, cultures, and religions, and beliefs do not.[38] Human beings have the right to freedom of "thought, conscience and religion" but the thoughts, consciences, and religions themselves have no rights.[39] This debate, based though it is on a concept unknown in law, has resulted in resolutions in the Human Rights Council and the General Assembly and has seriously distorted basic

---

[35] See the note prepared for national human rights institutions by the Office of the High Commissioner for Human Rights at www2.ohchr.org/english/bodies/hrcouncil/nhri.htm.
[36] NHRI Survey supra note 28.
[37] Universal Declaration of Human Rights, art 1.
[38] International Covenant on Civil and Political Rights, art. 17.1.
[39] International Covenant on Civil and Political Rights, art. 18.1.

principles of human rights, including their universality.[40] NHRIs could have made written and oral statements on this issue, individually and collectively. They could have sponsored parallel events with expert speakers to present the legal argument for universality. They could have contributed a combined voice affirming universal standards based on serious legal analysis. They could have broken down the political divisions among states in the Human Rights Council by speaking on a worldwide basis from different perspectives but with a common view. But they have failed to do so. This example illustrates both the opportunities national institutions have for positive, active engagement and their failure to take those opportunities. The international human rights system suffers as a result.

One difficulty national institutions face in making a significant contribution is the cost in financial and human resources required to do so. Geneva is an expensive town and it is far away from the ground where national institutions work. The annual program of work of the Human Rights Council is heavy, involving at least ten weeks of ordinary meetings spread over three sessions and an unknown number of special sessions. In addition there are six weeks of universal periodic review and many other weeks of working groups, committees and forums. Participation in all of this is impossible for any organization, state or nonstate, not based in Geneva. The Office of the High Commissioner for Human Rights does not provide financial support for national institutions to come to Geneva for the Council sessions. On some occasions, some funding has been sourced through regional associations of national institutions or from donors at the local level but almost all institutions have to find their own resources to enable their attendance and participation.

The Human Rights Council's institution-building year, 2006–07, provides a good example of the importance of national institutions' participation and a model for how it can be undertaken. This first year in the new Council was largely spent in

---

[40] The most recent resolution in the Human Rights Council was resolution 13/16 adopted by vote on March 25, 2010, with 20 votes in favor, 17 votes against, and 8 abstentions, as follows:

In favor: Bahrain, Bangladesh, Bolivia, Burkina Faso, China, Cuba, Djibouti, Egypt, Indonesia, Jordan, Kyrgyzstan, Nicaragua, Nigeria, Pakistan, Philippines, Qatar, Russian Federation, Saudi Arabia, Senegal, South Africa;

Against: Argentina, Belgium, Chile, France, Hungary, Italy, Mexico, Netherlands, Norway, Republic of Korea, Slovakia, Slovenia, Switzerland, Ukraine, United Kingdom of Great Britain and Northern Ireland, United States of America, Zambia;

Abstaining: Bosnia and Herzegovina, Brazil, Cameroon, Ghana, India, Japan, Madagascar, Mauritius;

Not present: Angola, Gabon.

This was a significantly closer vote than in March 2009 when the resolution was carried with 23 votes in favor, 11 against, and 13 abstentions.

The most recent resolution of the General Assembly was resolution 65/244 adopted on December 21, 2010, with 79 votes in favor, 67 votes against, 40 abstentions, and 6 states absent.

very difficult negotiations to develop the Council's methods and procedures. It was a critical process because it set the basis for the Council's operations for the indefinite future. It was also a time-consuming process, with the Council holding four ordinary sessions and working groups working in parallel for most of the year, seeking agreement on procedures for each of the major areas of Council activity. National institutions were active at critical moments during those negotiations. Admittedly most of their attention was directed toward their own role in the Council's work, because of the uncertainty already described. They succeeded in ensuring that the Council's Rules of Procedure incorporated Resolution 2005/74 of the Commission on Human Rights.

This success was due to astute advocacy in public sessions of the relevant working groups and in private. The experience demonstrated the potential for national institutions to influence decisions in Geneva. They were able to pursue two important strategies.

First, individual national institutions approached their own governments at the national level and encouraged them to support proposals in the negotiations for participation by national institutions. This local advocacy resulted in collaboration across the Council's traditionally divided regional groupings. So, for example, India and Indonesia were very vocal and active in supporting the participation of national institutions, as were Australia, Canada, Kenya, and Uganda. The collaboration of states with national institutions, that supported the participation of their national institutions, won the day when other states were either opposed or lacked interest. If national institutions coordinate their policies on critical human rights issues arising in the Council and then place more domestic pressure on their own governments, it may be possible to effect significant changes in state positions in the Council itself, across the regional groupings, with far better results.

Second, representatives of national institutions collectively were active in the lobbies in Geneva. The institution-building negotiations marked the first occasion on which the international and regional associations of national institutions played significant advocacy roles in Geneva on behalf of their member institutions. The International Coordinating Committee placed a full-time representative in Geneva during the latter part of the institution-building year. She was joined during the critical last six weeks of negotiations by the deputy director of the Asia Pacific Forum of National Human Rights Institutions. Together they provided a voice in the open working groups and behind the scenes. They were able to follow up the national level representations of individual institutions with meetings with the diplomats in Geneva. They met the president of the Council on several occasions to advance the position of the institutions. Feedback was provided to the national institutions on what was happening in Geneva so that there could be further pressure on states at the local level. Their advocacy efforts further secured active support for national institutions from nongovernmental organizations that otherwise might not have seen this as a priority concern in the negotiations.[41]

This two-pronged approach, domestic advocacy by individual institutions with their own governments and collective advocacy by their representatives in Geneva, is a good model that enables national institutions to play an effective role in the Council. It is cost effective too as it does not require individual institutions to travel to Geneva frequently for lengthy periods.

The International Coordinating Committee has responded to the opportunities now available by placing a permanent representative in Geneva, based with the National Institutions and Regional Mechanisms Section of the Office of the High Commissioner for Human Rights (OHCHR) but funded by the national institutions themselves through voluntary contributions. This representative acts both for the Committee as a whole, advocating policies and positions of national institutions collectively, and for individual institutions, making statements on their behalf to the Council.

The full potential of the position has not yet been realized, however, but the potential is there. The scope of the work is still restricted far too narrowly to the place, role, and work of national institutions themselves and has not to date extended to the key issues in contention relating to international human rights law or the international human rights system and mechanisms. The fact that the Office of the High Commissioner provides hosting ensures good communications between the representative and the Section but it might also act as a constraint if there is concern that a critical position taken by the representative will reflect badly on the Office. So, for example, if the representative became active on a highly controversial issue such as "religious defamation," the Office could well find itself in the middle of a very hostile debate about its role, including the support of national institutions, and its views.

The role of the permanent representative of the International Coordinating Committee is an important and a difficult one. The representative needs to be collaborative and consultative, always carefully ensuring that she or he knows and reflects the views of the Committee and individual national institutions. But the representative works virtually alone for most of the year, with national institutions far away, and so needs to be an independent worker, able to take initiatives and to react to developments as they occur, knowledgeable in international human rights law and the international mechanisms, and a good lobbyist and advocate with a strong sense of accountability to the Committee. A very tall order!

The Human Rights Council is a combat zone in which human rights often seem to be of least concern. States that approach the work of the Council with

---

[41] This is especially true of Amnesty International, Human Rights Watch, and the International Service for Human Rights.

seriousness for the protection of human rights find their motives challenged and their initiatives defeated more often than not. Nongovernmental organizations are often marginalized and their views dismissed or ignored. Because of their official status in national law and because of their practical work on the ground protecting human rights, national institutions can "speak truth to power" with credibility and authority. Many do but unfortunately most content themselves with interventions that are either self-promoting or largely irrelevant to the issues in dispute. On the whole they have failed to engage actively as key participants in the issues of hottest contention, for example, as already discussed, on the concept of "religious defamation."

National institutions should bring honesty and frankness to the deliberations of the most politicized forum in the international human rights system. They should also play an important role in affirming the universality of human rights law. In the context of repeated attempts to subject human rights law to cultural and religious particularities, they can affirm universality while speaking from all regions and all religious, cultural, political, and social systems. They are challenged to use their right of participation in the Council to contribute to the development and strengthening of international human rights law and the international human rights system and its mechanisms.

5.3.2. *Special Procedures*

Without doubt Special Procedures have been the most effective mechanisms of that part of the international human rights system that is based in the United Nations Charter, that is, the former Commission on Human Rights and the present Human Rights Council.[42] At the time of the Commission's end and the Council's establishment they were praised as the arms and legs of the Commission, its eyes and ears, and the jewel in the crown of the international human rights system.[43] Special Procedures can have responsibility for a human rights theme, such as health, education, torture, or arbitrary detention, or to a specific country situation, such as Myanmar or Sudan. They typically have wide functions. National institutions can interact with them in relation to all of their functions. National institutions have many opportunities to contribute to the work of these important mechanisms and,

---

[42] "Special Procedures" is a general term for all the independent mandates established by the former Commission or the Council to investigate, monitor, and report on a human rights issue or situation and occasionally to develop new human rights standards. The term includes mandate holders with various titles: Special Rapporteurs, Independent Experts, Representatives and Special Representatives, and expert working groups.

[43] See for example the statement by the Secretary General, Kofi Annan, at the Opening Ceremony of the Human Rights Council, Geneva, June 19, 2006, accessible at www2.ohchr.org/english/bodies/hrcouncil/statements.htm.

in turn, to receive international endorsement and support from these mechanisms for the national institution's own work.

Special Procedures investigate and report on human rights questions within the scope of their mandate. A national institution can provide them with general briefings on its own views of the mandate and on the specific relevance of the mandate to its own country. The briefings can be provided in writing or, where the Special Procedure is a working group that meets periodically, personally in oral form. These general briefings contribute to the Special Procedures' work, assisting in the development of the approach, focus, and work plan of the mandate holder. Where the mandate covers an issue of priority to the institution in its own work, the institution can look to the mandate holder's reports for assistance in defining the nature of the rights and the consequent obligation and for support in its work.

The cooperation of national institutions is especially important when Special Procedures undertake country visits. The mandates of the Special Procedures almost always provide for mandate holders to make country visits and most visit two to four countries a year. Each visit is followed by a report that is presented to and discussed in the Human Rights Council. The visits and reports provide opportunities to draw international attention to specific human rights issues within the countries visited. They also provide the countries with the benefit of advice and recommendations from eminent international experts on the particular rights. However, according to the survey by the Office of the High Commissioner for Human Rights, less than 35 percent of respondent national institutions provided information to a Special Procedure or met a mandate holder during a country visit.[44] The survey provides no clues as to the reason for this low level of interaction but it may be the result of the obstacles to engagement already discussed. An additional problem is inadequate notice of country visits and inadequate communications between a national institution and the staff servicing a mandate holder prior to a visit.

A national institution can be involved in a Special Procedure's visit from beginning to end. It can initiate and advocate a visit in the first place, encouraging a mandate holder to include in her or his work plan a visit to its country and lobbying its government to issue an invitation to the particular mandate holder. It can submit relevant information to the mandate holder before and during the visit. It can meet and brief the mandate holder early in the visit and propose and arrange meetings with key groups and individuals during the visit. It can propose issues to be examined during a visit and recommendations that the mandate holder could consider making to the government at its conclusion. After the mandate holder has reported, it has an important role in disseminating the conclusions and recommendations in

---

[44] NHRI Survey supra note 28. In the Asia Pacific region, the level of engagement was much higher at over 50 percent.

the report and following up implementation. All this is of assistance to the mandate holder but it also assists the institution in its own work. The visit can be an opportunity to raise awareness among the public of the particular issue. It can offer support for, even endorsement of, the institution's policies, views, and work on the issue. In these ways, the visit can be part of the institution's strategies in its work.

Special Procedures also take up individual cases. In doing so, they communicate with governments, seeking advice on the case and sometimes recommending some form of action to address it. Cases can be taken up on an urgent basis where required. Usually the cases are addressed confidentially but on occasion the Special Procedure will make a media statement to draw public attention to the matter. National institutions themselves can refer matters to Special Procedures for their attention. They can also assist victims of human rights violations to put their own concerns before a Special Procedure. They can follow up a case locally, before, during, and after the Special Procedure has taken it, particularly in promoting implementation of any recommendations that might be made. Again the institution's involvement both assists the Special Procedures in their work and enables international support for the institution in its own work.

National institutions have become most involved with Special Procedures during country visits. Very few have provided general briefings to the mandate holders or have assisted with individual cases. During country visits, however, they have often acted as briefers, facilitators, and commentators. Clearly they have seen benefit in engagement with the Special Procedures in this context but not in other contexts. Collaboration in visits has been important but it has not led national institutions to defend a Special Procedure when the Special Procedure has been under attack in the Human Rights Council for what she or he has said and done. Frequently, when the report of a country visit is discussed in the Council, the state concerned and its allies have responded with attacks on the mandate holder personally and his or her integrity. The substance of criticisms in the report is denied and the recommendations are rejected. National institutions have generally not participated in the Council discussion of reports of country visits and, as a result, they have not been able to rebut state denials.[45] They could do so with legitimacy and authority as official bodies.

In spite of the praise of the system of Special Procedures at the time of the Council's establishment, the system has been under sustained attack ever since. States seem to like the idea of Special Procedures but not the actuality of the work

[45] For example, the Nigerian government attacked the Special Rapporteur on Extra Judicial, Summary and Arbitrary Executions Professor Philip Alston, in the strongest terms when he reported at the Council session in September 2007 on his visit to Nigeria. The Nigerian Human Rights Commission had assisted the Special Rapporteur during the visit but it did not attend the Council session and did not defend the Special Rapporteur or his report.

they do. They express their support of the system in general while undermining, through formal controls and very personal abuse, the individuals appointed to perform the mandates and imposing tighter and tighter restrictions on their ability to do their jobs. In 2007 the Council adopted a Code of Conduct for Special Procedure mandate holders, allegedly to strengthen their role and their work but in fact to constrain their independence and control their activities.[46] A proposal at the time to adopt a complementary Code of Conduct for states was ignored. Special Procedures are routinely attacked in the Council and new resolutions passed to remind them of the Code of Conduct and threaten them with disciplinary action if they fail to apply it as some states want to see it applied, that is, by restricting their operations.[47]

National institutions have a strong interest in ensuring that the system of Special Procedures is as effective as possible. Unfortunately they have not become engaged in the debates and have generally not acted to defend either the system as a whole or individual mandate holders.[48]

5.3.3. *Universal Periodic Review*

In establishing the Human Rights Council in 2006, the General Assembly added one new mechanism to the international human rights system, the universal periodic review. The resolution required the Council to

> undertake a universal periodic review, based on objective and reliable information, of the fulfillment by each State of its human rights obligations and commitments in a manner which ensures universality of coverage and equal treatment with respect to all States; the review shall be a cooperative mechanism, based on an interactive dialogue, with the full involvement of the country concerned and with consideration given to its capacity-building needs.[49]

The resolution gave the Council a year to develop the modalities for the conduct of the review. During the negotiations there were heated exchanges about

---

[46] Human Rights Council resolution 5/2, adopted in June 2007, imposed a Code of Conduct on Special Procedures but not on states.

[47] Resolution 11/11, adopted in June 2009, reaffirms the application of the Code of Conduct with an implicit but clear warning to the mandate holders.

[48] For example, at the 11th session of the Council in June 2009, the Special Rapporteur on Freedom of Expression, reporting to the Council for the first time, was subjected to very personal attacks because of his rejection of the concept of "religious defamation." The Special Rapporteur on Extra Judicial, Summary and Arbitrary Executions was also accused of lacking integrity and objectivity. They were strongly defended by nongovernmental organizations but no national institution came to their defense. See International Service for Human Rights Council Monitor: Analytical Overview Human Rights Council 11th session 2, June 19, 2009, 15–16, at www.ishr.ch/council-monitor/session-overviews?task=view.

[49] General Assembly resolution 60/251, paragraph 5(e).

whether nongovernmental organizations and NHRIs should have any role in the review. Many states wanted to keep the review process entirely a state-run and state-controlled process. In the end, the modalities of the review make no specific mention of either nongovernmental organizations or national institutions. However, they refer to "relevant stakeholders" who should be consulted at the national level in the preparation of the state report, who may provide "[a]dditional, credible and reliable information" and who "have the opportunity to make general comments before the adoption of the outcome by the plenary."[50] National institutions are "relevant stakeholders" for both purposes. They can provide information for the review and comment on the draft report before its adoption by the plenary session of the Council. Like nongovernmental organizations, they can attend but are not permitted to participate in the working group interactive dialogue with the state under review.

National institutions have taken advantage of these opportunities to influence the review, though only to a limited extent. In fact, according to the survey by the Office of the High Commissioner for Human Rights, the Universal Periodic Review process has attracted the highest level of engagement by national institutions. Of the twenty-seven respondents whose states had been reviewed, all had participated in some capacity.[51]

Many national institutions have participated in national level consultations on the state report and many have provided information before the interactive dialogue, but few have become deeply involved in the process. They could propose issues to be pursued in the dialogue and recommendations that could be made in the report but generally they did not. The review provides very significant opportunities for an institution to have the international mechanism of the Council take up its identified priorities and policies.

The Council and its members have found the burden of the review very heavy. Having adopted a four-year cycle for reviewing all 192 member states of the United Nations, the Council must review forty-eight States each year, sixteen in each of the three sessions. Although there are strict limits on the volume of material officially put to the Council, in fact extensive material is made available directly and through the website of the Office of the High Commissioner for Human Rights. Even large delegations complain of the difficulty they face in digesting all the information and contributing effectively to the process. Small delegations have little chance of doing so. As a result, there is a limited focus on a small number of issues, and priority is given in preparation to states that are the most serious human rights violators. Some

---

[50] Human Rights Council resolution 5/1, annex para. 15(a), 15(c), and 31, respectively.

[51] NHRI Survey supra note 29, 58. Institutions in the Asia Pacific and the Americas reported consistent engagement with all stages of the process, perhaps again the result of the high levels of training in these two regions in the use of the international human rights system.

issues and some states receive little attention. National institutions have the opportunity to fill this vacuum. States are generally pleased to receive their information and many states welcome their informal advice on what issues to pursue and what recommendations to make.

The opportunity to influence recommendations is especially significant. The Council has adopted the practice of including in the report of the review every recommendation made by any state. Recommendations are not subject to a vote of the Council and so do not become Council recommendations. However, every recommendation made is included as part of the Council report and the state under review is expected to consider and respond to it. Any national institution can propose a recommendation to states undertaking the review and, because of the heavy workload, many states will receive the proposals sympathetically, treat them seriously because they come from the official institution, and then present the recommendations as their own during the course of the interactive dialogue.

National institutions, like nongovernmental organizations, are not permitted to make oral statements or ask questions during the interactive dialogue with the state under review in the Human Rights Council's working group. However, there could be an opportunity, that has not been explored, for them to become involved. A state under review has a set period of time allocated to it in the dialogue in the working group. The state could make some of that time available to its national institution to make its own report on the state's compliance with its human rights obligations. This has not occurred to date, probably because no national institution has asked for it. It is an example of more creative ways of engaging with the international human rights system that national institutions can pursue if they are committed to increasing their participation.

Though silenced during the working group's interactive dialogue with a state under review, national institutions can speak at the plenary session of the Human Rights Council that considers the reports of the review and adopts the recommendations. Many national institutions have participated effectively in this plenary discussion. Technically they could comment on any state and any report of the review but they have not done so. In practice, they have often commented on the human rights situation only in their own state and do so with greater honesty than the state. They have been able to endorse or criticize the conclusions and recommendations of the review and make a public commitment to monitor and report on state implementation.[52]

---

[52] See, for example, the comments by the Human Rights Commission of Malaysia in the Human Rights Council's plenary consideration of the report of the review of Malaysia in June 2009 – at http://portal. ohchr.org/portal/page/portal/HRCExtranet/11thSession/OralStatements/120609 and reported in "International Service for Human Rights Council Update," Item 6, Universal Periodic Review, June 9–12, 2009, 12–13.

5.3.4. *Treaty Monitoring Committees*

All the core human rights treaties have a treaty monitoring body that promotes and monitors compliance with the treaty. These bodies are made up of independent human rights experts elected by those states that have ratified the particular treaty. The treaty monitoring committees offer important opportunities for national human rights institutions to further their own work. Unlike the Human Rights Council they are bodies of independent experts, not of representatives of states. They are legal bodies, not political bodies. Their observations and recommendations are based on human rights law rather than on the interests of states. National institutions have engaged far more with these committees than with other parts of the international human rights system and there are many opportunities for them to increase and improve their engagement.[53]

Each of the nine major international human rights treaties has a committee of elected independent experts that promotes the treaty, assists in its interpretation and implementation, and monitors the compliance by states party to the treaty with their obligations under it.[54] The committees have increasingly seen NHRIs as important collaborators in their work. For the committees, national institutions have roles in encouraging ratification, promoting implementation, monitoring compliance, and assisting the committees in their monitoring and recommendatory roles.[55] Three committees have adopted General Comments on national institutions.[56] Others have referred to national institutions in wider General Comments.[57] National

---

[53] The role of national human rights institutions in the treaty body process was discussed at an international roundtable in Berlin in November 2006 – see "Conclusions of the International Roundtable on the Role of National Human Rights Institutions and Treaty Bodies," Berlin, November 23–24, 2006, UN doc. HRI/MC/2007/3. The roundtable made twenty recommendations to national institutions and adopted a draft harmonized approach to NHRI engagement with treaty body processes, which they recommended to treaty bodies for adoption. The treaty bodies have not yet adopted the draft.

[54] Each of the treaty monitoring committees is established by the treaty for which it is responsible except the Committee on Economic, Social and Cultural Rights, which is established by resolution of the Economic and Social Council. The Convention for the Protection of All Persons from Enforced Disappearances only commenced on December 23, 2010, and so the treaty committee under that treaty has not yet been established.

[55] The Paris Principles too, see the promotion of treaty ratification as an important function of national institutions: "Competence and responsibilities," paragraph 3(c). This is in addition to the more general function of cooperating with the international human rights system: "Competence and responsibilities," paragraph 3(e).

[56] Committee on the Elimination of Racial Discrimination, "General Recommendation XVII" 1993; Committee on Economic, Social and Cultural Rights, "General Comment 10," 1998; and Committee on the Rights of the Child, "General Comment 2," 2002.

[57] For example, Committee on the Elimination of Discrimination against Women General Recommendation 6, 1988 on "Effective National Machinery and Publicity."

institutions themselves have proposed common guidelines for their engagement with the committees.[58]

The level of engagement by national institutions in the treaty committees has been described as moderate but it covers every aspect of the implementation, reporting, and monitoring process. According to the survey by the Office of the High Commissioner for Human Rights:

> NHRI interaction with the UN treaty bodies was moderate overall. In Africa, almost 80 percent of respondents had contributed to a state report and 50 percent had participated in a session. However, few had submitted a parallel report or contributed to the list of issues. In the other three regions [that is, the Americas, Asia Pacific and Europe], fewer had contributed to a state report, but the level of parallel reports and contributions to the list of issues was higher (around 30–40 percent). In all regions, only 40–45 percent of respondents had disseminated concluding observations and conducted follow up activities and only around 20 percent had participated in the treaty bodies' general work.[59]

The reasons for the higher level of engagement are not clear. It may be related to the relative infrequency of the reporting, once every three to five years, but that disguises the fact that with so many treaties, most states now find themselves in a very regular cycle of reporting on one treaty or another. A second possible reason for the greater engagement is the greater confidence that national institutions, among others, have in the independent treaty bodies than in the Human Rights Council with all its politics. The basis of the treaty bodies' work is law, as expressed in an agreed text, and so the committees' deliberations are seen as strongly legally based and judicial.

National institutions encourage ratification of international human rights treaties.[60] Many institutions urge their governments to catch up. The first six of the principal human rights treaties have been ratified by at least three quarters of UN member states but the Convention on the Protection of the Rights of All Migrant Workers and Members of Their Families, adopted in 1990, has only forty-four states parties. The goal of universal ratification remains unfulfilled. National institutions have an especially important role when a new treaty is adopted. The Convention on the Rights of Persons with Disabilities has been ratified by ninety-seven states, but the Convention for the Protection of All Persons from Enforced Disappearances has only twenty-three, and only came into effect on December 23, 2010.[61]

---

[58] See "National Human Rights Institutions and UN Treaty Monitoring Bodies: A Recommendations Paper by the International Coordinating Committee of National Human Rights Institutions," at www.nhri.net/default.asp?PID=281&DID=0.

[59] NHRI Survey supra note 29, 58.

[60] The Paris Principles, "Competence and responsibilities," para.3(c).

[61] Numbers of states parties as of 1 January 2011.

National institutions then have a role in treaty implementation. They should offer "opinions, recommendations, proposals and reports on any matters concerning the promotion and protection of human rights."[62] They should "promote and ensure the harmonization of national legislation regulations and practices with the international human rights instruments to which the State is a party, and their effective implementation."[63] In fact this is at the heart of most of the work that they do. These domestic responsibilities are the principal focus of their programs and activities. Their legislation often incorporates international treaties directly, through specific inclusion, or indirectly, through the definition of "human rights," within the jurisdiction of the institutions.[64] The responsibility of cooperation with the international system extends further, however.

National institutions should play a role in the preparation of the state reports. There is tension here in that national institutions can contribute but should not take over state responsibility for the report. They must be careful to preserve their independence. Many institutions are consulted by their governments during the course of the preparation of the state reports. Some institutions have been invited, and at times even pressured, to take on the complete responsibility for the state report. They have almost always refused to do so. The Paris Principles provide for national institutions to "contribute" to state reports "with due respect for their independence."[65] This necessarily means that they should not take on the role of preparing the reports. That is a state responsibility under a treaty to which the state is a party.[66] If a national institution were to take that role, it would permit the state to distance itself from its obligations and to avoid its responsibilities. The Committee on the Rights of the Child has been explicit in affirming that reporting on the performance of treaty obligations is a state obligation that should not be delegated to a national institution.[67] The Committee on the Elimination of Racial Discrimination similarly sees one role of national institutions as "assist[ing] the government in the preparation of reports,"

---

[62] The Paris Principles, "Competence and responsibilities," para.3(a).

[63] The Paris Principles, "Competence and responsibilities," para.3(b).

[64] An example of the former is the Australian Human Rights Commission, which has jurisdiction in respect of certain international human rights instruments that are specified either in the establishing legislation or in governmental declarations: Australian Human Rights Commission Act 1986, sec. 3. An example of the latter is the Afghanistan Independent Commission on Human Rights for which the definition of human rights includes rights "enshrined in the Afghan Constitution, declarations, covenants, treaties, protocols, and other international human rights instruments ratified and acceded to by Afghanistan and to which Afghanistan is a party:" "Law on the Structure, Duties and Mandate of the AIHRC," art. 4.

[65] The Paris Principles, "Competence and responsibilities," para.3(d).

[66] International Coordinating Committee, "A Discussion Paper Regarding the Engagement of National Human Rights Institutions in the Treaty Body Process," para.8(c), at www.nhri.net/default.asp?PID=281&DID=0.

[67] Committee on the Rights of the Child General, "Comment 2," para.21.

not in preparing the reports for the governments.[68] The proper role for a national institution is to contribute issues and analysis for the governmental drafters to consider and then provide comments on drafts. The institution needs to remain free to prepare and submit its own report to the committee, with its own views.

The treaty monitoring committees look to national human rights commissions to provide objective, authoritative information to the Committees to assist them in monitoring states' compliance with the treaties. Most institutions forward information to the committees. Many prepare their own parallel or alternative or shadow reports so that the committees have information additional to and more objective than that provided by the states themselves.

The practice of committees in dealing with national institutions in the reporting process varies greatly. The International Coordinating Committee has described the optimum process. NHRIs should be encouraged to attend the various meetings of the Treaty Bodies, as appropriate, and in particular,

- Contribute to the information utilized in the drafting of the list of issues – either directly or in coordination with the National Institutions Unit of the OHCHR – or provide input into the country-analysis prepared by the Secretariat
- Participate in the Pre-Sessional Working Group to raise particular issues of concern (the modalities for such participation are not yet formally defined)
- Participate in the informal briefings with Members during the Session (similar to those held with NGOs)
- Be granted a right of reply similar to that of NGOs, following a State Party presentation
- Follow up on the Concluding Observations (the Concluding Observations are now systematically sent to NHRIs through a staff member within the National Institutions Unit whose main area of work relates to national institutions and treaty bodies).[69]

Most committees provide informal opportunities for the institutions to address them and discuss the states' reports and the institution's alternative reports. Some committees have a more formal process. The Committee on the Elimination of Racial Discrimination has suggested that representatives of national institutions be included in government delegations when the Committee examines state reports.[70] That is not generally considered desirable as it detracts from the independence of the institution. The Committee on Economic, Social and Cultural Rights offers the "best practice" here. It permits national institutions to participate in the formal

---

[68] Committee on the Elimination of Racial Discrimination, "General Comment 17," para.1.
[69] International Coordinating Committee, "The United Nations Treaty Bodies and National Institutions," at www.nhri.net/default.asp?PID=281&DID=0.
[70] Committee on the Elimination of Racial Discrimination, "General Comment 17," para.2.

state examination process. The national institution appears with but independently of the state delegation and addresses the Committee and answers questions from Committee members.

The treaty monitoring committees certainly consider that NHRIs are important mechanisms at the national level to promote implementation of treaty obligations and to monitor compliance. Over the past decade all committees have regularly made recommendations that concern national institutions, particularly directed toward the establishment of new institutions, where they do not already exist, and the strengthening of existing institutions.[71] Although national institutions have a higher level of engagement with these bodies than others in the international system, there is still a great deal of untapped potential in fostering greater collaboration at all levels of committee activity.

5.3.5. *Standard Setting*

National human rights institutions have taken a special interest in standard setting. This began during the final stages of the negotiation of the Convention on the Rights of the Child in 1988–89.[72] At that time, however, these institutions were barely recognized in international forums and their participation was generally required to be as part of government delegations.

Over the past decade, national institutions have played more prominent, independent roles. They were active in the negotiation of the Declaration on the Rights of Indigenous Peoples, where they were able to draw on their practical experience on the ground of working with those who had been dispossessed and were disadvantaged and suffered discrimination.

In many respects, however, the participation of national institutions in the Ad Hoc Committee of the General Assembly that negotiated the Convention on the Rights of Persons with Disabilities was the widest and most intense of any international instrument. National institutions were accepted as important experts who could contribute to the development both of the law and of the international system. They can be said to have come of age as international contributors.

National institutions certainly demonstrated their expertise. They brought into the negotiating sessions some of the foremost academic expertise on the issue available anywhere.[73] More than that, they demonstrated that they had internal expertise through the involvement of senior officials in the institutions with

---

[71] The International Coordinating Committee has prepared a compilation of these recommendations, arranged by treaty committee and region, at www.nhri.net/default.asp?PID=281&DID=0.

[72] The then Australian Human Rights Commissioner, Brian Burdekin, was a very active participant in the negotiation sessions during this period.

[73] Including Professor Gerard Quinn of Ireland and Professor Andrew Byrne of Australia.

disabilities.[74] At the final session of the Ad Hoc Committee, representatives of ten national institutions participated directly, in addition to the Asia Pacific Forum, the association of the seventeen institutions in the Asia Pacific region.[75]

5.3.6. *Other International Forums*

A secondary achievement through the process of the Ad Hoc Committee for the Convention on the Rights of Persons with Disabilities was the arrival of national institutions in the United Nations' New York headquarters. Previously the engagement between national institutions and the international system had been Geneva-focused and virtually exclusive to Geneva. For all their faults, the UN forums operating in Geneva have traditionally been far more open to participation by nongovernmental organizations and national human rights institutions than the UN forums operating in New York. In Geneva, nongovernmental organizations and national institutions have speaking rights in many bodies, including the Human Rights Council, and rights of access to the floors of meeting and conference rooms where they are able to mingle with state delegates and advocate their concerns and views. They can participate in open-ended consultations on draft resolutions and propose amendments, and they are more easily able to follow states' positions and hold them accountable. In New York, they have very little of this. They have no speaking rights in almost all New York–based forums and restricted access to meeting rooms and coffee shops where the state delegates gather.

The negotiation of the Convention on the Rights of Persons with Disabilities was the first occasion on which national institutions participated in significant numbers in a New York–based process. Through this process, UN officials and state delegations in New York for the first time became aware of these relatively new nationally based institutions and saw them in action and the significance of their contribution. There is no doubt that this strengthened the standing of national human rights institutions within the international system.

Certainly NHRIs had appeared previously in a number of international forums outside Geneva. They had played prominent roles in some of the most important international human rights conferences since 1990, including the Vienna World Conference on Human Rights in 1993, the Beijing World Conference on Women in 1995, and the Durban World Conference against Racism, Racial Discrimination, Xenophobia and Related Intolerance in 2001. At Vienna, they succeeded in

---

[74] For example, the Australian Human Rights Commission's Assistant Disability Commissioner and later Human Rights Commissioner, Graeme Innes, and the Indian Human Rights Commission's Special Rapporteur on Disability Rights, Anuradha Mohit, were persons with disabilities.

[75] The national institutions of Australia, Canada, France, India, Ireland, Morocco, New Zealand, Republic of Korea, Sierra Leone, and Sweden participated directly.

achieving recognition and endorsement for the first time. At each of the conferences they made contributions that focused especially on issues of implementation at the national level.

More recently, national institutions have sought to play larger parts in New York–based international human rights forums. They are already active in the Permanent Forum on Indigenous Issues, where some members and staff of some national institutions have participated regularly, and they are now seeking recognition from the Commission on the Status of Women to enable them to participate in meetings of that Commission on the same basis as their participation in the Human Rights Council. Each year for some years now, representatives of NHRIs have gone to New York to attend that Commission and advocate their status. They hope to achieve their objective at the 2011 session.

The Commission on the Status of Women, though a subsidiary body of the Economic and Social Council, as the Commission on Human Rights was, has never permitted the same level of participation of nongovernmental organizations and has never recognized the separate independent status of national institutions. As a result, national institutions have no direct say at meetings of the Commission on the Status of Women. In 2008 the Asia Pacific Forum passed resolutions directed toward achieving the same participation entitlements in the Commission on the Status of Women and in the Human Rights Council.[76] The International Coordinating Committee joined in this initiative and in March 2009 delegations from the national institutions of Australia, Indonesia, Korea, the Philippines, and Thailand attended the 53rd session of the Commission in New York, 2–13 March 2009. A second delegation, including the chairperson of the International Coordinating Committee and the deputy director of the Asia Pacific Forum, visited New York in December 2009 to pursue discussions with key people in the Commission, its secretariat, and the UN women's body. They have secured good support from a number of advocates both inside the United Nations secretariat and in the missions and delegations.

5.4. GREATER AND MORE EFFECTIVE ENGAGEMENT

National human rights institutions have many reasons for engaging with the international human rights system. In many states they owe their very existence to support, encouragement, and even pressure from the international system. The international system can continue to work to their advantage, promoting the establishment of institutions where they do not already exist and strengthening them where they are in place. The international system can also provide legitimacy and protection when

---

[76] See Asia Pacific Forum, "Report: NHRI Advocacy at the 53rd Session of the Commission on the Status of Women," at www.asiapacificforum.net/issues/womens-rights/downloads/commission-on-the-status-of-women-53rd-session/NHRI_Advocacy_53rd_Session_UNCSW.doc.

an institution is subjected to criticism from its own government and is threatened with abolition or weakening or a loss of independence.

In return, national human rights institutions can offer international mechanisms a credible, authoritative interlocutor that has detailed, direct knowledge of human rights situations on the ground. They can provide a bridge from the international level to the national level, taking the views, findings, and recommendations of international mechanisms to local actors and local people. They can be partners in country for mechanisms that have neither the resources nor the capacity to act locally.

National institutions are committed to extending their current engagement with the international system and expanding it to new international forums. They have successfully built on the practices of the former Commission on Human Rights to attain full participation rights in the new Human Rights Council. They have established a unique role in the Universal Periodic Review mechanism. For the first time they have been accorded explicit recognition in treaties under which they have special monitoring and preventive roles.[77] They are looking for much closer participation in and cooperation with treaty monitoring committees. They are working more and more with Special Procedures, especially in relation to country visits. They have established a presence in key meetings in New York for the first time and are seeking full participation in the Commission on the Status of Women.

The relationship between international mechanisms and national institutions can be one of mutual advantage. For that to be achieved, however, the engagement must be greater and more effective. It must overcome both the justifiable skepticism of national institutions about whether the international system has anything helpful to offer and the international system's distance from local and national levels, where national institutions do their work. The advantages that each can gain from the engagement will ensure that it continues to grow. Without doubt there will be more and better participation by national institutions in the international system, for the good of those who experience human rights violations.

---

[77] "The Convention on the Rights of Persons with Disabilities and the Optional Protocol to the Convention against Torture and other Cruel, Inhuman or Degrading Treatment or Punishment," UN doc. CAT/C/MNG/CO/1, January 20, 2011.

6

National Human Rights Institutions in Anglophone Africa

Legalism, Popular Agency, and the "Voices of Suffering"

Obiora Chinedu Okafor

6.1. INTRODUCTION

This chapter is grounded in a study of three of the national human rights institutions (NHRIs) that operate in "Anglophone Africa." In the main, it focuses on two objectives. The first goal is to understand the performance of the relevant NHRIs in terms of the extent of their legalism; facilitation of their own deployment and utilization by civil society agents; and attentiveness to the "voices of suffering" in whose interest they ought to function.[1] As explained in this chapter, these three factors together constitute a more holistic way of understanding NHRI effectiveness, beyond the usual "measures." The second main objective of the chapter is to probe for more general conceptual insights into the behavior, performance, and promise of these institutions and elaborate upon what these findings tell (or do not tell) us about NHRIs in Anglophone Africa.[2]

Methodologically, it is important to note that the particular Anglophone African NHRIs studied here are the Nigerian, South African, and Ugandan bodies. Each NHRI is chosen from one of the three geographical regions of the African continent

[1] I owe the term "voices of suffering" to Upendra Baxi's fecund imagination. See Upendra Baxi, "'Voices of Suffering' and the Future of Human Rights," *Transnational Law and Contemporary Problems* 8 (1998), 125.

[2] This whole exercise relies in part on my previous work. See Obiora Okafor and Shedrack Agbakwa, "On Legalism, Popular Agency and 'Voices of Suffering': The Nigerian National Human Rights Commission in Context," *Human Rights Quarterly* 24 (2002), 662. I have also benefited much from Linda Reif's earlier work in the area. See Linda Reif, "Building Democratic Institutions in Africa: Functions, Strengths and Weaknesses," *Harvard Human Rights Journal* 13 (2000), 1.

I should like to thank Opeoluwa Badaru and Vijayari Sripati, both doctoral candidates at Osgoode, and Sherifat Enikanolaiye, JD class of 2012, for their excellent research assistance. I am grateful to some officials of the National Human Rights Institutions of Nigeria, South Africa, and Uganda, and also to a number of NGO activists in those countries, for their help in accessing relevant information. This chapter is dedicated with very special gratitude to my wife, Atugonza, and our children, Ojiako and Mbabazi, for their extraordinary patience during its preparation.

where Anglophone countries exist – West Africa, Southern Africa, and East Africa (in that order). There are no North or Central African Anglophone countries. The temporal scope of the study is the decade between 1999 and 2009. The evidence on which the chapter is based was collected through a desk study, consisting of both a review of secondary sources and transcribed telephone interviews with NHRI officials and NGO activists in the relevant countries. The interviews focused on these actors because they are the best placed to comment on work of the NHRIs in their countries, and comparing the evidence supplied by one with the others ensured that a more accurate picture of the relevant NHRI's performance was obtained.[3] It is recognized, however, that there are limits to what a study of only three NHRIs can tell us about the thirteen or so NHRIs that exist in Anglophone Africa. Yet, as the three NHRIs studied here have been purposively selected from each of the three regions of Anglophone Africa, they suffice for the purposes of the current chapter.

The chapter also relies to some extent on the annual reports produced by the three NHRIs under study. Additionally and to a significant degree, it uses independent information, largely sourced from civil society groups (CSGs) and the media. This lessens the dangers of tendentiousness in the self-reported information contained in those NHRI documents. A skeptic may further ask whether these CSGs are themselves a reliable source of evidence about the relevant NHRIs, given that the CSG activists interviewed tended to report a degree of cooperation with the NHRIs under study. That would be a fair concern. However, as many of the interviewed activists offered significant criticisms of the relevant NHRIs, this concern is not really a serious one in this case.

This chapter has four main sections, the introduction included. In section II, I discuss the nature of the evaluation model that is applied throughout the chapter. Section III analyzes how each of the NHRIs under study has performed against each element of the evaluation model. The chapter concludes in section IV with a brief discussion of broader insights that can be derived from this analysis.

6.2. A MORE HOLISTIC EVALUATION MODEL

In combination with the UN Handbook and the UN Fact Sheet, the Paris Principles – the gold standard against which NHRIs tend to be assessed – constitute the dominant measure of NHRI value.[4] This is not wrong in and of itself. Indeed, many of its

---

[3] As was mandated by the ethics committee at the author's home university, the real names of the interviewees have been withheld. Instead, code names have been used to identify them.

[4] Centre for Human Rights, "National Human Rights Institutions: A Handbook on the Establishment and Strengthening of National Institutions for the Promotion and Protection of Human Rights," UN Training Series No. 4, U.N. Sales.E.95XIV.2; the "UN Fact Sheet on National Institutions for the Promotion and Protection of Human Rights, Fact Sheet No. 19"; and "The Paris Principles,"

elements are essential to the conception and establishment of ideal-type NHRIs and to their assessment.[5] However, as I have argued extensively elsewhere, the dominant NHRI evaluation model is so significantly limited and incomplete that it requires extension and enlargement so that the NHRIs that are animated by its vision might, in most contexts, have a higher transformative potential.[6] As I have also argued, a more holistic conception of NHRIs – one that (in addition to applying key elements of the dominant conception) eschews excessive legalism, accords much more priority to popular agency, and lays much greater emphasis on the nature of an NHRI's connection to the relevant society's most urgent "voices of suffering" – is a more well-rounded way of evaluating NHRIs.[7]

By "excessive legalism" I meant the erroneous notion that the more an NHRI approximates a court of law and the more effectively it exercises its court-like functions, the more effective or valuable it is as an institution. Here, too central and crucial a role is placed on the court-like features of NHRIs, and too marginal a role is assigned to the institution's other features.[8] By the phrase "according much more priority to popular agency" I contend that almost all of the focus in the relevant literature has been on assessing NHRIs according to what they can do *for* society, and too little space has traditionally been accorded to assessing what other agents are able to do *with* them (i.e., how they are able to utilize NHRI's as resources). Much more attention needs to be paid to this latter question.[9] And by emphasizing the depth of an NHRI's connection to the "voices of suffering," I mean assessing NHRIs on their performance in focusing on the human rights concerns of the most vulnerable people in the relevant societies.[10]

As important as other criteria for NHRI evaluation are, it is against these three (more holistic) measures that the NHRIs under study are evaluated in this chapter. The point of this approach is to assess how these NHRIs have fared against these particular criteria during the period under study, and thus to gain an alternative and more holistic insight into their effectiveness as human rights institutions.

U.N.G.A. Res. 48/134, December 20, 1993, Annex. Notice also that the Paris Principles have been supplemented and strengthened by the general comments that are produced by the International Coordinating Committee of National Human Rights Institutions. See sec. 3, art. 7, of the ICC Statute of Incorporation, adopted July 31, 2008, and as amended October 21, 2008, and March 24, 2009.

[5] Okafor and Agbakwa, "On Legalism, Popular Agency and 'Voices of Suffering'," 682–3. A recent study by the International Council on Human Rights Policy also arrived at the same conclusion. See R. Carver, *Assessing the Effectiveness of National Human Rights Institutions* (Versoix: ICHRP, 2005), pp. 7–9.

[6] Okafor, ibid., 682.

[7] Ibid.

[8] Ibid., 683.

[9] Ibid., 688–9.

[10] Ibid., 693–4.

6.3. APPLYING A MORE HOLISTIC MODEL: THE PERFORMANCE OF NHRIS IN ANGLOPHONE AFRICA

This part has four sections. In the first, the origins and background of each NHRI under study is briefly examined. The second deals with the question of the absence (or otherwise) of excessive legalism in the conceptual frameworks that guide the relevant NHRIs and in their actual work. In the third section, the extent to which the practice of each NHRI accords priority to popular agency is considered. The fourth section is devoted to an assessment of the extent to which each NHRI lays emphasis on the depth of its connection to the most urgent "voices of suffering" in the country in which it operates.

6.3.1. *Origins and Background*

A. The South African Human Rights Commission

The origins of the South African Human Rights Commission (SAHRC) and the impetus for its establishment can be traced to the end of the apartheid regime in South Africa and the strong desire of the new African National Congress (ANC) leadership to build institutions that would in the future help secure the human rights of its long-brutalized citizenry.[11] Originally authorized by South Africa's Interim Constitution, the SAHRC was first established in 1995 when the Human Rights Commission Act No. 54 of 1994 came into force.[12] It held its inaugural meeting in October of that same year.[13] Chapter Nine of the Final Constitution of 1997 confirmed its position as one of the bodies supporting constitutional democracy (the so-called Chapter 9 Institutions).[14] The SAHRC currently enjoys "Grade A" status at the International Coordinating Committee of National Institutions for the

---

[11] See John Kazoora, "The Human Rights We Fought for Still Elude Us," *Daily Monitor*, April 22, 2010, http://www.monitor.co.ug/OpEd/Commentary/-/689364/904170/-/view/printVersion/-/bpco29/-/index.html.

[12] Human Rights Watch (*hereafter* HRW), *Protectors or Pretenders? Government Human Rights Commissions in Africa* (New York: HRW, 2001).

[13] SAHRC, Annual Report 2000–2001, 1.

[14] Ibid. See also Kazoora, "The Human Rights We Fought for Still Elude Us"; James Matshekga, "Toothless Bulldogs? The Human Rights Commissions of Uganda and South Africa: A Comparative Study of their Independence," *African Human Rights Law Journal* 2 (2002), 68; C. E. Idike, "*Deflectionist Institutions or Beacons of Hope? A Study of National Human Rights Commissions in Anglophone Africa,*" unpublished Ph.D. dissertation, Osgoode Hall Law School (2006), 273–333; and P. E. Chabane, "*Enforcement Powers of National Human Rights Institutions: A Case Study of Ghana, South Africa and Uganda,*" unpublished LLM thesis, University of Pretoria (2007), 18–21.

Promotion and Protection of Human Rights (the ICC).[15] This is only one of the many possible measures of its international reputation, but a significant one nevertheless.

B. The Uganda Human Rights Commission

The origins of the Uganda Human Rights Commission (UHRC) are traceable to Uganda's long civil wars, near social and political chaos, and dismal human rights record in the decades before the 1986 forcible takeover of power in that country by President Yoweri Museveni's National Resistance Movement after the long "Bush War."[16] Museveni's government then embarked on a process of constitutional and sociopolitical reform that led to a new constitution.[17] Established and entrenched in Articles 51 to 59 of the constitution of Uganda of 1995, and later provided for in more detail by the Uganda Human Rights Commission Act No. 4 of 1997, the UHRC became functional in November 1996.[18] The UHRC's literature proclaims its compliance with the Paris Principles.[19] This self-assessment appears credible given the UHRC's grade "A" rating by the ICC.[20]As has already been argued, this is one significant measure of an NHRI's stature among its peers. As we shall see later in this chapter, the UHRC's high rating is also corroborated in part by the relatively strong reputation enjoyed by its immediate past chair and commissioners.

C. The Nigerian National Human Rights Commission

My earlier work on the Nigerian National Human Rights Commission (NNHC) dealt extensively and in depth with the Commission's origins, performance, and promise.[21] To avoid being repetitive, my treatment of the NNHC in this chapter will necessarily

---

[15] Annual Report of the United Nations High Commissioner for Human Rights and Reports of the Office of the High Commissioner and Secretary General, A/HRC/7/70, January 18, 2008, Annex I, 6 (*hereafter* OHCHR Report 2008).

[16] See Oliver Furley and James Katalikawe, "Constitutional Reform in Uganda: The New Approach," *African Affairs* 96 (1997), 9–11.

[17] Ibid., 37.

[18] Chabane, "Enforcement Powers of National Human Rights Institutions," 22; HRW, *Protectors or Pretenders?* 358; UHRC Annual Report, 2001–2002, 35; and "Interview with Alpha-UG" (Senior Official of the UHRC), July 16, 2009. For more on this body, see R. Murray, *The Role of National Human Rights Institutions at the International and Regional Levels* (Oxford: Hart, 2007); Matshekga, "Toothless Bulldogs?" Apollo Makubuya, "Breaking the Silence: A Review of the Maiden Report of the Uganda Human Rights Commission," *East African Journal of Peace and Human Rights* 5 (1999), 213; and John Hatchard, "A New Breed of Institution: The Development of Human Rights Commissions in Commonwealth Africa with Particular Reference to the Uganda Human Rights Commission," *Comparative and International Law Journal of South Africa* 32 (1999), 28.

[19] UHRC Annual Report, 2001–2002, 35.

[20] OHCHR Report 2008, 7.

[21] See Okafor and Agbakwa, "On Legalism, Popular Agency and 'Voices of Suffering.'"

draw on that study, reiterate its main findings where still valid, and build upon them. The NNHC was established in 1995 by the notorious Abacha-led military regime, became functional in 1996, and has operated under a civilian government since May 1999.[22] Although the Abacha regime established it under massive internal and external human rights pressure as a way to deflect some attention from the regime's poor human rights record, the Commission quickly emerged as an important ally of, and resource in the hands of, the local human rights community.[23] Previously ranked in the "A" category by the ICC, it now labors under a "B" rating.[24] This demotion resulted from the dismissal without due process of its then executive secretary Bukhari Bello; this dismissal was done under the NNHC's enabling law, which allows the president of Nigeria to dismiss any member of the NNHC, including the executive secretary, at his discretion if he or she deems such dismissal to be necessary in the national interest.[25] That offending legislation has recently been amended by the Nigerian National Assembly (Parliament) to guarantee, among other measures, the independence of the NNHC's governing boards and executive secretaries.[26]

6.3.2. *The Absence of Excessive Legalism*

The key question here is the extent to which an NHRI assigns too central a role to its "court-like" functions and features in its organizational framework, its sense of institutional self, and its practice. Clearly, the question here is one of relative, not absolute, weight. As suggested earlier, the problem with this form of excessive legalism is that it focuses too much attention on a role that is already performed by the courts and too little on the (non-court-like) roles that distinguish NHRIs and provide them a comparative advantage. The three NHRIs under study are assessed by the extent to which they are guilty or innocent of this error. While some consideration is also paid to the flip side of this question, namely, the issue of insufficient legalism, the dominant conception of NHRIs and their practice has historically tended to be excessively legalist in orientation. As such, much less attention is paid here to insufficient legalism, as it is not nearly as serious an issue in the case of Anglophone African NHRIs as excessive legalism.

---

[22] Ibid., 665, 699–701. See also Interview with ASA (Senior NNHC official), July 11, 2009.

[23] Ibid, 665–6.

[24] OHCHR Report 2008, 9.

[25] See International Coordinating Committee of National Institutions for the Promotion and Protection of Human Rights, "Report and Recommendations of the Sub-Committee on Accreditation," October 22–26, 2007, 10.

[26] See "NHRC Urges Jonathan to Sign Amended Rights Bill," *Guardian*, June 30, 2010; "Senate Passes Amendment to NHRC Act," *Punch*, February 11, 2010, http://www.punchng.com/Article2Print.aspx?th eartic=Art201002113542860; and "We've Removed Human Rights Commission from FG's Influence – Senate," *Tribune*, June 29, 2010, http://www.tribune.com.ng/index.php.news/7504.

A. The South African Human Rights Commission

One rough measure of an NHRI's adherence to excessive legalism is the domination in its ranks by persons with legal training. Unlike the equivalent Nigerian and Ugandan statutes, neither the South African constitution nor the relevant statute prescribes the nature of the professional training that members of the SAHRC must possess. In practice, however, at least three of the SAHRC's current five full-time members are lawyers or have legal training;[27] the Commission employs about thirty lawyers as part of its approximately 138 staff members (slightly over one-third of the staff)[28]; and its CEO is a lawyer.[29] Nevertheless, as suggested in part by these statistics, the Commission employs a significant number of non-lawyers.

Although certain court-like functions and powers are conferred upon the SAHRC by its enabling legislation, those instruments do not overemphasize these types of functions and powers over and above its educational, training, advocacy, research, monitoring, and other more non-judicial mandates. In practice, the Commission does not also overestimate the value of its court-like functions at the expense of the other equally important functions mentioned previously. As a senior SAHRC official has put it, the Commission's operational emphasis is

> more or less balanced, though if pushed personally, I may say the bulk of our work is on human rights awareness.... [T]he biggest department in the Commission is currently the Research Department.... The budget of the Research and Legal Departments are almost the same. The Education Program is also strong.[30]

This assessment is supported to varying degrees by independent sources and other evidence.[31] One key indicator is that the commission has expended a large amount of its resources on human rights education and other non-judicial functions.[32]

However, despite the SAHRC's significant accomplishments in these respects, some NGOs have complained that the Commission has not carried out enough

---

[27] Interview with Nze-SA (Senior SAHRC official), June 22, 2009.

[28] Ibid.

[29] See "New Human Rights CEO Named," *Pretoria News*, November 15, 2005. See also SAHRC, Annual Report (2005–2006), 2.

[30] Nze-SA (Senior SAHRC official), June 22, 2009.

[31] See Caroline Rees, "Overview of a Selection of Existing Accountability Mechanisms for Handling Complaints and Disputes," Harvard University, CSRI working paper publication, June 2007, 23; and David Horsten, "The Role Played by the South African Human Rights Commission's Economic and Social Rights Reports in Good Governance in South Africa," *Potchefstroom Electronic Law Journal* 12 (2006), 14. See also SAHRC, Annual Report (2001–2002), Appendix C, 2; SAHRC, Annual Report (2003–2004), 21–23, 36–37; SAHRC, Annual Report (2004–2005), 36; SAHRC, Annual Report (2006–2007), 23–25; and SAHRC, Annual Report (2007–2008), 29–31, 51, 61–62.

[32] See Horsten, "The Role Played by the SAHRC," 11–15. See also SAHRC, Annual Report (2005–2006), 42; SAHRC, Annual Report (2006–2007), 23–25; and SAHRC, Annual Report (2007–2008), 51.

human rights education, its main non-judicial function.[33] Indeed, an otherwise very supportive NGO activist has concluded that the SAHRC is preoccupied with its major court-like function – the treatment of complaints lodged before the Commission – and less occupied than it ought to be with its human rights awareness initiatives.[34] The truth, it seems, lies somewhere between this credible NGO perspective and the appreciable evidence of the Commission's attentiveness to its non-court-like functions.

Given this evidence, it would be unreasonable to conclude that the SAHRC has been insufficiently legalistic either in its self-conception or in the execution of its functions. For, as strong as its non-judicial efforts have been, it has also paid significant attention to handling and adjudicating complaints.

B. The Uganda Human Rights Commission

The UHRC is by law chaired by a person with legal training. In practice, although other members are not required to possess legal training, most of its commissioners have also been lawyers. More important, the Uganda Commission is perhaps the most court-like of the three NHRIs under study. It has in fact been much celebrated as such.[35] It is empowered as a tribunal to make legally binding decisions that can be enforced in the same way as judicial decisions.[36] In practice though, it appears that it has not overemphasized such powers to the significant detriment of its promotional and educational function.[37] For example, one NGO activist views the UHRC as mostly focused on its "preventive" work in trying to improve the conditions of prisons.[38] Another views it as "mainly" engaged in "promotional" work, and as placing "a lot of emphasis ... on human rights education and training of security officials who are prone to human rights violation."[39] The evidence suggests that in practice the UHRC is not excessively legalistic in its approach to its work.

Given that the UHRC is the most court-like of any of the NHRIs under study, the prominent role that the court-like "UHRC tribunal" plays in its work, its reasonably well-developed complaints process, the domination of the ranks of its board by lawyers, its dogged focus on awarding reparations and seeking governmental compliance with its decisions in that respect, it would seem quite unreasonable to accuse the UHRC of being insufficiently legalistic in the sense in which NHRI "legalism"

---

[33] For example, see Interview with BP (Senior Activist), July 6, 2009.
[34] Interview with NM (Senior Activist), July 9, 2009.
[35] Hatchard, "A New Breed of Institution," 31.
[36] Alpha-UG (Senior UHRC Official), July 16, 2009.
[37] Ibid.
[38] Interview with MF (Senior Activist), August 10, 2009.
[39] Interview with ECK (Senior Activist), October 20, 2009.

is used in this chapter. The UHRC is the most judicial of any of the NHRIs under study. The court-like "UHRC tribunal" functions prominently in the work of the Commission. It has a well-developed complaints process. Lawyers dominate the ranks of its board. And it has a dogged focus on awarding reparations and seeking governmental compliance with its decisions.

C. The Nigerian National Human Rights Commission

Both the statute under which the NNHC was established and its institutional self-conception and practice tend to avoid the pitfall of excessive legalism. The majority of the members of the NNHC, according to legislation, need not be lawyers (although about half of the members have been).[40] Moreover, although the NNHC does possess one or two court-like functions and has recently campaigned to be empowered to enforce its decisions,[41] top officials of the Commission have always recognized that its court-like powers should not be overemphasized at the expense of its educational and promotional functions.[42] Independent evidence confirms that this is so in practice.[43]

There is, however, a sense in which the NNHC can be said by some to have been insufficiently legalistic. The complaints assessment process is not as well developed as similar processes conducted by its South African and Ugandan counterparts. Furthermore, unlike the UHRC, it does not have a court-like "tribunal" that hears and determines complaints. However, in this author's view, because it does not have a tribunal and its complaints process is not as strong as it could be are not nearly as important as recognizing that there is significant room for improvement in the execution of its promotional and educational mandates. After all, while the regular courts can always perform a casework role, there is no existing institution that can replace the NNHC in the performance of at least one of its non-court-like roles: providing official cover and legitimacy to the agents of civil society groups in their attempts to conduct effective human rights education for law enforcement and

---

[40] National Human Rights Act, 1995, sec. 2 and sec. 7.

[41] See Kehinide F. Ajoni, "My Experience in Driving the Mandate of the National Human Rights Commission of Nigeria and the Challenges of NHRIs in the African Sub Region," paper presented at the Conference of Commonwealth National Human Rights Institutions, Marlborough House, London, February 26–28, 2007, 7. See also ASA (Senior NNHC official), July 11, 2009. The recent amendments to the NNHC Act do empower the NNHC in this way. See *Punch*, February 11, 2010.

[42] Okafor and Agbakwa, "On Legalism, Popular Agency and 'Voices of Suffering'"; and NNHC Public Service Announcement, March 10, 2010, http://www.alliancesforafrica.org/content_files/files/NHRC_HIV_Law.pdf.

[43] See Eze Anaba, "Law & Human Rights – Seminar Report – No Culture or Religion Supports Maltreatment of Children," *Africa News Service*, July 30, 2004; and Agha Ibiam, "Human Rights Our Common Heritage," *Africa News Service*, December 22, 2004.

other key government officials. As is shown in this chapter, without the NNHC, CSGs would have been far less successful at this task within the Nigerian context.

D. Assessment

Commendably, all three NHRIs under study have, on the whole, tended to eschew excessive legalism in their practice. Although all of these bodies appear to be led, and even dominated, by lawyers or persons with legal training, they have tended to emphasize their educational and promotional functions to the same, or even greater, degree as their court-like functions. In all three cases, a review of the evidence reveals that the relevant NHRI commissioners have tended to show a keen awareness of the necessity to emphasize these functions at least as much as the judicial ones. They have also, in practice, committed to this approach. In their practice and statements, the members and officials of all three NHRIs tend to recognize that duplicating the functions of the regular courts is outside their mandate and would, in any case, not emphasize key areas of comparative advantage over the courts. But, as set forth in the previous discussion, the UHRC is the most court-like of these generally non-judicial commissions. To its credit, the NNHC – which, on most measures, tends to compare unfavorably to the other two bodies – is the least guilty of the charge of excessive legalism. The SAHRC is placed a close second in this respect.

6.3.3. *The Adequacy of an NHRI's Attention to Popular Agency*

The main question here is the extent to which an NHRI shows its understanding that its value should not be limited to what it can do *for* civil society, but includes to a significant extent what these other agents are (with the NHRI's help) able to do *with* it.[44]

A. The South African Human Rights Commission

An important determinant of the adequacy of an NHRI's attentiveness to popular agency is the extent of its cooperation with the CSGs that operate in its country. For its part, the SAHRC has cooperated extensively with local NGOs, community-based organizations (CBOs), traditional leaders, and other groups that constitute civil society in South Africa, and the SAHRC tends to enjoy a cordial relationship with a very large number of them.[45] This much is acknowledged by the Commission and

---

44 See Okafor and Agbakwa, "On Legalism, Popular Agency and 'Voices of Suffering,'" 688–93.

45 Idike, *Deflectionist Institutions or Beacons of Hope?* 294–6. See also SAHRC, Annual Report (2000–2001), 44, 54; SAHRC, Annual Report (2001–2002), 12; and Linda Ochiel, "Communicating Human Rights: A Case Study of the South African Human Rights Commission and the Kenya National

many civil society actors.[46] For their own part, NGOs such as Black Sash (a respected socioeconomic rights group) tend to report generally warm and beneficial relationships with the Commission.[47] There does, however, seem to remain a noticeable gap in the web of relationships that the SAHRC has been creating over the years in an attempt to link up more densely and symbiotically with these civil society actors. For example, one prominent NGO, the Youth Empowerment Network (YEN), did not report any significant direct collaboration with the Commission.[48]

The SAHRC considers an imperative its deployment by civil society actors – so that these agents carry out initiatives with it – rather than waiting for the Commission to initiate the actions. As the Commission itself has noted, it "endeavors to be a resource for human rights practitioners and institutions internationally [and of course locally]."[49] Select examples will serve to illustrate this point. Although much of the SAHRC's work on the issue of poverty was undertaken outside the period under study, it is noteworthy that the South African National NGO Coalition (SANGOCO) deployed the SAHRC as a key resource to conduct hearings on poverty, which led to a landmark report on poverty and human rights in South Africa.[50] These hearings were held at the initiative of SANGOCO.[51] Also, both the mental disability community and the SAHRC mutually utilized each other's comparative resource advantages to develop and push submissions that the Commission sent to Parliament on the Criminal Law (Sexual Offences) and Related Matters Amendment Bill.[52] Here, the SAHRC facilitated the flow of CSG concerns into the parliamentary debate and, in fact, into the bill, providing a special value to the latter's campaign.[53] Furthermore, the Youth Empowerment Network has attempted to deploy the SAHRC's complaints mechanism as a resource in the execution of its advocacy work.[54] Although it reports some dissatisfaction with the delay in resolving such complaints,[55] the key point is that in exercise of its agency it was able to utilize the Commission. Not every such deployment of the SAHRC has to be successful for it to count. The fact that the Commission is aware of the role it plays as a civil society

---

Commission on Human Rights Communication Programmes," unpublished report, 25, www.britishcouncil.org/sep_linda_kenya.doc.

[46] Nze-SA (Senior SAHRC official), June 22, 2009.
[47] Interview with NM (Senior Activist), July 9, 2009.
[48] Interview with BP (Senior Activist), July 6, 2009.
[49] SAHRC, Annual Report (2004–2005), 5. See also Charlotte McClain-Nhlapo et al., "Disability and Human Rights: The South African Human Rights Commission," in B. Watermayer et al. (eds.), *Disability and Social Change: A South African Agenda* (Cape Town: HSRC Press, 2006), 100.
[50] Idike, *Deflectionist Institutions or Beacons of Hope?* p. 296.
[51] Human Rights Watch, supra note 11.
[52] SAHRC, Annual Report (April 2006–March 2007), 10.
[53] Ibid.
[54] Interview with BP (Senior Activist), supra note 33.
[55] Ibid.

resource is illustrated by a rather telling comment by one of its high officials, that "NGOs use the Commission more for their benefit" than anything else – meaning that the SAHRC realizes that these CSGs consider the Commission a resource to be utilized, to the extent possible, as these CSGs see fit.[56]

Although the SAHRC should be commended for its self-conscious adherence to this "best practice" of facilitating its deployment by civil society actors, there are indications of a continuing need for the Commission to enhance its attentiveness to this imperative. Consider that even a senior activist who recounted many ways in which the SAHRC had been useful to her organization still said, "it is not that clear to our organization the various ways we can use them as a resource, but they are very welcoming on an individual basis. Perhaps they need to do some clear communication on how they could be used in this way."[57]

B. The Uganda Human Rights Commission

Cooperation with civil society groups tends to enhance the creative deployment of NHRIs by these groups. The UHRC is well known for its cooperation with CSGs in Uganda. As one of its former senior officials noted:

> We don't have a specific legal provision requiring us to cooperate with civil society groups but we do it as a matter of practice. We work with civil society organizations.... We form coalitions with civil society, e.g. [the] Coalition against Torture. We do campaigns together. We have a very good working relationship with civil society.[58]

Additional evidence supports this conclusion. For example, the Foundation for Human Rights Initiative has worked closely with the UHRC.[59] Other NGOs have reported a meaningful level of cooperation with the Commission.[60] Equally important, the UHRC does not cooperate only with human rights NGOs. For example, it has established some (limited) links with village and clan leaders.[61]

As reported by both the UHRC and the NGOs, the UHRC is very attentive to its availability as a resource to civil society actors. NGOs have tended to deploy the UHRC to facilitate their own work. As one activist put it, "in instances where we have needed to deal with certain particularly difficult agencies of government it

---

[56] Nze-SA (Senior SAHRC official), June 22, 2009.
[57] Ibid.
[58] Alpha-UG (Senior Official of the UHRC), July 16, 2009.
[59] See Global Forum on MSM and HIV, "A Narrative Report on OHCHR Workshop on Strategies for Human Rights Protection and Promotion in Uganda," October 22, 2008 (on file with the author). See also UHRC, Annual Report 2003, 81–82.
[60] MF (Senior Activist), August 10, 2009; also ECK (Senior Activist), October 20, 2009.
[61] See Global Forum on MSM and HIV, "A Narrative Report." See also UHRC, Annual Report (2001–2002), 43.

has proved fruitful to elicit the assistance of the Commission."[62] Just as important, use of the Commission has been fruitful to the institutional practices of both sides, resulting, for instance, in the joint UHRC/NGO drafting of the "Prohibition and Prevention of Torture Bill."[63]

C. The Nigerian National Human Rights Commission

The NNHC is virtually beyond reproach in the area of cooperation with NGOs. Indeed, this is one of its strengths.[64] As a senior official of the NNHC has put it:

> Because some of these local NGOs have been in existence before the Commission (e.g. CLO, CRP), we use them particularly when it relates to their expert areas. We use them to build capacity. In fact, there is no activity of the Commission without NGO involvement.[65]

NGOs tend to strongly agree with the Commission's perspective. For example, one activist has reported that "[we have] done some work with the Commission.... [M]y organization and the Commission have worked together on meetings, capacity building, women's rights and participation in governance."[66] Other groups have reported a similar experience.[67] The close professional relationship that tends to exist between NGOs and the NNHC was well portrayed by one activist who noted that "the commission is like an umbrella body for civil society organizations and works closely with NGOs."[68]

Additionally, the NNHC has, without doubt, paid adequate attention to popular agency, especially to the extent that this commitment is reflected in the participation of NGOs and other civil society groups.[69] These groups have tended to deploy the NNHC successfully to achieve some of their own human rights goals, such as securing access to government data and obtaining the cooperation of government and law enforcement officials.[70] The vast majority of NGO activists will agree

---

[62] ECK (Senior Activist), October 20, 2009; MF (Senior Activist), August 10, 2009.

[63] Ibid.

[64] Okafor and Agbakwa, "On Legalism, Popular Agency and 'Voices of Suffering,'" 708; and NNHC, "Activities of the Commission," http://www.nigeriarights.gov.ng/index.php?option=com_content&view=article&id=37&It; NNHC, *State of Human Rights in Nigeria 2005–2006* (Abuja: NNHC, 2006), iv–vi; Kehinide F. Ajoni, "Statutory Report 2007" (on file with the author), 6; and HRW, *Protectors or Pretenders?* 363.

[65] Interview with ASA (Senior NNHC Official), July 11, 2009.

[66] Interview with OO (Senior Activist), July 20, 2009.

[67] Interview with LM (Senior Activist), July 8, 2009; and interview with OV (Senior Activist), July 6, 2009.

[68] OV (Senior Activist), July 6, 2009.

[69] Okafor and Agbakwa, "On Legalism, Popular Agency and 'Voices of Suffering,'" 713–14.

[70] OO (Senior Activist), July 20, 2009.

that the Commission has "facilitated a lot of [NGO] programs."[71] Also, in many such instances, it was the NNHC that approached the relevant group and established a channel through which that group was able to utilize the Commission as a resource.[72] This openness to being deployed as a resource by civil society groups has, in this author's view, been the NNHC's greatest strength.

D. Assessment

Several insights can be drawn from this analysis. First, the success enjoyed by a given NHRI in cooperating with CSGs and the level of the institution's attentiveness to popular agency depends in part on the reputation of its leadership among the relevant segments of civil society. And the reputation of an NHRI's leaders partly depends on their personal character and credibility. In those respects, the question of their professional background is not as relevant as one might suppose. What is more important is their reputation. Analysis of the relevant literature on the leadership of the SAHRC (especially NGO commentaries) indicates that these leaders are much more commended than criticized, and are now generally viewed as dedicated, visible, and outspoken. For example, one senior NGO activist was of the view that "the current head of the [South African] Commission is developing visibility and is asked to comment and speak out on important issues in the media."[73] But acknowledging the gap that remains to be filled in this connection, another activist stated that "my personal opinion is that they [the SAHRC's leadership] need to become more media savvy in creating spaces to put out their positions and actions."[74] The following view epitomizes the generally positive but cautious and nuanced overall assessment of the UHRC by Ugandan NGOs:

> Considering the vibrancy of the last set of [UHRC] commissioners and the perception that they came out very strong against the government, it was assumed that the new set of commissioners may be government stooges. It is still too early to state one way or the other but it would appear that the new commissioners aware of the criticisms against them are trying to be seen as effective.[75]

Regarding the NNHC, NGO activists tend to single out Bukhari Bello's tenure as executive secretary as a period during which the NNHC "did a lot" for human rights in Nigeria.[76] As courageous and competent as she eventually turned out to

---

[71] LM (Senior Activist), July 8, 2009.
[72] OV (Senior Activist), July 6, 2009.
[73] NM (Senior Activist), July 9, 2009.
[74] Ibid.
[75] Interview with ECK (Senior Activist), October 20, 2009.
[76] LM (Senior Activist), July 8, 2009.

be, Bello's successor – Kehinde Ajoni – assumed office under the cloud of strong suspicion and disappointment that ensued following Bello's summary dismissal from office without due cause by the country's president well before the expiration of his contract.[77] Thus, although Ajoni quite deservedly came to be seen as personally credible by many, she never came to enjoy the same level of credibility as Bello.[78] The NNHC has still not recovered fully from the damage done to its credibility by the sacking of Bello.[79]

Additionally, it is somewhat intriguing that the NNHC, which tends to compare unfavorably to the other NHRIs under study, significantly outperforms these other commissions in the extent to which it has been utilized as a key resource by local civil society groups. One might have ordinarily expected the more resourced SAHRC, which has operated in a much more democratic context, to have done better in this regard than a less resourced NNHC that has had to function for all of its institutional life under military and semi-democratic regimes. This is not to suggest, of course, that the SAHRC and the UHRC have not performed credibly in this area, but to offer a comparative evaluation and calibration of their respective strengths in that regard.

However, one potential tension may arise from the density of the engagement of these NHRIs with CSGs, and the large measure of attentiveness of the NHRIs to popular agency. The insertion of an NHRI into a preexisting human rights CSG network (e.g., when the NHRI is deployed by an NGO as a resource) may have the unintended effect of displacing some of the independent capacity of these CSGs to affect the conduct of state and society, thus negatively impacting their maturation into more effective actors. Another potential displacement effect is that the relevant NHRI may consume a significant amount of limited donor funding that is available in some countries for human rights work. That said, given the added value that these commissions have provided to the CSGs, shortfalls in donor support to the latter are likely to be canceled out by positive institutional support from the Commission.

6.3.4. *The Level of an NHRI's Connection to the "Voices of Suffering"*

A fundamental issue is the extent to which the legal framework and operations of the NHRIs under study reflect a connection to the "voices of suffering," who depend on the institution the most. The concept of "voices of suffering" is concerned with those whose need for protection is greatest, who are society's most vulnerable elements,

---

[77]   OO (Senior Activist), July 20, 2009.
[78]   See Josephine Lohor, "Global Human Rights Bodies Move against Nigeria," *Pambazuka News*, 261, June 29, 2009, http://pambazuka.org/en/category/comment/35491. See also NNHC, Annual Report 2007, 32.
[79]   OO (Senior Activist), July 20, 2009.

and who survive at the bottom end of the scale of human freedom from want and deprivation.[80] Specific sub-issues that are dealt with under this heading concern the extent to which the relevant NHRI has promoted and protected gender equality; ensured or enjoyed a measure of social plurality in the composition of its board or governing body; established and deepened connections with the more marginalized groups in its country (such as ethnic minorities, indigenous peoples, migrants, the disabled, and HIV/AIDS sufferers); adopted an ethnographic (i.e., fieldwork-based) approach to its work; striven to physically locate itself at the grassroots level; and tackled poverty and the denial of economic, social, and cultural rights (ESCR) as a key goal. Greater (but not exclusive) attention is paid to ESCR rights here, not because ESC rights are viewed as superior to civil and political rights, but simply as a result of the salience of material poverty in the relevant countries and the historic neglect of ESCR in human rights praxis. In any case, the issues of gender equality, disability rights, and non-discrimination raised above, and discussed in this section of the chapter, are in many respects connected to the protection of civil and political rights.

A. The South African Human Rights Commission

The constitutional provision for a Commission on Gender Equality in South Africa has meant that the SAHRC has not been the only (or even principal) institution charged with the promotion and protection of gender equality in South Africa.[81] This fact may have contributed, somewhat paradoxically, to the very low rates at which gender complaints have been treated by the Commission. For example, in 2007–08, only 2 percent of all of the equality complaints dealt with by the SAHRC raised issues of gender equality.[82] By contrast, a full 82 percent of equality rights complaints concerned racial discrimination, while another 4 percent were grounded in disability rights.[83]

Unlike its Nigerian counterpart, there are no reserved positions on the SAHRC for the representatives of civil society (such as NGOs and the privately owned media). However, civil society is involved – although somewhat peripherally – in the process of appointing SAHRC commissioners, and civil society representatives also work closely with the commissioners and are included on an advisory basis in the SAHRC's committees.[84] Nevertheless, the systematic and fuller representation of civil society on the Commission would help to deepen its connection with the

---

[80] See Okafor and Agbakwa, "On Legalism, Popular Agency and 'Voices of Suffering,'" 694. See also Baxi, "Voices of Suffering," 125.

[81] Constitution of the Republic of South Africa, sec. 187.

[82] SAHRC, Annual Report (2007–2008), 135.

[83] Ibid.

[84] Nze-SA (Senior SAHRC Official), June 22, 2009.

voices of suffering who regularly approach and are more frequently served at the grassroots level by many of these CSGs.

To its credit, the SAHRC has laid great emphasis on deepening its connections with the more marginalized communities in South Africa, such as the all-too-often neglected majority rural dwellers; the poor; immigrants (especially detained or impoverished ones); the largely marginalized Khomani-San ethnic minority; the disabled; and HIV/AIDS sufferers.[85] The Commission also works in the most remote regions of South Africa.[86] All of the SAHRC's nine provincial offices are equipped with four-wheel-drive vehicles so its staff can get to remote rural areas.[87] One of its officials noted:

> The focus of the Commission in the last three years … [has been] poverty and equality and this is mostly addressed at the rural level. Hearings are held and interpretation is provided. Even the *Mail & Guardian* which criticizes the Commission acknowledges its work in the rural areas. Three years ago, the Commission decided it would devote 60 percent of its budget on the rural areas, though this may not be totally the case in practice but there is a will to improve its work there. Recently, the Commission investigated the granting of mining licenses in the Eastern Cape, which is a very remote area.[88]

The "ethnographic" approach that the Commission has tended to take has served it well as it has strived to deepen and intensify its connections to the grass roots. For example, as one of its annual reports correctly suggests,

> The Commission's capacity to reach rural and marginalised communities across the country has increased, with the consolidation of the Omnibus Training approach, whereby the Commission conducts several week-long visits in an area. There were an average of 8 interventions per month in rural areas.[89]

The training manual on the rights of farmworkers is another example of the efforts it has made to deal with human rights issues that touch more directly on the lives of the majority rural population.[90] The rights of immigrants in South Africa, especially

---

[85] See "South Africa Rights Body to Probe Police over Shooting," *Panafrican News Agency*, August 25, 2005, http://www.accessmylibrary.com/coms2/summary_0286–13140645_ITM; SAHRC, Annual Report (2000–2001), 2–3, 11; and SAHRC, Annual Report (2004–2005), 5.

[86] Nze-SA (Senior SAHRC Official), June 22, 2009.

[87] Ibid.

[88] Ibid.

[89] See SAHRC, Annual Report (2003–2004), 6. See also South African Parliament, "Constitutional Literacy Campaign, Appendix 4, Annexure B," Minutes of Meeting recorded by the Parliamentary Monitoring Organization on June 9, 2003, http://www.pmg.org.za/minutes/20030608-public-submissions-report-annual-report-2002-committee-programme-considerations.

[90] SAHRC, Annual Report (2000–2001), 30. See also "Report Reveals Dire Conditions Facing Farm Workers," October 2, 2003, http://www.wsws.org/articles/2003/oct2003/farm-002.shtml.

of those who have been detained in the notorious Lindela facility[91] and those who live in the poorer neighborhoods in the country, have also occupied a significant amount of the SAHRC's time.[92] As part of its work in this area, the Commission has focused on preventing and redressing attacks on migrants and violations of their human rights in general.[93] The SAHRC conducted work during the period under study on the status of the largely marginalized Khomani-San ethnic minority. The Commission held hearings and prepared a major report on the human rights situation of this group, which was submitted to the government.[94] However, in 2004, a separate SAHRC-like body was established to take care of this issue.[95] The promotion and protection of the rights of the disabled is another way through which the SAHRC has enhanced its capacity to more systematically connect to the voices of suffering within South Africa. It has long produced its human rights material in Braille, making information accessible to the visually impaired.[96] And 4 percent of the equality rights complaints lodged with the Commission in 2007–08 raised disability rights issues. For years the Commission has appointed one of its staff as a focal point for the human rights issues that tend to concern disabled persons the most.[97] As important, the SAHRC has also continued to work very hard to address the human rights needs of older persons and HIV/AIDS sufferers.[98]

As the Commission has strived over the years to attain its stated goal of taking its work closer to those communities most in need of its services and good offices, it has of course had to work increasingly at the grass roots (and not just in the rural areas) including – as we have seen – through the decentralization of many of its

---

[91] The Lindela facility is one of the main detention centers where undocumented or offending migrants in South Africa are held prior to deportation from that country. According to one report, with a maximum capacity of 6,000, it has over the years been home to hundreds of thousands of detainees. According to the same report, the SAHRC has lodged many complaints about this center. See Michael Appel, "MPs Assess Conditions at Lindela Centre," *BuaNews*, August 1, 2007.

[92] SAHRC, Annual Report (April 2004–2005), 26; SAHRC, Annual Report (2005–2006), 35; and SAHRC, Annual Report (2006–2007), 19; "Migrants Badly Treated Says Human Rights Body," *IRIN News*, December 12, 2000, http://www.irinnews.org/Report.aspx?ReportId=889.

[93] SAHRC, Annual Report (2000–2001), 2–3.

[94] Nze-SA (Senior SAHRC Official), June 22, 2009; SAHRC, Annual Report (2003–2004), 4; SAHRC, Annual Report (2004–2005), 5; and SAHRC, Annual Report (2004–2005), 26. See also *Panafrican News Agency*, August 25, 2005.

[95] See *Panafrican News Agency*, August 25, 2005; SAHRC, Annual Report (2000–2001), 2–3, 11; and Nze-SA (Senior SAHRC Official), June 22, 2009.

[96] See *BUA News*, "SA Banks Urged to Consider Disabled People," March 17, 2008, http://www.hellonam.com/human-rights/8104-south-africa-sa-banks-urged-consider-disabled-people.html. See also SAHRC, Annual Report (2000–2001), 11

[97] See Nhlapo et al., "Disability and Human Rights," 100. See also SAHRC, Annual Report (2000–2001), 33.

[98] See "Migrants Badly Treated Says Human Rights Body," *IRIN News*, December 12, 2000, http://www.irinnews.org/Report.aspx?ReportId=889; and "Govt. Defends Development Record," *IRIN News*, http://www.irinnews.org/Report.aspx?ReportId=43233; SAHRC, Annual Report (2004–2005), 20.

operations.[99] Equally important, as part of this grassroots work, the SAHRC has continuously worked hard to create and maintain linkages with South Africa's traditional leaders, who tend to operate and wield considerable influence at the grassroots level.[100] The Commission also publishes many of its booklets, pamphlets, and posters in all of the eleven official languages of South Africa, most of which are local languages which are more accessible to those at the grass roots.[101] For many years now, the Commission has also placed an emphasis on utilizing community radio stations to reach the grass roots more deeply.[102]

However, as commendable as the work of the Commission has been in this area, some in the local NGO community feel that the reach of its grassroots efforts could be significantly enhanced. As one activist has put it:

> I know the Commission sometimes distributes booklets on rights but the truth is people still read these booklets and not understand what is there. It is not enough to cite laws and clauses. These laws have to be broken down and explained to the public before they can understand it. A lay person cannot just understand clauses or sections of laws listed in the booklets. Young people should be taught what the specific law is and not only told where to find the law.... [T]he Commission needs to really educate the public.[103]

In a society in which poverty is as prevalent as in South Africa, the protection and promotion of ESCR is a key way of connecting to the needs – and therefore the minds – of most ordinary people. It is commendable, therefore, that section 184 of the Constitution charges the SAHRC with monitoring the steps that the various organs of the South African state have taken toward the progressive realization of ESCR.[104] The SAHRC is thus obliged to – and does – undertake ESCR work.[105] It has continually made great effort to discharge this mandate effectively. To this end, it prepares and disseminates reports on the status of ESCR in South Africa and on the measures taken or not taken by the government to realize such

---

[99] On its own stated commitment to reach the marginalized, see SAHRC, Annual Report (2003–2004), 4; SAHRC, Annual Report (2004–2005), 5, 9.

[100] See "Anglo Standoff Resolved," *Sunday Times*, September 1, 2009; see also SAHRC, Annual Report (2000–2001), 44, 54.

[101] For the official languages of South Africa, see sec. 6 of the Constitution. See also SAHRC, Annual Report (2000–2001), Appendix C, 2; and SAHRC, Annual Report (2004–2005), 9. See also Jennifer Parsley, "We Are Not Treated Like People: The Roll Back Xenophobia Campaign in South Africa," *Humanitarian Exchange Magazine* 17 (2002), http://www.odihpn.org/report.asp?id=2208.

[102] See Parsley, ibid. See also SAHRC, Annual Report (2004–2005), 22.

[103] Interview with BP (Senior Activist), July 6, 2009.

[104] See Chabane, "*Enforcement Powers of National Human Rights Institutions*," 19.

[105] See Kader Asmal, "Report of the Ad Hoc Committee on the Review of Chapter 9 and Associated Institutions," Report to the National Assembly, 167 (*hereafter* Kader Asmal Report); Horsten "The Role Played by the South African Human Rights Commission's Economic and Social Rights Reports," 3. See also SAHRC, Annual Report (2000–2001), 26.

rights.[106] These reports now appear on a three-yearly rather than annual cycle.[107] Much of the data on which these reports are based are gathered through fieldwork.[108] The SAHRC also holds conferences, workshops, and seminars on ESCR and handles sizable numbers of ESCR-grounded complaints.[109] For example, in 2000–01, although equality and other civil and political rights complaints formed the majority of claims processed, 31 percent of such complaints were ESCR-based (and were founded in particular on health, labor, and education rights violations).[110] Similar trends were recorded in 2001–02, 2004–05, 2006–07, and 2007–08.[111] As should be clear, the focus of the SAHRC for a few years now has been on poverty and equality, requiring an intensification of its preexisting treatment of the promotion and protection of ESCR as one of its tasks.[112] This focus does not seem to have abated.[113] For example its 2006–07 annual report records innovative poverty-alleviation activities such as the "school fees dialogue" which the Commission organized.[114] To be clear, it is worth re-emphasizing that the predominant focus on ESCR work – as a key measure of the SAHRC's attentiveness to the voices of suffering – is necessitated by contextual factors involving the salience of material poverty in that country. It is of course recognized that civil and political rights and ESCR are interdependent and ultimately indivisible from one another.

Although the SAHRC received only about 6,000 complaints between 2000 and 2001,[115] by 2008 the annual number of complaints had grown to over 11,000 complaints.[116] Moreover, its complaints "docket" has averaged about 10,000 per annum for the last few years.[117] This is indicative of the growing tendency among

---

[106] See Kader Asmal Report, 167; SAHRC, Annual Report (2000–2001), 26; and SAHRC, Annual Report (2003–2004), 31.

[107] SAHRC, Annual Report (2006–2007), 47.

[108] See Horsten, "The Role Played by the South African Human Rights Commission's Economic and Social Rights Reports"; "SAHRC to Focus on Eastern Cape for Human Rights Week," *Asia Africa Intelligence Wire* (2003), http://www.accessmylibrary.com/coms2/summary_0286–22699894_ITM. See also SAHRC, Annual Report (2004–2005), 31; and SAHRC, Annual Report (2005–2006), 32–38.

[109] See *Mail and Guardian*, "Partners for Change," April 9, 2008. See also SAHRC, Annual Report (2000–2001), 28; and SAHRC, Annual Report (2003–2004), 31.

[110] See SAHRC, Annual Report (2000–2001), 14.

[111] See SAHRC, Annual Report, (2001–2002), 24; SAHRC, Annual Report (2004–2005), 28; SAHRC, Annual Report, (2006–2007), 45; and SAHRC, Annual Report (2007–2008), 35.

[112] See "HRC Shifts Focus under New Leadership," *Mail and Guardian*. October 10, 2002; see also Nze-SA, June 22, 2009; SAHRC, Annual Report (2003–2004), 4, 6; and SAHRC, Annual Report (2005–2006), 39.

[113] See *Mail and Guardian*, "What It Means for Business," April 9, 2008; and *Mail and Guardian*, "Making Markets Work for the Poor," April 10, 2008. See also SAHRC, Annual Report 2006–2007, iv, 7; and SAHRC, Annual Report 2007–2008, 15.

[114] SAHRC, Annual Report 2006–2007, 8.

[115] SAHRC, Annual Report, 2000–2001, 14.

[116] SAHRC, Annual Report 2007–2008, 134.

[117] Nze-SA (Senior SAHRC Official), June 22, 2009; and SAHRC, Annual Report (2006–2007), 43–44.

the victimized (usually constituted by the more vulnerable members of society) to approach the Commission for succor. And it is an impressive figure when compared to the far fewer petitions received by the Nigerian NHRI from a population that is more than three times the size of South Africa's.[118]

Despite the SAHRC's strenuous and highly commendable efforts to vastly decrease the distance between it and ordinary South Africans, it appears that an appreciable gap remains. Since its resources are invariably limited, there may always be some gap between the SAHRC and the South African grass roots. If the SAHRC is to optimize its contribution to the fundamental transformation of the human rights situation in South Africa, the task that confronts it is to continuously narrow that gap. The Commission appears to be strongly committed to pursuing that goal.

B. The Uganda Human Rights Commission

Although men have tended to submit a significant majority of the complaints received by the UHRC in any one year, the Commission has done a fair amount of work on women's human rights, especially in the area of domestic relations.[119] For example, its work on the right of women to receive child support from the fathers of their children has been a consistently prominent feature of its promotional and protective activities.[120] As important is the fact that three of the seven commissioners in the immediate past group of members of the UHRC (whose tenure expired in 2008) were female.[121] The chair of the UHRC during that era was also female.[122] These facts indicate, to some extent, that gender perspectives were not absent at the top echelons of the UHRC.

However, there are no formally reserved spots for women on the UHRC – although the constitution does encourage gender equity in all institutions of governance.[123] In this sense, the UHRC is no different from its South African and Nigerian counterparts. But unlike the Nigerian body, there are no reserved positions on the

---

[118] See Okafor and Agbakwa, "On Legalism, Popular Agency and 'Voices of Suffering,'" 716.

[119] Sarah Forti, "Challenges in the Implementation of Women's Human Rights: Field Perspectives," conference paper: "The Winners and Losers from Rights Based Approaches to Development," February 2005, 21; "Forced Circumcision Illegal, Says Social Affairs Minister," *Africa News Service*, June 27, 2008; "Culture-Uganda: Muslims Demand Changes in Bill on Women's Rights," *Africa News Service*, April 7, 2005; and "Women Decry Dowry," *Asia Africa Intelligence Wire*, February 21, 2004. Also UHRC, Annual Report (2003), 3; and UHRC, Annual Report (2007), 17.

[120] UHRC, Annual Report (2001–2002), 3; and UHRC, Annual Report (2007), 13–29, 71.

[121] See Francis Kagolo, "UHRC Term Expires," *New Vision* [Uganda], November 23, 2008; also UHRC, Annual Report (2007), v.

[122] See Kagolo, ibid.

[123] Constitution of Uganda, sec. 3(VI); Alpha-UG, July 16, 2009.

Commission for representatives of human rights NGOs and the private media.[124] The law is basically silent on who may be appointed to the UHRC.[125]

The UHRC has conducted a fairly significant amount of work in favor of those Ugandans who are among the most vulnerable and/or marginalized – especially rural dwellers, ethnic minorities, the poor, children (including orphans), the disabled, internally displaced persons, and HIV/AIDS sufferers.[126] For example, the Commission has persuaded a growing number of district authorities to set up district human rights committees to help reach the majority rural population more easily;[127] consistently attempted to reach ordinary Ugandans in their own local languages[128]; and doggedly fought for the enactment of a law establishing a living minimum wage in Uganda to avoid the exploitation of vulnerable groups.[129]

Aligning with the UHRC's concern for poverty alleviation, the Commission has undertaken a significant amount of work on the implementation of economic ESCR.[130] Examples of its work are the concerted, multifaceted campaign to expand social security to needy orphans; provide government aid to persons with disabilities; institute a health insurance system; and provide public care for the aged.[131] The Commission has also promoted the rights of pensioners as an ESCR.[132] Yet, it is civil and political rights (and not ESCR) complaints that have tended to dominate the Commission's complaint docket.[133] It appears that this situation has begun to change, as in 2007, civil and political rights and ESCR complaints each amounted to about 50 percent of the UHRC's caseload.[134] As important, the

---

[124] Ibid. at sec. 51(4); and Uganda Human Rights Commission Act, sec. 2.

[125] Alpha-UG (Senior UHRC Official), July 16, 2009.

[126] See "Rights Body Starts Project for Ex-IDPs," *Africa News Service*, April 5, 2010; see also UHRC, Annual Report (2005), 86–111.

[127] See Robert LeBlanc et al., *Country Level Evaluation: Uganda*, European Commission, November 2009; and UHRC, Annual Report 2006, 134.

[128] UHRC, Annual Report 2005, 30–31.

[129] See Moses Mulondo, "DP Hails Human Rights Commission," *New Vision* [Uganda], September 1, 2008; and Milton Olupot, "Human Rights Commission Seeks Wage Limit," *Asia Africa Intelligence Wire*, December 16, 2003; see also UHRC, Annual Report 2001, 10; and UHRC, Annual Report 2007, 117.

[130] See also Josephine Maseruka, "Uganda: Activists Urge Government on Human Rights," *New Vision*, December 3, 2009; UHRC, Annual Report 2001–2002, 1; and UHRC, Annual Report 2007, xix.

[131] See Conan Businge, "Uganda: Health Rights Unit Launched," *New Vision*, September 30, 2008; Halima Shaban, "Uganda: Rights Chief Asks for Health Laws," December 13, 2006; and UHRC, Annual Report (2001–2002), 16.

[132] See "Retired Teachers Appeal to Human Rights Commission," *New Vision*, June 8, 2001 (on file with the author); and UHRC, Annual Report 2001–2002, 3.

[133] See "Uganda: Human Rights Abuse Cases Decline," *New Vision*, July 23, 2008; also UHRC, Annual Report 2007, xx.

[134] See *New Vision*, ibid; and UHRC, Annual Report (2007), 14.

momentum appears to be on the side of ESCR because, as a former senior official of the UHRC has noted:

> We used to focus mainly on civil and political rights but we recently started emphasizing economic, social and cultural rights, e.g. we now have a Right to Health Unit.... We just did a research [project] on the Right to Food. Eventually, we are going to do more.[135]

The increase in its ESCR work is important given the historical bias in favor of civil and political rights in human rights work, and the materially impoverished circumstances in which most Ugandans find themselves. Reflecting its commitment to work "throughout Uganda," the UHRC has tended to work at the grass roots.[136] It has consistently networked with local councils and village leaders[137]; and it communicates with Ugandans in the local languages that dominate interaction at the grass roots.[138] Its tendency (however imperfect it may be) to employ ethnographic methods in its routine investigations and other work is also noteworthy in this respect.[139]

As crucial for assessing its connection to the voices of suffering is the fact that the trend has been generally upward in terms of the number of complaints the Commission receives per annum.[140] This is one measure of the extent to which the victimized trust and rely on the UHRC to provide some redress for the wrongs they have experienced. Also noteworthy, the Commission has initiated investigation of many human rights violations without receiving any prior complaint.[141]

Despite these accomplishments with respect to the Commission's connections to the voices of suffering, much remains to be done if the Commission is to optimize its potential. The UHRC members realize this. Indeed, it is a crucial reason that the Commission wants to increase its efforts at mass education.[142]

C. The Nigerian National Human Rights Commission

While the gender-related work of the NNHC is still not optimal, the Commission has accomplished a lot of work to date in this area. It lists "women and gender matters"

---

[135] Alpha-UG (senior UHRC Official), July 16, 2009.
[136] See Simon Mugenyi, "Extend to Villages, RDC Asks NGOs," *New Vision*, March 9, 2004; see also UHRC, Annual Report (2005), 22.
[137] UHRC, Annual Report (2001–2002), 43.
[138] UHRC, Annual Report (2007), 11.
[139] See "Tap Karamoja Resources to Stop Conflicts – UHRC," *Africa News Service*, September 27, 2004; UHRC, Annual Report (2004), 127–34.
[140] UHRC, Annual Report (2007), 20.
[141] See "Rights Body Starts Project for Ex-IDPs," *Africa News Service*, April 5, 2010; "Probe Kiboko Squad, Says UHRC," *Monitor*. June 20, 2010; also UHRC, Annual Report (2004), 127.
[142] See Chris Kiwawulo, "Rights Group Ready for 2011 Polls," *New Vision*, October 5, 2008; and UHRC, Annual Report (2007), 9.

as one of its thematic areas of focus; it has undertaken significant work in relation to child support[143]; and its related promotional efforts have been commendable. As important, a significant proportion of the NNHC's membership (including the immediate past executive secretary) has been female.[144] This has been one way in which the NNHC has remained well connected to the female "voices of suffering" that dominate Nigeria's social landscape. Another such bridge is the statutory requirement that at least five members of the sixteen-person NNHC board be representatives of NGOs and the independent media.[145]

The substantial, if still insufficient, attention paid by the Commission to vulnerable groups within Nigerian society has also deepened its connection to the voices of suffering. The Commission has made some effort to work within the usually neglected but majority rural areas of the country.[146] It has been an advocate for the rights of children and HIV/AIDS sufferers.[147] It works for the rights of the aged and disabled.[148] It has earned a well-deserved reputation among NGOs and other observers for its work with prisoners.[149] And it takes its anti-poverty work seriously.[150]

Closely related to the NNHC's work in this area is its effort to promote and protect ESCR in Nigeria. Although civil and political rights still unduly dominate its agenda and practice,[151] the Commission appears committed to the advancement of the ESCR of Nigerians. For example, twelve of its sixteen thematic areas of focus can be described as ESCR-related, and a large proportion of the complaints it has dealt with over the years have concerned ESCR.[152]

As relevant a measure of the NNHC's connection to the voices of suffering is the fact that it has established six zonal offices designed to increase access at the grassroots level.[153] In the same vein, the Commission has shown an awareness that it needs to work with traditional leaders so as to bring its human rights work to the

---

[143] ASA (Senior NNHC Official), July 11, 2009; "'Lawmakers' Intolerance and the Rights of the Child," *Vanguard*, December 14, 2002; "UNICEF, NHRC, CRS Implement Child Rights Act," *Vanguard*, August 24, 2009.

[144] See Okafor and Agbakwa, "On Legalism, Popular Agency, and 'Voices of Suffering,'" 714.

[145] Ibid.

[146] OO (Senior Activist), July 20, 2009; ASA (Senior NNHC Official), July 11, 2009; Ajoni, "My Experience," 2.

[147] See R. Ewubare, "Statutory Report 2009" (on file with the author), 3, 7. See also *Vanguard*, August 24, 2009.

[148] *Vanguard*, April 11, 2008.

[149] OV (Senior Activist), July 6, 2009.

[150] Ajoni, "My Experience."

[151] See Agha Ibiam, "Nigeria: Mass Poverty, Misery: Whither Human Rights?" December 4, 2005; ASA (Senior NNHC Official), July 11, 2009.

[152] Ajoni, "Statutory Report 2008," 6.

[153] NNHC, Annual Report (2007), 16. See also "NIGERIA: Defending Human Rights: Not Everywhere, Not Every Right," *Observatory for the Protection of Human Rights Defenders*, May 11, 2010, 17.

local level.[154] Although the NNHC can and does act *suo motu*, the fact that its complaints docket has grown modestly but steadily over the years is an indicator of the Commission's increasing connection to the populations who need it the most.[155]

On balance, however, a significant gap remains between the Commission's aspiration to connect more deeply to the voices of suffering and its current performance. As one NGO activist put it, "I don't think the woman frying *garri* [a local staple] in the village knows about the commission."[156]

D. Assessment

The three NHRIs under study have all made considerable effort to deepen their connections to the most vulnerable groups in their societies. All three NHRIs have been led by a female CEO at some point during the last decade, and each of the commissions has welcomed a significant number of women to their governing boards or councils. All have paid considerable attention to other vulnerable groups such as HIV/AIDS sufferers, the disabled, the aged, and children. Each NHRI has struggled to advance ESCR. All three commissions have undertaken significant, explicit anti-poverty work (although the SAHRC and the UHRC appear to have been more focused on this area than the NNHC). And each NHRI has made an appreciable effort to reach out increasingly to the grass roots. Nevertheless, a significant conceptual and material gap remains between each of these commissions and the voices of suffering that cry out continually for succor in the relevant country.

6.4. NHRIS IN ANGLOPHONE AFRICA: TWO TENTATIVE INSIGHTS

In light of the foregoing discussion, two main points may be made regarding the performance and promise of NHRIs in Anglophone Africa. First, the "popular legitimization factors" that play important roles in NHRI evaluation – including the absence of excessive legalism, sufficient attention to popular agency, and the depth of an NHRI's connections to the voices of suffering – are at least as important as the NHRI's legal and administrative framework and its broader political context in forming an accurate and holistic assessment of NHRI value. This conclusion is important, because the more an NHRI enjoys popular legitimization within the society in which it operates, the more credibility it commands, and the more it is able to

---

[154] Ewubare, "Statutory Report 2009," 9.

[155] Ajoni, "My Experience," 3; and Ajoni, "Statutory Report 2008," 4. See also UN Commission on Human Rights, "Promotion and Protection of Human Rights Defenders Report of the Special Representative of the Secretary-General on Human Rights Defenders: Addendum, Mission to Nigeria," January 30, 2006.

[156] OO (Senior Activist), July 20, 2009.

augment its capacity to persuade or pressure the government and other powerful actors to change their mind-sets or conduct. To be sure, the formal structure of the NHRIs under study (especially their structural independence) is a very important factor in their effectiveness. Yet, these more formal factors do not by themselves "*determine* ... [NHRI] performance on the ground."[157]

Second, the less democratic the governance framework within which a given NHRI must operate, the greater necessity there appears for that NHRI to be open to the possibility of being utilized more as a resource deployed by civil society agents and less as an institution that acts "autonomously" for civil society or the general population.[158] Perhaps this insight partly explains why the NNHC (which has operated for all of its institutional life within either a military or a semi-democratic polity) is more notably accomplished in this regard than the SAHRC (which has functioned entirely within a democratic context). However, as made clear earlier in the chapter, this kind of beneficial relationship between an NHRI and civil society agents (employing popular agency) can also be observed, albeit in a less pronounced way, in significantly more democratic countries like contemporary South Africa. Again, the fact that this phenomenon is less observable in the Ugandan context – which can be viewed as even less democratic than the Nigerian polity during relevant periods[159] – provides reason to exercise caution in developing this hypothesis. More research is needed on Anglophone African NHRIs before either of these two conceptual insights can be confirmed. These insights do, however, point to important dimensions along which NHRI performance should be evaluated.

---

[157] See R. Carver, "Assessing the Effectiveness of National Human Rights Institutions," (Versoix: ICHRP, 2005), 7.

[158] This argument is broadly consistent with Enrique Peruzzotti's conclusion in this volume that accountability deficits in weak democratic regimes can be addressed to some extent by cooperation between civil society and certain horizontal agencies. See Enrique Peruzzotti in this volume, "The Socialization of Horizontal Accountability: Rights Advocacy and the Defensor del Pueblo de la Nación in Argentina."

[159] For example, an important indicator of how much more personally dominant and authoritarian Ugandan president Museveni is when compared to his Nigerian counterparts is that while Museveni was able to change the Ugandan constitution to abolish the term limits that impeded him from remaining in power after over two decades as president, then President Obasanjo's attempt to follow in Museveni's footsteps was roundly and loudly defeated by members of his own party (who held two-thirds of the seats in Parliament).

7

National Human Rights Institutions in the Asia Pacific Region

Change Agents under Conditions of Uncertainty

Catherine Renshaw and Kieren Fitzpatrick

7.1. INTRODUCTION

In 1996, within the Asia Pacific region, there were only five national human rights institutions (NHRIs): the Australian Human Rights and Equal Opportunity Commission,[1] the National Human Rights Commission of India,[2] the Indonesian National Commission on Human Rights,[3] the New Zealand Human Rights Commission,[4] and the Philippines Commission on Human Rights.[5] In July 1996, representatives from the NHRIs of Australia, India, Indonesia, and New Zealand met in Darwin, Australia, to attend a meeting sponsored by the United Nations Office of the High Commissioner for Human Rights (OHCHR).[6] The meeting was also attended by representatives of eight governments considering the establishment of NHRIs (Fiji, Mongolia, Nepal, Pakistan, Papua New Guinea, Solomon Islands, Sri Lanka, and Thailand) and representatives of several nongovernmental

[1] The Australian Human Rights and Equal Opportunity Commission was initially established in 1981, reconstituted in 1986, and renamed in 2008 as "the Australian Human Rights Commission."
[2] Established in 1993.
[3] Established in 1993.
[4] Established in 1977.
[5] Established in 1987.
[6] The Philippines Commission on Human Rights was also invited to the meeting but could not attend.

In 2007, the Australian Research Council provided funding for a Linkage Project with the Asia Pacific Forum of National Human Rights Institutions (LPO776639 "Building Human Rights in the Region through Horizontal Transnational Networks: The Role of the Asia Pacific Forum of National Human Rights Institutions"). As part of this Project, between 2008 and 2010, interviews were conducted with human rights commissioners, government representatives, and civil society members, in Australia, New Zealand, Thailand, Malaysia, Nepal, Samoa, Jordan, and South Korea. This chapter, in part, draws on that research. The authors would like to thank Professor Andrew Byrnes for his assistance in preparing this chapter.

organizations (NGOs).[7] The NHRI participants at the Darwin meeting decided to form the Asia Pacific Forum of National Human Rights Institutions (APF), a network to enhance regional cooperation and capacity building among NHRIs. The conclusions of the Larrakia Declaration, which emanated from that first meeting of NHRIs from the Asia Pacific region, stated that

- The promotion and protection of human rights is the responsibility of all elements of society and all those engaged in the defense of human rights should work in concert to secure their advancement;
- NHRIs should work in close cooperation with nongovernmental organizations and wherever possible with governments to ensure that human rights principles are fully implemented in effective and material ways;
- Regional cooperation is essential to ensure the effective promotion and protection of human rights; and
- To ensure effectiveness and credibility, the status and responsibilities of NHRIs should be consistent with the Principles relating to the status of national institutions adopted by the General Assembly that provide that NHRIs should be independent, pluralistic and established wherever possible by the Constitution or by legislation and in other ways conform to the Principles.

Since 1996, a further fourteen NHRIs have been established in the Asia Pacific region. Presciently, the Larrakia Declaration identified the key issues that would come to mark the complex and variegated history of NHRIs in the Asia Pacific: first, the importance of collaboration between NHRIs, NGOs, and government; second, the necessity for regional cooperation to support the establishment and strengthening of NHRIs in the Asia Pacific region; and third, the importance of the Paris Principles as a standard for NHRIs to obtain or preserve legitimacy in a region which (at present) possesses no supranational system of oversight of state adherence to human rights standards.[8] In the thirteen years of the APF's existence, these three issues have emerged as common threads in the very different experiences of NHRIs within the region.

This chapter picks up each of these threads and explores their significance in the context of the implementation of international human rights standards in the Asia Pacific. In the first section, we provide a brief history of the establishment of

---

[7] At the first meeting, representatives of attending NHRIs discussed matters of common interest to NHRIs in the region, including their independence, their functions and powers, their investigation and conciliation processes, community education, and media relations.

[8] Principles relating to the Status and Functioning of National Institutions for the Protection and Promotion of Human Rights (*hereafter* "The Paris Principles"), endorsed by the United Nations General Assembly on December 20, 1993. See Office of the High Commissioner for Human Rights, http://www.unhchr.ch/html/menu6/2/fs.19htm#annex.

NHRIs in the region and note how the different circumstances in which individual NHRIs were created have influenced their form and subsequent diverse experiences. In the second part of the chapter, we explore the history of NHRI and NGO engagement and note that, in a development distinctive to the Asia Pacific region, engagement between NHRIs and NGOs has evolved into sophisticated and formalized processes for interaction. In the third part of the chapter, we consider the impact of the regional network of NHRIs, the APF, in establishing new NHRIs, strengthening existing NHRIs, providing opportunities for transnational collaboration on human rights issues, and enabling NHRIs within the region to act in concert in international forums. Finally, we consider the challenges to the legitimacy of NHRIs in the region, most visibly (1) in circumstances where the NHRI has become "politicized" (the Fiji Human Rights Commission), (2) where the government has reduced budget or staffing of the institution (South Korea, Australia), and (3) where the government fails to provide the NHRI with the political, financial, and infrastructure support necessary to give the institution legitimacy within the political and social context in which it operates (Nepal).

The experience of NHRIs in the Asia Pacific suggests that the transformative potential of the institutions will depend on a range of variables, which include the physical capabilities of the institution relative to the degree of human rights violations the institution is expected to address (by civil society, by the international community, by the government); the preexisting receptiveness of the political order to the changes being proposed; the support the institution receives from other actors such as the parliament, judiciary, and media; and the caliber and tenacity of the commissioners appointed during different periods of the institution's life. We consider the significance of these variables through our study of the three central issues that have defined the NHRI experience in the Asia Pacific region: NHRI/NGO interaction, the influence of the regional network, and the enduring question of compliance with the Paris Principles and institutional legitimacy in political situations that range from stable democracies to authoritarian regimes.

7.2. THE EMERGENCE OF NHRIS IN THE ASIA PACIFIC REGION

The APF and the International Coordinating Committee of National Human Rights Institutions (ICC) define the "Asia Pacific region" almost by default; it is the region containing all those countries that do not lie within the other regions of the world (Europe, Africa, and the Americas). The Asia Pacific region, therefore, stretches from the Occupied Palestinian Territories in the Middle East to the Small Island States in the South Pacific such as Samoa. The region contains within it at least five subregions, which differ from one another markedly in terms of their demography, geographic characteristics, history, culture, politics, and economic development. Yet since 1977, in each of these subregions, at least one NHRI has been created. In West Asia, NHRIs have been established in Palestine (1993), Jordan (2002), Qatar (2002), Bahrain (2009), and Oman (2009), and NHRIs are being established in Lebanon and Iraq. In South Asia, NHRIs have been established in India (1993), Sri Lanka (1996), Nepal (2000), Afghanistan (2002), the Maldives (2006), and Bangladesh (2009); an NHRI is being created in Pakistan. In Southeast Asia, NHRIs have been established in the Philippines (1987), Indonesia (1993), Malaysia (2000), Thailand (2001), and Timor Leste (2004). In East Asia, NHRIs have been established in Korea (2001) and Mongolia (2001), with one being created in Japan. In Oceania, NHRIs have been established in New Zealand (1977), Australia (1981), and Fiji (1999), and an NHRI is being established in Samoa. The growing momentum in the region toward the establishment of these institutions seems unlikely to abate; several governments within the region have drafted legislation to establish NHRIs,[9] and several governments have made commitments – before the United Nations Human Rights Council, as part of the Universal Periodic Review mechanism, and/or in other forums – to establish NHRIs.[10]

NHRIs established within the Asia Pacific region have applied to join the APF, which holds compliance with the Paris Principles as the sole criterion for full membership.[11] NHRIs that do not fully comply with the Paris Principles, but which may do so within a reasonable period of time, are entitled to become "candidate members." NHRIs that do not comply with the Paris Principles and which are unlikely to do so within a reasonable period can become "associate members" of the APF.[12]

As the circumstances in which NHRIs are created helps to explain why these institutions may sometimes fail to meet the expectations generated by their establishment, it is useful to briefly trace the factors that have influenced the emergence of human rights institutions in the Asia Pacific region. Here we consider first the international influences that have been and remain a significant influence on states

---

9   Papua New Guinea, Solomon Islands.

10   These include Bahrain, Cambodia, Nauru, Samoa, and Yemen.

11   At its annual meeting held in August 2009, in Amman, Jordan, the Forum Council agreed to adopt the accreditation decisions of the ICC as its criterion for membership. Thus, institutions accredited with "A" status by the ICC are entitled to become full members of the APF. "B" accredited institutions are entitled to become associate members of the APF.

12   As a result of the decision of the Forum Council to adopt ICC decisions, the NHRIs from Jordan, Palestine, and Qatar are full members of the APF. The National Society for Human Rights of the Kingdom of Saudi Arabia applied for full membership in the APF in 2006, but when it appeared that its membership application would be refused and the institution deemed not to be an NHRI, the National Society for Human Rights of the Kingdom of Saudi Arabia did not pursue its membership application. In 2008, the Iranian Islamic Human Rights Commission applied for full membership in the APF; it too withdrew its application when it was offered associate membership rather than full membership. The Maldives and Sri Lankan Commissions are currently associate members.

considering the establishment of an NHRI and, second, the domestic impulses that have encouraged the establishment of NHRIs.

7.2.1. *International Influences on the Establishment of NHRIs*

In the Asia Pacific region, as Cardenas argued in 2002, the impetus for creating NHRIs has generally emanated from international actors.[13] Citing the examples of India, Indonesia, and the Philippines, as well as Nepal and Sri Lanka, Cardenas argued that international actors (the OHCHR, APF, International Non-Governmental Organizations [INGOs], such as Amnesty International, and donor agencies), have played a significant role in inducing states to establish domestic institutions for protecting and promoting human rights – institutions that challenge the state's monopoly on "agenda setting, rule creation, accountability and socialization."[14] Cardenas also argued that because domestic human rights institutions were created by governments largely to appease an international audience, the institutions created by the state have been weak,[15] and state concession of sovereignty has been half-hearted.

The history of the creation of new NHRIs in the Asia Pacific region since 2002 supports Cardenas's analysis but reveals some complicating dimensions to her explanation. International actors, in particular the United Nations, have remained a significant influence on states' decisions to establish NHRIs. Indeed, the process of the Universal Periodic Review has been used to add further pressure on states to establish NHRIs.[16] However, it has also become clear, when viewed through the lens of subregional analysis, that the existence of an NHRI in a powerful nation within certain subregions is also a factor that has inspired other nations within the region to emulate that nation in the creation of NHRIs.[17] Thus, the National Human Rights

---

[13] Sonia Cardenas, "National Human Rights Commissions in Asia," *Human Rights Review* 30 (2002), 48. See also Sonia Cardenas, "Emerging Global Actors: The United Nations and National Human Rights Institutions," *Global Governance* 9 (2003), 23–42; Sonia Cardenas, "National Human Rights Institutions in the Middle East," *Middle East Journal* 59 (2005), 411.

[14] Cardenas, "National Human Rights Commissions in Asia."

[15] Although, as Cardenas argues, their impact has been more influential than initially expected. Ibid., 42.

[16] In April 2008, the United Nations Human Rights Council held the first session of the Universal Periodic Review. In written questions presented in advance, fifteen of the sixteen states under review were asked whether they possessed an NHRI and whether this institution complied with the Paris Principles. In each of the four successive sessions of the UPR, questions about the existence and status of NHRIs have been a staple feature.

[17] Our research suggests that nations within a subregion view an NHRI (established under the auspices of a country's ministry of justice or ministry of foreign affairs) as an actor with an international presence, able to maintain relationships with the United Nations (through the Human Rights Council) and its regional neighbors (through networks such as the APF); they view the possession of such an institution as desirable, as it confirms their status as equally progressive as their neighbors. It also enables states to work collaboratively with similar regional institutions to achieve joint goals; see the discussion on human trafficking at Section 7.4.2 of this chapter.

Commission of India (1993) has served as an inspiration for the establishment of institutions in Nepal (2000), Sri Lanka (1996), the Maldives (2006), and more recently in Bangladesh (2009) and the current Pakistan proposals. Within the Pacific subregion, New Zealand and Australia were influential in encouraging the establishment of the Fiji Human Rights Commission in 1999. When the Malaysian government established the Malaysian National Human Rights Commission (SUHAKAM) in 2002, it did so with an eye on the recent or imminent establishment of commissions in its ASEAN (Association of Southeast Asian Nations) neighbors – Thailand, the Philippines, and Indonesia. In the subregion of West Asia, the human rights institutions of Qatar and Jordan were established within a short time of one another. It appears that within the Asia Pacific's subregions, the establishment of an NHRI by a "leader nation" within the region indicates to other states that the institution can be incorporated into the (similar) political and social fabric of their own country without causing undue ruptures.

Analysis of the emergence of NHRIs by reference to examples set by subregional leaders, however, fails to account for the sometimes considerable influence of connections made across different subregions in the lead-up to the establishment of commissions. In the Asia Pacific region, these connections are facilitated by the APF. The successful establishment of NHRIs in the predominantly Islamic states of Indonesia and Malaysia, for example, was studied by government representatives in (also predominantly Islamic) Afghanistan. In 2001, the APF arranged for a representative of SUHAKAM to travel to Kabul to participate in discussions with leaders of the Afghan government about the creation of NHRIs in Islamic countries.[18] Recently, considerable interest in establishing NHRIs has been expressed by several Pacific Island states. Concerns have centered on the ability of these sparsely populated, economically undeveloped island states to comply with Paris Principles requirements of independence from government and adequate resourcing. At an APF-OHCHR workshop on the establishment of NHRIs held in Samoa in 2009, representatives of the NHRIs of the Maldives and Timor Leste worked with representatives of Pacific Island governments on addressing these issues and shared their experiences of the challenges of resourcing, staffing, and maintaining independence in the face of powerful governments and underdeveloped democratic institutions. The common bonds were not geographic or drawn from identified subregional similarities of culture, geography, or politics but from shared challenges related to size, level of economic development, and similar demographics. Consequently, the governments of Samoa and the Solomon Islands have begun the process of establishing NHRIs or hybrid human rights institutions/ombudsmen, modeled on the Office of the

---

[18] See Statement by Mary Robinson, United Nations High Commissioner for Human Rights at the Opening of the 58th Session of the Commission on Human Rights, Geneva, March 18, 2002.

Provedor of Timor Leste.[19] Examples such as these suggest that exposure to successful institutional models can serve as a catalyst for the establishment of NHRIs.

Thus we suggest that two strands of international influence have shaped the form of NHRIs within the Asia Pacific region. The first is the work of the OHCHR and the APF in advising on the institutional structure of nascent NHRIs so that they are compliant with the Paris Principles. The second is the example of other countries with NHRIs within the region and subregion, whose NHRIs have been considered and, where appropriate, used as the basis for shaping new NHRIs. These influences have left a clear impression on the form of NHRIs in the region. All NHRIs within the region aspire to Paris Principles compliance, even if all have not yet attained that status with the ICC or the APF. In addition, all the NHRIs within the Asia Pacific region have protective complaint-handling and investigation functions with quasi-judicial competence,[20] as well as the normal monitoring and promotional functions. These two factors – the guarantee of an independent institution through adherence to the Paris Principles and the institution's ability to provide individual remedies – are particularly significant in the Asia Pacific, where the region's inhabitants lack recourse to any regional system of oversight and redress. Nationally based institutions are therefore well placed to become significant human rights actors.

7.2.2. *Domestic Impulses toward the Establishment of NHRIs*

In countries that have established NHRIs in the wake of civil conflict, the primary catalyst for the creation of an NHRI is the need for an institution to fulfill the role of an independent commentator on past human rights violations, which were often carried out by both parties to the conflict, in circumstances where political power is (often tenuously) held by the victor. In post-conflict states such as Afghanistan,[21] Timor-Leste,[22] and Iraq,[23] the catalyst for the creation of an NHRI is often the

---

[19] See Catherine Renshaw, Andrew Byrnes, and Andrea Durbach, "Institutions for Human Rights Protection in the Pacific," *New Zealand Journal of Public International Law* 8 (2010).

[20] See Chris Sidoti in this volume explaining the distinction between "quasi-jurisdictional" features (in Paris Principles text) and "quasi-judicial" features (as the intent of Paris Principles drafters).

[21] See Section III(C) (6) of the Bonn Agreement, signed by Afghan military commanders, representatives of the exiled monarch, and members of Afghanistan's different ethnic groups on December 5, 2001.

[22] The Democratic Republic of Timor-Leste achieved independence from Indonesia on May 19, 2002. In 2003, the Office of the High Commissioner for Human Rights reported that a Working Group had been established for the creation of the Office of the Provedor, composed of the Human Rights adviser to the prime minister, representatives of the judiciary, NGOs, and United Nations Mission of Support in East Timor (UNMISET). See the Report of the High Commissioner for Human Rights on the situation of human rights in Timor-Leste, E/CN.4/2003/37 (March 4, 2003), para. 28.

[23] In October 2005, Iraqis approved by referendum a new constitution. Chapter 4, Article 99, of the Constitution provides for the creation of a "High Commission for Human Rights," as well as an

inclusion of a provision regarding the institution's establishment in the peace agreement sanctioned by the international community. Here, the interests of the international community in building institutions that can help to support a democratic peace are seen as coinciding with the interests of those who hold political power within the state at the time.

In Afghanistan, Dr. Sima Samar, first human rights commissioner and former deputy chair of the Afghanistan Interim Administration led by President Karzai, has identified four principal reasons that she and others in the 2001 Afghanistan government of President Karzai considered the establishment of an NHRI a priority for the new government. First, there was the imperative of establishing an institution capable of redressing past human rights violations. Samar states that those who held power in Afghanistan in 2001 were determined not to repeat the experience of 1992, when the granting of a general amnesty after the departure of the Soviet Union generated reprisals that undermined the stability of the new political order. Second, there was the need to ensure that an agency was established to undertake independent monitoring of human rights abuses carried out by the different powers operating within Afghanistan (e.g., the Afghan Independent Human Rights Commission has issued reports on both insurgent abuses against Afghan civilians and the operation of pro-government forces within Afghanistan). Third was the necessity of raising human rights awareness among the people in order to decrease impunity and the toleration of abuse, particularly against women and children. Finally, there was the imperative to address the issue of women's rights.[24]

NHRIs established in the wake of conflict inevitably face resource shortages (human, financial, infrastructural) and enormous workloads, which, combined with the necessity of maintaining relationships with multiple international agencies, place a high degree of stress on the institution's ability to fulfill its mandate and to be seen as doing so by its domestic constituency. In countries that have established NHRIs largely at the behest of external interest groups, the institutions also face the challenge of domestic legitimacy: how can this imported institutional model address the unique difficulties of the context in which it operates? The governments of states emerging from authoritarian rule, such as the Philippines, Bangladesh, and Pakistan, view the establishment of an NHRI as a symbol (to a domestic constituency and to an international audience) of political commitment to the recently (re)generated, democratic aspirations of the new political order. But in these circumstances, the

Independent Electoral High Commission and a Commission on Public Integrity, which are to be independent commissions, subject to monitoring by the Council of Representatives.

[24] Interview with Dr. Sima Samar by Catherine Renshaw, Amman, August 4, 2009, copy of interview on file with authors. In 2002 Dr. Samar was appointed chairperson of the Afghanistan Independent Human Rights Commission. She also held a cabinet post in the Afghan Transitional Administration led by Hamid Karzai.

institution is likely to meet resistance from two different interest groups – from elements within the new government itself, who view criticism from a national commission as undermining its tenuous hold on power, and from civil society groups, who have long worked to achieve human rights and who view the new institution as a state-sponsored and ephemeral effort to appease an international constituency.

7.2.3. *Final Thoughts*

The different international and domestic impulses behind the establishment of NHRIs in the Asia Pacific provide part of the explanation for the varied experiences of those institutions. Most of the NHRIs in the Asia Pacific were established after the adoption of the Paris Principles by the UN General Assembly in 1993, and the influence of the APF and OHCHR is evident in the legislative framework of national human rights institutions within the region. NHRIs in the region that formally comply with the Paris Principles have protective (as well as monitoring and promotional) functions, something that distinguishes NHRIs in the Asia Pacific from other institutions, particularly in Europe, where the research and promotional functions of NHRIs are emphasized. Compliance with the Paris Principles and the international recognition from bodies such as the ICC and APF that follows such compliance, as well as the strong protective functions of the NHRIs, have meant that the institutions occupy a prominent position in the legal, political, and social framework of their countries.

But unfavorable domestic political conditions at the time of an NHRI's establishment can restrict its ability to fulfill its mandate. Political instability, for example, makes it difficult for NHRIs to develop strategies for ensuring that governments respond to their recommendations, and the weakness of other institutions (in particular the judiciary and the police) places an unrealistic burden on NHRIs to address human rights violations. The consequent disillusionment of civil society and its trenchant critiques of the NHRI serve to compound the problem the institution faces in effectively fulfilling its mandate: governments are less likely to respond to discredited institutions and NGOs are less likely to cooperate with institutions they perceive as ineffectual.

7.3. NHRIS AS SIGNIFICANT ACTORS WITHIN THE ASIA PACIFIC: THE RELATIONSHIP BETWEEN NHRIS AND CIVIL SOCIETY

One gauge of the importance of NHRIs in the Asia Pacific region is the significance attached to their work by national and regional NGOs. The Paris Principles "Methods of Operation" delineate an important role for NHRI-NGO cooperation in light of "the fundamental role played by non-governmental organizations in expanding the work of the national institutions."[25] NGOs, which are often able to reach groups suffering discrimination in ways that state institutions are not, and to focus uniquely on particular disadvantaged groups, are clearly a crucial partner for NHRIs. Members of the APF recognized the importance of NGO-NHRI collaboration in 1999 when they agreed upon the Kandy Program of Action: Cooperation between National Institutions and Non-Governmental Organizations. The Kandy Program, which emanated from a workshop held in Kandy, Sri Lanka, hosted by the APF and the OHCHR, provided a detailed agenda for structures and mechanisms of cooperation between NGOs and NHRIs, in relation to education, procedures for handling complaints and investigations, public inquiries, relations with legislatures, reviewing legislation to ensure consistency with human rights law, and the establishment of new national institutions.

From its inception, the APF has invited representatives of national and international NGOs to attend its annual meeting and conference, where NGOs and INGOs contribute to the debate and to the final statement emanating from the conference. The annual meetings of the APF are the largest regular human rights events in the region and they bring together APF members and other NHRIs, United Nations agencies, national governments, NGOs, and donors "in a cooperative setting to discuss and share expertise on the pressing human rights issues in the region."[26] The Kandy Program also agreed that national institutions and NGOs would provide brief annual reports to the APF on measures taken to give effect to the program.[27] This invitation has been taken up with alacrity by NGOs.

The desirability of cooperation between NGOs and NHRIs applies to the operation of national institutions in all regions. Distinctive to the Asia Pacific region, however, is the formalized process of engagement between NHRIs and NGOs that has occurred at a national and regional level. In December 2006, the Asian Forum for Human Rights and Development (Forum-Asia), an alliance of forty-eight NGOs from across the Asia Pacific, held a Regional Consultation on Cooperation between NHRIs and NGOs. Participants at the Consultation[28] agreed to establish "The Asian NGOs Network on National Human Rights Institutions" (ANNI). Participants were of the view that

> national human rights institutions hold an important role in the promotion and protection of human rights in the region, considering the fact that Asia has yet to

---

[25] The Paris Principles, "Methods of Operation," g.

[26] Catherine Renshaw and Katrina Taylor, "Promoting and Protecting Human Rights in the Asia Pacific; The Relationship between National Human Rights Institutions and Non-Governmental Organisations," *Human Rights Defender* 17 (2008), 5–7.

[27] Kandy Program of Action: Cooperation between National Institutions and Non-Governmental Organizations, para. 9(3).

[28] Held in Bangkok, Thailand, and hosted by the Asian Forum for Human Rights and Development (FORUM-ASIA).

set up a human rights mechanism that would cover the region. National human rights institutions are the primary protection mechanisms for human rights defenders working on the ground. They also hold the potential of developing a regional jurisprudence on human rights that would conform to international human rights principles.[29]

ANNI has evolved to coordinate the submissions of NGOs, to develop strategies for influencing NHRIs, and to share information about how NGOs can develop productive relationships with NHRIs. ANNI's membership includes the major NGOs from countries within the region that have established NHRIs[30] and from countries that have yet to establish NHRIs but have made commitments to do so or where governments are being lobbied by NGOs to establish an NHRI.[31] In 2007, ANNI published its first report, "The Performance of National Human Rights Institutions in Asia 2006: Cooperation with NGOs and Relationship with Governments." In this and its subsequent reports, ANNI has consistently acknowledged the potential power of NHRIs as "the practical link between international standards and their concrete application, the bridge between the ideal and its implementation,"[32] but has also questioned the independence and effectiveness of individual NHRIs in Asia.

ANNI's network mirrors the APF network; ANNI's annual meetings occur before the annual meeting of the APF, and ANNI publishes a yearly assessment of the independence and effectiveness of NHRIs in Asia. Just as APF members meet on a yearly basis and discuss shared challenges, explore possibilities for joint projects, and develop regional strategies for addressing transnational human rights issues, ANNI's members meet to share their experiences of working with NHRIs and to learn from each other about effective techniques for engagement. The APF's annual meetings thus bring together civil society and NHRIs in the largest human rights conference of the region. In March 2009, ANNI produced its first quarterly newsletter, detailing issues facing individual commissions.

Of great significance is the decision on the part of the largest and most active NGOs in the region[33] to devote resources and energy to (1) ensuring the independence and increasing the effectiveness of NHRIs and (2) increasing the level

---

[29] The Asian NGOs Network on National Institutions (ANNI), 2008 *Report on the Performance and Establishment of National Human Rights Institutions in Asia* (Bangkok: Asian Forum for Human Rights and Development, 2008), 11 (*hereafter* ANNI, *2008 Report*).

[30] This includes India, Indonesia, Malaysia, the Maldives, Mongolia, Nepal, the Philippines, South Korea, Sri Lanka, and Thailand.

[31] Bangladesh, Taiwan, Japan, Hong Kong.

[32] Cardenas, "Emerging Global Actors," 23.

[33] For example, Ain O Saliah Kendra (ASK) (Bangladesh), Hong Kong Human Rights Monitor (Hong Kong), People Watch (India), Indonesian Human Rights Working Group (Indonesia), Centre for Human Rights and Development (Mongolia), Libertas (the Philippines), Law and Society Trust (Sri Lanka), and the Taiwan Association for Human Rights (Taiwan).

of engagement between NGOs and NHRIs. It reflects a conviction on the part of those NGOs that "NHRIs remain the key bodies for the promotion and protection of human rights in the region."[34] The forthright criticism that has accompanied ANNI's reports on NHRIs is part of its goal to establish and develop accountable, independent, effective, and transparent NHRIs in Asia. This formal process and the energy dedicated to it by NGOs is, in part, a result of the lack of any regional supranational human rights monitoring body in the Asia Pacific and the consequent imperative that NHRIs reach the standard of independence from the state necessary for them to fulfill their functions.[35]

Recently, ANNI has pursued a strategy of engaging with the re-accreditation process of the ICC. The first, and dramatically effective, example of this strategy occurred in 2008 in relation to SUHAKAM, the national human rights commission of Malaysia.[36] In March 2008, a coalition of Malaysian NGOs, led by ERA Consumer and Suara Rakyat Malaysia ("Voice of the Malaysian People"), sent a letter to the ICC claiming that in the view of Malaysian civil society, Malaysia's human rights commission, SUHAKAM, was not in compliance with the Paris Principles. NGOs anticipated that the ICC's potential demotion of SUHAKAM would encourage the Malaysian government to strengthen the institution's powers, its independence, and the breadth of its mandate.

In April 2008, the ICC Sub-Committee on Accreditation informed SUHAKAM of its decision to downgrade SUHAKAM from an "A" status institution to a "B" status institution.[37] The Sub-Committee gave SUHAKAM one year to provide evidence of

---

[34] ANNI, *2008 Report*, 22.

[35] In Africa, Europe, and the Americas, each of these regions has a supranational oversight mechanism for human rights; however, they do not at present have as highly developed a network of NHRIs as the APF, though there are moves in all regions to develop further the nascent networks that exist. Outside of the Asia Pacific region, NGOs have not formalized their process of engagement with NHRIs, as ANNI has done. It could be argued that the APF's evolution results, in part, from the lack of any formal regional mechanism for the promotion and protection of human rights. In this regard, it is interesting to note the evolution of the ASEAN inter-governmental human rights monitoring body, which was driven by the "ASEAN Four" – those NHRIs that exist within the ASEAN region (Thailand, Malaysia, Indonesia, Philippines). Kal Raustiala's argument, that networks may facilitate the institutions of traditional liberal internationalism, is relevant here. Kal Raustiala, "The Architecture of International Cooperation: Transgovernmental Networks and the Future of International Law," *Valparaiso International Law Journal* 1 (2003), 43.

[36] This section draws on a paper by Catherine Renshaw presented in July 2009 at a workshop on NHRIs hosted by Melbourne University: "Creating Change?: NHRIs (In)Action in the Asia Pacific Region." The title of the paper is "The National Human Rights Commission of Malaysia, Civil Society and the Malaysian Government; Exploring the Dynamics of Change" and is available at http://iilah.unimelb. edu.au/index.cfm?objectid=796E6CDE-FE38–0609-D2B1B041E27C22E6.

[37] SUHAKAM was accredited with "A" status by the ICC and in 2002 was admitted as a full member of the APF. See Amanda Whiting's work on SUHAKAM's early years: "Situating Suhakam: Human Rights Debates and Malaysia's National Human Rights Commission," *Stanford Journal of International Law* 39 (2003), 59.

its continued conformity with the Paris Principles. The Sub-Committee noted four areas of concern:

- The lack of clear and transparent appointment and dismissal processes for commissioners in the founding legal documents, which weakened the independence of the institution;
- The short term of office of the members of the commission (two years);
- The Paris Principles requirement of pluralism and the importance of ensuring the representation of different segments of society and their involvement in recommending candidates to the governing body of SUHAKAM; and
- The requirement that a national commission interact with the International Human Rights System.

SUHAKAM's commissioners objected to the proposed demotion, arguing that at the time of SUHAKAM's establishment in 1999, the ICC had seen fit to accredit SUHAKAM with "A" status, and the only thing that had changed by 2008 was that SUHAKAM had a list of commendable reports to its name and could demonstrate the hard work of many dedicated commissioners, who had done everything within the power granted to them under SUHAKAM's founding legislation to improve the human rights of Malaysian citizens. SUHAKAM's commissioners took the view that NGOs were "targeting the government but pointing the barrel of the gun at SUHAKAM."[38]

On 24 March 2009, two days before the ICC was due to make its decision on SUHAKAM's re-accreditation, the Malaysian government tabled the Human Rights Commission of Malaysia (Amendment) Bill 2009, for first reading. The Explanatory Memorandum accompanying the Human Rights Commission of Malaysia (Amendment) Bill stated that the legislation was intended "to make the process of appointment of the members of the Human Rights Commission of Malaysia more transparent."[39] Section 5(2) of the Amendment Act provided that SUHAKAM commissioners were to be appointed by the Yang Di Pertuan Agong (king) on the recommendation of the prime minister, who must now, before tendering his advice, consult with a Selection Committee. Section 11(A)(6) of the Amendment Act also provided, however, that the views and recommendations of the Selection Committee were not binding on the prime minister. The Amendment Act also changed the criteria for selection of commissioners, stipulating that "members of the Commission shall be

---

[38] Interview with Tan Sri Simon Sipaun by Professor Andrew Byrnes and Associate Professor Andrea Durbach, Kuala Lumpur, August 5, 2008, copy of interview on file with authors. Tan Sri Simon Sipaun was one of the first commissioners appointed to SUHAKAM, the Malaysian Human Rights Commission, in 2002. In 2003 he was appointed vice-chairperson of SUHAKAM.

[39] Explanatory Memorandum Human Rights Commission of Malaysia Act 1999 ("Act 597"), http://www.suhakam.org.my/web/guest/home.

appointed from amongst men and women of various religious, political, racial back-grounds who have knowledge of, or practical experience in, human rights matters."[40] The period of tenure for commissioners was also extended in the Amendment Act from two years with possible reappointment for a further two years, to three years with possible reappointment for a further three years.[41]

On 25 March 2009, the bill was passed, amid protests from the opposition that the bill had been tabled and passed in unseemly haste (and in contravention of the Standing Orders of the House). No notice of the bill had been given, and there had been no consultation about it. Opposition MP Lim Kit Siang was tem-porarily suspended from Parliament when the "vigorous debate" about the bill's hasty passage descended into "an exchange of insults" between government and opposition MPs.[42]

The day after the Amendment Act was passed ANNI sent another letter to the ICC Sub-Committee on Accreditation. The letter stated:

> The hasty manner [in which] the amendments were passed clearly illustrated the government's will to bulldoze this bill through Parliament in time for the review of SUHAKAM by the ICC Sub-Committee on Accreditation, on March 26, 2009. Moreover, this also manifests an intention by the government to avoid a debate over the amendments.[43]

ANNI's letter stated that the amendments were "superficial," that they did not ensure pluralism in the appointment process, as required by the Paris Principles, and that they gave the prime minister absolute discretion over the appointment of new mem-bers of the Commission. ANNI argued that

> should the Sub-Committee on Accreditation maintain the "A" status of the SUHAKAM based on these amendments, this would set a precedence [*sic*] that would negatively affect future accreditation reviews of other NHRIs. Moreover, should the Sub-Committee maintain the "A" status of the SUHAKAM based on these amend-ments, it would be difficult to push forward more substantial amendments that would truly make SUHAKAM an independent, effective and accountable NHRI.[44]

The ICC Sub-Committee on Accreditation apparently concurred with ANNI's view. In April 2009, the Sub-Committee informed SUHAKAM that the

---

[40] Clause 5(3), Human Rights Commission of Malaysia Act 1999 (Amendment) Bill (2009)
[41] Sec. 5(4) Human Rights Commission of Malaysia Act 1999 (Amendment) Bill.
[42] ANNI, "SUHAKAM Bill Hastily Passed in Malaysian Parliament," March 30, 2009, http://groups.google.co.th/group/anni21?hl=en.
[43] Letter from Emerlynne Gil, coordinator, Asian NGOs Network on National Human Rights Institutions (ANNI) to Mr. David Langtry, ICC Sub-Committee on Accreditation, dated March 26, 2009, http://suarampg.blogspot.com/2009/03/malaysia-ngos-letter-to-sca-on-suhakams.html.
[44] Ibid.

government's legislative amendments were inadequate. As a result, the Sub-Committee deferred its decision on SUHAKAM's re-accreditation, and provided a twenty-eight-day window for the Malaysian government to consider further legislative amendments.

The Malaysian government took this opportunity. On May 8, 2009, de facto law minister Datuk Seri Nazri Abd Aziz announced that the government would again amend the Human Rights Commission Act 1999 in a bid to ensure SUHAKAM's compliance with the Paris Principles.[45] The further amendments would involve two substantial changes. First, the clause providing that the prime minister was not bound by the opinions, views, or recommendations of the Selection Committee would be deleted. Second, the clause referring to the composition of the Selection Committee would be amended from "three eminent persons" to "three members of civil societies of human rights." The bill was read for the first time in the Malaysian Parliament on June 22, 2009 and passed on July 2, 2009, despite protests by opposition Members of Parliament. ANNI issued a statement asserting that the amended act still does not fully address SUHAKAM's lack of compliance with the Paris Principles and cautioning that the amendments might not be sufficient to prevent SUHAKAM from being downgraded by the ICC. On November 23, 2009, the ICC Sub-Committee on Accreditation informed SUHAKAM's chairman that the institution would maintain its "A" status.

The attempt by Malaysian NGOs to use the ICC and its procedures to effect change introduces a new dynamic into the relationship of state, civil society, and the institution that sits between them, the NHRI. In his statement to the 14th Annual Meeting of the APF, held in August 2009, the OHCHR representative, Dr. Homayoun Alizadeh, acknowledged "the important role played by NGOs from the Asia Pacific region for their exemplary advocacy for and commitment to making NHRIs throughout the region stronger and more effective."[46] ANNI has resolved to continue its engagement with the ICC. In response, since March 2008, ICC procedures have evolved to meet this new civil society engagement; NGO reports to the ICC Sub-Committee on accreditation are encouraged and are now required to be submitted four months before the date of review, to allow NHRIs time to respond to the NGO report.[47]

---

[45] "Two More Changes to Suhakam Act," *Star Online*. May 8, 2009.

[46] Available http://www.asiapacificforum.net/about/annual-meetings/14th-jordan-2009.

[47] The Rules of Procedure for the ICC Sub-Committee on Accreditation, adopted by the members of the International Coordinating Committee at its 15th session, held on September 14, 2004, Seoul, Republic of Korea, and amended by the members of the ICC at its 20th session, held on April 15, 2008, Geneva, Switzerland, provide at 3.6: "Any civil society organization wishing to provide relevant information pertaining to any accreditation matter before the Sub-Committee shall provide such information in writing to the ICC Secretariat at least four (4) months prior to the meeting of the Sub-Committee."

The (relatively) successful example of the ANNI network has inspired subregional offshoots. In August 2009, Jordan hosted the 14th Annual Meeting of the APF, the first time a country in the Middle East had hosted the meeting. Proximity permitted civil society representatives from organizations in Syria, Palestine, Iraq, Jordan, Qatar, and Iran to attend the meeting, to witness the engagement between NGOs and NHRIs, and to participate in the discussions on issues such as human rights and religious belief and human rights and corruption. Following the event, participants from the Middle East decided to establish their own NGO network, the Arabic NGOs Network on National Human Rights Institutions (ARNNI). Networks such as ANNI and ARNNI are significant parts of civil society's aim to challenge NHRIs to be independent and effective protectors and promoters of human rights.

7.4. THE REGIONAL NETWORKS OF NHRIS: THE ASIA PACIFIC FORUM OF NATIONAL HUMAN RIGHTS INSTITUTIONS

Unlike Africa, the Americas, and Europe, the Asia Pacific has to date no formal intergovernmental regional human rights mechanism. This lacuna has had two major implications for the implementation of international human rights standards in the region. First, human rights advocates have attached increased importance to the strength and independence of NHRIs. Second, it has become necessary for human rights actors involved in addressing cross-border or transnational issues to evolve new ways of coordinating approaches and acting in concert to address human rights issues. The regional network of NHRIs, the APF, has emerged to address both challenges.

The APF, as a membership organization, has established incentives for states to create institutions that conform to the Paris Principles.[48] Membership in the APF brings with it the domestic political benefits a state receives as a result of creating a human rights institution eligible for full membership status (Paris Principles–compliant) in its regional organization. In addition, there are often tangible benefits (e.g., in the attitudes of donors) which flow from a government representing, by its establishment of a credible NHRI, that it has a genuine commitment to improving the institutional protection of human rights.

Equally important is the opportunity the APF network presents for NHRIs to collaborate on transnational human rights issues. Below we consider – as representative of a positive model – the efforts of the ASEAN NHRIs to advance human rights goals in the area of human trafficking.[49]

---

[48] See Andrew Byrnes, Andrea Durbach, and Catherine Renshaw, "Joining the Club: The Asia Pacific Forum of National Human Rights Institutions, the Paris Principles and the Advancement of Human Rights Protection in the Region," *Australian Journal of Human Rights* 14 (2008), 63–98.

[49] This section of the paper draws on the research presented by Catherine Renshaw at the 25th Annual Law and Society Australia and New Zealand Conference held at the University of Sydney December

7.4.1. *The APF's Role in Assisting the Establishment of Paris Principles–Compliant NHRIs*

In 1996 the APF began its life as an informal regional forum of NHRIs, whose members agreed to share expertise and information on best practice, to undertake joint projects, to develop joint positions on issues of common concern, and to hold periodic regional meetings.[50] By 2002, the APF's work was defined by three core activities: strengthening the capacity of individual APF member institutions to enable them to undertake their national mandates; assisting governments and NGOs to establish NHRIs in compliance with the minimum criteria contained in the Paris Principles; and promoting regional cooperation on human rights issues. The APF describes its role as "opening up important new avenues for strengthening human rights observance and advancing human rights protection for the peoples of the region in a constructive and cooperative environment."[51]

The secretariat of the APF, located in Sydney, Australia, provides advice to NHRIs seeking APF membership, so that necessary adjustments to their legislative basis, structure, or mandate can be made prior to their formal application. Once a government has issued a formal request for assistance in establishing an NHRI, the APF conducts an extensive "needs assessment mission" to the country seeking to establish the institution. In determining the need and scope of assistance required, the APF consults with relevant members of government, civil society, United Nations officials, and international NGOs. Governments provide the APF with copies of draft legislation for the establishment of an NHRI, and APF comments have formed the basis for legislative amendments to ensure the institution's conformity with the Paris Principles.[52] The APF has also developed a set of "Best Practice Principles" outlining the steps that should be taken by both governments and civil society in the pre-establishment phase of creating an NHRI. The APF's assistance has been fundamental to the successful establishment and admission to the APF of the NHRIs of Afghanistan, Malaysia, Mongolia, South Korea, and Timor Leste. In addition, the APF has provided assistance and advice, on request, to a range of governments

---

10–12, 2008: see "The Globalisation Paradox and the Implementation of International Human Rights: The Function of Transnational Networks in Combating Trafficking in the ASEAN Region," Proceedings of the 25th Annual Law and Society Australia and New Zealand Conference, http://ses.library.usyd.edu.au/handle/2123/4045?mode=full&submit_simple=Show+full+item+record.

[50] See Andrea Durbach, Catherine Renshaw, and Andrew Byrnes, "A Tongue but No Teeth? The Emergence of a Regional Human Rights Mechanism in the Asia Pacific Region," *Sydney Law Review* 31 (2009), 211–38.

[51] Asia Pacific Forum, APF website (2006), http://www.asiapacificforum.net/.

[52] For example, in 2002, the APF Secretariat provided detailed legislative and legal advice to the recently elected Constituent Assembly, NGOs, and representatives of the East Timor administration and the United Nations transitional administration in East Timor on the possible mandate, role, and functions of a future NHRI.

including Bangladesh,[53] Cambodia, China, Japan, Pakistan, Samoa, Solomon Islands, Taiwan, and Vietnam[54] in relation to the future establishment of NHRIs.

The criterion applied in the APF's membership application process is whether an institution complies with the Paris Principles.[55] The APF's Forum Council – a committee of the institution's regional peers – is responsible for the decision on compliance. Reviewing the history of applications for membership of the APF, it is clear that full membership of the APF has been an incentive for governments to bring their NHRIs into conformity with the Paris Principles. The example that follows in relation to Jordan bears similarities to the cases of Afghanistan and Timor-Leste, with APF membership providing an incentive for governments to improve their NHRI's compliance with the Paris Principles.

The Jordan National Centre for Human Rights (JNCHR) was established by executive decree in 2002. The legislation relating to the appointment and termination of appointment of the chair and board of trustees permitted termination by royal decree on recommendation of the prime minister, without qualification. When it applied for APF membership in 2004, the APF Council took the view that establishment by executive decree did not satisfy the requirements of article 2 of the Paris Principles, which specify that the mandate of a national institution "be clearly set forth in a constitutional or legislative text, specifying its composition and sphere of competence" and that the provisions relating to termination of the chair and board of trustees did not comply with article 6 of the Paris Principles, which provides that the appointment of members to a national institution shall be by an "official act which shall establish the specific duration of the mandate." The APF Council awarded the JNCHR "Associate Membership" and undertook to assist the JNCHR to take whatever steps were necessary to become fully compliant with the Paris Principles.[56] In 2006, Jordan's National Assembly passed a law which placed the JNCHR on a firm legislative basis and removed the king's unqualified power to remove its members. In September 2007 the APF Council admitted the JNCHR to full membership.

---

[53] Many years may elapse between an overture to the APF by a government considering the establishment of an NHRI and the institution's creation. In 1997, the Australian Human Rights and Equal Opportunity Commission and New Zealand hosted a senior delegation from Bangladesh, who wished to establish an NHRI. In June 1998, officers from the Human Rights Project team of the Bangladesh Department of Law, Justice and Parliamentary Affairs commenced a human rights training internship in Australia for three months. The members of the Bangladesh team were placed within three functional units of the Australian Commission – conciliation, human rights, and public affairs. Bangladesh's NHRI was not established until 2009.

[54] A group of experts within the prime minister's research group for Vietnam conducted a study tour to New Zealand, November 2–9, 1997, and explored several aspects of the New Zealand government including its human rights commission.

[55] See the discussion above at note 12 concerning recent changes to APF's membership criteria, to align APF membership status with ICC accreditation status.

[56] APF Concluding Statement, Ninth Annual Meeting, September 13, 2004, Seoul, Korea, art 2, para 7.

At its annual meeting in 2009, the APF Council decided that it would adopt the accreditation decisions of the ICC as its membership criterion: ICC "A" accredited institutions would be entitled to become full members of the APF; "B" accredited institutions would be entitled to associate membership only. The NHRIs of Palestine and Qatar, previously only associate members of the APF, became, as a result of this decision, full members, and the Sri Lankan Commission was reduced from full to associate membership.

The APF's decision to adopt the ICC accreditation system is significant. In the period since its inception, the APF has developed a rigorous process of peer-accreditation that was intended to guard against states establishing NHRIs that were not truly independent. Until recently, this process was considered by APF members to be more rigorous and sophisticated than the ICC process of accreditation, which tended to be a test of "paper compliance" only. Reform of the procedures of the ICC's Sub-committee on Accreditation (in part, a result of efforts by the APF secretariat) has convinced the APF's Council that its own separate accreditation procedure is no longer necessary or desirable.

7.4.2. *The APF's Role as a Network Facilitating Transnational Collaboration*

Within the broader regional network of the APF, sub-networks of NHRIs have emerged to enable institutions to act in concert to achieve joint goals. Since 2005, NHRIs in the Arab region (Algeria, Egypt, Jordan, Mauritania, Morocco, Palestine, Qatar, Saudi Arabia, Tunisia) have met annually to discuss issues of shared concern.[57] Of particular significance, however, are the efforts of the NHRI network (Thailand, Malaysia, Philippines, and Indonesia) of the Association of Southeast Asian Nations (ASEAN). This network has been prominent in advocating the creation of a strong and independent human rights monitoring body for the ASEAN region. It has also developed a network approach to addressing the issue of human trafficking, which we examine as an example of subregional collaboration to address a human rights issue in a region that has been marked by reluctance to ratify international treaties on the subject.

At the 1999 meeting of the ICC, the United Nations High Commissioner for Human Rights noted that NHRIs are "an underutilized resource in the fight against trafficking."[58] That same year, at the Fourth Annual Meeting of the APF, Anne Gallagher, adviser to the High Commissioner on Trafficking, spoke to the APF's

---

[57] See Office of the High Commissioner for Human Rights and Advisory Council for Human Rights UN Doc. E/CN.4/2005/G/34, April 8, 2005.

[58] Quoted in Anne Gallagher, "A Case Study on Trafficking in the Asia Pacific Region," presented at APF, *Fourth Annual Meeting: Women and Trafficking*, September 6–8, 1999, 7.

members in an address titled "The Role of National Institutions in Advancing the Human Rights of Women; a Case Study on Trafficking in the Asia Pacific region." In response, the APF Council asked its Advisory Council of Jurists (ACJ)[59] to prepare a reference guide on trafficking; regional workshops on the issue were held and a Trafficking Focal Point Network was established among member institutions of the APF. The APF recognized that the issue of human trafficking required a multifaceted response: a domestic legal framework within the state and a multilateral approach at the regional level.

The network structure of the APF was well suited to this purpose. The mandate of NHRIs – to promote and protect human rights – generated a response to the issue of human trafficking that placed the protection of human rights at the center of any measures taken to prevent or respond to trafficking. The networking activities of the four ASEAN NHRIs on the issue of trafficking have been notable. In 2004, the "ASEAN Four" decided to hold regular consultation meetings among themselves, build closer cooperation, and develop practical and feasible plans to promote and protect the human rights of trafficked persons at the regional level. In June 2007, the ASEAN Four agreed to carry out a series of programs and activities in relation to five human rights issues of common concern: (1) suppression of terrorism while respecting human rights; (2) human rights aspects of trafficking in persons; (3) protection of the human rights of migrants and migrant workers; (4) implementation of economic, social, and cultural rights and the right to development; and (5) enhancement of human rights education. The ASEAN Four also agreed to encourage other ASEAN countries to establish NHRIs, so that the cross-border dialogue on key issues of concern could engage other nations in the region as well.

One of the major functions of an NHRI is to review prospective government legislation to ensure that laws comply with a state's international human rights obligations. Where no formal obligations exist, NHRIs encourage states to draft laws that meet the expectations of the international community in relation to human rights standards. Each of the ASEAN nations that possess an NHRI has recently passed anti-trafficking legislation, as has Cambodia. In June 2008, Thailand introduced new legislation, the Anti-Trafficking in Persons Act, which replaced the Measures in Prevention and Suppression of Trafficking in Women and Children Act, B.E 2540 (1997). The new act extends protection to male victims of trafficking, and significantly strengthens the protection for victims of trafficking. In 2003, the Philippines passed the Republic Act 9208 or the Anti-Trafficking in Persons Law of the Philippines. This act sets the issue of trafficking within a human rights framework and also provides a broad definition of "trafficking," deeming issues of "consent"

---

[59] The Advisory Council of Jurists (ACJ) comprises jurists and academics from the Asia Pacific region who are nominated by an NHRI to sit on the body for a five-year period. Each year, the ACJ considers a human rights issue of relevance to the region. See http://www.asiapacificforum.net/acj.

irrelevant. In April 2007, Indonesia's president signed into law a comprehensive anti-trafficking bill that defines the act of human trafficking in consonance with the Trafficking Protocol. The Malaysian House of Representatives passed the Anti-Trafficking in Persons Act in May 2007. This act also provides an expansive definition of trafficking, deems consent irrelevant and provides some measures for the care and protection of trafficked persons (Anti-Trafficking in Persons Act, Malaysia, 2007, Part V).

Among the ASEAN nations that have NHRIs and are members of the APF, there is thus evidence of a "policy convergence" in relation to the issue of trafficking that has ultimately generated domestic legislation compatible with that of other states within the "NHRI network" and which largely conforms to international standards. A shared understanding of the problems of international trafficking and shared approach to addressing them, through similar legislative measures, is the basis for effective cooperation in addressing transnational problems. These measures and this effect have been largely outside the orbit of international law reflected in the United Nations Trafficking Protocol.

7.4.3. *Final Thoughts*

The APF network has served its members well in the provision of advice, information, and assistance in the management of independent and effective NHRIs. As the membership of APF increases and subregional networks emerge, it may be that the sense of identity currently held by NHRIs of the "Asia Pacific" region will be subjugated to a subregional identity currently emerging in ASEAN and the Middle East. Several Pacific Island states have begun the process of establishing NHRIs,[60] and a network of Pacific Island NHRIs, following the political grouping of the Pacific Islands Forum, would seems to be a natural evolution. If the APF is to continue to maintain the level of support it has currently provided to NHRIs, it may in the future require the establishment of subregional offices to service its members.

7.5. LEGITIMACY AND THE EFFECTIVENESS OF THE PARIS PRINCIPLES STANDARDS OF INDEPENDENCE

The legitimacy and credibility of an NHRI rests on its independence from government. An NHRI that is not independent of government (and thus not engaged in scrutiny of state action and robust critique of government action, policy, and legislation) will not be a credible human rights actor. In the Asia Pacific, the independence of NHRIs has been questioned in three main contexts, which we explore next.

---

[60] These include Samoa, Nauru, Solomon Islands, and Papua New Guinea.

In the first, NHRIs have overtly supported a political position taken by the government, most clearly evident in the case of the Fiji Human Rights Commission. In the second, government has reduced the funding of an NHRI, consequently curtailing its activities. In the third, governments have failed to provide the crucial initial support necessary for an NHRI to establish itself as an independent actor within the domestic political and social context.

7.5.1. *Maintaining Political Independence: The Experience of the Fiji Human Rights Commission*

The Pacific region's only NHRI, the Fiji Human Rights Commission (FHRC), was established under the 1997 Constitution of the Republic of the Fiji Islands.[61] The Constitutional Review Committee that recommended the establishment of the FHRC anticipated that the institution would make a significant contribution to achieving the interracial harmony and consequent political stability that Fiji hoped to obtain after the introduction of the 1997 Constitution. It was intended that the primary functions of the FHRC would be to educate the public about the nature and content of the Fiji Bill of Rights and to make recommendations to the government about matters affecting compliance with human rights. The Constitutional Review Committee, presciently, advised that

> this is a role that needs to be exercised with extreme caution. Opinions may legitimately differ on whether proposed ways of dealing with a recognized evil is or is not consistent with human rights. That question is properly a matter for public debate. But a body devoted to the protection of human rights should express its concerns only after undertaking adequate research and seeking to ensure that its recommendations will achieve a proper balance between human rights principles and the problem that the government is trying to address. Otherwise its efforts could be counterproductive.[62]

The Fijian Parliament passed the Human Rights Commission Act in 1999 to give effect to the provisions of the Constitution establishing the Commission. The FHRC was established with a broad range of powers and duties, including the central functions of providing education about human rights, conducting inquiries and investigations into possible infringements of human rights, encouraging governmental

---

[61] Our discussion of the Fiji Human Rights Commission draws on Catherine Renshaw, Andrew Byrnes, and Andrea Durbach, "Implementing Human Rights in the Pacific through National Human Rights Commissions: The Experience of Fiji," *Victoria University of Wellington Law Review*, 40 (2009), 251–78.

[62] Sir Paul Reeves, Tomasi Rayulu Vakatora, and Brij Vilash Lal, "The Fiji Islands – Towards a United Future: Report of the Fiji Constitution Review Commission Parliament of Fiji" (Parliamentary Paper No 34, 1996), 125.

compliance with Fiji's international human rights obligations, advising the government of the human rights implications of its actions and policies, and resolving complaints by conciliation or by referral to the courts.[63] The FHRC continued to function during and after the abortive coup of George Speight in 2000 and the state of emergency that followed, focusing its attention on "investigating allegations of human rights violations and breaches of the Bill of Rights by the police, military and prison authorities during the State of Emergency."[64]

On 5 December 2006 Military Commander Bainimarama of the Royal Fiji Military Forces assumed executive power in Fiji and dismissed President Rate Josef Iloilo, Vice-President Rate Joni Madraiwiwi, and Prime Minister Laisenia Qarase. On January 4, 2007 Commander Bainimarama restored executive authority to President Iloilo, who on January 5, 2007 appointed Commander Bainimarama as interim prime minister. Elections in Fiji, which Commander Bainimarama undertook to hold in February 2009, have been postponed until 2014.

In January 2007, the FHRC released its report: "The Assumption of Executive Authority on December 5th 2006 by Commodore J. V. Bainimarama, Commander of the Republic of Fiji Military Forces: Legal, Constitutional and Human Rights Issues" (the "Shameem Report").[65] Dr. Shameem, who authored the report as director of the FHRC, stated that it was written "in response to the number of requests the Commission has received from the public to determine legality issues"[66] and was based on

> an assessment of the Commander's assumption of executive authority as well
> as on the apparently singular view of both local and international observers and

[63] Fiji Human Rights Commission Act 1999, sec. 7.

[64] By 2002, Dr. Shaista Shameem, director of the FHRC, was able to claim "the Commission has dealt with just about every single right protected in Chapter Four of the Constitution." Notable among its achievements was successfully arguing that the sentence of the convicted leader of the May 2000 civilian coup, George Speight, should be commuted from the death penalty to life imprisonment. The FHRC was also successful in lobbying Parliament to have the death penalty removed from the penal code. "Country Report of Fiji," delivered at the Seventh Annual Meeting of the Asia Pacific Forum of National Human Rights Institutions, November 13, 2002, Delhi, India. An overview of the protection function of the FHRC, written by Dr. Shameem, is provided in B. G. Ramcharan (ed.), *The Protection Role of National Human Rights Institutions* (Boston: Martinus Nijhoff, 2005).

[65] Shaista Shameem, "The Assumption of Executive Authority on December 5, 2006 by Commodore J. V. Bainimarama, Commander of the Republic of Fiji Military Forces: Legal, Constitutional and Human Rights Issues," January 4, 2007 (*hereafter* Shameem Report), www.humanrights.org.fj/ publications/2007/Investigations. See also Shameem's second report on the subject, "The Assumption of Executive Authority on December 5, 2006 by Commodore J.V. Bainimarama, Commander of the Republic of the Fiji Military Forces: Legal, Constitutional and Human Rights Issues, Part II: Report to the UN High Commissioner for Human Rights on Alleged Breaches of International Law and the 1997 Constitution of Fiji in the Removal of the Prime Minister, Laisenia Qarase on December 5, 2006," August 29, 2007, www.humanrights.org.fj.

[66] Ibid, 2.

commentators that the Commander of the [Royal Fiji Military Forces] illegally overthrew the democratically elected and legitimate Government of Fiji on December 5, 2006.[67]

The Shameem Report received the imprimatur of the chair of the Commission, Mr. Acraman, although it appears that it had been written before his term of office began. The report stated that "the Qarase Government was involved in massive violations of human rights in Fiji, constituting crimes against humanity, and made serious attempts to impose ethnic cleansing tactics in Fiji."[68] It further stated that "the crimes against humanity that were committed in Fiji 2001–2006 were condoned not only by the NGOs but also by UN agencies."[69]

The Shameem Report's legal analysis of the assumption of power by Commander Bainimarama in December 2006 was that it was legally justified under the doctrine of necessity; the commander "stepped into the President's shoes" to remove the prime minister and others and to dissolve Parliament.[70] According to the report, the Royal Fiji Military Forces "overthrew an illegally constituted, unconstitutional Government which was acting against the public interest in violation of public security and public safety protections in the Constitution."[71] The report stated that the Royal Military Forces had the "capacity to invoke certain human rights and welfare powers under section 94 of the 1990 Constitution and section 112 of the 1997 Constitution Amendment Act"[72] and that

> since it has the constitutional power to ensure security and protect people, the military does not act unlawfully as long as it keeps to this objective. In view of the rampant abuse of power, privilege, illegalities and wastage of wealth of the Qarase regime, as well as its proposed discriminatory legislation which, if enacted, would have constituted a "crime against humanity" under the International Law Commission's definition, and limited scope for an immediate judicial solution, there appeared to be few options remaining to protect the people of Fiji from an illegal, unconstitutional, anti-human rights, and despotic regime.[73]

Shameem's assessment that the Royal Military Forces "overthrew an illegally constituted, unconstitutional government which was acting against the public interest in violation of public security and public safety protections in the Constitution"[74] was at odds with the assessment of United Nations observers, domestic and international

---

[67] Ibid.
[68] Ibid. 15.
[69] Ibid.
[70] See *Republic of the Fiji Islands v. Chandrika Prasad* [2001] FJCA 2 and cases cited there.
[71] Shameem Report, 30.
[72] Ibid., 6.
[73] Ibid., 31.
[74] Shameem Report, 31.

NGOs, and Fiji's neighbors in the Pacific Islands Forum, all of whom called upon Commander Bainimarama to relinquish power and restore Fiji to democracy. The FHRC's support for Commander Bainimarama led to its politicization and consequent isolation, not merely from its regional and international networks (Fiji resigned from the APF and the ICC following decisions by both bodies to review its compliance with the Paris Principles), but from part of its own domestic constituency, who did not support what was commonly viewed as the coup d'état of the military leader.[75] In the Asia Pacific region, the example of Fiji remains the clearest case of an NHRI's lack of independence in a situation of political conflict.

7.5.2. *Independence and Financial Support from Government*

The Paris Principles require a government to provide its NHRI with adequate funding, the purpose of which is to "enable it to have its own staff and premises, in order to be independent of the government and not be subject to financial control which might affect its independence."[76] A government's withdrawal of significant financial support for an NHRI will of course impede the NHRI's effectiveness, but the significance of funding cuts also lies in the message being sent by government to a commission: that power to define the NHRI's work rests in the hands of government and that government will use this power to constrict an NHRI's autonomy.

The National Human Rights Commission of Korea (NHRCK), established in 2001, has until recently enjoyed the reputation of being an independent and effective commission. ANNI's 2008 report on the NHRCK listed several reasons the Commission's recommendations were respected by government "although these have no legal impact:"

> First, the government is conscious of the fact that society is more aware of human rights. Second, human rights organisations advocate the implementation of the recommendations. Third, the media publishes articles that portray the perspectives of the Commission and human rights organisations. Fourth, former Minister of Foreign Affairs, Ban Ki Moon is now the UN Secretary General while the Republic of Korea is a member of the UN Human Rights Committee [*sic*] (Council) – as such, there is an increasing pressure for the country to pay respect to international human rights law.[77]

As a presidential candidate in 2007, conservative politician Lee Myung-bak pledged to remove the independence of the NHRCK and place the institution under the

---

[75] In *Qarase v Bainimarama* [2009] FJCA 9; Fiji Court of Appeal Civil Appeal No ABU0077 of 2008, April 9, 2009, the Court supported the view that Bainimarama's appointment was unconstitutional.
[76] The Paris Principles, "Composition and Guarantees of Independence and Pluralism."
[77] ANNI, *Report 2008*, 154.

Office of the President.[78] Lee's attempts to fulfill this pledge after his election as president in December 2007 were strongly objected to by the OHCHR, the ICC, the APF, and domestic NGOs. President Lee did not proceed with his proposal. Then in February 2009, South Korea's Minister of Public Administration and Security announced plans to reduce the staff of the NHRCK from 208 to 146, to close three of the Commission's regional offices,[79] and to merge the policy and education divisions of the Commission.[80] The staff reductions were announced in the wake of the mass protests and police use of force to disperse the protests that occurred in South Korea in December 2008[81] and January 2009,[82] of which the NHRCK had been critical.

On 24 March 2009, the (then) chairperson of the APF, Tan Sri Abu Talib Othman, wrote to the South Korean Minister of Foreign Affairs and Trade Yu Myung-hwan, noting "concern that the proposed reductions target the important work of a National Human Rights Institution."[83] Tan Sri Abu Talib Othman urged the minister to ensure that changes are commensurate with reductions to other public agencies: "to do otherwise may be considered indicative of an attempt to interfere with the independent operation of an NHRI, in contravention of the requirements of long-standing and universally accepted international standards."[84] ANNI also wrote to the ICC, urging the body to "take strong action to protect the National Human Rights Commission of Korea, not only to ensure the independence of this institution, but also to send a clear message of support to NHRIs everywhere struggling against efforts to constrain their capabilities."[85] ANNI requested

---

[78] See Forum Asia, *Asian Human Rights Defender* 1 (5), May 2009, http://www.forum-asia.org/news/in_the_news/pdfs/2009/AHRD%205-1.pdf.

[79] In Busan, Gwangju, and Daegu.

[80] ANNI pointed out in a letter addressed to the chairperson of the ICC that the reduction of personnel would mean that virtually all staff members who were recruited from the NGO sector and academe would lose their jobs. NHRCK staff are classified under three categories: (a) General Public Service, (b) Contractual Public Service, and (c) Specific Public Service. Civil servants fell within category A and were guaranteed security of tenure. Staff recruited from the NGO sector or academe were classified under (b) or (c) and had no security of tenure – it was therefore these groups who would be most likely to lose their jobs.

[81] Mass candle-light vigils were held from May to September 2008 to protest the government's decision to approve the importation of U.S. beef. NGOs claimed that police used unnecessary force to disperse the protestors.

[82] The South Korean government's plan to redevelop the Yongsan area in central Seoul as a business district and the evictions and demolitions that followed were met with fierce resistance by protestors. On January 20, 2009, six people died in a fire that broke out in an apartment building during police attempts to end a sit-in by demonstrators.

[83] Letter dated March 24, 2009, from Tan Sri Abu Talib Othman, in his capacity as APF chairperson, to Yu Myung-hwan, www.asiapacificforum.net/files/issues/APF_Letter_To_Korean_Government.pdf/view.

[84] Ibid.

[85] ANNI: letter to ICC from the ANNI on NHRCK Personnel Reductions. The UN High Commissioner for Human Rights, Ms. Navanethem Pillay, also sent an official letter to the Korean Government asking that the independence of the National Human Rights Commission of Korea be guaranteed.

that the ICC place the NHRC under review, in accordance with article 16.2 of the
ICC Statute, relating to situations where circumstances have changed in a way
which might affect compliance with a commission's "A" status.[86] Member of the
ruling Grand National Party in the National Assembly of the Republic of Korea,
Mr. Jun Seon Park, has stated:

> Of course it would be a very big matter to the current government if there was a
> change in the status I think, because the current government keeps a very keen eye
> on the opinions of the international organisations and other human rights organisa-
> tions around the world. It would be very important to us.[87]

Funding cuts have also occurred within the region in other wealthy, developed states
with stable democracies, such as Australia and New Zealand. NHRIs in these countries supplement the work of an independent and (largely) accessible judiciary and
a democratically accountable government. Government responsiveness to the recommendations of the Australian Human Rights Commission and the New Zealand
Human Rights Commission has largely depended on government perceptions of the
political benefits to be gained from implementing the NHRI's recommendations.[88]
The challenge for these institutions is to influence public debate on human rights
issues and to create a political climate in which governments are prepared to respond
to recommendations. Government reduction of funding for an NHRI provides an
indication of the government's attitude toward the importance of an NHRI's work.

In 1998, Australian Human Rights Commissioner Chris Sidoti published "For
Those Who've Come across the Seas,"[89] a 282-page report on Australia's practice
of holding in detention people who arrive without a visa pending a determination
of their refugee status. The report found that the treatment of detainees under the
policies of Prime Minister John Howard, particularly of children, was in violation
of human rights. The report recommended that alternatives to detention – such as
release subject to residency and reporting obligations or guarantor requirements – be

---

[86] See http://www.asiapacificforum.net/services/international-regional/icc/sub-committee-on-accreditation.

[87] Interview with Mr. Jun Seon Park by Catherine Renshaw, Seoul, South Korea, August 23, 2010; copy
on file with authors. Mr. Park is member of the Grand National Party of Korea and representative in
the National Assembly of the Republic of Korea.

[88] For example, in the 1997 report of the Human Rights and Equal Opportunity Commission, "Bringing
Them Home," on the separation of Aboriginal and Torres Strait Islander children from their families,
a key recommendation was that reparation, including an apology and compensation, should be made
to indigenous people affected by policies of forced removal. Both recommendations were rejected by
the Liberal government of then prime minister John Howard. The Labour government of prime minister Kevin Rudd, elected in 2007, made an unreserved apology to the "Stolen Generations" but has
rejected any suggestions to compensate victims.

[89] Human Rights and Equal Opportunity Commission, *For Those Who've Come Across the Seas:
Detention of Unauthorized Arrivals* (Sydney: HREOC, 1998). The title is a reference to a line in the
second verse of Australia's national anthem, "Advance Australia Fair": "For those who've come across
the seas we've boundless plains to share."

pursued. The government's response to the Commission's report, tabled in the Commonwealth Parliament the same year that the report was released, was that "The Chief General Counsel of the Australian Government Solicitor has advised that detention of asylum seekers is not in principle an infringement of Australia's human rights obligations." In 2003, the Australian Commission reported that its budget had been reduced by around $7.3 million during the three years between 1996 and 1999 and that as a result staff numbers had been cut and the positions of some of the commissioners had remained unfilled.[90] Australia's practice of mandatory detention of asylum seekers had bipartisan support and was not amended until the election of a new government in 2007.

The ability of a human rights commission to influence government policy depends on government perceptions of the political desirability of implementing a particular recommendation. It also depends on whether the commission operates within a system of political accountability, with a free media and an independent judiciary. If a government wishes to curtail the influence of an NHRI, it need not necessarily take the politically difficult steps of restricting an NHRI's mandate or amending legislation to limit the powers of commissioners. There are other effective pressure points through which government control can be exercised, such as the reduction of an NHRI's funding (which indicates to a domestic audience and to civil society interest groups that the government discounts an NHRI's recommendations and critique) and the appointment of commissioners who are believed to be sympathetic to government positions on human rights.

7.5.3. Government Support for the Independence and Effectiveness of its NHRI

NHRIs must be independent of the state yet maintain a working relationship with government in order to effect change.[91] The status of an NHRI as a state institution with access to the government is the institution's distinguishing feature vis-à-vis civil society; NGOs perceive one of the primary strengths of an NHRI to be the support and access that an NHRI enjoys from government. Writing in 1998 about the establishment of the Sri Lankan Human Rights Commission, Mario Gomez noted the paradox inherent in an institution's credibility: it is state-sponsored and

[90] During this period, the positions of the Disability Discrimination commissioner and Race Discrimination commissioner were not filled when they became vacant. See Australian Human Rights Commission, "Questions on Notice Arising from Evidence Given to the Senate Legal and Constitutional Legislation Committee's Reference on the Australian Human Rights Commission Legislation Bill 2003," HREOC's response May 8, 2003, http://www.hreoc.gov.au/legal/submissions/qon/8may.html.

[91] Anne Smith, "The Unique Position of National Human Rights Institutions: A Mixed Blessing?" *Human Rights Quarterly* 28 (2006), 904–46

state-funded; at the same time, some of its major functions are to scrutinize state action, educate state actors, and advise state entities.[92]

The experience of NHRIs in the Asia Pacific region, especially in cases where NHRIs have had to operate in post-conflict situations or situations of civil strife, demonstrates that an NHRI's role – as an independent body, capable of robust critique of state institutions, but nonetheless constructively engaged with government – can be fulfilled only when the independent nature of an NHRI is understood by and has the support of government. NHRIs will have difficulty fulfilling their role of facilitating the cooperative efforts of government, the legal profession, NGOs, and international aid organizations if the institution's relationship with and the support it can expect to receive from government is uncertain.

This possibility is particularly acute in the early days of an NHRI's existence. The consequences of uncertainty surrounding a government's support for an NHRI can lead to the institution's being marginalized by international human rights organizations and domestic civil society, and this can adversely affect the ability of the NHRI to enlist the support of these actors in promoting and protecting human rights. Here, we explore the consequences of an NHRI's failure to receive support from government in the early days of its existence. These examples suggest that in some cases, it may be preferable to defer the establishment of an NHRI until there is political stability sufficient to enable an NHRI to fulfill its mandate and that the international community's insistence on the early creation of these institutions may be misplaced.

Nepal's Commission was formally established under the 1997 Interim Constitution, with considerable powers of investigation, the power to provide compensation in cases of human rights violations, and the ability to publicize the names of those who fail to implement NHRC recommendations. The government, however, initially failed to appoint commissioners until litigation was commenced and a court ordered that appointments be made in 2000. In 2005, King Gyanendra dismissed the government and made new appointments to the commission. These commissioners resigned on 9 July 2006, when the Maoist People's Movement came to power.

The government of the People's Movement failed to appoint new commissioners and failed to provide the Commission with funds. It was not until September 2007 that new commissioners were appointed. The NHRC was expected to investigate and provide redress for human rights violations committed during ten years of civil war and to prevent the ongoing violence still occurring in Nepal's seventy-five districts. These factors were combined with a well-publicized dispute between the

---

[92] Mario Gomez, "Sri Lanka's New Human Rights Commission," *Human Rights Quarterly* 20 (1998), 281–302.

under-resourced NHRC and the well-resourced Office of the High Commissioner for Human Rights, which was exacerbated when the OHCHR hired several key NHRC staff members, cementing the hostile nature of the relationship between the two bodies.[93]

In the case of Nepal, the government's lack of commitment to an independent, adequately resourced NHRI resulted in the disaffection of civil society and the marginalization of the NHRI as a significant human rights actor. In April 2006, the ICC placed the "A" status of Nepal's National Human Rights Commission under review.[94]

There is still some debate about when NHRIs should be set up – during a transitional phase or only when a stable government has been established. This question has been (and continues to be) raised in a number of cases in the Asia Pacific.[95] One view is that the lack of support from other nascent institutions (judiciary, media, legal profession) coupled with high expectations that the NHRI will address the massive human rights violations of the past make the effective functioning of a commission extremely difficult. Often, government is not in a position to support the institution financially, and donors must provide the support, adding an additional layer of complexity to the work of the commission. There are also questions about whether civil society participation can properly be harnessed during such a period of turmoil. A related issue is whether the process of establishing the institution will be dominated by international and United Nations agencies involved in constructing the peace; when an institution is created at the behest of the international community, often very quickly, there is less likelihood that it will reflect the priorities and needs of the people.

On the other hand, the existence of an NHRI is one of the indicia of a government able to handle its own human rights obligations and hence signals (to the international community and to its own population) the reclaiming of sovereignty. The work that an NHRI can do in the period of transition to democracy is important, and arguably better done by an institution embedded within the state than an international institution.

---

[93] On February 20, 2009, The OHCHR-Nepal and the NHRC signed an agreement to collaborate and cooperate in promoting and protecting human rights.

[94] In November 2008, the ICC Sub-Committee decided that the NHRC could maintain its "A" status.

[95] The Human Rights Commission of Bangladesh provides another example of chaotic beginnings. The Commission was established by ordinance on September 1, 2008, under the military regime's caretaker government. Its staff of four consisted of a secretary, government joint secretary, computer operator, and office orderly. No premises were provided for the Commission. Commissioners were appointed to assume office on December 1, 2008. After national elections held in December 2009, the newly elected government passed the National Human Rights Commission Act (July 9, 2009), which increased the number of commissioners from four to six. However two commissioners resigned in April 2010 and new commissioners were not appointed until June 22, 2010.

7.6. CONCLUSION

It is unsurprising that NHRIs appeal to states within the Asia Pacific region. NHRIs offer a link between international human rights standards and enforceable national protection in a domestic context, a promising development in a region that has not developed a regional human rights mechanism and which (arguably) lacks the homogeneity to do so, a region in which many states retain some vestige of their recent colonial past and are exploring the parameters of their sovereignty, and in which there is still talk of "Asian values" (although in more muted terms since the Asian financial crisis of 1997). At the same time these factors impel states to preserve their dominion in relation to human rights, many states within the region maintain a desire to prove themselves international citizens, dedicated to implementing the human rights norms of international society. The establishment of NHRIs promises an answer to these complex needs.

Writing in 1998 about the establishment of Sri Lanka's Human Rights Commission, Mario Gomez wrote that "one cannot suppress the cautious optimism that greets the creation of any new human rights institution."[96] "Cautious optimism" is an appropriate phrase: against the positive evolution of civil society's increasingly sophisticated engagement with NHRIs at the regional level and the benefits which have flowed from the work of the region's energetic network of NHRIs must be balanced serious and continuing threats to the institution's independence, which have troubled NHRIs operating within both stable democratic conditions and in the aftermath of civil turmoil.

[96] Gomez, "Sri Lanka's New Human Rights Commission," 302.

8

National Human Rights Institutions in Central and Eastern Europe

The Ombudsman as Agent of International Law

Richard Carver

8.1. INTRODUCTION

The sudden proliferation of national human rights institutions in the Eastern European transition from Communism went largely unremarked at the time.[1] Two decades later, when NHRIs are a more frequent object of study, it is not just the number of NHRIs in the region that is noteworthy but the general uniformity of their structure and function. In the former communist states of Eastern Europe and the Soviet Union – 28 in all[2] – only three have yet to establish an NHRI: Belarus, Tajikistan, and Turkmenistan.

Some political scientists have understandably sought to classify the ombudsman institutions depending on the thoroughness of the democratic transition.[3] The approach taken in this chapter is somewhat different, however. The creation of these institutions coincided with a significant and deliberate turn by the East European states to embrace international legal norms, especially in the field of human rights. The ombudsman institutions have as a principal function the investigation of

---

[1] The general discussion in this chapter largely refers to all the successor states of the former Soviet Union, including those of Central Asia, as well as the former socialist countries of Central Europe. For ease and brevity "East European" is often used in place of the more correct "Central and Eastern European"; no political significance should be read into this terminology.

[2] Kosovo is not included for these purposes.

[3] The Central and Eastern Europe region displays examples of states where democracy has been established securely, partially with the retention of strong authoritarian tendencies, or hardly at all, with ombudsman institutions functioning with varying degrees of effectiveness in each. Alexander Sungurov, "Human Rights Institutionalization in the Former USSR Countries: Development of Ombudsman Institutions," *Pushkin*, October 2008.

Much of the field research that is reflected in this chapter was conducted under the auspices of the United Nations Development Programme Regional Centre based in Bratislava. The author is grateful to the staff there, as well as to the representatives and staff of ombudsman institutions visited in Moldova, Georgia, Lithuania, the Russian Federation, Uzbekistan, and Croatia.

individual complaints from members of the public. Has it been possible for them to embrace standards of international law, which presupposes a broad and systemic approach to human rights, at the same time as providing a remedy for individual grievances?

The first wave of NHRIs in Central and Eastern Europe, beginning in Poland in 1987 and continuing to the mid-1990s, came as part of an overall package of constitutional reform. The most important element of this was that it was underpinned by a notion of *constitutionalism* that contrasted sharply with the instrumentalism that had characterized the application of law under communism. One aspect of this new constitutionalism was a recasting of the relationship between international and municipal law in the new and reformed East European states. Without exception, international human rights standards now became directly applicable within the domestic legal orders. Another reform was the creation of constitutional courts, empowered to review the consistency of statutes and official actions with constitutional standards and, in some instances, also with international law. Part of this package was the national human rights institution, often explicitly empowered to apply international law in its monitoring work and able to refer matters to the constitutional court and recommend legislative reform.

In almost every instance, the institutional model that has been followed has been the ombudsman, usually with an explicit reference to the Scandinavian model in modes of operation but with a broader human rights mandate. The nomenclature varies widely – People's Defender, Parliamentary Advocate, Authorized Person, and so on – yet the structure, mandate, and powers of these institutions are remarkably similar. The selection of a model where a major function is to handle individual complaints from the public is not theoretically inconsistent with being a guardian of constitutionalism or an agent of international human rights law – after all, most NHRIs worldwide have a complaints-handling role.

In practice, however, the deluge of individual petitions from a citizenry that had previously lacked any avenues for complaint and remedy has often been a diversion from the role of the NHRI in the new constitutional order. The complaints brought to ombudsman institutions are not necessarily about the most important human rights issues.[4] Almost certainly they do not emanate from those sections of society most vulnerable to human rights violations. Making complaints-handling the top priority may be to ignore the most serious human rights issues and to neglect the ombudsman's functions in relation to international law.

---

[4]   In Croatia, the largest proportion of complaints to the ombudsman address an issue – delays in the judicial system – that does not even fall within the institution's mandate, yet still the complaints must be processed and referred to the correct agency.

In this chapter I conclude that the best institutions – often also the best-resourced – are the ones that have succeeded in managing a creative tension between the complaints they receive and a systemic approach to human rights issues. These are the ones that have been most effective in applying international law within the domestic sphere.

8.2. NHRIS IN THE NEW CONSTITUTIONAL ORDER

The collapse of the Soviet Union and the other communist states of Central and Eastern Europe was rapid and almost completely unpredicted.[5] The consequence of this surprising historical turn of events was that few plans had been made for post-communist institutional development, either by the international community or at the national level.[6] Zygmunt Bauman noted of the upheavals that overthrew communism:

> It is a constant and the constitutive attribute of systemic revolutions that the forces that destroy the ancien regime are not consciously interested in the kind of change which would eventually follow the destruction.[7]

The transitions that took place in 1989 and the years that followed were not a single, uncomplicated move from communist autocracy to capitalist democracy. The move to a more accountable governmental system, of which NHRIs were part, was accompanied by the destruction of a comprehensive system of social welfare and great hardship for much of the population, especially in the early to mid-1990s. Even today, the removal of the communist pension system creates social problems that fall to the ombudsman institutions to address. Most of the political transitions had additional dimensions that had an impact on all newly created institutions, including the ombudsmen. Most evidently, in the Soviet Union, Yugoslavia, and Czechoslovakia the breakup of multinational states created the need for new national institution-building and created a host of individual issues involving matters such as citizenship and property ownership. These too continue to constitute an important part of the caseloads of the ombudsman institutions in successor states. Finally, while some of the transitions were indeed "velvet revolutions" accomplished entirely peacefully, elsewhere the new states were born out of violence. The states of the former Yugoslavia provide the most obvious example, but the Baltic states, Moldova, and the countries of the Caucasus also saw violent transitions in the early 1990s. In the

---

5 Srđan Dvornik, *Actors without Society* (Berlin: Heinrich Böll Foundation, 2009), 100.
6 Howard Elcock, "The Polish Commissioner for Citizens' Rights Protection: Decaying Communism to Pluralist Democracy through an Ombudsman's Eyes," *Public Administration* 75 (1997), 359–78.
7 Z. Bauman, *Intimations of Postmodernity* (London: Routledge, 1992), 158.

latter instances, the redrawing of national boundaries has not been completed to universal agreement and the status of minorities and the existence of secessionist enclaves continue to confront the work of human rights institutions.[8]

Given the chaotic and unexpected character of the transition it is perhaps surprising that in three important respects the new institutional and legal regimes were almost entirely uniform across the new states of Central and Eastern Europe. First, the ombudsman model was adopted almost universally. Second, the socialist doctrine of dualism in the incorporation of international treaties gave way across the board to a monist approach, whereby ratified treaties are directly enforceable in national courts. Third, many states of Central and Eastern Europe established constitutional courts empowered to conduct abstract and centralized reviews of legislation and governmental practice. The reasons such a diverse group of states hit upon a common set of legal and institutional solutions are beyond the scope of this chapter. They are probably connected, paradoxically, with the unforeseen character of the transitions and the rapid intervention of external actors.[9] The new, or newly democratic, states were simply presented with a short menu of good examples – constitutional courts from Germany, ombudsmen from the Nordic countries – that seemed ready to be transplanted into new soil.[10]

8.2.1. *Choosing the Ombudsman Model*

The rapid spread of ombudsman[11] institutions in the post-communist states might be attributable to the hostility of communist ideologues to these bodies. They appeared to belong to a capitalist system in which the relationship of the citizen to the state was fundamentally different from that under communism, where two institutions in particular supposedly regulated this relationship. First, the Communist Party itself represented the rights of the citizenry in the event of failures of the administration.[12] (The problem here was the difficulty of making any effective separation between actions of the party and the state.) Second, the *Prokuratura* was a

[8] This can be seen in the lingering mutual hostility between the ombudsman institutions of Armenia and Azerbaijan. Since the seating plans at international meetings are always determined alphabetically, the two institutions are destined to continue to enjoy their enmity at close quarters.
[9] See R. H. Linden (ed.), *Norms and Nannies: The Impact of International Organizations on the Central and East European States* (Lanham: Rowman & Littlefield, 2002).
[10] An interesting irony is that the former East Germany finds itself the only post-communist entity outside the former Soviet Union lacking a human rights ombudsman. By virtue of reunification with its capitalist Western neighbor it has a statutory human rights institute with no power to handle individual complaints.
[11] See generally L. Reif, *The Ombudsman, Good Governance and the International Human Rights System* (Boston: Brill, 2004), 155–69.
[12] Richard Carver and Alexey Korotaev, *Assessing the Effectiveness of National Human Rights Institutions* (Bratislava: UNDP, 2007), 4.

mechanism for regulating the legality of administrative actions and the consistency of court decisions. Far broader in scope and powers than the procuracies of Western Europe, which are essentially prosecutorial bodies, the *Prokuratura* was an essential tool of communist governance.[13] Its origin, however, lay not in Marxist doctrine but in empire. The *Prokuratura* was a creation of Peter the Great in the early eighteenth century to ensure uniformity in the application of law throughout the Russian Empire.[14] In its communist reincarnation too, the *Prokuratura* was concerned with legality and uniformity rather than justice, although there is an evident overlap with the traditional function of the ombudsman as an overseer of administrative probity. The post-communist procuracies have sometimes struggled to come to terms with their more limited mandate, and their relationships with ombudsman institutions have often been tense.

It is not, however, entirely correct to state that the ombudsman had no place in communist Central and Eastern Europe. The first such institution in Eastern Europe was established in Poland in 1987.[15] As will be discussed later, Poland was also (at least nominally) monist in its interpretation of the relationship between international and municipal law and had also established a constitutional court before the fall of communism.[16] The reasons for the creation of the ombudsman and constitutional court lie in the peculiarities of semi-democratic reform in Poland during the 1980s,[17] but both were to be highly influential in institutional development throughout the region. The Polish legal system is similar to the civil law systems of Western Europe and the desire for political acceptance by the government after the suppression of the Solidarity trade union in the early 1980s led it to look westward for legal and institutional models and to flirt with the notion of the rule of law. The office of the Commissioner for Citizens' Rights Protection – the ombudsman – was deliberately modeled on West European examples, with the important exception that the commissioner was only permitted to determine the legality of administrative actions (like the Soviet *Prokuratura*) and not adjudicate on the merits of any

---

[13] Jane McGregor, "Mechanisms for Redress of Citizens' Grievances in Russia," in R. Müllerson et al. (eds.), *Constitutional Reform and International Law in Central and Eastern Europe* (The Hague: Kluwer Law International, 1998), 123–32.

[14] Bill Bowring, "Sergei Kovalyov: The First Russian Human Rights Ombudsman – and the Last?" in R. Müllerson et al. (eds.), *Constitutional Reform and International Law in Central and Eastern Europe* (The Hague: Kluwer Law International, 1998), 235–54.

[15] Eva Letowska, "The Polish Ombudsman (The Commissioner for the Protection of Civil Rights)," *International and Comparative Law Quarterly* 39 (1990), 206–17; Howard Elcock, "The Polish Ombudsman and the Transition to Democracy," *International and Comparative Law Quarterly* 45 (1996), 684–90.

[16] Wladyslaw Czaplinski, "International Law and Polish Domestic Law," in R. Müllerson et al., *Constitutional Reform and International Law in Central and Eastern Europe* (The Hague: Kluwer Law International, 1998), 15–36.

[17] Elcock, "The Polish Commissioner for Citizens' Rights Protection," 361.

particular decision.[18] In other words, the commissioner, unlike Western European ombudsman institutions, does not address (or redress) maladministration unless the act in question was illegal. A legal act or decision resulting in an unfair outcome was not covered by the 1987 law. The competencies and powers assigned to the Polish commissioner for Citizens' Rights Protection in 1987 were to become a model for most of the region in the post-communist period.[19]

8.2.2. The Paris Principles and the Legal Powers of Ombudsman Institutions

Most ombudsman institutions in Central and Eastern Europe have powers, mandates, and guarantees of independence that conform, at least on paper, to the requirements of the Paris Principles.[20] The Paris Principles do not require that the existence of an NHRI be enshrined in the constitution, merely stating that "A national institution shall be given as broad a mandate as possible, which shall be clearly set forth in a constitutional or legislative text, specifying its composition and its sphere of competence."[21] More often than not in Central and Eastern Europe the ombudsman institution is contained in the constitution,[22] although one of the institutions specifically studied for this chapter, the Parliamentary Advocates in Moldova, is not. All ombudsman institutions in the region are established by primary legislation.

Officeholders are generally appointed by and are answerable to the legislature. Candidates for the post of ombudsman are generally nominated by either the executive, usually in the person of the president of the Republic, or by a group of parliamentarians. The extent to which parliament exercises oversight of the selection of candidates varies considerably. In Moldova, for example, there is little transparency in the selection of candidates. There is usually only one set of nominees for the three posts of Parliamentary advocate and these are approved automatically. In Slovenia, the ombudsman is directly nominated by the president, though endorsed by the

---

[18] Ibid., 363.

[19] My own discussions with ombudsmen in the region have confirmed the importance of the Polish example, not only in states where this might be expected, such as neighboring Lithuania, but also more remote places such as Georgia.

[20] Principles relating to the status and functioning of national institutions for protection and promotion of human rights (endorsed by UN Commission for Human Rights Res. 1992/54 and UNGA Res. A/RES/48/134 20 December 1993). The Paris Principles, adopted by a conference of national human rights institutions have come to be regarded as the benchmark for NHRIs and provide the main criteria for accreditation by the International Coordinating Committee of NHRIs, which in turn provides speaking rights at the UN Human Rights Council.

[21] Ibid., Principle 2.

[22] For example, in Russia, Ukraine, Poland, Georgia, Croatia, Albania, Bosnia-Herzegovina, Hungary, Kyrgyzstan, Lithuania, Macedonia, Romania, Slovakia, and Slovenia.

legislature.[23] Elsewhere, the process is competitive, with greater transparency and the likelihood of increased public confidence in the outcome.

A common issue, however, is the extent to which civil society groups might participate in nominating candidates for office. In many countries, as noted, nomination is not the sole prerogative of the legislature, since the executive may also put forward its preferred names. In some countries, such as Georgia and Lithuania, nongovernmental organizations are able informally to suggest their preferred candidates to parliamentarians or to comment on those already nominated. Nowhere in the region, however, is civil society participation formally built into the process of selection and nomination.

In some countries, such as Poland and Moldova, there is a formal precondition of legal education or expertise for candidates to the ombudsman post, while elsewhere, as in Georgia, Russia, or Ukraine, there is none. The requirement that the ombudsman be a lawyer is understandable, particularly in situations such as the Polish one, where the institution is required to review the *legality* of administrative decisions. Yet the success of ombudsmen without a legal qualification – such as the public defender in Georgia – suggests that this knowledge is not a sine qua non for the effective defense and promotion of human rights.

Ombudsmen in the region are generally provided with reasonable guarantees of tenure of office. The Polish Commissioner is appointed for a four-year term and can only be recalled if mentally or physically incapable or in breach of the oath of office.[24] The Croatian People's Ombudsman is given a renewable eight-year term, while the Georgian has a renewable five-year term, but also an extensive set of immunities. The Croatian ombudsman may be removed "if the Chamber of Representatives decides,"[25] which assigns it a potentially dangerous discretion. The Croatian official, as is the common practice,[26] must submit an annual report to the legislature. The latter may choose to accept the report, merely to note its submission, or to reject it. Recently, the legislature decided to "note" a critical report rather than approve it,[27] which may function as a form of pressure on the ombudsman. Rejection of the report, which has not so far occurred, would be possible grounds for the legislature to remove the ombudsman. In most instances, however, the reality of reporting back to the legislature seems to be rather different. Several ombudsmen have complained that there is inadequate consideration of their reports, which are

---

[23] Istvan Bizjak, "The Human Rights Ombudsman of Slovenia," in K. Hossein et al. (eds.), *Human Rights Commissions and Offices: National Experiences throughout the World* (The Hague: Kluwer International Law, 2000), 373–7.

[24] Act of July 15, 1987 on Commissioner for Civil Rights Protection, art 5.

[25] Act on the Ombudsman of September 25, 1992, art 19(3).

[26] The Georgian People's Defender has the rather onerous obligation to present six-monthly reports.

[27] *Republic of Croatia Ombudsman: Report on Work for 2008.*

seldom discussed in full session of parliament, but only by the committee responsible for human rights issues.

The primary significance of the adoption of the ombudsman model is that the institutions are built around the consideration of complaints from members of the public. The Polish ombudsman is empowered to consider only complaints against public authorities, but institutions elsewhere in the region, including Moldova, Georgia, and Lithuania, may also consider complaints against private bodies in certain circumstances. (This is most often the case where, as in Lithuania and Croatia, for example, there are specialized institutions addressing the rights of specific vulnerable groups such as women and children.) Croatia provides an interesting example of an institution whose mandate has recently been expanded to address discrimination issues across both public and private authorities.[28]

Ombudsman institutions generally have adequate powers to allow them to consider and investigate complaints. They can generally compel the attendance of witnesses and the production of evidence. They have powers to visit administrative offices and, in most instances, police and military offices, and prisons and other closed institutions. Where there is a frequent problem, however, is in ensuring a response from the relevant authorities to the ombudsman's recommendations. In common with most such institutions, the Central and Eastern European ombudsmen do not have the power to enforce a remedy to the complaints they receive. They make a finding and a recommendation to the relevant authority. In the event that there is a finding that a criminal offense has been committed, the matter may be referred to the procuracy (although not necessarily with great positive effect). In the vast majority of cases, however, the ombudsman is dependent on the good faith of the body complained against to implement any adverse recommendation. In practice, authorities that choose to ignore the recommendations may do so with impunity. There are two main reasons for this. First, in some instances the law does not require the authority to respond or imposes no penalty for failure to respond. Second, ombudsman institutions have such a heavy caseload that they are generally unable or unwilling to monitor response to recommendations, preferring to move on to new cases.[29]

8.2.3. *Constitutional Courts and Review of Legislation*

In one other important respect, most Central and East European states have followed the Polish model. By a 1982 law, Poland established a constitutional court to review

---

[28] See discussion later in the chapter.

[29] Typically a case file will remain formally open until a final response has been received from the authority complained against. My interviews with complaints staff in four different institutions suggest that in most cases there is no active monitoring of what action the authority takes.

legislation and regulations to determine their conformity with the constitution. The court came into existence in 1986, just a year before the establishment of the commissioner for Citizens' Rights Protection. In fact the power of the Polish constitutional court was limited by the fact that the legislature, the Sejm, could overrule its findings by a two-thirds majority. Nevertheless, it provided some indication of a move toward the notion of a *Rechtstaat*, a state based upon the rule of law, a shift that was reflected in the 1989 constitution. Many other Central and East European states have followed Poland in adopting the constitutional court model. The template for the constitutional court is Germany, although France and other West European civil law countries have a similar system. In common law systems such as the United States, constitutional review is concrete and decentralized. Judicial review of the constitutionality of a law or action is triggered by litigation in a specific case within the regular justice system. The German and East European process of constitutional review is generally abstract and centralized. It is not necessarily related to the consideration of any particular case. Indeed, the constitutional courts stand outside the regular judicial system – unlike, say, the U.S. or British Supreme Court, which stands at the apex of a judicial pyramid. East European constitutional courts are sometimes considered not to belong properly to the judicial branch at all, enjoying as they do a form of legislative veto.[30] Some constitutional courts – for example, in Poland, the Czech Republic, the Slovak Republic, and Hungary – are empowered to annul statutes that do not comply with the state's treaty obligations.[31]

Since constitutional review is abstract rather than being driven by individual litigation, the court requires a reference from some other body to alert it to constitutional issues that may require review. Ombudsman institutions play this role rather effectively.

One other relevant power is that of legislative initiative – to be able to propose draft laws directly to the legislature. Most ombudsman institutions in the region do not fully enjoy this power, in contrast to several similar human rights ombudsman institutions in Latin America.[32] In practice, in most countries in the region, legislative proposals are made in three different ways. First, they can be made indirectly by reference to the constitutional court, as already described, at

---

[30] See the discussion in W. Sadurski (ed)., *Constitutional Justice, East and West: Democratic Legitimacy and Constitutional Courts in Post-communist Europe in a Comparative Perspective* (The Hague: Springer, 2002).

[31] Theodor Schweisfurth and Ralf Alleweldt, "The Position of International Law in the Domestic Legal Orders of Central and Eastern European Countries," *German Yearbook of International Law* (1997), 164–80.

[32] An exception, prior to the amendment of the institution's founding statute in 2004, was the Authorized Person of the Oliy Majlis on Human Rights in Uzbekistan who, by virtue of herself being a deputy in the legislature, was provided with legislative initiative. Since the amendment, the Authorized Person need not be a deputy of the Oliy Majlis and has no ex officio legislative initiative.

least in terms of reviewing legislation. Second, they may be made informally, by reviewing existing or draft laws and making proposals to the executive. Or third, several ombudsman institutions enjoy what might be described as a power of "soft" legislative initiative. That is, they may draft proposals for laws or amendments to existing legislation and present them to sympathetic parliamentarians – such as members of the committee responsible for human rights – who will then formally present them. Although these options lack the formality and certainty of the power of legislative initiative proper, they generally appear to have been used effectively and with discretion.

8.3. THE EAST EUROPEAN OMBUDSMAN AND INTERNATIONAL LAW

One of the most important functions of national human rights institutions is as a means of domesticating international human rights law.[33] It is a truism that international law itself prescribes no particular means whereby obligations, whether contained in treaties or in general or customary international law, are applied within the domestic legal system. Article 27 of the Vienna Convention on the Law of Treaties states that national law may not be used as a reason that a state fails to meet its treaty obligations.[34] Yet the means whereby this is achieved is left to the state itself. Likewise, the International Covenant on Civil and Political Rights, for example, requires states parties to take "legislative or other measures" to give effect to the rights contained in the treaty, including the right to a remedy.[35]

The two main approaches to domesticating international law are usually described, somewhat imprecisely, as "monism" and "dualism." Monism posits that international and domestic law constitute a single seamless system. The implication is that ratified treaties and customary international law are directly applicable within the national legal system. Dualism is the doctrine that international and domestic law occupy different spheres of application, with the consequence that international law can only be applied domestically when it is explicitly enacted into national law. There are considerable variations within these two broad approaches and, most important, an apparently infinite range of ways in which these doctrines apply in practice. Hence, for example, the theoreticians of monism would appear to suggest that international law stands at the apex of the legal system, yet the judicial systems

---

[33] Richard Carver, "A New Answer to an Old Question: National Human Rights Institutions and the Domestication of International Law," *Human Rights Law Review* 10 (2010), 1–32.

[34] Vienna Convention on the Law of Treaties (adopted May 23, 1969, entered into force January 27, 1980), 1155 UNTS 331, art 27.

[35] International Covenant on Civil and Political Rights (adopted December 16, 1966, entered into force March 23, 1976), 999 UNTS 171, art 2.

of "monist" states will, more often than not, consider international law in a subordinate position to the national constitution.

The role of NHRIs has increasingly been to provide an avenue whereby international human rights standards are applied directly within the national sphere, regardless of the means by which international law is domesticated. The Paris Principles set out various means whereby NHRIs would interact with the international system, including advocating the ratification of relevant human rights treaties, scrutinizing national legislation for consistency with international human rights standards, and participating in state reporting to human rights treaty bodies and UN Charter mechanisms. To this list can be added at least two more ways in which NHRIs in recent years have attempted to apply international standards domestically. First, they increasingly refer directly to internationally guaranteed human rights, rather than just constitutional rights, in their monitoring and complaints-handling. Second, the recent trend in human rights treaty law has been to designate a specific role for national human rights mechanisms in monitoring or implementing a state's treaty obligations.[36] Ombudsman institutions in Central and Eastern Europe have actively implemented international law obligations in all of these ways.

This increased assertion of international standards in the work of NHRIs has been primarily driven by the intense promotional work carried out by UN bodies and other transnational actors.[37] It has been embraced by many of the institutions themselves because invoking international human rights may provide textual and interpretative guidance that goes beyond mere reference to domestic constitutions and laws. Arguably there is a danger here: that reference to international standards may create a distance from homegrown priorities and values. In the East European context, however, both the public and officialdom view human rights issues with constant reference to the "Europeanization" of their societies. The prospect of accession to the European Union – or at least of a closer relationship with the EU – constitutes a sort of looming human rights conditionality that allows international, or at least regional, human rights discourse to be readily accepted.

The notion of the individual asserting rights under international law against his or her own state is a recent one. It was certainly one that had no place within the communist legal systems, which had a conservative view of international law as serving simply to regulate relations between states, regardless of their internal political and

---

[36] Optional Protocol to the Convention against Torture and other Cruel, Inhuman or Degrading Treatment or Punishment (adopted December 18, 2002, UNGA Res 57/199, entered into force June 22, 2006), Convention on the Rights of Persons with Disabilities (adopted December 13, 2006, entered into force May 3, 2008).

[37] Sonia Cardenas, "Emerging Global Actors: The United Nations and National Human Rights Institutions," *Global Governance* 9 (2003), 23–42.

social system.[38] Hence they were instinctively and reflexively, if not always explicitly, dualist in their approach to the relationship between international and municipal law. The two partial exceptions to this were Poland and Yugoslavia. The Polish legal system, like that of other states in non-Soviet Eastern Europe, was a civil law system that resembled those of Western Europe. According to the pre-communist constitution of 1921, ratified treaties automatically became part of the internal legal order, as would generally be the case in Western civil law systems. The Communist Constitution of 1952 was silent on the issue, leading to considerable debate as to whether ratified treaties were part of the domestic legal system. The scholarly consensus was that the previous monist approach prevailed, yet the interpretation given by the courts was, rather more significantly, that ratification of treaties had consequences only in the international sphere, not domestically.[39] It was not until 1990, after the fall of communism, that a Polish court, the Supreme Administrative Court, found that ratified treaties "require neither transformation nor incorporation and are binding *ex proprio vigore*." The court also found that in the event of conflict, treaties took precedence over domestic law. These views were echoed by the constitutional court two years later.[40]

This trajectory from de facto dualism to explicit monism was one followed by all the ex-communist states, both inside and outside the former Soviet Union.[41] However, the mere doctrinal statement that international law forms part of the internal legal order is not a complete answer to the problem of how to implement or enforce rights domestically. For example, it may frequently be the case – especially in those states that did not fully overhaul their legal systems and legislation after communism – that laws remain on the statute book that are inconsistent with international human rights obligations. In some instances ratified treaties enjoy a constitutional status, but more often they are in a mid-ranking position in the hierarchy of law, above domestic statutes but below the national constitution.[42] Invariably there is also a need to elaborate the specific content of internationally guaranteed rights. In both of these areas ombudsman institutions in Central and Eastern Europe have played a leading role.

It is noteworthy that along with the shift to monism, there has been a strong tendency in Central and Eastern Europe to assign ombudsman institutions an explicit role in promoting and protecting *international* human rights standards, not merely those rights contained in national constitutions. Table 8.1, covering selected ombudsman institutions in Central and Eastern Europe, indicates the nature of

---

[38] G. I. Tunkin, *Theory of International Law* (London: Wildy, 2003).
[39] Czaplinski, "International Law and Polish Domestic Law," 17.
[40] Schweisfurth and Alleweldt, "The Position of International Law," 167.
[41] Ibid., 179.
[42] Ibid., 179.

TABLE 8.1. *The source of protected rights in selected ombudsman laws*

Country	Year established	National	Treaty	Unspecified	ICC status
Albania	1999			1	A
Armenia	2003		1		A
Bosnia	1999		1		A
Croatia	1992			1	A
Czech Republic	1999			1	n/a
Georgia	1996		1		A
Kazakhstan	2002			1ᵃ	n/a
Kosovo	2000		1		n/a
Lithuania	1994		1		n/a
Macedonia	2003		1		n/a
Moldova	1997		1		B
Montenegro	2003		1		n/a
Poland	1987	1			A
Romania	1997			1	C
Russia	1997		1		A
Slovakia	1993			1	B
Slovenia	1993			1	B
Total		0	9	7	n/a

ᵃ However, Kazakhstan does have a mandate to promote ratification of international human rights treaties. Statute on Commissioner for Human Rights, art. 3.

the mandate assigned to the institution in its founding statute. The distinction is between a mandate explicitly confined to national constitutional rights, an explicit mention of international human rights, or generic and unspecified human rights without reference to their source. None of the institutions is confined to national constitutional rights, with 53 percent explicitly referring to international law. By way of comparison, this table is drawn from a larger database that I compiled of seventy national human rights institutions drawn from all geopolitical regions. In that database, 10 percent of the *total* number (indicating the Central and East European NHRIs) had mandates that were confined to rights contained in the national constitution or bill of rights.[43]

The law establishing the Protector of Human Rights and Freedoms in Montenegro refers to "generally recognized rules of international law,"[44] and the Kosovan ombudsman law to "international human rights standards."[45] The Russian ombudsman

---

[43] Carver, "A New Answer to an Old Question." Of the total surveyed, 45 percent had a mandate to defend human rights generically (unspecified mandate), and the remaining 45 percent had a mandate to apply international human rights law.

[44] Law on the Protector of Human Rights and Freedoms, 2003, art. 1.

[45] On the Establishment of the Ombudsperson Institution in Kosovo, UNMIK/REG/2000/38.

statute refers to "universally recognized principles and norms of international law" – a far cry from Soviet dualist doctrine. And so on.

The Moldovan statute also provides interpretative guidance:

> In the event of any inconsistencies between international treaties and agreements on basic human rights to which the Republic of Moldova is a party and its domestic laws, the international laws shall prevail.[46]

This is a particularly strong statement, both because it is explicitly contained within the law establishing the national human rights institution and because it asserts not merely the direct applicability of international treaties within the domestic legal order but also their primacy. However, it is generally understood throughout the region that ombudsman institutions will be directly involved in the implementation of treaty-based rights.

It might be argued, of course, that no particular significance is to be attached to the fact that ombudsman institutions apply international rather than domestic rights. The transition has already been effected from dualism to monism and in monist legal regimes the courts are obliged to apply international law as part of the internal legal order. Yet, as the example of pre-1989 Poland indicates, it is by no means automatic that courts will arrive at such an interpretation – a particular problem when there are residual inconsistencies between domestic legislation and international standards (which national human rights institutions are well placed to identify). In any case, the actual status of international standards within the domestic legal hierarchy may be unclear. Second, it could be argued that the rights protected in international law are not significantly different from those contained in the democratic constitutions of Central and Eastern Europe. On a day-to-day basis, does it actually make any practical difference that ombudsman institutions can invoke international law? There is obvious merit in this skeptical observation, yet the importance of international law for NHRIs in monist jurisdictions is that it elucidates the *content* of rights. For NHRIs in dualist jurisdictions, by contrast, references to international law tend rather to be used to expand the *scope* of rights.[47] The ombudsman institutions of Georgia and Lithuania, for example, can ensure that the rights protected are indeed the same as the rights contained in the treaties to which their states are party.

This application of international law occurs, *mutatis mutandis*, in four principal ways: applying international law in monitoring and case-handling; reviewing

---

[46] The Law of the Republic of Moldova on Parliamentary Advocates, No 1348, October 17, 1997, art.10(2).

[47] Such is the case, for example, with the Australian Human Rights and Equal Opportunity Commission which is empowered, in its complaints-handling and monitoring, to invoke rights contained in various specified treaties, regardless of whether they are actually ratified by Australia, still less transformed into municipal law.

legislation for compliance with international law; participating in reporting to international treaty bodies; and in direct implementation of treaty obligations.

8.3.1. *International Law in Monitoring and Case-Handling*

It is not unusual for ombudsman institutions in the region to refer to international standards in their handling of individual complaints. For example, the Moldovan Parliamentary Advocates have found that discrimination alleged in individual petitions breaches not only the rights guaranteed in the national constitution, but also the "Universal Declaration of Human Rights, the European Convention for Protection of Human Rights and Fundamental Freedoms and other international and regional instruments."[48]

The Georgian Public Defender's Office (PDO) frequently invokes international standards. For example, in the case of an individual prisoner who was not released on completion of his sentence, the PDO's report referred to treaties that Georgia had ratified or acceded to (the European Convention on Human Rights and the International Covenant on Civil and Political Rights) and the Universal Declaration of Human Rights.[49] In the case of a journalist compelled to reveal a confidential source of information, the PDO referred to the jurisprudence of the European Court of Human Rights (ECtHR) in *Goodwin v. United Kingdom.*[50]

Goodwin is a good example of how references to international law elucidate the content of rights. Freedom of expression is, of course, guaranteed in the Georgian Constitution. Reference to the ECtHR clarifies that protection of journalists' sources is part of the content of that right. However, invocation of international law occurs more often – and more effectively – in relation to the institutions' general monitoring activities. The Georgian PDO also makes extensive use, for example, of international standards in its monitoring of places of detention. The UN Standard Minimum Rules on the Treatment of Prisoners and other soft law international sources are used to give substance to the Public Defender's recommendations on conditions of detention.

8.3.2. *Reviewing Legislation for Compliance with International Law*

In practice, no ombudsman institution in the region has the capacity to conduct a comprehensive audit of legislation to ensure conformity with international law. What happens instead is that the need for legislative reform arises on an ad hoc

---

[48] Centre for Human Rights of Moldova, *Annual Report 2005*, 18.
[49] Centre for Human Rights of Moldova, *Annual Report 2007*, 20.
[50] Ibid., 76–77.

basis, usually prompted by particular complaints submitted to the institution or from monitoring activities. These are then dealt with in one of four ways.

First, the ombudsman institution usually has the opportunity to review all draft legislation that may bear upon human rights. The institution usually has a close relationship with the human rights structures within the legislature, to which it is accountable, which helps ensure that there is early warning of impending draft laws. More often, however, government departments submit drafts to the institution for review. In Uzbekistan, for example, the ombudsman has bilateral agreements to this effect with relevant ministries.

Second, the matter may be referred to the constitutional court. The Moldovan Parliamentary Advocates, for example, may apply to the constitutional court "seeking a ruling on the constitutionality of any laws, decisions of parliament, decrees of the president of the Republic of Moldova, decisions and orders of the government, and their consistency with generally accepted human rights principles and international law."[51] A decision of the constitutional court on such an application would have binding effect[52] and clearly is an effective mechanism for ensuring the compatibility of municipal law and practice with human rights standards. Between 1999 and 2006, the Parliamentary Advocates made fifty-one such applications. As of 2007, the court had ruled on twenty of these, finding wholly or partially in favor of the applicants on twelve occasions.[53]

Third, the ombudsman institution may make its own proposal for legislative reform, in the form of a draft submitted either directly to the legislature or to the relevant government department.

Fourth, and perhaps most commonly, the ombudsman institution may simply make a recommendation for legislative reform. The Georgian PDO has done this particularly forcefully. In 2004, for example, its biannual report analyzed the inconsistency of the prohibition of torture in Georgian law with the state's obligations under the UN Convention against Torture (CAT), including the failure of Georgian law to include any of the key elements of the definition of torture contained in the CAT.[54] The ombudsman's advocacy resulted in amendments to the constitution and the criminal procedure code, strengthening the prohibition of torture. The following year the PDO recommended a change in the definition of a child in Georgian law to bring it into line with the state's obligations under the UN Convention on the Rights of the Child.[55] Similarly, the Lithuanian Children's Ombudsman made recommendations that succeeded in bringing

[51] The Law of the Republic of Moldova on Parliamentary Advocates 1997, art. 31.
[52] Constitution of the Republic of Moldova, art. 140.
[53] Carver and Korotaev, *Assessing the Effectiveness*.
[54] Public Defender's Office, *Report on Conditions of Human Rights in Georgia in 2004*, 15.
[55] Public Defender's Office, *Report on Conditions of Human Rights in Georgia in 2005*, 132.

the criminal code into conformity with the CRC. The cases represent a more general practice.

8.3.3. *Engagement in Treaty Body Reporting*

Until recent years ombudsman institutions in Central and Eastern Europe have not been centrally involved in reporting to treaty bodies (or in relations with the UN special mechanisms). There have probably been three reasons for this absence. The first has been a reluctance to take on an additional workload. This has certainly been the explanation for the low profile of the Georgian PDO in treaty body reporting, confining itself to responding to requests for information from the Ministry of Foreign Affairs.[56] It should be noted that the Georgian institution already has a particular heavy reporting burden, with the requirement for biannual reports to parliament.

Second, there is a strong residual reluctance among some ombudsman institutions in the region to criticize their governments on the international stage. The Russian ombudsman has stated that the country should speak with "one voice" in international forums, while the Uzbekistan ombudsman has been a member of the government delegation to the Universal Periodic Review.

The third reason for the low priority in reporting to treaty bodies is perhaps the lack of clarity in the Paris Principles on the precise obligations of NHRIs in this regard.[57] The relationship between NHRIs and treaty monitoring bodies is clearly crucial if the former are to play an effective role in implementing and monitoring treaty obligations. Yet the relationship is in reality a triangular one – treaty body-state-NHRI – the exact nature of which has never been very precisely articulated. The Paris Principles stated the role of the NHRI thus:

> To contribute to the reports which States are required to submit to United Nations bodies and committees, and to regional institutions, pursuant to their treaty obligations, and, where necessary, to express an opinion on the subject, with due respect for their independence.[58]

The meaning here is opaque. Since the process of contributing to states' reports would, of necessity, involve some expression of opinion, this principle is presumably intended to refer to two separate roles that NHRIs might play: *first*, contributing to states' reports and, *second*, expressing an opinion directly to the treaty body separate from that contribution. It is also unclear whether the final qualifier, "with due

---

[56] Carver and Korotaev, *Assessing the Effectiveness*.
[57] One East European ombudsman has requested of the author a note clarifying precisely this point in order to help in formulating the policy of his institution.
[58] The Paris Principles, A(3)(d).

respect for their independence" is intended to refer to the expression of opinion or to the totality of the NHRI's role in the reporting process. Although syntactically the former appears more likely, this is tautologous, since the only purpose of expressing a separate opinion would be when this differed from the position of the state. So the intention was presumably that the overall role of NHRIs in treaty reporting was to be conducted in a manner that does not compromise their independence.

The lack of clarity was not initially helped by the mixed messages emanating from the treaty bodies themselves. In 1993 the Committee on the Elimination of Racial Discrimination recommended that NHRIs "should be associated with the preparation of reports and possibly included in government delegations in order to intensify the dialogue between the Committee and the State party concerned."[59] The more recent opinion of the Committee on the Rights of the Child appears now to reflect the predominant position among UN treaty bodies: "it is not appropriate to delegate to NHRIs the drafting of reports or to include them in the government delegation when reports are examined by the Committee."[60] A much more active approach by the treaty bodies in soliciting the views of NHRIs has prompted the beginnings of a more active engagement on the part of the ombudsman institutions of Central and Eastern Europe. A recent case in point would be the (highly critical) shadow report by the Lithuanian Children's Ombudsmen on the implementation of the Optional Protocol to the CRC on the sale of children trading, child prostitution, and child pornography.[61]

8.3.4. Treaty Implementation: OPCAT and the CRPD

An important impetus to the engagement of NHRIs in treaty monitoring has been the recent drafting of treaties in which the implementation role of the national institution is written into the text of the treaty itself. In one sense this represents a full circle – returning to the idea floated in the 1940s whereby national committees would monitor adherence to human rights norms.[62] Yet it goes further, since the new role for NHRIs is in relation to treaties rather than customary obligations alone, with states parties to these two instruments required to give the relevant national institutions the necessary powers to carry out various functions specified in the treaty itself. This is a radical new method of implementing treaties. Hence the Optional

[59] CERD General Recommendation XVII, "On the Establishment of National Institutions to Facilitate the Implementation of the Convention," UN Doc A/48/1993 18 1(e).

[60] CRC General Comment No. 2, "The Role of Independent National Human Rights Institutions in the Promotion and Protection of the Rights of the Child," CRC/GC/2002/2 2002.

[61] *The Children's Rights Ombudsman of the Republic of Lithuania*, Annual Report of 2008, 37.

[62] A. Pohjolainen, *The Evolution of National Human Rights Institutions: The Role of the United Nations* (Copenhagen: Danish Institute for Human Rights, 2006), 30.

Protocol to the Convention against Torture requires states parties to establish a national preventive mechanism (NPM) within a year of ratification.[63] While there is nothing to say that an NPM is coterminous with an existing NHRI, in practice this has generally been the case, a situation clearly envisaged by OPCAT, which makes reference to the Paris Principles.[64]

The Convention on the Rights of Persons with Disabilities is a very different type of instrument from OPCAT. Whereas the latter has the limited and specific aim of preventing torture, largely through visiting places of detention, the former is a treaty of very wide scope. It does not aim to create new rights but to provide a mechanism for guaranteeing the existing range of human rights to people with disabilities.[65] Hence the role assigned to national institutions is broader than in OPCAT and is not prescribed in any detail. Article 33(2) simply requires states parties to "designate or establish" independent mechanisms to "promote, protect and monitor implementation" of the Convention. As in OPCAT, reference is made to the Paris Principles for guidance on the status and functioning of national institutions.[66] In some East European countries, such as Croatia, a new Disabilities Ombudsman has been created to fulfill the state's obligation under Article 33(2), along the lines of the Children's Ombudsman institutions that have been strongly promoted in the region to monitor implementation of the CRC.

However, it is in the designation of national preventive mechanisms under OPCAT that the region has had greatest experience. Seventeen states in Central and Eastern Europe have ratified the OPCAT, of which nine have so far designated their national preventive mechanisms.[67] All those that have identified their mechanism have made the ombudsman institution the sole or principal NPM. In most instances ombudsman institutions already carry out the visits to closed institutions that are the main function of an NPM. However, the existing ombudsman statutes are not always adequate, failing to provide the full range of powers specified in the OPCAT. Hence new legislation has or will be required expanding the institution's formal competencies.

Assigning a major additional responsibility to the existing national human rights institution has often been controversial. Ombudsman institutions in the region

[63] OPCAT, art. 17.

[64] Ibid., art. 18(4).

[65] Frédéric Mégret, "The Disabilities Convention: Human Rights of Persons with Disabilities or Disability Rights?" *Human Rights Quarterly* 30 (2008), 494; Rosemary Kayess and Phillip French, "Out of Darkness into Light? Introducing the Convention on the Rights of Persons with Disabilities," *Human Rights Law Review* 8 (2008), 1.

[66] CRPD, art. 33(2).

[67] Albania, Armenia, Azerbaijan, the Czech Republic, Estonia, FYR Macedonia, Moldova, Poland, and Slovenia are the nine that have designated NPMs. Source: Association for the Prevention of Torture, *OPCAT Country Status: Ratification and Implementation*, June 2009.

(as elsewhere) are invariably underfunded and overworked and have not always welcomed the extra role. One such was the Parliamentary Advocates in Moldova, where designation as the NPM coincided with discussion of the creation of an additional Parliamentary Advocate with responsibility for children's rights (but utilizing the existing infrastructure of the institution). There was an understandable reluctance within the institution to assume the additional responsibility. Finally, Moldova adopted a mixed model, with the Parliamentary Advocate at the core of an NPM that also comprises a new Consultative Council.[68] A similar approach has been adopted in Slovenia and is under discussion in Georgia. This has provided a framework for cooperation with civil society that was previously lacking, while the profile and prestige of the Parliamentary Advocates have been heightened and the institution has acquired new detention monitoring skills. Most important, perhaps, amendments to the founding statute of the Parliamentary Advocates expanded the institution's legal powers to carry out visits to places of detention.[69]

8.4. APPLYING INTERNATIONAL LAW: THE PRACTICAL OBSTACLES

The adoption of ombudsman institutions with the power to invoke and implement international law represents, at least on the face of it, a considerable advance on the situation before the fall of communism where there was no independent institution to protect citizens' rights and no mechanism for invoking international legal protections. The question of the actual impact of these institutions on the enjoyment of rights is a far trickier issue that has not so far been studied with any depth or rigor. I would argue, however, that two main obstacles to effectiveness may be easily identified. The first, self-evidently, is the slow pace of democratization throughout the governmental institutions as a whole (combined, in many instances, with a lack of political will at the top). Although ombudsman institutions are endowed with certain legal powers of investigation, they have no capacity to enforce their recommendations. Ultimately they depend upon the goodwill of other governmental bodies for their effectiveness.[70] The second obstacle, I argue, derives from the choice of institutional model for NHRIs in Central and Eastern Europe. The ombudsman model, driven as it is by individual complaints from members of the public, may not be the most effective way of tackling systemic human rights problems.

---

[68] Law on Modification and Completion of the Law, No. 1349-XIII of October 17, 1997, on Parliamentary Lawyers, No. 200-XVI of 26.07.2007, Official Gazette No. 136–140/581, August 31, 2007.

[69] Ibid.

[70] It is generally not regarded as possible for NHRIs to have direct powers of enforcement (with one or two exceptions). However, several East European ombudsmen are seeking to acquire the power to apply to the courts to enforce their recommendations. As well as guaranteeing procedural fairness, such a mechanism would also retain the relative informality and accessibility of the ombudsman's complaints process, which is part of the strength of such institutions.

8.4.1. The Slow Pace of Democratization: The Example
of the Security Sector

Lack of accountability of the entire state bureaucracy was an obvious characteristic of the communist systems of Central and Eastern Europe (though not of them alone) and one that was not ended overnight by the change of political system. Of their very nature, ombudsman institutions aim to increase the responsiveness of state bureaucracies, at least on an individual, case-by-case basis. The security sector provides a particularly striking example of the difficulties of enforcing accountability. The security sector, for these purposes, is assumed to include all state agencies that have legitimate authority to use or order the use of force. These would normally include the military, paramilitary units, border guard, police, and prison authorities.

In the former Soviet Union, the percentage of the overall caseloads involving complaints against security sector agencies varies enormously, from 43 percent in Georgia, down to around 20 percent in the Baltic states of Latvia and Lithuania. A very low figure of 16 percent in Uzbekistan is probably explained by the absence of legal powers for the Uzbek ombudsman to compel security sector institutions to provide evidence, with a corresponding public perception of ineffectiveness. At the other end of the scale, the Georgian Public Defender has a high public profile and is perceived as an outspoken critic of the authorities.

In the countries of the Caucasus and Central Asia, the main security sector agency against which complaints are lodged is the police. Further west, in Moldova, Latvia, and Lithuania, prisons and other correctional facilities generate the highest number of complaints. In the case of the Baltic states this may reflect the progress in police reform that will have been a condition of membership of the European Union. In Moldova, the high proportion of complaints from prisoners may have been generated by a vigorous and extensive program of prison visiting. In all countries surveyed, complaints against the military, paramilitary forces, and border guards figured low on the list.

Ombudsman institutions surveyed stated that they received the highest degree of cooperation from police and the staff of pre-trial detention centers and prisons. This contrasted with a general lack of interaction with the military, paramilitary, and border guard.

The ombudsman institutions' own perceptions of the problems that they encounter in exercising oversight of the security sector provide interesting indications of the nature of the issue. Security sector agencies are often unwilling to recognize that they have committed human rights violations or to comply with recommendations from the ombudsman institution, such as recommendations to start an investigation or discipline an official. It was felt to be easy for security sector officials to conceal and remove evidence of human rights violations. Security sector agencies were perceived to contain strong internal networks that were not readily susceptible to influence from outside. It was also noted that ombudsman institutions face particular difficulties in gathering information about human rights violations affecting officials from the security sector itself, such as the abuse of conscripts in the military.

These observations are interesting, but perhaps not very surprising. What was encouraging was that ombudsman institutions felt that the power most of them enjoyed to make unannounced visits to security facilities was a particularly effective way of gathering relevant information.[71] The increase in visiting powers that will be enjoyed by institutions that are designated as OPCAT NPMs is thus a promising sign. On the other hand, respondents to the survey indicated a low level of response to their recommendations from government institutions. Given that NHRIs are unable to enforce recommendations – or indeed broader reform of the security sector – they are only ultimately as effective as the response they receive from government, legislature, and procuracy.[72]

8.4.2. *Systemic Reform: Hobbled by the Ombudsman Model*

"The [ombudsman institution] is like a post office. They receive mail and transfer it to the relevant institution."[73]

The Paris Principles do not require that an authentic national human rights institution handle individual complaints or petitions. This is rather curious, given the almost universal assumption that this will be the primary means by which NHRIs address human rights problems.[74] Certainly in Central and Eastern Europe the assumption has been that NHRIs should be primarily complaints-handling bodies. Hence, as suggested, the adoption of the ombudsman model, which, while not exclusively geared to addressing complaints, is nonetheless built around that central function. The primacy of complaints can be seen in almost all the founding statutes of NHRIs in the region.

Yet there is a very strong case for saying that complaints-handling is actually one of the least effective means of addressing human rights issues; that the most effective NHRIs are those that address in a systemic fashion the most important human rights problems.[75] The experience of ombudsman institutions in Central and Eastern Europe appears to validate this proposition. It is not so much that the institutions have

[71] Of the institutions surveyed, Uzbekistan and Latvia did not have this power.

[72] My own interviews with prosecutors in several countries suggest a poor level of cooperation with ombudsman institutions.

[73] An NGO human rights activist describes the work of the ombudsman in one Eastern European country.

[74] R. Carver, *Performance and Legitimacy: National Human Rights Institutions* (Versoix: International Council of Human Rights Policy, 2000), 110.

[75] Ibid., 71–4.

been ineffective – rather that the most useful ways of effecting reform and improvements have been departures from their central work of complaints-handling.

A. Complaints-Handling

The Parliamentary Advocates of Moldova have presented a fairly clear example of an institution sinking in a mire of complaints. The Parliamentary Advocates received 1,913 petitions of complaint by mail in 2006. For 2005, the total was 1,271 in the capital, Chisinau, of which the largest numbers concerned matters under the headings for personal security and dignity, the right to work, free access to justice, and the right to social assistance and protection. The largest number of petitions came from prisoners (658 or more than half the total). A further 151 petitions were addressed to the three branch offices outside the capital.[76]

The four years 2003–06 generally saw an annual rise in the number of petitions, from 1215 in 2003, with the largest jump between 2005 and 2006.[77] Additionally, some 1,500 complaints annually were received by the Parliamentary Advocates personally during their reception hours (from 1,422 in 2003 to 1,715 in 2006).[78] The institution maintains that the rise in petitions was evidence of its success, although this conclusion cannot be supported without qualitative data indicating, for example, why complainants had approached the institution. Whatever the explanation for the rise, it seems clear that the institution's complaints-handling process is meeting a considerable need.

The importance of a proactive approach was underlined by the Parliamentary Advocates themselves in their 2005 report:

> The methods of psychological influence are usually applied on persons, by infringing the right to petition. Due to the situation of the persons in custody, they do not have the possibility to address petitions to the Centre for Human Rights of Moldova or to other institutions describing the cases of inadequate treatment of criminal prosecutors. This possibility appears later after the event has happen and the things invoked by the petitioners cannot be proved.[79]

This is precisely the reason an exclusively complaints-based approach is inadequate. Certain types of human rights issue are less likely to be the subject of complaints, while certain categories of people are less likely to complain. Petitioners to national human rights institutions are generally less likely to be from the most vulnerable social groups and are less likely to have suffered human rights violations of a type

---

[76] *Report on Human Rights Observance in the Republic of Moldova in 2004, 2005, 2006, 2007.*

[77] Ibid.

[78] Ibid.

[79] Centre for Human Rights of Moldova, *Report on Human Rights Observance in the Republic of Moldova in 2005* (Chisinau: Centre for Human Rights, 2005), 14.

that depend on secrecy (torture being a prime example). This is why it is so important for a national human rights institution to set its own priorities for monitoring and investigation, utilizing, but not wholly dependent upon, the data yielded by the complaints process.

The elements of a systemic approach to human rights issues would include the following:

- The identification of priority human rights issues, whether from analyzing complaints or from monitoring the human rights situation
- The allocation of resources for work on priority issues (including raising funds where necessary)
- Initiating monitoring of the priority issues
- Conducting public information campaigns (for example, through the mass media) on these same issues
- Reviewing laws related to these issues
- Training officials in skills required to protect human rights in the identified priority areas

In its initial years the Lithuanian Children's Rights Ombudsman did not take this approach, instead focusing largely on complaints. With the arrival in 2005 of a new incumbent, Rimantė Šalaševičiūtė, however, a distinct change in approach could be seen. A major priority was identified each year and made a focus of the institution's work. From 2005 to 2008 these priority issues were care institutions, adoption and care in the family, education and schools, and poverty.

The systemic approach to children's rights issues does not apply only to the issues identified as a major priority each year. Complaints are analyzed on a regular basis. Three complaints on the same issue constitute a "problem," which is the trigger for the institution to conduct systematic monitoring. In this way, the Children's Rights Ombudsman avoids the twin pitfalls of, on the one hand treating complaints as isolated or discrete issues, or on the other hand failing to attend adequately to the individual concerns of complainants. The Children's Rights Ombudsman has had an apparent impact in these priority areas, as well as communicating policy on these issues, both to stakeholder institutions and to the general public.

Croatia presents an interesting example of an ombudsman institution that has made a deliberate effort, largely under the pressure of external factors, away from a complaints-driven reactive approach, toward one that is systemic and proactive. Three changes in the status of the Croatian People's Ombudsman (CPO) have prompted this shift.

First, a new Anti-Discrimination Act came into force in January 2009. This assigned a new role and powers to the CPO as an equality body – that is, a body that would be responsible for developing policy proposals on anti-discrimination issues, rather than merely handling complaints of discrimination. The act also defined, in broad terms, the CPO's relationship with the other statutory ombudsman institutions.

Second, the CPO has been designated a Status A national human rights institution by the International Coordinating Committee of National Human Rights Institutions, under the terms of the Paris Principles. The implication of this, as understood by the institution's leadership, is that the CPO will need to take on certain broader functions of an NHRI, beyond complaints-handling, and that its legal responsibilities and powers should be reviewed.

Third, Croatia has ratified the OPCAT. The Croatian government has indicated that the CPO will be designated as that country's National Preventive Mechanism, although no formal announcement has been made at the time of writing.

These three developments all point toward a more active approach for the CPO, moving somewhat away from the past centrality of complaints-handling. Typically, however, there are several other factors that suggest that the burden of complaints will actually increase. The passage of a Free Legal Aid Act, by introducing more stringent standards for registration as a legal aid provider will exclude many NGOs and probably correspondingly increase the burden on the CPO. It is proposed that the mandate of the CPO be expanded to allow the institution to deal with complaints about the functioning of the judiciary and thereby address the chronic delays that have been the subject of cases against Croatia in the European Court of Human Rights. At the same time, the decision to create two regional offices for the CPO is likely to increase the number of complaints received, by promoting the visibility and accessibility of the institution.

Each of these three examples – Croatia, Lithuania, and Moldova – features an institution that understands the need to identify priority human rights issues rather than being driven by complaints. But only one of these, Lithuania, by virtue of being relatively well resourced and in a relatively favorable human rights environment, has actually managed to make the transition.

B. Interaction with Civil Society

Another almost universal feature of effective national human rights institutions is a high level of interaction with civil society bodies, including human rights non-governmental organizations.[80] Such an approach is strictly in line with the Paris Principles. The Principles refer to "necessary guarantees to ensure the pluralist representation of the social forces (of civilian society) involved in the protection and promotion of human rights."[81] The Paris Principles then go on to enumerate

[80] Carver, *Performance and Legitimacy*, 97–9.
[81] Paris Principles, B1.

the relevant bodies in civil society, including nongovernmental organizations, trade unions, lawyers, doctors, and scholars.

This discussion is specifically in relation to the appointment process (where, as discussed earlier, there is generally scant involvement of civil society in Central and Eastern Europe). The Paris Principles "refer to the fundamental role played by the non-governmental organizations" and require national human rights institutions to develop a working relationship with such organizations.[82]

The objective problem in Central and Eastern Europe, however, is the continuing weakness of civil society as a long-term consequence of the "Communist (de) construction of society."[83] Srđan Dvornik notes the paradox of the "late-communist 'awakening' and the postcommunist 'disappearance' of civil society."[84] This may result in part from a deliberate demobilization of civil society by the elites that have ruled since the fall of communism.[85]

Arguably, NHRIs that have a strong emphasis on complaints-handling will be less likely to work extensively with NGOs, although the Croatian CPO has used the nongovernmental human rights sector as a means of outreach to communities outside the capital, Zagreb, where hitherto it has had its only office. Nevertheless, it is common in many Central and East European countries (including Croatia) to hear strong criticism of the ombudsman institution for its failure to engage adequately with NGOs.

In Moldova, the Parliamentary Advocates hold consultations with nongovernmental organizations (described by the former as regular and by the NGOs as infrequent). The complaint from NGOs is that such meetings take place only to discuss specific agenda items (such as joint meetings or training events). NGO activists tend to favor such consultations on a regular basis. The paradox in Moldova is that NGOs generally appear to have better funding than the national human rights institution and, in a reverse of the usual situation, it is in the financial interests of the Parliamentary Advocates to seek partnerships with NGOs. As noted above, the designation of an OPCAT NPM that includes both the Parliamentary Advocates and NGOs will perforce lead to more regular collaboration.

Elsewhere in the region some of the more effective ombudsman institutions have also opted for a more structured relationship between themselves and civil society. A month after her appointment, the present Lithuanian Children's Ombudsman

---

[82] Paris Principles, C7.
[83] The phrase is Srđan Dvornik's: *Actors without Society*, 32.
[84] Ibid., 100.
[85] Bill Lomax identified a deliberate *trahison des clercs* in post-communist Hungary, where the new ruling intelligentsia appropriated the mantle of civil society and displayed a particular hostility to autonomous social activism: Bill Lomax, "The Strange Death of 'Civil Society' in Post-communist Hungary," *Journal of Communist Studies and Transition Politics* 13 (1997), 41–63.

gathered all NGOs together and agreed on an agenda for their future collaboration. Since then, the ombudsman convenes a roundtable on strategic planning twice a year. This also includes other stakeholders – including ministries and other institutions. The outcome of these planning sessions is the formation of working groups to address the different issues relating to children's rights.

The Lithuanian children's NGOs representatives also credit the ombudsman with an improvement in the relationship between NGOs and parliament. She has gained them access to the social affairs committee of the Seimas. Also, again in a reversal of the usual situation, the children's NGOs, many of them service providers funded by the Ministry of Social Affairs, seem reluctant to criticize the government. They appreciate the outspoken and critical stand taken by the ombudsman.

The Georgian Public Defender's Office has also developed a more formalized model for collaboration with civil society. In late 2005 and early 2006 the institution established a National Council of Ethnic Minorities (comprising some eighty NGOs from all over Georgia) and a Council of Religions, which includes representatives of twenty-three religious denominations functioning in the territory of Georgia (except the Georgian Orthodox church and the Jehovah's Witnesses). They meet every two to three months with various thematic working groups meeting weekly. There is also a Monitoring Council for Psychiatric Hospitals under the Patients' Right Centre, which includes representatives of most NGOs working in this area.

The National Council of Ethnic Minorities in particular has made an important contribution on a human rights issue that heads the list of priorities for many NHRIs in the region.[86] The council developed a set of recommendations for the Georgian government on implementation of the Framework Convention for the Protection of National Minorities, which entered into force in Georgia on April 1, 2006. These recommendations were met with interest by the representatives of the relevant state bodies and came under active consideration, although subsequent political events have made the situation of Georgian minorities even more difficult.

Another particular strength of both the Lithuanian and Georgian institutions has been their readiness to use the mass media, not only for the generic "awareness-raising" undertaken by most NHRIs but also to mobilize public concern about major human rights issues. In the Georgian case this was undoubtedly helped by having a former journalist in the position of public defender for several years. In the absence of direct enforcement powers for the ombudsman – and with generally weak civil society structures – the media take on a particular importance in the work of NHRIs. However, many Central and East European ombudsmen have been strikingly poor in their use of the media.

---

[86] The Croatian CPO, for example, still receives the majority of its complaints from members of ethnic minorities.

In both the Lithuanian and Georgian examples, much of the positive outreach to civil society could be attributed to the character of the incumbent ombudsman. The importance of factors like a systemic approach to human rights issues and collaboration with civil society are illustrations of how a formalistic legal analysis of the structure and competencies of NHRIs will not provide complete answers as to their impact and efficacy. However, the vulnerability of these approaches to a change in the leadership of the institution shows how some of the formal, structural characteristics – such as the appointment process and the maintenance of effective independence – remain preconditions for effective national human rights institutions in the longer term.

National human rights institutions in general are highly dependent on the quality and independence of their leadership in order to be effective. When leadership resides in a single member, as in most of the region's ombudsman institutions, these bodies may be vulnerable to outside pressure and inconsistent in their performance over time. An independent appointment process is more likely to ensure the right caliber of leader, but this is by no means assured. Civil society involvement in the process is a further step in the right direction. Strengthening the staff capacity of the ombudsman institutions goes some way toward institutionalizing the independence and vigor of a strong leadership, yet it does not really overcome the risk that replacing the head of a single-member NHRI can easily render it much less effective.

8.5. CONCLUSION

The institutional model, mandate, and powers assigned to the ombudsman institutions of Central and Eastern Europe have displayed one overriding positive characteristic: they have established the ombudsman as an agent of international human rights law. The institution is rooted in the new constitutional order and has domestic legitimacy – in both the formal and social sense. Hence the institution is able to expand the scope of domestic rights protection and act as a stimulus to further reform of the legal order.

On the other hand, however, the adoption of a model for NHRIs where complaints-handling is perceived as the central function has diverted many institutions away from their role in implementing international human rights law. Of course, it is possible to apply international standards in the processing of individual complaints and examples in this chapter show how some East European ombudsmen have successfully done so. Yet the sheer arithmetic of scarce resources means that a heavy caseload diverts them from a more systemic approach.

This creates a genuine dilemma for ombudsman institutions. For each individual complainant, their own matter is the priority. For decades they were denied an effective means of righting and redressing maladministration, illegality, or human rights violations by the state bureaucracy. The ombudsman provides the most accessible and effective means for doing so. Yet the petitions that come before the ombudsman are not necessarily the most important human rights issues. They come from those with ready access to the institution about issues where there is a reasonable expectation of success. The ombudsman has an obligation to try to satisfy these expectations – but also a broader obligation to direct the institution's resources toward overall improvements in respect and enjoyment for human rights. The two obligations are in tension, and often in conflict.

The most effective institutions in the region have succeeded in imposing their own priorities, using complaints as an indicator of systemic issues rather than a series of discrete problems to be resolved in isolation. Such, for example, has been the achievement of the Lithuanian Children's Ombudsman, always with an eye to the need to apply the international standards for the protection of human rights contained in the Convention on the Rights of the Child.

At the other end of the spectrum is an institution such as the Authorized Person in Uzbekistan, where the complaints processed bear very little relationship to the very serious human rights violations conducted by the state security sector, which are effectively out of bounds. The fine words in the founding statute about international treaties and general principles of international law count for little in practice.

Of course, Lithuania is a European Union state with a stable democratic framework, while Uzbekistan remains an authoritarian oligarchy and this may provide sufficient explanation for the different functioning of the two institutions. Yet examples that are midway between the two may also be instructive. The Georgian PDO has succeeded in applying international law on the issue of torture, largely outside the framework of its complaints caseload. Its systemic approach and willingness to build alliances in civil society has proved an effective way of bringing international standards to bear. Institutions like those in Moldova and Croatia, which have been largely complaints-driven hitherto, are trying to change direction, well aware that a different approach is needed if the international standards are to be applied.

9

National Human Rights Institutions in Latin America

Politics and Institutionalization

Thomas Pegram

9.1. INTRODUCTION

This chapter offers an in-depth study of the institutionalization of national human rights institutions (NHRIs) in Latin America, institutions that are often created under adverse political conditions. The analysis demonstrates the variable institutionalization of the Iberian model of the NHRI – the Defensoría del Pueblo – showing its distinctive political accountability function as a potential bridge between state and society.[1] More specifically, relying on extensive primary material, including interviews with key participants, the analysis disaggregates the formal and political dimensions that shape NHRI institutionalization within Latin America. The empirical evidence assembled here indicates that development of formal design principles is important in explaining Defensoría institutionalization. However, the political dimensions of the Defensoría's interactions with organized state and social actors are often decisive.

The chapter adopts a distinct understanding of institutionalization, one that incorporates not only formal design principles but also the ability of informal rules, norms, and practices to decisively shape behavior and outcomes. Investigation into the political significance of informal rules, norms, and practices animate some of the most promising contemporary scholarship on democracy.[2] The analytical framework for evaluating the development of NHRIs in Latin America's democratic regimes focuses on three interrelated, but distinct, features of institutionalization: formal

---

[1] This chapter uses the generic Spanish title Defensoría del Pueblo ("Human Rights Ombudsman"), or Defensoría for short, to refer to the organization in Latin America and Defensor or Defensora to refer to the individual throughout. Other titles for these entities in the region include Procuraduría de los Derechos Humanos ("Human Rights Attorney") and Comisiones de los Derechos Humanos ("Human Rights Commissions").

[2] Steven Levitsky and María Victoria Murillo, "Variation in Institutional Strength," *Annual Review of Political Science* 12 (2009), 115–33.

design principles, relations with organized state and social actors, and rules of access across institutional arenas. This frameworks draws upon political accountability theory to locate the position of the Defensoría in relation to three significant clusters of actors: vertical (executive branch), horizontal (state checks and balances), and social (organized civil society).[3]

Despite the prominence of these organizations in political systems throughout Latin America, political and institutional scholarship has largely neglected NHRIs as a subject of analysis. A principal objective of this chapter and the volume more generally is to address such theoretical and empirical deficits, exposing limitations in conventional approaches toward understanding the political accountability function of an institution that generally lacks coercive faculties. Through case study analysis, what emerges is a highly contextualized picture of an institution sometimes capable of bridging an often problematic state-society divide characterized by the failure of democratic regimes to meet social needs and demands. However, this chapter also demonstrates that the institutionalization of the Defensoría can be compromised by volatile processes of democratization in Latin America, reflected in unstable rights frameworks, political conflict, and insistent demands for more responsive government.

The chapter begins with a review of Defensoría formal design features and their modification. This is followed by an evaluation of the office's interaction with organized state and social actors. The third section analyzes the Defensoría's access to formal and informal accountability arenas within and outside state structures. The chapter concludes by reflecting on the implications of this study for understanding how the experience of Defensorías and institutional development more broadly is informed by the complex interplay of actors based within and outside of state structures.

9.2. FORMAL DESIGN PRINCIPLES

According to formal analyses, the robustness of formal design principles is important to the institutionalization of NHRIs. However, the dynamic experience of Defensoría institutionalization in Latin America suggests that some re-specification of formal analytical frameworks is necessary. The section addresses five key formal

---

[3] See Guillermo O'Donnell, "Horizontal Accountability in New Democracies," *Journal of Democracy* 9 (1998), 112–26. Also E. Peruzzotti and C. Smulovitz (eds.), *Enforcing the Rule of Law: Social Accountability in the New Latin American Democracies* (Pittsburgh: University of Pittsburgh, 2006). A remaining category of relations is external. Without denying their significance and evolution in recent years, external relations are generally a secondary consideration for the local activity of Latin American Defensorías and not directly addressed in this chapter. See Chris Sidoti in this volume, "National Human Rights Institutions and the International Human Rights System."

design principles: (1) constitutional status; (2) mandate and powers; (3) budgetary autonomy; (4) operational autonomy; and (5) appointment procedures.

9.2.1. *Constitutional Status*

Scholars argue that constitutional status grants the Defensoría enhanced stability due to the elevated cost of repeal. The empirical evidence is broadly consistent with the claim that constitutional entrenchment is conducive to institutional stability. However, constitutional status does not always deliver the associated benefits, with cases in Latin America deviating from the dominant claim on at least two counts: (1) Defensorías included within the constitution but subject to interference, and (2) Defensorías not in the constitution, or without such status for a significant time, that nevertheless display relative autonomy.

A general trend toward assigning constitutional status to Defensorías in the region is apparent with all six offices originally created by legislation or executive decree, except for Costa Rica and Uruguay, subsequently elevated to constitutional rank.[4] No office in the region has been stripped of constitutional status once assigned. A number of cases are illustrative of the protection afforded by constitutional status. For instance, the Honduran Commission was created in 1990 by executive decree as an adjunct office to the secretary of state and remained under executive auspices until its inclusion within the constitution in 1995. A subordinate position prior to 1995 limited the autonomy of the office, with wider ramifications for the activity of the office. The first commissioner, Leo Valladares, characterized the time leading up to 1995 as "years of preparation."[5]

Similar to Honduras, other offices display lengthy time lags between initial establishment and constitutional reform. The Panamanian Defensor experienced a seven-year interlude between legislative creation in 1997 and constitutional elevation in 2004. Feedback loops resulting from its inferior status were highly negative, with a 1998 ruling by the Supreme Court declaring various articles of the instituting law to be unconstitutional.[6] Despite continuing to meet resistance from within the judiciary,[7] the 2004 reform has rectified many structural limitations, not least in the transfer of Defensor appointment powers from the executive to the legislature.[8] As such, this empirical material does appear to support the claim that constitutional entrenchment is preferable.

---

4 These cases include Argentina, Ecuador, Honduras, Mexico, and Panama.
5 Carlos Quesada, *En Procura de la Paz: Tercer Informe Sobre las Procuradurías de Derechos Humanos de Guatemala, El Salvador y Honduras* (San José: CODEHUCA, 1996), 22.
6 Ruling by the Supreme Court of Panama, February 12, 1998.
7 See *La Prensa* [Panama], April 3, 2001.
8 Reformatory Act, No. 1, 2004 altering art. 129 and 130, Chapter 9, Title III of the Constitution.

However, other experiences in the region complicate the picture. Defensorías have been created by variably democratic regimes in response to a range of different incentives. Contexts defined by high levels of political conflict, power asymmetries, and only a loose adherence to the constitutional order pose a formidable challenge to functionalist assumptions. A number of Defensorías installed within the constitution at point of origin fit this profile, notably the Colombian, Guatemalan, Mexican, and Peruvian offices, which were created by authoritarian regimes or in the midst of armed conflict. Under such conditions, constitutional status may do little to safeguard, let alone guarantee, independence.

The case of Mexico provides a good illustration. Created by executive decree in 1990, the commission was included by amendment within the 1992 Constitution in the context of a highly managed transition to democracy by an authoritarian regime. The elevation of status may have provided the office with the appearance of greater autonomy, but executive influence remained considerable.[9] In this instance, the process of constitutional elevation was used by the governing regime to further constrain the commission's jurisdiction and mandate.[10] The office was finally granted autonomy in the 1999 constitutional reform. This could be interpreted as a sign of institutional strengthening one year prior to formal transition to electoral democracy. However, the 1999 constitutional reform was used by the Mexican Senate as an opportunity to dismiss the presiding commissioner, casting this reform as a "false positive."[11]

In contrast, the Costa Rican Defensoría has been repeatedly frustrated in its wishes for constitutional status.[12] Nevertheless, the institution has experienced no significant formal interference. This relative stability reflects a political context that, in regional perspective, is highly institutionalized. As Rodrigo Carazo, a former Defensor, puts it, "It is very nice to have [constitutional rank] but it is not necessary. At least not in Costa Rica, where there is no fear that Congress will shut down the institution tomorrow."[13] Nevertheless, the experience of the Defensoría does reveal, albeit to a lesser extent, similarities to other cases that lack constitutional status, with oversight robustly resisted by the judiciary and a lack of safeguards, such as immunity, informing the relationship of the entity with elected officials.[14]

9 J. M. Ackerman Rose, *Organismos Autónomos y Democracia: El Caso Mexicano* (México, D.F.: Siglo XXI Editores, 2007), 130.
10 Ibid.
11 See *La Jornada* [Mexico], October 15, 1999.
12 Defensoría de los Habitantes [Costa Rica], *Informe Anual 2002* (San José: DHR), 3.
13 Rodrigo Alberto Carazo, Costa Rican Defensor 1993–1997, interview by author, San José, Costa Rica, August 31, 2007.
14 See *Diario Extra* [Costa Rica], January 3, 2003, 15.

9.2.2. *Mandate and Powers*

Defensorías lack legal enforcement powers. However, they do generally have a broad mandate, comprehensive powers of investigation, and certain legal prerogatives. Unsurprisingly, the distributional potential of such powers has been noticed by other powerful actors and has prompted attempts to constrain the Defensoría following activation. For instance, the decision by the Panamanian Supreme Court in 1998 noted above also removed the Defensoría's supervisory mandate.[15] Similarly, the constitutional reform of the Mexican office in 1992 restricted the office's jurisdiction and imposed a strict interpretation of its mandate with a focus on case reception.[16] However, actual modification of powers is rare despite indications to the contrary. Threats by public officials to formally constrain Defensorías are often not followed through, as occurred in Honduras following criticism by the commission of government handling of humanitarian aid.[17]

In turn, more unusually, offices have been subject to positive modification. In Costa Rica, the regulative law that followed constitutional insertion significantly expanded the scope of the Defensoría's mandate.[18] The 2006 reform of the Mexican Commission giving the office constitutional review powers is highly significant for the most constrained office in the region.[19] Nevertheless, formal strengthening of Defensorías is not necessarily positive when placed in context. In the Mexican case, reform is likely to conform to a process of political bargaining more than to an attempt to actually empower the office.[20] Specifically, the outgoing administration may have sought to constrain its successor, elected months later. Other instances of empowerment, such as new mandates, also warrant critical appraisal, especially when such expansion is not accompanied by new resources. In Nicaragua and Guatemala, the Procuraduría has been designated the formal legal redress mechanism for Laws of Access to Public Information without a commensurate increase in resources.

9.2.3. *Budgetary Autonomy*

Interference through budget allocation has proved to be a popular means of exerting control over Defensorías in the region. The regional norm is for the Defensoría's budget to be allocated by the legislature. The removal of direct influence by the

---

[15] Ruling by the Supreme Court of Panama, February 12, 1998.
[16] Ackerman, *Organismos Autónomos y Democracia*, 130.
[17] Michael Dodson, "The Human Rights Ombudsman in Central America: Honduras and El Salvador Case Studies," *Essex Human Rights Review* (2000) 3, 29–45.
[18] Executive Decree no. 22266-J, June 15, 1993.
[19] Cámara de Diputados, Boletín 2931, April 20, 2006.
[20] Private communication with John Mill Ackerman Rose by email July 21, 2009.

executive in budget allocation is often cited as an important formal safeguard.[21] Interference or not, Defensorías throughout Latin America are uniformly under-funded given the scope of their mandates. A notable exception to this rule is the Mexican office with a budget for 2008 of $75 million.[22] Table 9.1 summarizes the (not readily available) budgetary information for six of fourteen cases under analysis.

These figures demonstrate how governments can use budget freezes and cuts to exert control over the Defensoría. Often under the pretense of austerity measures, governments have imposed punitive budget cuts, as in Colombia and Panama in 2003, with reductions of 25 and 20 percent, respectively. Honduras may be the poorest office among those surveyed in Table 9.1. However, available data show Nicaragua is the poorest Defensoría in the region. Repeatedly subject to budget freezes and cuts, the Nicaraguan Procuraduría was subject to a 50 percent reduction in 2001, an attempt, according to one observer, to "asphyxiate" the institution.[23] The situation has not improved in recent years, with the budget for 2008 standing at a lowly $1,454,545 or $0.26 per capita.[24]

Per capita and percentage of GDP expenditure figures for these Defensorías indicate that, with the possible exceptions of Bolivia, Mexico, and Peru, all offices labor under inadequate financial support from the state, and many rely heavily on international funding. Honduras has traditionally enjoyed the highest levels of international funding in the region, with state provision finally matching international donations in 2003. Originating primarily from Scandinavia and Spain, international aid is a vital source of support. However, dependency on foreign donations can also pose risks, offering little long-term security as well as establishing disincentives for adequate provision by the state. For instance, the Danish and Swedish governments withdrew all funding from the Nicaraguan Procuraduría in 2006, citing non-compliance with attached conditions.[25] The withdrawal of $1,800,000 from the Peruvian Defensoría's budget in 2006 by USAID led to a narrowly averted crisis.[26]

9.2.4. *Operational Autonomy*

Operational autonomy means the Defensoría is not subject to any imperative mandate, does not receive instructions from any authority, and carries out its function with autonomy. More specifically, the Defensoría ideally has autonomy over recruitment, can define its internal structures, and can develop a strategic plan. Reflecting

---

[21] In Colombia, Ecuador, Honduras, Nicaragua, and Venezuela the budget forms part of state expenditure, essentially controlled by the executive.
[22] *The Economist*, "Big, Expensive and Weirdly Spineless," February 14, 2008.
[23] *El Nuevo Diario* [Nicaragua], October 10, 2000.
[24] *El Nuevo Diario* [Nicaragua], February 15, 2008.
[25] *El Nuevo Diario* [Nicaragua], May 9, 2006.
[26] See Defensoría del Pueblo [Peru], *Informe Anual* (La Paz: DP, 2007), 24.

TABLE 9.1. *Budgetary and operational data on defensorías in Latin America 2002–2006*

Year	2002	2003	2004	2005	2006
Bolivia					
Budget (total $)	4,049,934	4,462,464	4,040,482	3,975,462	4,879,813
GDP (% of)	0.05	0.06	0.05	0.04	0.04
Per capita ($)	0.46	0.49	0.44	0.41	0.50
International cooperation (%)	53.3%	62.7%	54.6%	61.2%	66.1%
Number of regional offices	5	8	8	8	8
Costa Rica					
Budget (total $)	2,738,132	2,976,833	3,092,388	3,559,847	3,511,457
GDP (% of)	0.02	0.02	0.02	0.02	0.02
Per capita ($)	0.67	0.71	0.73	0.82	0.80
International cooperation (%)			11%		2.2%
Number of functionaries			144	151	152
Number of regional offices	4	4	4	4	4
Guatemala					
Budget (total $)	4,514,890	5,046,256	5,983,851	8,733,658	9,093,804
GDP (% of)	0.02	0.02	0.02	0.03	0.03
Per capita ($)	0.38	0.42	0.48	0.69	0.70
International cooperation (%)	1.2%	2.5%	2.7%	1.9%	2.4%
Number of functionaries	61	59	69	62	84
Number of regional offices	28	28	28	33	36
Honduras					
Budget (total $)	1,300,000	1,400,000	1,400,000	1,500,000	1,700,000
GDP (% of)	0.02	0.02	0.02	0.02	0.02
Per capita ($)	0.20	0.21	0.21	0.22	0.24
International cooperation (%)	69.2%	50.0%	42.8%	46.7%	41.2%
Number of functionaries	94	114	119	126	129
Number of regional offices	14	15	16	16	16
Panama					
Budget (total $)	2,800,000	2,325,000	2,325,000	2,345,000	2,437,000
GDP (% of)	0.02	0.02	0.02	0.02	0.01
Per capita ($)	0.92	0.75	0.73	0.73	0.74
International cooperation (%)		1.2%			
Number of functionaries	125	124	122	126	138
Number of regional offices	3	1	0	0	0
Peru					
Budget (total $)	22,469,134	27,698,322	31,989,180	33,499,228	35,935,647
GDP (% of)	0.04	0.05	0.05	0.04	0.04
Per capita ($)	0.85	1.04	1.19	1.23	1.30
International cooperation (%)	26.2%	29.0%	38.2%	41.9%	18.9%
Number of regional offices	23	28	28	28	28

Sources: Database compiled by author with information received directly from individual offices, with the exception of Bolivia, which was compiled from annual reports 2002–2006. All per capita data are from the Economic Commission for Latin America and the Caribbean (CEPAL). GDP data are from IMF World Economic Outlook Database, October 2009.

concern over operational autonomy, many Defensorías have drafted their own regulative laws in consultation with civil society. In Costa Rica, the regulative law was drafted by Defensoría personnel and endorsed by executive decree, thereby avoiding congressional negotiation. This outcome may be widely viewed as positive for institutional autonomy but it also raises important questions as to the accountability of the Defensoría itself. Similarly, the Peruvian regulative law was drafted in large part by civil society jurists.[27] Even in Mexico, as a concession of "semi-independence," the Commission was permitted to draft its own internal regulation.[28]

Despite such formal safeguards, operational autonomy is subject to broader informal practices such as clientelism. Considering the area of recruitment: a vertical organizational culture common to Latin America's civil administration and with little public service ethos often combines to undermine meritocratic procedures. This can be particularly damaging in a context of deep ambivalence or hostility between state structures and society. For instance, the Guatemalan Procuraduría has been criticized for a general lack of transparency over internal procedures and accused, as late as 1996, of recruiting personnel with links to the military.[29] In contrast, transparent recruitment of highly qualified personnel can quickly become a potent source of organizational credibility under difficult operating conditions.[30] Operational autonomy appears to be reflective of the leadership of individual Defensors more than of formal rules, with individuals rejecting or perpetuating norms of patronage upon appointment.[31]

In terms of internal structures, a key area of development is decentralization. Decentralizing structures can serve to raise the national profile of the Defensoría through penetration at the sub-national level. Local presence can also convert into a source of political leverage against elected officials.[32] Table 9.1 shows that all the Defensorías sampled have developed local infrastructure to some extent or used mobile units to reach remote areas. Guatemala and Peru stand out as highly decentralized offices. However, in the smaller territory of Costa Rica, decentralization has also been actively pursued. One way in which powerful actors may constrain Defensoría expansionism is through the budget. The Nicaraguan office's precarious

---

[27] Renzo Chiri, Secretary General of the Comisión Andino de Juristas (CAJ), interview by author, Lima, Peru, July 8, 2005.

[28] Ackerman, *Organismos Autónomos y Democracia*, 122–24.

[29] Comisión para la Defensa de los Derechos Humanos en Centroamérica, "Procuradurías de Derechos Humanos: La fuerza de la presión," *Brecha: Informe Especial* 1 (1994), 22.

[30] See Carlos Quesada, *Entre la cal y la arena: IV Informe sobre las Procuradurías de Derechos Humanos en El Salvador, Guatemala, Honduras, Nicaragua y Costa Rica* (San José: CODEHUCA, 1997), 19.

[31] See Michael Dodson and Donald Jackson, "Horizontal Accountability in Transitional Democracies: The Human Rights Ombudsman in El Salvador and Guatemala," *Latin American Politics and Society* 46 (2004), 10–15.

[32] Successful financial negotiations by the Peruvian Defensora in 2006 can be partly attributed to the unpopularity of threatened local office closures.

financial situation has meant that only one local office has been created. Similarly, in Panama a program of decentralization was aborted in 2004 due to budget cuts.[33]

9.2.5. Appointment Procedures

Many observers lament the influence of political partisanship in the election of Defensors. Appointments constitute a key battleground for political actors competing to shape the nature and direction of Defensoría institutionalization. Formal safeguards including appointment by the legislature rather than by the executive and security of tenure are common.[34] Disregarding whether finite terms actually constitute security of tenure,[35] the empirical evidence demonstrates that formal rules surrounding appointment are often supplemented by informal norms and practices. In particular, as the political capital of Defensorías has increased in recent years, so has political conflict surrounding candidates for Defensor.[36]

In order to ensure a modicum of plurality, many cases in the region require a legislative two-thirds majority for successful appointment.[37] In practice, this arrangement frequently leads to protracted horse-trading among political blocs in Congress and the designation of interim officeholders who lack the legal status of elected Defensors.[38] Defensorías throughout the region have repeatedly experienced delayed appointments.[39] Formal rules stipulating a compulsory time frame for election, such as a limit of thirty days in Bolivia, are routinely violated.[40] Where conflict is high, political actors may use the opportunity presented by appointment to severely undermine the office. For instance, in El Salvador, Congress reformed the regulative law in 1998 to ensure that a highly effective Procuradura was unable to serve as interim, leaving the office in limbo.[41]

---

[33] *Martes Financiero* [Panama], November 8, 2005.

[34] Two prominent outliers are Colombia where the executive presents a list of candidates to the Senate and El Salvador where tenure is limited to three years.

[35] Compare an average of five-year term limits to lifetime terms for U.S. Supreme Court justices, for instance.

[36] The Honduran Commission successfully evaded an attempt by Congress in 1999 to reduce the term of office from six to four years.

[37] A two-thirds majority is desirable to the degree to which it encourages cross-party consensus in the selection of the Defensor. In contrast, election by simple majority may allow powerful political factions to more easily impose their own preferred candidate. Pluralist legislative endorsement of the new Defensor's candidacy can serve not only to safeguard his or her independence but also, importantly, to confer political authority upon the individual mandate-holder.

[38] A four-year deadlock in Peru was finally resolved through informal negotiations within Congress prior to its being put to a vote guaranteeing the election of a new Defensora in 2005.

[39] These include Costa Rica in 2005, El Salvador in 1998 and 2001, Ecuador in 1999, Peru in 2001, Bolivia in 2003 and 2008, and Colombia in 2003.

[40] Although Waldo Albarracín's term in office expired in December 2008 a new Bolivian Defensor was not appointed until May 2010.

[41] Dodson and Jackson, "Horizontal Accountability in Transitional Democracies," 9–10.

The influence of the executive within the legislature should also not be under-estimated. The appointment of partisan candidates can severely undermine the credibility of formal procedures and the Defensoría more generally, as occurred in Argentina where the first Defensor was closely associated with the Menem government.[42] In order to safeguard against opaque political influence, some cases in the region promote plural and meritocratic procedures. For instance, candidates for the Costa Rican Defensor are selected according to a meritocratic point system. In Nicaragua and Ecuador the legislation explicitly states that civil society or human rights organizations must be consulted on the selection of candidates.[43] Nevertheless, adherence to such requirements is limited at best. The 2009 election of Defensor in Costa Rica was widely criticized when a highly qualified candidate was awarded a zero rating by a government-aligned congressperson on the nomination committee.[44]

Emerging trends regarding appointment practices are also worthy of a brief look. In an earlier phase, many Defensorías were effectively decommissioned through electoral maneuvering. In Paraguay, a nine-year delay in the appointment of a Defensor was finally overcome in 2001 with the appointment of a regime proxy.[45] Similarly, the Ecuadorian congress went through a succession of Defensors from 1997 to 2000 before finally leaving the position vacant until 2005.[46] Other sources of opposition have also effectively blocked appointment, including the Nicaraguan Supreme Court in 1996.[47] In Bolivia, social actors effectively mobilized to end the brief incumbency of the government-aligned Defensor in 2003.[48] However, a contemporary phase since 2004 sees a concerted turn toward influence through appointment and, specifically, re-election of incumbents. Defensors in Colombia, El Salvador, Guatemala, Honduras, and Mexico have all been re-elected in recent years. Viewed in a positive light, this trend may indicate institutional stability.[49]

---

[42] The first Defensor, Jorge Luis Maiorano, of Argentina, while a respected jurist, was also a former justice minister, member of the Peronist Party, and advisor to President Carlos Menem's brother.

[43] See Article 96 of the NHRI law in Ecuador.

[44] See *La Nación* [Costa Rica], December 12, 2009.

[45] Hugo Valiente, "Defensoría del Pueblo: polémica elección," *Informativo Mujer* 16 (2004), 19–25.

[46] Julio César Trujillo, elected in 1997 as Defensor, promptly quit in 1998 following a sudden reduction in his term by congress from four years to one. This was followed by the election of Milton Alava Ormaza, who abruptly succumbed to allegations of financial irregularities in 2000. The position of Defensor was subsequently left vacant until 2005.

[47] The 1996 election of a Nicaraguan Procuradora was annulled by a Supreme Court ruling the following month, leaving the office vacant until 1998.

[48] The decisive rejection of the government candidate for the Bolivian Defensoría in 2003 by the powerful Federated Neighborhood Committees of El is an example of an effective intervention from outside the system. Marina Vargas Sandoval, functionary of the El Alto office of the Bolivian Defensor (1998–2005), interview by author, La Paz, Bolivia, July 17, 2008.

[49] The Danish Ombudsman remarking on the Guatemalan re-election stated: "when an ombudsman is re-elected it demonstrates recognition of their work, indicating that those in positions of power

However, a more circumspect appraisal might note that these individuals tend to be less combative than their predecessors and more acquiescent to governing regime interests.

9.3. RELATIONS

The Defensoría offers a point of intersection between state and society, of a kind relatively scarce in Latin America. This section highlights the importance of relations in understanding the institutional development of the Defensoría. The following discussion focuses on three clusters of significant relations: (1) vertical (executive branch), (2) horizontal (state checks and balances), and (3) social (organized civil society).

9.3.1. *Vertical (Executive Branch)*

The position of the Defensoría within the political system at point of origin has a bearing on relations with the executive. The executive has wide powers of designation and internal organization across ministries but also legal and investigative agencies, including the public prosecutor's office.[50] Many Defensorías were initially created by executive decree and incorporated into the executive branch.[51] All Defensorías have subsequently been relocated from this vertical command and control structure to the legislature. Such origins continue to influence relations moving forward, especially where executive encroachment in the public sector is extremely entrenched, as in Mexico.[52]

The Defensoría has a novel doctrinal function, able to operate through vertical channels similar to those of elected officials. The direct receipt of complaints, ex officio powers of investigation, and policy and legislative prerogatives have been characterized by one senior functionary in Peru as "quasi-executive."[53] Such a wide-ranging mandate sets the institution apart from other horizontal agencies. It also presents an arena of overlap with elected officials and a potential challenge to their democratic authority. However, the latent potential for conflict also presents opportunities for coordination. Executives in the region have recognized

recognize the function of the Procurador and respect it." Hans Gammeltoft, quoted in *Prensa Libre* [Guatemala], April 12, 2007.
[50] For instance, in Argentina the attorney general is designated by the president following ratification by a two-thirds majority in the Senate. See Article 5 of the Organic Law of the Public Prosecutor's Office (Ministerio Público).
[51] This is the case in Costa Rica, Honduras, Mexico, Argentina, Ecuador, and Panama.
[52] See *Fundar* [Mexico], October 26, 1999.
[53] Eduardo Vega, Defensor for Human Rights and the Disabled, interview by author, Lima, Peru, June 30, 2008.

Defensorías as viable frameworks through which to pursue their own interests. For example, in Peru the Defensoría appealed to the Fujimori regime's discourse of renewal and internationalism and its promotion of a new public service culture.[54] In the highly conflictive context of Colombia, the government has requested the assistance of the Defensoría as a means to publicly affirm its commitment to human rights.[55]

However, Defensorías perceived as a threat to, or which directly challenge, official interests are often subject to backlash. This is particularly true in the aftermath of intervention in core arenas of political competition, such as elections and corruption. Possibly most disconcerting for political elites is the high public standing of many Defensorías.[56] A sense of popular competition is further exacerbated by Defensors running for public office, including the presidency.[57] Conflict is observed in Nicaragua, where the first Defensor's opposition to electoral reform was described as the one "dissonant note" in the Alemán-Ortega pact of 1999 and led to the appointment of a regime proxy in 2004.[58] Highly publicized clashes between the executive and the Defensor in Colombia over internally displaced persons and crop eradication programs has led to attempts to subordinate the Defensoría to the attorney general's office and the early exit of the Defensor in 2003.[59] These cases highlight the dangers inherent in directly challenging executive authority.

The executive may seek to exert a direct command and control over the Defensoría through informal channels. Principally, this has been achieved through appointment of regime proxies. As noted earlier, the trend is toward increasingly government-aligned appointees. This is most evident in Nicaragua and Venezuela. In Nicaragua, a vocal regime loyalist was appointed in 2004.[60] In Venezuela, successive Defensors have promoted a partisan agenda and the current Defensora has close ties to the official party of government.[61] Other governments have attempted to exert control indirectly by isolating the Defensoría or creating

---

54 *El Peruano* [Peru], April 29, 1997.
55 "Presidente pide a Defensor del Pueblo tramitar ante Fiscalía denuncias de indígenas sobre violación de DD.HH," Press Release of the President's Office, November 2, 2008.
56 Public opinion mobilization is discussed further below.
57 In highly unusual circumstances, the former Guatemalan Procurador, Ramiro Leon de Carpio, was appointed president in 1993. Similarly, Peruvian Defensor, Jorge Santistevan, made a failed bid for the presidency in 2000.
58 *La Prensa* [Nicaragua], February 11, 2001.
59 See Center for International Policy, "CIP Memo: Colombia's Álvaro Uribe – The First 100 Days," November 18, 2002.
60 The Procurador, Omar Cabezas, is an ally of President Daniel Ortega and a former military commander within the Ortega-led Sandinista movement of the 1980s.
61 The first Defensor, Germán Mundaraín, declared in 2004 that "in Venezuela there are no political prisoners, only politicians in prison." *BBC Mundo*, March 26, 2004. Also see *El Universal* [Venezuela], November 27, 2007.

directly competing agencies with rights mandates.[62] Dodson and Jackson draw a distinction between marginalization due to perceived threat (in El Salvador) and just plain indifference (in Guatemala).[63] Relations between the executive and the Defensoría are also subject to broader informal structures. In particular, powerful special interests such as the military and the church have also had a significant influence across cases.[64]

9.3.2. Horizontal (State Checks and Balances)

Initial executive influence over Defensoría reform has often led to subsequent difficulties in the new office's negotiation of a stable position within preexisting horizontal accountability frameworks, with tensions arising from the ability of Defensorías to enable, displace, or undermine other accountability actors. In settings where the Defensoría is inserted into a dense cluster of horizontal agencies, the activity of the office is more constrained than where it is inserted into an institutional vacuum. In this regard, an articulated Colombian state can be contrasted with the dysfunctional apparatus found elsewhere.[65] However, a lack of stable, credible, and routinized practices in Latin America means that the supplementary role of the Defensoría alongside other agencies is often undermined by political conflict. A critical perspective might even frame the Defensoría as parasitic, exploiting broader systemic failings. In turn, Defensorías are not themselves always immune to wider institutional pathologies. For instance, Brett argues that the Guatemalan office has succumbed to widespread institutional racism.[66]

In relation to the legislature, the notion that "public office belongs to the political parties" is widespread among Latin America's political classes and commonly leads to the Defensoría being regarded as competitor rather than a collaborator.[67]

---

[62] For instance, in Guatemala the mandate of the Presidential Coordinating Commission for Executive Policy on Human Rights (COPREDEH) overlaps with that of the Procuradoría.

[63] Dodson and Jackson, "Horizontal Accountability in Transitional Democracies," 21.

[64] The Mexican Commissioner, José Luis Soberanes (2000–2009), was accused of aligning policy with the interests of Opus Dei, a conservative Catholic organization. See *El Universal* [Mexico], August 4, 2009. A number of local functionaries of the Colombian Defensoría have been assassinated and subject to death threats. In Guatemala, the wife of the Procurador, Sergio Morales, was kidnapped in March 2009 by masked assailants shortly after the publication by the Procuraduría of a report into crimes committed by the National Police during the country's civil war.

[65] The Colombian Defensor, created in 1991, inserted into a formally robust and extensive horizontal apparatus, dominated by the Presidential Council for the Defence of Human Rights, the Attorney General's Office, and Constitutional Court.

[66] Roddy Brett, "Confronting Racism from within the Guatemalan State: The Challenges Faced by the Defensoría of Indigenous Rights of Guatemala's Human Rights Ombudsman's Office," paper presented at the conference "How Can the Law Help Reduce Group-Based Inequalities?" Keble College, Oxford, May 14–15, 2009.

[67] Dodson and Jackson, "Horizontal Accountability in Transitional Democracies," 14.

As such, relations are guided not so much by formal rules but rather by inter-personal norms of reciprocity and the receptiveness of individual legislators and committees.[68] More often, Defensorías are subject to particular partisan interests within Congress and have surprised politicians by resisting conventional practices of political patronage.[69] Reflecting a learning process, many notably independent first-generation Defensors have been replaced by individuals with ties to the polit-ical class as the significance of the office grows.[70] Nevertheless, political vocation is not necessarily bad for the Defensoría. Rather, it is the appointment of partisan or incompetent individuals that poses the greatest threat. Such actions can also back-fire on the legislature; the election of Eduardo Peñate in 1998 was later described by El Salvador's main opposition party as "one of our greatest mistakes" following his dismissal for misconduct.[71]

As with all horizontal agencies, the judiciary is not monolithic, and differentiation among actors and processes is important. That said, Defensoría relations with a branch of the state widely perceived in Latin America to be inefficient, inaccessible, and corrupt are often highly problematic.[72] Of particular note is the relationship between Defensorías and Constitutional Tribunals as normatively complementary custodians of the constitution.[73] Highly activist Constitutional Tribunals, such as those found in Costa Rica and Colombia, have increasingly intervened in matters of public policy, leading scholars to note a "judicialization of politics."[74] Such new legal openings may provide structures of opportunity for Defensorías.[75] Domingo has pointed to the potential of the Bolivian Defensoría to push judicial activism

[68] Collaborative Defensors are often former members of Congress or members of other state bodies, such as the former Bolivian Defensor, Waldo Albarracín, previously a member of the Permanent Commission on Human Rights in the Constituent Assembly.

[69] Defensora Ana Maria Romero Campero of Bolivia recalls having to firmly refuse attempts by legisla-tors to exchange votes for jobs (for family members) shortly after her election in 1998. Ana María Romero Campero, former Bolivian Defensora 1998–2003, interview by author, La Paz, Bolivia, July 15, 2008.

[70] Notably independent and effective first-generation Defensors are found in Bolivia, Colombia, Costa Rica, Honduras, and Peru.

[71] Farabundo Martí National Liberation Front (FMLN) representative Miguel Saenz quoted in *Inforpress Centroamericana*, "El Salvador: Human Rights Ombudsman Resigns under Pressure," *Central American Report* 27 (2000), 3. Peñate was dismissed from office in 2000 following a legislative investigation into allegations of corruption. The investigation found that Peñate had violated Article 194 of the Constitution, which establishes the requirements of "honesty, professional capacity, and the highest level of integrity."

[72] W. Prillaman, *The Judiciary and Democratic Decay in Latin America* (Westport, CN: Praeger, 2000).

[73] Constitutional Tribunals have been created throughout Latin America, including Chile in 1980, Costa Rica in 1989, Colombia in 1991, Peru in 1993, and Bolivia in 1999.

[74] R. Sieder, L. Schjolden, and A. Angell (eds.), *The Judicialization of Politics in Latin America* (London: Palgrave Macmillan, 2005).

[75] See Alicia Yamin and Oscar Parra-Vera, "How Do Courts Set Health Policy? The Case of the Colombian Constitutional Court," *PLoS Medicine* 6 (2009), 1–4.

into "potentially controversial social and economic rights issues."[76] An accessible and activist constitutional authority may also pose challenges for a Defensoría not wishing to duplicate the role of existing institutions. Nevertheless, the dismantling of such a resource, as occurred under the Fujimori regime in Peru, poses a much greater impediment to the office.[77]

The Defensoría also intersects with an array of appointed horizontal agencies with investigative and auditing authority. Together with the offices of the attorney general and the comptroller general, these offices exercise legal control and investigative accountability through horizontal channels. A further tier of specialized, advisory, and regulatory agencies, among them the Defensoría, constitute a second level of appointed agencies. This highly diverse patchwork of appointed agencies is a significant arena of strategic interaction for the Defensoría. However, coordination depends, on the one hand, upon the compatibility of respective agency mandates and scope of enforcement authority. On the other, relations are affected by informal norms and practices, specifically the ability and willingness of agencies to coordinate accountability actions and hold powerful actors to account.

Finally, relations of the Defensoría at the sub-national level merit more attention than is possible here. It is often in remote areas where the state is largely absent that the greatest gaps between formal rules and informal practices exist.[78] Defensorías throughout Latin America have decentralized, and the dynamics that govern horizontal relations are applicable to the microcosm of local politics. In particular, the level of political conflict and the balance of power between state and social actors are crucial in this arena. This subject takes on a special significance in federalized states where the national and local Defensorías are autonomous agencies, as in Argentina and Mexico. Preliminary evidence suggests that federalized autonomous Defensoría systems can be problematic when characterized by jurisdictional overlap, a dilution of leadership and authority, and conflict, as opposed to coordination, among offices. Notably, the autonomous Mexico City Human Rights Commission has provided a highly credible rights counterpoint to a regime proxy national-level federal commission.[79]

---

[76] Pilar Domingo, "Weak Courts, Rights and Legal Mobilization in Bolivia," in R. Gargarella et al. (eds.), *Courts and Social Transformation in New Democracies: An Institutional Voice for the Poor?* (Burlington: Ashgate, 2006), 242.

[77] See Thomas Pegram, "Accountability in Hostile Times; The Case of the Peruvian Human Rights Ombudsman 1996–2001," *Journal of Latin American Studies* 40 (2008), 51–82.

[78] Local government municipalities are the source of thousands of annual complaints to Defensorías throughout the region.

[79] In Mexico, the Commission of Mexico City has clashed with the National Commission over jurisdiction and human rights. See *La Jornada* [Mexico], June 1, 2007.

9.3.3. *Social (Organized Civil Society)*

Social relations refer to interaction with organized actors exercising accountability over elected officials from outside the state, notably human rights nongovernmental organizations (NGOs), media, and civic organizations. Such relationships have been a crucial addition to the activities of many Latin American Defensorías, highlighting the ability of the office to operate through vertical as well as horizontal channels. However, the quality of these relations varies considerably across cases. Notably, in contexts with a recent history of authoritarian government, human rights abuse, and generally deficient representative institutions, the challenge of bridging the state-society divide is particularly acute.

The extent to which social actors have been engaged in Defensoría reform at point of origin is significant for future relations. In the cases of El Salvador, Honduras, Mexico, and Paraguay, there was little or no participation of social actors in the design or establishment of the Defensoría.[80] In contrast, the Nicaraguan reform involved consultation with over sixty civic organizations.[81] Social participation at the design stage may have material consequences for formal structures, injecting an element of plurality.[82] More broadly, an insular process of institutional design conducted by political elites is likely to color social relations following activation. For instance, the Bolivian Defensor was initially viewed with deep skepticism by social actors as part of a regime-managed "neo-liberal project."[83]

The ability of the Bolivian Defensor to overcome popular skepticism and to decisively "move away from the [neo-liberal] category" is attributed to the election of individuals with strong interpersonal ties to social actors.[84] Relations with social actors based on established "relationships of opportunity" are likely to facilitate coordination. The appointment of broadly representative nonpartisan (i.e., without militant or radical profiles) Defensors explains the rapid social legitimization of many of these entities.[85] Even for Defensorías emerging from elite political pacts, overtures to civil society actors by the leadership can significantly alter social

---

[80] See Dodson, "The Human Rights Ombudsman in Central America," 32.

[81] The Nicaraguan consultation process was heavily promoted by the Norwegian government, the chief financiers of the Defensoría reform. See Quesada, *Entre la Cal y la Arena*, 31.

[82] In Nicaragua and Ecuador, the legislation explicitly states that civil society or human rights organizations must be consulted on the selection of candidates.

[83] Diego Pary Rodríguez, Senior advisor to Confederación Sindical Unica de Trabajadores y Campesinos de Bolivia (CSUTCB), interview by author, La Paz, Bolivia, July 17, 2008.

[84] Ibid. The first Defensora, Ana Maria Romero Campero (1998–2003), was a journalist. Her successor, Waldo Albarracín (2003–2008), was a human rights activist and member of the Permanent Assembly on Human Rights.

[85] Nonpartisan Defensors in El Salvador, Honduras, Peru, and elsewhere have drafted highly credible civil society activists as a method of "signaling" solidarity with social constituencies.

relations for the better.[86] Conversely, the appointment of a regime proxy as Defensor will effectively close off social relations, even resulting in direct conflict between the office and autonomous civil society actors.[87] In other instances, despite vocal criticism of official policy by the Defensor, relations remain distant due to interpersonal mistrust or broader structural issues of competition over resources.[88]

Similar to Defensoría insertion within state structures, the Defensoría also can enable, displace, or undermine actors within social accountability arenas.[89] Crowding out of social actors is a concern, with Defensorías potentially diverting international funding away from civil society actors as well as enticing highly qualified personnel away from the human rights sector.[90] Despite initial tensions, some Defensorías have cultivated good relations by using resources, coupled with official recognition, to bolster the profile of social actors.[91] Other cases have been less successful. Argentina has arguably the most highly organized human rights communities in the region. However, due to multiple factors, relations with the Defensor have been defined primarily by indifference and competition.[92]

That said, a proposal to strengthen the human rights profile of the Argentinean Defensor, led by a coalition of human rights organizations in 2009, followed incipient signs of a new willingness on the part of the Defensoría to mobilize alongside social actors to advance human rights claims.[93] In contrast, similar attempts by social actors in Mexico to publicly challenge a failing institution have had far less impact, due to a lack of political will within Congress and a political system relatively unresponsive to wider social needs and demands.[94]

---

[86] The first Procurador of Nicaragua, Benjamín Pérez, discreetly sought alliances within civil society.

[87] Vocal attacks by the Nicaraguan Procurador in 2008 against regime opponents have led to the organization's alignment with regime sympathizers in society against human rights defenders. See Centro Nicaragüense de Derechos Humanos, *Derechos Humanos en Nicaragua 2008* (Managua: CENIDH, 2008), 171.

[88] Dodson and Jackson, "Horizontal Accountability in Transitional Democracies," 17.

[89] See Peter Rosenblum in this volume, "Tainted Origins and Uncertain Outcomes: Evaluating NHRIs."

[90] See Coletta Youngers, "Promoting Human Rights: NGOs and the State in Peru," in J. Crabtree (ed.), *Making Institutions Work in Peru* (London: ISA, 2006).

[91] Leo Valladares, the first Honduran Procurador, was careful to assure social actors that "we do not want to create large structures that substitute the work that must be done by civil society." Quoted in Quesada, *En Procura de la Paz*, 22.

[92] The appointment of successive partisan Defensors, its restricted jurisdiction over non-federal matters and the military, as well as the self-sufficiency of the NGO community are all material to explaining this outcome. Gaston Chillier and Diego Morales, executive director and Litigation and Legal Defense director of CELS, Center for Legal and Social Studies, interview by author, Buenos Aires, Argentina, August 11, 2008.

[93] See Enrique Peruzzotti in this volume, "The Societalization of Horizontal Accountability: Rights Advocacy and the Defensor del Pueblo de la Nación in Argentina."

[94] See generally work produced by Programa Atalaya (Análisis académico sobre la CNDH) since 2003: http://atalaya.itam.mx/.

Reflective of an ongoing and dynamic process, Defensoría social relations are continually subject to renewal as circumstances change. Defensoría relations are affected by broader conditions of power asymmetries and conflict between state and society. For instance, the rights work of the Guatemalan office received growing recognition throughout the 1990s. Nevertheless, commenting in 1996, one NGO worker claimed, "This work is not exploited by human rights NGOs, who still view the Procuraduría as a government entity and therefore uninterested in getting to the bottom of the matter."[95] Criticism of Defensoría timidity toward government policy on sensitive issues is widespread, even if the independence of the office is acknowledged.[96] Most dramatic for the Defensoría is where the balance of power between state and society shifts decisively. With the election of Evo Morales in Bolivia and ascendance of the traditionally excluded into the heart of government, social actors have begun questioning the need for a Defensor "when we [the people] defend the community."[97]

The ability of a Defensoría to appeal to the interests of organized social actors relies to a large extent on media exposure. Indeed, the media constitute a critical relationship for the office. High profile coverage of the Defensoría can significantly raise the public credibility of the office and, in turn, its leverage over the behavior of elected officials. Defensorías throughout the region use the media as a means to mobilize public opinion around violations. Notably, mobilizing public opinion does not conform strictly to either vertical or horizontal dimensions. The Defensoría may channel public opinion vertically through public censure of elected officials. Simultaneously, the Defensoría can transmit public opinion horizontally through its advisory role to the legislature. Most important, the force of the Defensoría's words lies not with formal rules but rather its ability to generate publicity and mobilize public opinion. Notwithstanding legitimate concern over the validity of public opinion polling on Defensorías,[98] in many countries in Latin America much of the time this is an organization held in high public esteem in political systems that are generally not trusted.[99] Such public legitimacy constitutes a powerful instrument of accountability that overlies and supplements the Defensoría's vertical and

---

[95] Quoted in Quesada, *En Procura de la Paz*, 11.

[96] See Quesada, *Entre la Cal y la Arena*, 15.

[97] Sonia Cuentas, functionary in the Bolivian Defensor del Pueblo since 2002, interview by author, La Paz, Bolivia, July 17, 2008.

[98] As Ackerman argues in relation to the Mexican Commission, "high public approval ratings bear little resemblance to more concrete indicators of legitimacy." Ackerman, *Organismos Autónomos y Democracia*, 148.

[99] Public polls consistently give Defensorías approval ratings of 50 percent or higher. See, for example, Pegram, "Accountability in Hostile Times," 73; Dodson and Jackson, "Horizontal Accountability in Transitional Democracies," 7–8; and in this volume Fredrik Uggla, "Through Pressure or Persuasion? Explaining Compliance with the Resolutions of the Bolivian Defensor del Pueblo."

horizontal characteristics. Mobilizing a collective awareness around an issue may be the crucial instrument for getting things done, so far as anything can be done.

Conversely, media neglect of the office can effectively consign it to oblivion. National media environments pose a number of challenges, not least countervailing interests among powerful commercial proprietors.[100] Unaccountable corporate actors operating within liberalized markets and capable of setting the political agenda present a complex, opaque, and largely unstudied arena of accountability politics for the Defensoría. Also, reflective of a highly heterogeneous social sphere, powerful constituencies within the media, state and broader society may actively oppose the institution's human rights agenda. Evidence of this is apparent in Colombia, Peru, and elsewhere.[101] In Honduras, the Defensor has noted that its work on the extrajudicial killing of street children is hampered by public opinion toward these children becoming increasingly aggressive.[102]

9.4. RULES OF ACCESS

This section turns its attention to the formal and informal rules that govern Defensoría access to accountability arenas. In the absence of legal enforcement powers, the Defensoría relies on third parties to enforce compliance. Nevertheless, it has a range of legal, investigative, and advocacy prerogatives that may incur material consequences, if not legal sanction. Rules of access refers to three principal arenas: (1) vertical access (executive arenas), (2) horizontal access (state checks and balances), and (3) social access (organized civil society).

9.4.1. *Vertical Access*

The Defensoría has a range of policy and legislative advisory powers that shares comparisons with an executive function. In particular, the Defensoría may act through vertical channels to influence the political agenda – for instance, by publicly offering opinions on official policy through the media. Under certain conditions, the Defensoría may access vertical channels with the support of the executive where interests converge. The Defensoría, with its access to channels of vertical accountability, offers a potential ally to elected officials in their quest for popular legitimacy. In turn, for the Defensoría, responsiveness to such a powerful actor carries risk but

---

[100] Erick Torrico, National Coordinator of Communication and Investigation for UNIR Foundation, interview by author, La Paz, Bolivia, July 28, 2009.

[101] See, for example, *BBC Mundo*, September 9, 2003. In Peru, Human rights NGOs have faced severe hostility from government officials and politicians linked to the previous Garcia (1985–1990) and Fujimori (1990–2000) administrations.

[102] Report of the Special Rapporteur on extrajudicial, summary, or arbitrary executions (Ms. Asma Jahangir), Mission to Honduras, UN Doc. E/CN.4/2003/3/Add.2, June 14, 2002, 20.

may also yield dividends. For instance, Defensorías have been incorporated into a wave of sometimes controversial National Human Rights Plans across the region with variable results.[103] In general, working alongside the executive is rare in Latin America and will be conditioned by the nature of the accountability objective, the violators in question, and the expected consequences of action.

An important caveat to this claim is where the Defensoría is effectively captured by the executive. One important indicator of independence is the extent to which the Defensoría holds the executive accountable through vertical channels. In this regard, the Mexican Commission is notable for its reticence in criticizing executive policy. The commission issued its first recommendation directly addressed to the president in 2001, eleven years following its activation and one year after the transition to democracy.[104] This intervention was significant, resulting in the appointment of a special prosecutor by the president to investigate and prosecute crimes committed during the "dirty war" of the 1960s and 70s.[105] However, the commission subsequently failed to follow up on its recommendations or provide support to an isolated and ineffectual prosecutor.[106] In this instance, the Defensoría may be more an obstacle to accountability for violations than an enabler, failing to ensure proper scrutiny. Similar concerns apply to the alleged conduct of the Honduran office during the military coup of 2009.[107]

More commonly, Defensorías access vertical accountability channels unilaterally or in coordination with social actors, as discussed later. However, given the potential for backlash from the executive through formal or informal channels, access and exercising of vertical accountability in direct confrontation with the executive is rare and likely to result in powerful opposition. Indeed, actions by the Defensorías to constrain the executive are likely to have immediate or delayed repercussions.[108] That said, independent Defensorías who directly criticize official policy may, even under adverse conditions, sometimes bridge the divide between the executive and civil

---

[103] This is the case in Colombia, Ecuador, and Peru.

[104] Recommendation No. 26/2001, November 27, 2001.

[105] Order of the President of the Republic, November 27, 2001.

[106] See Human Rights Watch, *La Comisión Nacional de los Derechos Humanos de México: Una Evaluación Crítica* (Mexico D. F.: Human Rights Watch Americas Division, 2008), 33–4.

[107] Further study to trace how the situation has evolved is necessary. However, the Honduran Commissioner endorsed the interim coup government and allegedly failed to provide assistance to victims of military repression. See Comité de Familiares de Detenidos Desaparecidos en Honduras, *Informe Preliminar: Violaciones a Derechos Humanos en el Marco del Golpe de Estado en Honduras* (COFADEH: Tegucigalpa), July 15, 2009, 10.

[108] A dramatic example is that of the hunger strike conducted by the Bolivian Defensora, Ana Maria Romero, in 2003, shortly after stepping down from office. The then sitting vice-president, Carlos Mesa, has remarked that this action by the Defensora "resulted in the destruction of the government's support base within the middle classes" and precipitated the fall of the government. Mesa and the political elite refused to support the re-election of Romero installing a regime proxy in her place. See C. Mesa, *Presidencia Sitiada: Memorias de mi Gobierno* (La Paz: Editores Plurales, 2008), 64.

society. For instance, the groundbreaking report by the Honduran Commission in 1993 on forced disappearances during the 1980s gained the support of then President Roberto Reina. By directly implicating the military and old political guard in the killings, the commission assisted Reina in overcoming powerful opposition to establishing a High Level Ad Hoc Commission for Institutional Reform.[109] In turn, the report cemented the Defensoría's profile as a rights defender.

Nevertheless, more often than not, relations defined by mistrust and hostility translate into limited access to vertical accountability arenas within the state. Beyond influencing the public agenda, the Defensoría can also monitor the public bureaucracy, including ministries and agencies, through "reflexive" channels of persuasion. However, Defensorías are poorly equipped to effect systemic change. Rather, they have focused on pursuing amicable resolution with public officials through informal horizontal channels. For this form of pressure to be effective, however, it appears to be closely related to the high public standing of the Defensoría and the implicit threat that non-compliance will result in damaging public criticism. As the Bolivian Defensora recalls:

> As we entered our third year of operations, we began a new initiative to "shame" state functionaries into cooperating with the Defensoría. We produced lists of uncooperative functionaries and published it widely within the media. The following year, there was a marked rise in cooperation and responsiveness.[110]

However, in more conflictive settings, Defensorías have struggled to change the behavior, let alone preferences, of state officials. This is especially the case where the office lacks presence and authority within its social setting, as reflected in the views of the first Nicaraguan Procurador:

> With reference to human rights, there is much ignorance among public functionaries.... We have tried to maintain a working relationship and good communications, which is the first step in order to reach solutions to the many problems we confront. However this just does not exist.[111]

Beyond the receptiveness of non-elected bureaucracy to the mandate of the Defensoría, such internal channels of accountability may be problematic in a Latin American context where, too frequently, formal rules are overlooked in favor of personal discretion. The use of informal channels of influence also risks reinforcing what is already often an opaque arena of accountability. Furthermore, from an empirical perspective, it is hard to quantify the impact of such internal channels of redress and the extent to which individual claimants are satisfied with the result.

---

[109] Dodson, "The Human Rights Ombudsman in Central America," 30.
[110] Ana María Romero Campero, July 15, 2008.
[111] *El Nuevo Diario* [Nicaragua], December 30, 2001.

9.4.2. Horizontal Access

Reflecting its status as a horizontal institution, the Defensoría has a range of administrative, regulatory, legal, and investigative prerogatives despite its lack of enforcement powers. Working within, across, and apart from state checks and balances, the Defensoría does rely on other actors with compliance authority to advance legal claims. Ideally, Defensoría access to this arena is reflective of a highly articulated horizontal apparatus, with clear division of labor among actors. However, in Latin America access is often governed by informal norms as well as by political conflict among agencies. This presents a severe challenge to the legal mandate of the Defensoría. It can also impede horizontal powers more broadly; for instance, the Mexican Commission submitted a constitutional review action in 2009 against a new law governing the prosecutor's office which places restrictions on the commission's requests for information.[112]

Unsurprisingly, many Defensorías have advocated greater transparency within the state, with the Panamanian and Costa Rican offices formally coordinating interinstitutional networks of transparency.[113] However, the Mexican example just cited needs to be qualified in light of the commission's own dubious record in this area. The Mexican Commission was considered to be one of the least transparent public institutions in 2008 and has repeatedly denied information requests from civil society actors.[114] Similarly, the Honduran Commission presented its 2010 annual report to Congress in a private session, denying public scrutiny of its controversial actions in the wake of the military coup of July 2009.[115] In these instances, it is the Defensoría itself which is undermining access to horizontal arenas for social actors. More generally, offices have been criticized for narrow interpretations of their mandate that effectively close off or underutilize access to horizontal accountability. For instance, in Guatemala, successive Procuradors throughout the 1990s imposed a narrow interpretation on investigative powers.[116] In Nicaragua the Procuraduría has been criticized for not recognizing that judicial administration falls within its mandate.[117]

Conversely, other Defensorías have actively sought to expand horizontal access through creative interpretation of formal mandates. In El Salvador, under the leadership of Velázquez de Avilés, the Procuraduría exercised an aggressive investigative

---

[112] *UPI* [Mexico], July 27, 2009.
[113] Domingo writes on the Bolivian Defensor: "Reliable data is hard to come by, and only recently have there been efforts to build databases. One of the more reliable sources since 1998 is the information generated by the human rights Ombudsman (and to some extent by the Constitutional Tribunal)." Domingo, "Weak Courts, Rights and Legal Mobilization in Bolivia," 238.
[114] *El Universal* [Mexico], November 20, 2008.
[115] *Tiempo* [Nicaragua], March 18, 2010.
[116] Dodson and Jackson, "Horizontal Accountability in Transitional Democracies," 15.
[117] *El Nuevo Diario* [Nicaragua], April 3, 2001.

mandate that gained the institution widespread recognition.[118] Defensorías have also expanded the range of legal powers at their disposal. For example, in 2001 the Argentinean Defensor launched a class action (amparo colectivo) after reasoning that despite a lack of explicit provision such a faculty was compatible with its legal mandate.[119] Defensorías have frequently argued for a broad interpretation of their mandate on the ground of public interest. Notably, Defensorías in Costa Rica and Panama have successfully overcome judicial resistance to their oversight of judicial administration. A similar logic underpins the intervention of the office in the electoral arena throughout the region, often emphasizing due process and universal suffrage rights.[120] The role of Defensorías in monitoring elections is often subject to dispute, especially when offices are highly critical of the electoral process and the conduct of political parties.[121]

Intervention in such sensitive policy terrain will affect the receptiveness of partisan forces within the legislature to the Defensoría. A key arena of horizontal accountability is the legislature, and Defensorías generally have a mandate to advise Congress on draft legislation, introduce legislative projects, and present annual reports.[122] In practice, informal access to plenary, committees, and individual legislators and their staff is a highly negotiated affair. Despite the prevalence of conflict in this relationship, Defensorías have achieved material outcomes in this arena.[123] In particular, Defensoría technical expertise can enhance legislation's conformity with democratic and rule of law principles. Jurists consider this as a legitimate task given the mediocrity of much legislation.[124] However, Defensorías must also give due regard to independence when exercising an advisory function. The Mexican

---

[118] See Lawrence Michael Ladutke, "Freedom of Expression and Human Rights Violations in Postwar El Salvador: The Vilanova Case," paper delivered at Latin American Studies Association Conference, Washington, DC, September 6–8, 2001.

[119] See Eduardo Mertehikian, "Jurisprudencia comentada: La legitimación del Defensor del Pueblo de la Nación Argentina y una sentencia de alcance general contra el corralito bancario," *Revista Argentina del Régimen de la Administración Pública* 286 (2002), 222–5.

[120] Many offices are mandated to intervene in electoral matters with express prohibition only in Costa Rica, Ecuador, Mexico, Panama, and Paraguay.

[121] See Guillermo Escobar, "Defensorías del Pueblo y Democracia," *Quórum: Revista de pensamiento iberoamericano* 13 (2005), 80.

[122] The Colombian Defensoría has recently begun to exercise this function, working closely with Congress to pass an Anti-Discrimination Statute in 2008. See Law Project No.: 66 2008 and Law Project No.: 197/2007.

[123] The Bolivian Defensor del Pueblo received or initiated reviews of twenty-seven Supreme Decrees, preliminary texts, and drafts of laws during 2008. Of these, fifteen were approved by the Defensoría, eleven rejected, and in one case the institution recommended a technical work group be set up to study the proposal. Of eight cases where the Defensoría intervened in the legislative process, five proposals were approved as norms by the Congress. See Defensoría del Pueblo [Bolivia], *Informe Anual* (La Paz: DP, 2008), 28.

[124] "It is important legal projects are well informed as we all know bad law could be worse." César Landa, president of the Peruvian Constitutional Tribunal (2006–2008), interview by author, Lima, Peru, June 20, 2008.

Commission has been criticized for focusing on the application of existing norms and neglecting advocacy for legislative change.[125]

Defensorías also have a range of legal prerogatives. But access to this arena of accountability is complicated by the variably dysfunctional character of judiciaries throughout the region. Broadly speaking, Defensorías do not exercise their legal powers in a systematic manner and internal offices are often under-resourced in manpower and technical expertise.[126] Obstacles to legal accountability for Defensorías are not only structural but also political. Strategically, Defensorías may be reluctant to pursue legal action due to a range of factors including excessive time delays and the potential for adverse outcomes. The Argentinean case provides a good example of the risks entailed in accessing legal arenas. The Supreme Court has rejected multiple submissions by the Defensoría on procedural grounds. For instance, the court has repeatedly rejected class actions presented by the Defensor, in marked contrast to other associations with similar legal status under Article 43 of the constitution.[127]

However, Defensorías have worked alongside actors such as Constitutional Tribunals to advance progressive jurisprudence.[128] Throughout Latin America, Defensorías have submitted cases to constitutional authorities and achieved significant rulings. In Peru, a landmark ruling by the Constitutional Tribunal in 2003 curtailing the jurisdiction of military justice followed years of advocacy by the Defensoría.[129] Defensorías have also made gains in economic, social, and cultural rights recognition. As Domingo writes of the Bolivian Defensoría, "to the degree [the Constitutional Tribunal] has had to engage with potentially controversial social and economic rights issues, this somewhat reflects the 'judicial activism' pushed by the Ombudsman."[130] Across these cases, as well as others such as Colombia and Costa Rica, formal access to this arena constitutes a rare area of relative stability. However, access to justice and enforcement of legal decisions remain deeply problematic across settings.

9.4.3. Social Access

One of the more novel features of Defensorías in Latin America is their extensive access to, and use of, social accountability mechanisms. Strong relations with

---

[125] Programa Atalaya, *Análisis de Gestión de la CNDH en 2003* (Mexico City: ITAM, 2003), 30.

[126] See Quesada, *En Procura de la Paz*, 18.

[127] Crocioni notes, "The Court has displayed a far less hostile attitude toward associations, accepting in various cases their legitimacy to defend collective rights." Francisco Crocioni, "Los Procesos Constitucionales Colectivos en el Derecho Constitucional Argentino," *Temas de Derecho Procesal Constitucional* 1 (2008), 118.

[128] Constitutional Courts have been created alongside Defensorías in Bolivia, Colombia, Ecuador, Guatemala, and Peru.

[129] See Defensoría del Pueblo [Peru], *Informe Anual* (Lima: Defensoría del Pueblo, 2009), 519.

[130] Domingo, "Weak Courts, Rights and Legal Mobilization in Bolivia," 242.

nonstate actors can provide the Defensoría with crucial ballast against hostile state actors. In turn, interaction often proves mutually reinforcing, scaling up an array of accountability strategies. Specifically, Defensorías can provide resource-stretched social actors with legal and technical expertise and access to the legislative process.[131] Defensorías also benefit from association with credible social actors who bring with them mobilization strength and publicity. This has its clearest expression in the signing of formal inter-institutional agreements between Defensorías and prominent NGOs pioneered by the El Salvadorian Procuraduría and now common throughout Latin America.

Defensorías have often issued special reports on compelling human rights topics likely to resonate among the broader public. This serves to maximize impact with limited resources and also encourages the media to report upon the findings. More broadly, Defensorías can facilitate information exchange to enable mobilization and increase political pressure upon elected officials. Throughout Central America, Defensorías have publicly confronted the state over past massive violations of human rights. The Honduran 1993 report, "The Facts Speak for Themselves," on forced disappearances of the 1980s pioneered this highly public accountability activity.[132] It was subsequently emulated later in El Salvador in 2002 and Guatemala in 2009. Not only do such initiatives raise the profile of the office but they can also legitimate human rights mobilization more broadly. In the case of Guatemala, the report constitutes a valuable advocacy tool, building on unearthed official documents and years of advocacy by social actors. As the Procurador remarked upon publication:

> [This] archive was condemned to a slow death and with it would have disappeared an infinity of signs, clues and keys essential to understanding the national tragedy from which we are still yet to recover.[133]

Defensorías can also use their media profile to publicly censure elected officials over current human rights violations. Denouncing official policy through social mechanisms of accountability is also an effective means of signaling independence from the state. The El Salvadorian Procuraduría under the leadership of Velasquez de Aviles frequently criticized President Armando Calderón, resulting in high public approval ratings.[134] Similarly, the actions of the Peruvian Defensoría during

[131] See Obiora Chinedu Okafor in this volume, "National Human Rights Institutions in Anglophone Africa: Legalism, Popular Agency and the "Voices of Suffering."
[132] Dodson, "The Human Rights Ombudsman in Central America," 33.
[133] Guatemala Procuraduría de los Derechos Humanos, *El Derecho a Saber* (Guatemala City: PDDHH, 2009), 7.
[134] M. Popkin, *Peace without Justice: Obstacles to Building the Rule of Law in El Salvador* (Philadelphia: Penn State University Press, 2000), 173.

the fraudulent elections of 2000 cemented its public profile as a leading democratic actor.[135] Defensorías can scale up human rights claims to the national level in a way few NGOs can and turn individual grievances into public issues. In turn, Defensorías can offer a rare human rights counterpoint to official state policies. For instance, the Colombian Defensoría issued its policy recommendation on the prevention of massive violations of human rights to coincide with the government's "democratic security" policy of 2002.[136]

However, Defensorías are also often subject to robust criticism by NGOs for not going far enough in holding officials to account. The Honduran Commission's preference for public announcements as opposed to formal resolutions which carry an enforceable obligation to cooperate has been criticized as weakening the influence of the office.[137] More seriously, the Guatemalan Procurador has been accused of delaying the publication of the 2009 report concerning past violations as well as censoring its content.[138] Defensorías operating under highly conflictive conditions face a dilemma in this regard: do too little and disappoint social actors; do too much and risk backlash from hostile state actors. Cautionary tales abound. For instances, a campaign by the Colombian Defensoría questioning the legality of U.S. government-backed coca crop eradication in 2002 was followed by the reassignment of the Defensor and an alleged "softening of the position against the spraying program."[139] In the worst case scenario, partisan appointments may actively undermine regime opponents within society.[140]

Beyond access to the media and mobilization through public advocacy, the Defensoría can also facilitate access to the legal system for rights claimants, through ex officio submissions and participation in amicus curiae briefs. In facilitating legal expertise, the Defensoría brings "value added" support to NGO efforts to seek justice through the courts.[141] Conversely, where civil society is highly expert in legal

---

[135] See "Organizaciones que Cumplen un Papel Importante en el Fortalecimiento de la Democracia," survey conducted by DATUM Internacional, August 2000.

[136] Defensoría del Pueblo [Colombia], *Informe Anual* (Bogota: DP, 2004), 82.

[137] Quesada, *Entre la Cal y la Arena*, 28.

[138] The Procurador allegedly removed evidence of U.S. involvement in counterinsurgency operations; the control exercised by the Guatemalan military over the National Police; specific information on command structures within the police; and the removal of scrutiny of nine human rights cases. See *El Periódico* [Guatemala], June 25, 2009. For the Procurador's response see *El Periódico* [Guatemala], June 25, 2009.

[139] See Aida Memorandum to Tim Rieser, Inter-American Association for Environmental Defense, December 12, 2003, 3.

[140] In 2006 the Nicaraguan Procurador launched defamation proceedings against journalists of the newspaper *El Nuevo Diario* after their investigations highlighted a series of anomalies within the Procuraduría. See *El Nuevo Diario* [Nicaragua], April 1, 2006.

[141] Ana Leyva, Environmental Officer for FEDEPAZ, an NGO based in Lima, interview by author, August 23, 2005, Lima, Peru.

advocacy, such as in Argentina, the services of the Defensoría are not as much in demand.[142] In turn, the Defensoría may use litigation strategies, not only to win individual cases but also to set the parameters of public debate. As Human Rights Watch has stated, Defensoría intervention may become "a decisive factor in the multifaceted process through which the ... state determines the rights of individuals."[143] In contexts with high levels of impunity for human rights violations, Defensoría litigation, when combined with an internal political dimension, can produce results. For instance, pressure by the Colombian Defensoría alongside social accountability actors finally led to the sanctioning of the responsible military commander for the massacre of Bojayá, Chocó.[144]

9.5. THE DEFENSORÍA DEL PUEBLO IN LATIN AMERICA: POLITICS AND INSTITUTIONALIZATION

This chapter has unpacked the internal actors, processes, and interactions of each of the three core features of institutionalization identified by the study. The analysis has drawn on available material, including primary sources and others. Limited available evidence explains the uneven coverage of some Defensorías in the chapter, such as those of Ecuador and Paraguay. In the absence of additional evidence, the study has relied upon what few reliable accounts of these offices are available. In any case, the objective of the chapter is not to enter into the intricacies of individual Defensorías' experiences but rather to highlight the dynamic nature of their institutionalization across variable settings in Latin America.

The analysis demonstrates that each feature of institutionalization has its own internal actors, processes, and patterns. In other words, modification of one design principle can have spillover effects elsewhere: the absence of constitutional status in the Panamanian case effectively robbed the Defensoría of its formal budgetary autonomy and immunity. The more dynamic features of institutionalization, relations, and access also present individually complex arenas of interaction. For example, working relations with one group of organized actors are likely to have important effects upon the character of other relationships. In this sense, we see a rapid realignment of the Bolivian Defensoría away from the "neo-liberal category" promoted by its original designers toward the interests of powerful social actors following activation.

[142] See Jean Grugel and Enrique Peruzzotti, "Grounding Global Norms in Domestic Politics: Advocacy Coalitions and the Convention on the Rights of the Child in Argentina," *Journal of Latin American Studies* 42 (2010), 29–57.

[143] Human Rights Watch, *La Comisión Nacional de los Derechos Humanos de México*, 27.

[144] The Bojayá massacre of 119 civilians occurred in May 2002 during a battle between Revolutionary Armed Forces of Colombia (FARC) and United Self-Defence Forces of Colombia (AU). The potent "political echo" of this, the worst massacre in forty years of conflict, to the present day was recognized by President Uribe. See *Primera Pagina* [Colombia], February 6, 2005.

Access across accountability arenas presents an additional complex terrain, with the enabling or denial of access in one arena likely to determine the nature of access in another. For instance, the dismantling of horizontal institutions under Fujimori in Peru effectively forced the Defensoría to seek access to accountability arenas outside the state, or resign itself to obsolescence.

The analysis also highlights the importance of interaction effects across formal and informal dimensions of institutionalization. More specifically, how do particular processes, actors, and patterns in one arena significantly affect others, simultaneously or in sequence? This inquiry draws attention to questions of timing and temporal factors, as well as to broader institutional conditions. Placed in context, the Mexican reform process of 1999, which granted the Commission autonomy, poses problems for formal theoretical assumptions. In this instance, the Senate used the reform process as a pretext to initiate a technical procedure and to dismiss the incumbent Defensora without adequate explanation for its actions.[145] Rather than framing this episode of formal strengthening as a positive step, a focus on hostile relations with powerful state actors casts the reform process in a negative light. Alternatively, positive development in one arena may open up new structures of opportunity in another. For instance, effective social mobilization around the Bojayá massacre increased the likely political costs for vertical and horizontal actors of ignoring the Colombian Defensoría and legal petitions on behalf of victims' families.

Furthermore, different formal and informal factors, and their component parts, may have an equal or distinct bearing on institutionalization outcomes. For instance, the evidence suggests that formal design principles provide little protection against interference when confronted by entrenched and adverse informal norms and practices. This was the case for the Paraguayan Defensoría, which was effectively paralyzed by partisan negotiations within Congress for nine years. Following activation, formal appointment safeguards made little impact in preventing the installation of a regime proxy as Paraguay's first Defensor. Indeed, excessive focus on formal rules can neglect important questions of context and resources. The impressive budget of the Mexican Commission, for example, says more about the partisan status of the office than the formal robustness of its budgetary autonomy. A further factor of considerable consequence that emerges from the analysis is the individual leadership of Defensors. Forceful and effective leadership can quickly reverse the fortunes of failing offices, as witnessed in El Salvador under Velasquez de Aviles. The precariousness of such institutional strength is sadly also demonstrated by the experience of the El Salvadorian Procuraduría following de Avile's departure.

---

[145] A report issued by the Mexican Defensoría in 1998 (44/98) on killings in Juarez directly charged the PAN-led state and municipal governments of failing to prevent, protect, or guarantee the rights of the victims in an electoral year.

As such, it is necessary to pay attention to the nature of the precarious balance between formal and informal dimensions across cases to explain institutionalization. Nicaragua demonstrates this interplay between vying political forces and formal rules, with the Procuraduría initially led by a Defensor intent on establishing a tentative zone of independence from powerful political forces. The office nevertheless quickly succumbed to interference through appointment procedures in 2004. Various cases highlight the potential for Defensorías to be undermined by broader turf wars within their institutional settings. This dynamic is compounded by the widespread mistrust and hostility of elected officials in the region toward horizontal accountability actors in general. Such systemic dynamics can have the indirect effect of curtailing the Defensorías' ability to build plural coalitions of support. In other situations, the Defensoría can itself become the direct target of hostilities by powerful political forces.

In sum, a major conclusion of this chapter is that two crucial factors explain the diverse institutionalization outcomes of Defensorías in Latin America: (1) the relative stability and enforceability of formal versus informal rules within local settings, and (2) narrow versus expansive mandate interpretation. Regarding the first factor, under conditions of relatively stable and enforced formal rules, organizational form may take on heightened significance. We find evidence for this in the effects of constitutional status, or lack thereof, in Costa Rica and Panama. Also, the Argentinean Defensor's conflict with the courts indicates a relatively highly institutionalized, if not also politicized, judicial sector.[46] Where formal rules are extremely unstable and subject to routine norm violations, informal practices are likely to be the dominant factor for understanding political outcomes. This takes its most extreme form in Ecuador where political fragmentation ensured that the Defensoría was repeatedly decommissioned prior to 2005.

Local conditions of rule stability and enforcement also have a significant impact upon the second conclusion identified in this study: creative interpretation of the *content* of formal rules. Simply put, there is a great deal of elasticity in the interpretation of formal mandates among Latin American Defensorías. That said, the density of preexisting institutional frameworks will affect the office's scope of activity. For instance, while offices in El Salvador and Peru developed an election oversight mandate following activation, this was expressly prohibited in Costa Rica and Mexico where specialized electoral oversight institutions already existed. In Argentina, the Defensoría's attempt to expand upon the letter of the law was decisively rebuffed by powerful actors through formal channels. However, importantly, interpretation of mandates appears to correspond as much, if not more, to internal factors, especially

---

[46] See Pilar Domingo, "Judicialization of Politics or Politicization of the Judiciary? Recent Trends in Latin America," *Democratization* 11 (2004), 104–26.

individual leadership. In this sense, the restrictionist orientation of Defensors in Guatemala and Nicaragua in the 1990s can be contrasted to the ambitious expansionism pursued by De Avilés in El Salvador.

Across all of the Latin American cases analyzed it is the interactions between formal and informal dimensions that count most. Even in relatively highly institutionalized settings, informal norms and practices assume primacy: witness the questionable meritocracy of the Costa Rican appointment process in 2009. In turn, even under unstable conditions Defensorías can use formal rules of access to constrain powerful actors directly or indirectly. Most clearly, the use of petition powers to Constitutional Tribunals has led to decisive accountability outcomes against powerful actors. It is important to acknowledge that notwithstanding uneven stability and enforcement of formal rules at the aggregate level, there may still be significant pockets of reasonably reliable formal opportunity structures.

In this sense, Defensorías are well placed to strategically exploit the reputational concerns of those political elites keen to maintain at least the formal appearance of rule abidance, especially in the areas of political, human rights, and regulatory frameworks. This observation can be applied, for instance, to regimes with only a loose adherence to constitutional democracy, which constitutes the majority of cases in Latin America. However, the claim is also pertinent to illiberal democracies, such as Mexico and Peru in the 1990s, which were nevertheless often punctilious about the observance of formal rules. Consequently, this study is intended to draw out some of these more fine-grained distinctions among political regimes in Latin America, as opposed to falling back on the conventional dichotomy between strongly institutionalized constitutional democracies and their opposite.

A further finding of the chapter is that in no case does one feature of institutionalization acting in isolation, or in combination, guarantee the institutionalization of the Defensoría in a permanent manner. The continual production and reproduction of institutional form over time challenges conventional formalist analytical frameworks. If we discount the possibility of stabilizing the institutional development of the Defensoría over the indefinite long term, can we therefore specify some of the limiting conditions which might encourage stabilization over change? Factors that encourage stability include structural developments such as decentralization of operations. Most decisive, however, appear to be the more contingent aspects of institutional development; notably effective leadership by the first and successive Defensors. Notwithstanding the methodological difficulties of quantifying this highly particularistic and elusive feature of institutionalization, the personality of individual Defensors can make a huge difference to both the internal functionings and the external reputation of the institution.

PART III

NHRIs and Compliance

Beyond Enforcement

10

The Societalization of Horizontal Accountability

Rights Advocacy and the Defensor del Pueblo de la Nación in Argentina

Enrique Peruzzotti

10.1. INTRODUCTION

The democratic period that Argentina embarked upon in 1983 is characterized by a new form of relationship between citizens and politicians that sets it apart from earlier democratic experiences. Perhaps the best-known novelty is the emergence of a more sophisticated and demanding citizenry intent on redefining preexisting ideals of democratic representation and molding them into a new civic concern for governmental accountability. The dramatic experience of state terrorism under the last military dictatorship that governed the country (1976–1983) has given rise to a new actor, the human rights movement, which has played a crucial pedagogic role within Argentine society, introducing a profound concern for rights and the rule of law into the political culture.[1]

As a result, a new agenda of institutional reform has taken hold in Argentine society, one that demands the strengthening of agencies of accountability over state authorities and a more balanced relationship between the executive, the legislature, and judiciary. The Alfonsín administration that oversaw Argentina's transition to democracy placed human rights at the center of its political agenda. Actions

A first version of this chapter was presented at the workshop "Multi-Disciplinary Perspectives on National Human Rights Institutions, State Compliance and Social Change," jointly organized by Harvard Law School Human Rights Program and New York University Center for Human Rights and Global Justice, September 10–11, 2009. I am grateful for the valuable comments I received from participants at the meeting. I also want to thank Ryan Goodman and Thomas Pegram for their insightful suggestions, which were crucial in improving my arguments. Finally, I wish to acknowledge the research assistance of Silvie Varela for this chapter. All interviews were conducted by Silvie Varela in Buenos Aires between July and November 2009.
[1] Enrique Peruzzotti, "Towards a New Politics: Citizenship and Rights in Contemporary Argentina," *Citizenship Studies* 6 (2002), 77–93; Enrique Peruzzotti, "The Nature of the New Argentine Democracy: The Delegative Democracy Argument Revisited," *Journal of Latin American Studies* 33 (2001), 133–55.

included creating an executive-appointed national human rights commission (CONADEP), which collected information about the innumerable acts of human rights violation committed by the military dictatorship, promoted the ratification of international human rights treaties, and helped bring about the historic trial of the military juntas and the eventual conviction of five of the leading members of the dictatorship. During the presidency of Carlos Saul Menem, the 1994 constitutional reform granted constitutional status to all human rights treaties and expanded the catalogue of rights. New accountability agencies were also created such as the national human rights institution (NHRI) – or Defensor del Pueblo de la Nación[2] – and the Anticorruption Office[3] to complement and enhance the activities of existing mechanisms of accountability.

The emergence of a novel civic sensibility in large sectors of Argentine civil society focused attention on breaches of the law by public officials and gave rise to a new breed of civic politics engaged in promoting government accountability. The public space in Argentina throughout the 1990s featured a growing array of social movements and regular mobilizations denouncing governmental wrongdoing. Several high profile violations, in particular the murder of the schoolgirl Maria Soledad Morales in the northwestern province of Catamarca,[4] the death of Army private Omar Carrasco in an isolated garrison of the Patagonian province of Neuquén,[5] and the assassination of the news photographer José Luis Cabezas in the summer resort of Pinamar,[6] galvanized large sections of the population to march in their thousands

---

[2] The Defensor del Pueblo de la Nación (Human Rights Ombudsman) was introduced in 1993 and included in the 1994 constitution as an organ appointed by the National Congress oriented to protect constitutional rights and guarantees. For a description of this institution, see Linda C. Reif, "Building Democratic Institutions: The Role of National Human Rights Institutions in Good Governance and Human Rights Protection," *Harvard Human Rights Journal* 13 (2000), 57–61.

[3] The Anticorruption Office was established in 1998 with the goal of elaborating and coordinating anti-corruption programs as well as investigating alleged cases of governmental corruption.

[4] The Maria Soledad case refers to the demand for justice in the case of the rape and murder of a high school student in the northwestern province of Catamarca in September 1990. For an analysis of the case, see Catalina Smulovitz and Enrique Peruzzotti, "Societal and Horizontal Controls: Two Cases of a Fruitful Relationship," in Scott Mainwaring and Christopher Welna (eds.), *Democratic Accountability in Latin America* (Oxford: Oxford University Press, 2002), 309–31.

[5] The Carrasco case refers to the mistreatment and murder of conscript Omar Carrasco by military officers in March 1994 while he was doing the then mandatory military service in a remote barrack in the province of Neuquén. For an analysis of the case, see Jacqueline Behrend, "Mobilization and Accountability: A Study of Social Control in the 'Cabezas' Case in Argentina," in Enrique Peruzzotti and Catalina Smulovitz (eds.), *Enforcing the Rule of Law: Social Accountability in the New Latin American Democracies* (Pittsburgh: University of Pittsburgh, 2006), 213–45.

[6] The case refers to the murder of press photographer Jose Luis Cabezas in January 1997. From early on, his murder was linked to his photographs of a businessman Alfredo Yabran, the head of a vast business empire who was keen to avoid public exposure. For a detailed analysis of the case, see Jacqueline Behrend, "Mobilization and Accountability: A Study of Social Control in the 'Cabezas' Case in Argentina," in Peruzzotti and Smulovitz, *Enforcing the Rule of Law*, 213–45.

in support of justice.[7] A driving motivation for these popular protests was to exert pressure on the courts and other state agencies to activate proceedings and pursue sanctions against the wrongdoers.

Most of these accountability initiatives represented a continuation and deepening of the rights struggles that the human rights movement had begun in Argentina. In most cases these struggles were molded around the confrontational "society versus state" model characteristic of human rights struggles: autonomous movements based in civil society demand an adequate response from the mandated accountability agency. Many analyses have documented this wave of confrontational activism and shed light on its accomplishments and shortcomings.[8] The focus of this chapter, however, is on a different type of accountability initiative that has more of a mixed character and rests on the cooperative efforts of both state agencies and civil society. The Matanza-Riachuelo case, pursued by a coalition of social actors alongside the Defensor del Pueblo, refers to an extreme situation of environmental degradation affecting thousands of citizens who populate a river basin close to Buenos Aires. The case study presented in the chapter is particularly relevant to the debate on the workings and interrelationships of different kinds of accountability mechanisms, highlighting one way in which horizontal and social mechanisms can reinforce each other and jointly collaborate in the exercise of accountability. What sets this case apart from other accountability initiatives is the distinctive combination of social and horizontal resources being brought to bear in a coordinated fashion.

The chapter is divided into two sections. Section one discusses the different types of accountability mechanisms that have been the focus of recent debate, paying particular attention to the contribution of social mechanisms and appointed agencies, such as the Defensor del Pueblo. Section two analyzes the specificities of the Matanza-Riachuelo initiative. It shows that the concerted action of horizontal and social mechanisms has raised public awareness on environmental rights. The establishment of a mixed network of accountability has further improved the monitoring capability of both state agencies and civil society organizations. The concluding section evaluates the contribution of this study to an evolving research agenda on state compliance and accountability with consideration for national bodies such as NHRIs.

---

7   For example, between 1990 and 1996, demands for justice in the case of Maria Soledad Morales led to the organization of eighty-two marches in the city of Catamarca. The number rises to 107 if we count the mobilizations that took place outside Catamarca. The mobilizations in Catamarca city drew large numbers, reaching at some point 30,000 people in a province whose total population is 210,000. See Smulovitz and Peruzzotti, "Societal and Horizontal Controls," 309–31.

8   See the bibliography quoted in footnotes 5 to 8. For a more general and updated overview, see Enrique Peruzzotti, "Accountability Struggles in Argentina: From the Human Rights Movement to Kirchner," *Laboratorium: A Russian Review of Social Research* 2 (2010), 65–85.

10.2. VERTICAL AND HORIZONTAL MECHANISMS OF
ACCOUNTABILITY AND THEIR INTERRELATIONSHIPS

The concept of accountability involves the assurance that public officials are answerable for their behavior, that they can be compelled to inform and justify their decisions, and that they may be subject to sanctions for those decisions. The functioning of accountable government rests on a combination of formal and informal mechanisms. On the one hand, the institutional design of representative democracy includes a series of mechanisms such as regular elections, separation of powers, checks and balances, and due process to ensure state compliance with legal and administrative norms. On the other hand, constitutional guarantees facilitate the development of an autonomous public sphere and civil society, which also play a crucial accountability role as informal watchdogs.[9]

Guillermo O'Donnell has classified accountability mechanisms in two categories: horizontal and vertical. Vertical mechanisms refer to accountability initiatives undertaken by citizens, either as voters or as members of civil society.[10] Vertical accountability can be exercised through the institutional mechanism of regular, free, and competitive elections or through the informal influence of civil society and the media in the public sphere. Horizontal mechanisms are located within the intrastate system of checks and balances and do not rely on the actions of an external social agent.

10.2.1. *Horizontal Accountability*

The concept of horizontal accountability refers to the different institutional components that make up the complex machinery of intrastate controls.[11] Within the realm of horizontal mechanisms, O'Donnell distinguishes two distinctive forms of agencies which he designates as *balance* and *appointed* agencies. The concept of balance agencies refers to the classical system of separation of powers and checks and balances among the executive, legislature, and judiciary. Appointed agencies

---

[9] Enrique Peruzzotti, "Civil Society, Representation and Accountability: Restating Current Debates about the Representativeness and Accountability of Civic Organizations," in L. Jordan and P. Van Tuijl (eds.), *NGO Accountability: Politics, Principles and Innovation* (London: Earthscan, 2006), 44–5. For a good conceptual discussion on accountability, see R. Mulgan, *Holding Power to Account: Accountability in Modern Democracies* (London: Palgrave, 2004).

[10] For further elaboration of the distinction between horizontal and vertical accountability, see Guillermo O'Donnell, "Horizontal Accountability in New Democracies," in A. Schedler et al. (eds.), *The Self-Restraining State. Power and Accountability in New Democracies* (Boulder: Lynne Rienner, 1999), 29–52; Guillermo O'Donnell, "Horizontal Accountability: The Legal Institutionalization of Mistrust," in G. O'Donnell (ed.), *Dissonances: Democratic Critiques of Democracy* (Notre Dame, IN: University of Notre Dame Press, 2007), 77–98.

[11] O'Donnell, "Horizontal Accountability in New Democracies."

are a set of agencies specifically created to address some of the shortcomings of the classical system of separation of powers.[12] These agencies may fall within the jurisdiction of any of the three principal branches of power or have autonomous status. They include prosecutors, ombudsmen, human rights commissions, auditors, anticorruption agencies, and state councils. Both balance and appointed institutions integrate within a network of state agencies that, in theory, work in a coordinated and complementary manner.[13]

Balancing and appointed institutions differ in the ways in which they operate. According to O'Donnell, they exhibit different institutional logics. Agencies of balance, he argues, tend to be reactive and intermittent: they generally intervene only after a transgression has occurred. Such an intervention tends to be costly in political terms for it usually involves a conflict between different branches of state power.[14] Appointed agencies, on the other hand, generally regard themselves as apolitical agencies structured around professional criteria. In this sense, their interventions tend to be less conflictive and do not provoke the public hype that conflict among state powers usually generates.[15] As functionally specialized agencies of accountability specifically designed to address certain shortcomings of balancing institutions, appointed agencies can fully devote themselves to monitoring activities. The goal of appointed agencies is to prevent eventual acts of corruption or legal transgressions on the part of government, and their accountability activities might assume either a "police patrol" or a "fire alarm" modality.[16] Some agencies such as auditors engage in methodical and detailed police patrols to determine whether a certain public

---

[12] Guillermo O'Donnell, "Notes on Various Accountabilities and Their Interrelations," in Peruzzotti and Smulovitz, *Enforcing the Rule of Law*, 337.

[13] National human rights institutions are part of a horizontal network of accountability agencies. There are, however, different interpretations over which domestic human rights institutions qualify as "national human rights institutions" (see Linda Reif in this volume). Within this list of appointed horizontal institutions, only ombudsmen are unequivocally considered NHRIs in accordance with the Paris Principles. All national ombudsmen offices in Latin America are accredited with the International Coordinating Committee: http://www.nhri.net/.

[14] O'Donnell, "Notes on Various Accountabilities," 338.

[15] O'Donnell, "Notes on Various Accountabilities," 338. The description of appointed agencies as "apolitical" is a questionable one: the activities of many of them, like the Defensoría, are inherently political. Furthermore, many appointed agencies such as ethics committees, national human rights institutions, or privacy commissions have a mandate that extends beyond a legal accountability sphere of corruption or violation of legal norms to encompass violations of political accountability (i.e., actions that are not illegal per se but are considered politically unacceptable). I thank Tom Pegram for raising this point. It might be also argued that Defensorías, like other), do not strictly fit a horizontal depiction of interactions but also include an important vertical dimension. I return to this point in a later section.

[16] Matthew McCubbins and Thomas Schwartz, "Congressional Oversight Overlooked: Police Patrols versus Fire Alarms," *American Journal of Political Science* 28 (1984), 168; Kal Raustiala, "Police Patrols & Fire Alarms in the NAFTA Environmental Side Agreement," *Loyola Los Angeles International and Comparative Law Review* 26 (2004), 389–413.

budget fulfills all the formalities required by law. Other agencies instead are activated on demand. The Defensor combines both the capacity to act ex officio or to act as a receptor of claims.

The monitoring activities of appointed agencies can be accompanied by the power to enforce formal sanctions. In the absence of formal sanctioning powers, such agencies must rely on the activation of other state actors with the authority to impose legal or administrative sanctions. As such, an agency, such as the ombudsman, which lacks the power to make legally binding decisions has to rely on the willingness of other horizontal mechanisms "with teeth" to impose sanctions on wrongdoers.[17]

O'Donnell's analysis of appointed agencies, however, needs to be further developed as it includes a variety of state institutions that perform different institutional roles. There are at least three sets of literature that specifically address the nature of appointed agencies: one focused on national human rights institutions, of which this volume provides clear examples; another on auditing supervision bodies; and a third on institutions tackling the problem of government corruption.[18] The first set of literature focuses on domestic institutions that have an express human rights mandate such as human rights commissions, human rights ombudsmen, and human rights institutes. The literature on auditing bodies is largely interested in specialized agencies with responsibility for auditing and supervising public accounts, such as the public audits offices and controllers. Finally, the third set of studies focus on those agencies specifically designed to prevent and investigate corruption, such as anticorruption offices and administrative prosecutors.[19]

Most horizontal mechanisms are inserted within a broader web of accountability agencies and therefore their success is dependent, to a certain extent, on the proper and coordinated functioning of the whole network.[20] The exercise of governmental

---

[17] In the particular case of the Argentine Defensor del Pueblo, the agency does not have the capacity to impose sanctions. That said, any agency that refuses to answer its requests will be considered in violation of article 240 of the Penal Code and can thus be liable to legal sanctions on the ground of "disobedience." This gives the Defensor's requests a degree of legal force similar to those of other Defensorías in Costa Rica, Ecuador, Nicaragua, and Paraguay. See Lorena González Volio, "The Institution of the Ombudsman: The Latin American Experience," *Revista IIDH* 48 (2003), 240. I am grateful to Mariana Torres-Garcia for this observation (interview with Silvie Varela).

[18] For literature on supervisory bodies and government corruption, see "Poder Ciudadano," *El Fortalecimiento de la Responsabilidad de los Funcionarios Públicos: Construyendo Puentes entre Organismos de Control y la Sociedad Civil* (Buenos Aires: Poder Ciudadano, 2008); and Organización Latinoamericana y del Caribe de Entidades de Fiscalizadoras Superiores (OLACEFS), "Declaración de Asunción – Principios sobre Rendición de Cuentas": www.olacefs.net/uploaded/content/event/1158846820.pdf.

[19] In principle, the ombudsman or Defensor can be involved in all three issue-areas. A broader mandate than other "appointed agencies" means the Defensor is not easily pigeonholed.

[20] The effectiveness of such networks very often depends in the last instance upon the courts, particularly on the apex court where the final rulings are handed down. O'Donnell, "Notes on Various Accountabilities," 336.

accountability cannot be conceived as resting on the determination of a sole actor or agency; instead it relies upon a relatively complex chain of interactions among different horizontal institutions.[21] The workings of horizontal mechanisms will vary to the extent to which different agencies involved are able to generate a positive articulation between them. As O'Donnell argues

> For horizontal accountability to work, in particular over powerful segments of the state and government, the convergent and coordinated work of an entire network of institutions with legal authority, decision-making autonomy, and determination has to exist.[22]

If agencies are not properly structured as a network and, as a consequence, the relationship among them is not one of cooperation but of distrust or competition, the whole system of horizontal accountability will suffer. The analysis of accountability politics should thus adopt a relational perspective with a focus on points of access between different horizontal agencies as well as with other relevant, yet informal, actors such as civil society organizations.

10.2.2. *Vertical Social Accountability*

In contrast to the intrastate nature of horizontal mechanisms, vertical forms of accountability rely on the actions of an external actor: the citizenry. Elections are the paradigmatic institutional mechanism of vertical accountability. For elections to perform their accountability role, certain preconditions must be met. Only when a democracy institutionalizes regular, competitive, and free elections is the electorate able to use the vote as a mechanism of political accountability. Such features of electoral life, often taken for granted in consolidated democracies, have a particular significance in a region such as Latin America, which displays a long history of institutional instability and democratic breakdowns.[23] Only in those regimes where elections are a regular feature of political life, where viable political alternatives to official candidates exist, and sufficient guarantees are in place for citizens to exercise their political rights freely can the electorate make use of the vote as an accountability mechanism.

Outside of the state, citizens, the media, and civil society organizations in the public sphere can contest governmental decisions and denounce the unlawful actions

---

[21] This complex set of interactions is not necessarily limited to horizontal dynamics but may also involve social accountability mechanisms, particularly in the form of cooperation between social and horizontal actors.

[22] O'Donnell, "Notes on Various Accountabilities," 336.

[23] Enrique Peruzzotti, "From Praetorianism to Democratic Consolidation: Argentina's Difficult Transition to Civilian Rule," *Journal of Third World Studies* 21 (2004), 97–116; Marcelo Cavarozzi, "Political Cycles in Argentina since 1955," in G. O'Donnell et al. (eds.), *Transitions from Authoritarian Rule: Latin America* (Baltimore: Johns Hopkins University Press, 1986), 19–48.

of public officials.[24] Constitutional guarantees provide a framework for the development of an organizational substratum of associations and movements that can act as informal watchdogs over government. This component of accountable government has undergone significant development since Argentina's return to democracy, with civic struggles for more accountable government becoming an established feature of the political landscape in the new Argentine democracy. Demands are being made through a wide array of citizen initiatives, from professionalized nongovernmental organizations (NGOs) to informal grassroots movements, for effective rights, greater governmental transparency, and exposure of official wrongdoing.

Recent decades have witnessed the development and consolidation of a significant network of public interest NGOs committed to promoting the ideals of the rule of law and of responsible government. At the same time, demand for rights and the rule of law are present in a wide range of grassroots protests. Issues such as police violence, environmental hazards, and discrimination have triggered the mobilization of different constituencies to demand that authorities address their grievances. Finally, the development of a more autonomous and critical media has resulted in numerous exposés of governmental wrongdoing and a proliferation of political scandals that, in some cases, have assumed dramatic proportions.

These related developments are indicative of the emergence of a new brand of citizen politics whose goal is to ensure the subordination of elected officials to legal and constitutional norms. The term *social accountability* attempted to provide a conceptualization of such a brand of politics, on the ground that this set of actions and relationships represents an informal mechanism of vertical accountability that needs to be incorporated into the broader debate on governmental accountability.[25] In this way, the concept introduces into the classical understanding of accountability focused on the workings of state mechanisms or on isolated voters an intermediate dimension: civil society.[26]

---

[24] Peruzzotti and Smulovitz, "Social Accountability," 3–33.

[25] "Societal accountability is a non-electoral, yet vertical mechanism of control of political authorities that rests on the actions of a multiple array of citizens' associations and movements and on the media. These actions monitor the action of public officials, expose governmental wrongdoing, and can activate the operation of horizontal agencies. Societal accountability employs both institutional and non-institutional tools. The activation of legal actions or claims before oversight agencies are examples of institutionally channeled actions, social mobilizations and media exposés of non-institutional ones." Enrique Peruzzotti and Catalina Smulovitz, "Social Accountability: An Introduction," in E. Peruzzotti and C. Smulovitz (eds.), *Enforcing the Rule of Law*, 10.

[26] There are two ways in which civil society might complement and expand the workings of existing mechanisms of accountability. First, civil society enhances representative government by adding new voices and concerns to the political agenda and criticizing existing public policies and legislation. Second, civil society can contribute to improve the quality of representative arrangements by denouncing violations of rights or breaches of law and due process by public officials, as well as by developing strategies oriented to improve the mechanisms and agencies that regulate the behavior of political representatives. The first group of actions refers to the political dimension of the concept of

The politics of social accountability is a direct outcome of the development of human rights politics in Argentina. A second generation of civic claims has focused attention on the betterment of the quality of democracy. More specifically, social accountability initiatives aim to strengthen the rule of law and checks on government with a view to addressing a central issue of any rights politics: the building of a legal state. Rights cannot be made effective if there is no autonomous judiciary and no effective checks on public officials. Effective rights thus require the *constitutionalization* of state authority. In fact, many social accountability claims point to the persistence of human rights violations under democratic rule, such as police execution of civilians.[27] Yet not all of these sorts of initiatives explicitly refer to cases involving human rights violations; they also address other forms of state illegality such as corruption or violations of legal process.

Social accountability politics involve civic efforts whose goals are to (1) monitor the behavior of public officials and agencies to ensure that they abide by the law; (2) expose cases of governmental wrongdoing involving corruption and human rights violations; and (3) activate, in many instances, the operation of horizontal agencies, such as the judiciary or legislative investigation commissions, that would otherwise not act or would act in a biased manner. In exposing cases of governmental wrongdoing, activating reluctant state agencies of accountability, and monitoring the operation of those agencies, civic actors are making a crucial contribution to the enforcement of the rule of law.

Generally, the politics of social accountability is carried out by two different types of civic actors: protest movements and NGOs. Protest movements are normally born out of the mobilization of groups directly affected by breaches of law by public officials. Usually such protests are initiated by the communities or actors that perceive their rights to be violated by state actors or agencies. Families and friends of the victims of human rights violations or the victims of environmental degradation, for example, organize and mobilize to denounce, respectively, police violence or the inaction of state agencies mandated to enforce environmental controls. Neighborhood or family networks also often mobilize to demand the activation of horizontal agencies. These actors, when they attain media visibility, can be very

accountability and has been widely analyzed by the literature on social movements and by the public sphere approach. It is the second group of actions – those that revolve around the legal dimension of the concept of accountability – that are conceptualized as the politics of social accountability. Peruzzotti, "Civil Society, Representation and Accountability," 43–58.

[27] See María del Carmen Verdú, *Represión en Democracia: De la "Primavera Alfonsinista" al "Gobierno De Los Derechos Humanos"* (Buenos Aires: Herramienta Ediciones, 2009); M. Denissen, *Winning Small Battles, Losing the War: Police Violence, the Movimiento del Dolor, and Democracy in Post-authoritarian Argentina* (Amsterdam: Rozenberg, 2008); Ruth Stanley, "Controlling the Police in Buenos Aires: A Case Study of Horizontal and Vertical Accountability," *Bulletin of Latin American Research* 24 (2005), 83–105.

successful in gaining the support of the general public. That support can translate into mass mobilizations on their behalf. Given their grassroots and reactive origins, many of these movements are usually short-lived and unspecialized. They provide, however, a very vivid illustration of how accountability deficits directly affect the behavior and livelihood of ordinary citizens.

A second type of actor is the NGO or citizen association. Unlike grassroots protest movements, NGOs potentially represent a permanent and professionalized presence in the domestic landscape of many democracies. To be effective, NGOs must undergo a process of professionalization and specialization since they are frequently tasked with highly technical issues and are in permanent contact and negotiation with qualified public officials. A network of specialized NGOs can contribute to generating alternative and autonomous sources of information, diminishing asymmetries of information between the citizenry and their political representatives, and developing independent proposals for institutional reform.

In this sense, an important watershed in the agenda of social accountability is the consolidation of a network of specialized social organizations that can serve as a resource for non-specialized and grassroots civil society actors.[28] For example, a chronic problem with police violence in Argentina has led to the formation of an NGO "Coordinator against Police and Institutional Repression" (CORREPI), which produces statistics on police violence and challenges official data.[29] The organization has played a crucial role in providing legal assistance and media contacts to the family and friends of victims of police violence.

The establishment of a network of thematically specialized social watchdog organizations with significant professional skills has also contributed to the development of monitoring capacity outside the state, particularly important in democracies where horizontal accountability mechanisms tend to be weak and reluctant to fulfill their function. Informal watchdogs can effectively supervise the behavior of public officials and activate fire alarms whenever a breach of rights or process has occurred. While they might not be the most visible actors of social accountability politics, permanent societal watchdogs provide a professional and much valued infrastructure for other type of actors and movements that are frequently successful in attracting media attention and popular support.[30]

---

[28] In those cases in which the domestic watchdog network is weak or underdeveloped, global institutions or actors can play a crucial leveraging role, providing political and technical support to civic actors that might find it difficult to establish significant domestic partnerships with other sectors of society or who encounter open resistance or social indifference toward their cause. In many areas, like the environment or human rights, domestic civic actors have developed crucial linkages and coalitions with global actors to strengthen their domestic voice and influence.

[29] See http://www.correpi.lahaine.org/.

[30] The presence of an independent or watchdog journalism is essential for the success of any action of social accountability; protest movements or advocacy organizations commonly view the mainstream

10.2.3. *Analyzing the Interrelationships between Horizontal and Vertical Mechanisms*

The proper working of accountable government requires the articulation and collaboration of all mechanisms of accountability, horizontal and vertical, formal and informal. It is thus central to study accountability issues from a relational perspective that emphasizes the degree to which the entire web of accountability agents that exist in a democracy are willing and able to act in a "convergent and coordinated" fashion. Such an approach should not restrict its focus to horizontal agencies alone but should also evaluate the contribution of informal social mechanisms. Consequently, any comprehensive agenda of research on accountability should include analysis of the different types of interaction and forms of collaboration that vertical and horizontal mechanisms establish with one another.[31] The adoption of a comprehensive approach to accountability is particularly relevant for the analysis of new democracies, especially those such as Argentina where the horizontal network of agencies is weak or unable to perform its formal function adequately.[32] Under those conditions, certain forms of collaboration between horizontal and social mechanisms can emerge to address some of these deficits.

The preceding analysis has already stressed the relevance of social accountability initiatives for horizontal mechanisms in that they generally seek to activate reluctant state agencies of accountability.[33] A scenario in which social mechanisms are strong provides an important source of *stimulation* for horizontal agencies to fulfill their responsibilities. At the same time, the existence of horizontal agencies that are willing to perform their duties and responsibilities is an important facilitator of social accountability *induction*.[34] The analysis of accountability struggles in new democracies must pay particular attention to these different types of interactions

media as a potential "strategic ally." The public impact of any movement or NGO campaign may be directly proportional to the amount of media visibility it is able to gather. Peruzzotti and Smulovitz, "Social Accountability," 23–4.

[31] O'Donnell, "Notes on Various Accountabilities," 337–9.

[32] There has been a great deal of debate on the alleged malfunctioning of horizontal controls in several of the new Latin American democracies. Guillermo O'Donnell even classified them as a distinctive type of democratic regime characterized by the extreme weakness of horizontal checks on the executive. Guillermo O'Donnell, "Delegative Democracy," *Journal of Democracy* 5 (1994), 55–69.

[33] Civil society actors tend to make multiple openings on the "board game" of horizontal agencies with a view to gauging which agency might show receptiveness to their claims. Lemos and Zaverrucha refer to such a strategy as the "multiple activation" of horizontal agencies. Ana Tereza Lemos and Jorge Zaverrucha, "Multiple Activation as a Strategy of Citizen Accountability and the Role of the Investigating Legislative Commissions," in Peruzzotti and Smulovitz, *Enforcing the Rule of Law*, 75–114.

[34] O'Donnell uses the terms induction and stimulation to conceptualize the interactions between vertical and horizontal mechanisms. O'Donnell, "Notes on Various Accountabilities," 339.

that mechanisms of accountability may establish with one another. As O'Donnell forcefully put it, "it is in these interactions, both of induction and stimulation, where chances to move forward in the much-needed democratization of these countries can be found."[35]

10.2.4. *The Defensor del Pueblo and Social and Horizontal Mechanisms*

The case study presented in this chapter elucidates a joint initiative involving appointed agencies of horizontal accountability (principally, the Defensor del Pueblo de la Nación and the Supreme Court of Justice) as well as grassroots and NGO organizations. This case merits special attention: it takes us beyond cycles of induction and stimulation to highlight how horizontal and social mechanisms have mutually reinforced one another in the joint exercise of accountability. The case is drawn from Argentina, a country where, as argued above, social accountability initiatives have proliferated in the contemporary democratic period, with civic demands for more accountable government a constant presence in the public arena. It is important to note, however, that most accountability initiatives have assumed a confrontational character with social actors seeking to activate mechanisms of state accountability through popular mobilization and public exposés of wrongdoing. By raising the political stakes of conflict, social actors have attempted to exert moral and political pressure on public authorities.

However, this chapter illustrates an alternative form of collaborative accountability between civil society actors and NHRIs, in this case the Defensor del Pueblo. As noted earlier, the Defensor is a distinctive appointed agency. Not only does the Defensor have a broader mandate than many other appointed agencies (and thus can be involved in a wider range of issues from human rights violations to government corruption); it also combines horizontal and vertical elements with the result that the Defensor is not solely an intrastate mechanism of accountability but also closely related to, and to a large extent activated by, society.[36] The Defensor del Pueblo, created in 1993 as an independent organ appointed by Congress, is mandated to initiate investigations to shed light on the actions and omissions of the public administration as well as private actors.[37] As such, the Defensor has taken up cases involving human rights violations, consumer rights protection, the environment, the right to information, and inadequate provision of public services, among other issues.

---

[35] Ibid.
[36] See footnote 21.
[37] In fact, during the tenure of the first Defensor, Jorge Maiorano, the agenda was strongly oriented toward economic issues such as public service tariffs, consumer protection, and the establishment of a regulatory framework for the newly privatized public services sector.

The Defensor can either act ex officio or upon receiving a complaint. A large part of its legitimacy is built upon the idea that it is an institution that is particularly receptive to citizens' demands and expectations. For instance, the Defensor's involvement in the Matanza-Riachuelo case is the result of a claim brought by a community organization to the office. This is not the first environmental claim to reach the Defensor. Indeed, the institution has intervened on behalf of environmental causes since its earliest years. In 1995 it took part in a campaign against the docking of a vessel containing plutonium. It was also involved in the case of the contamination of the *Sali Dulce* basin and was active in several other matters relating to environmental claims.[38] During the tenure of Eduardo Mondino (1999–2009), environmental issues have assumed a greater significance, reflected in the creation of an environmental division within the Defensor.

What makes the Matanza-Riachuelo case distinctive is not so much the nature of the claim as the type of response it has generated on the part of the Defensor, specifically, the institution's decision to shift from a confrontational model to a strategy that required a significant effort of articulation with other actors both within the state and civil society. The Matanza-Riachuelo is a complex accountability initiative that involves various types of horizontal and social actors acting in concert to address a very difficult environmental issue. The focus of this chapter now turns to this case study and shows how Argentine civil society has not only pressured horizontal agencies from "outside" but has also positioned itself as an integral part of the controlling mechanism. The case demonstrates one way in which the dynamics of induction and stimulation identified by O'Donnell can play out, leading to the institutionalization of cooperation between formal and informal agencies of accountability.

10.3. ANALYZING NEW FORMS OF COORDINATION BETWEEN APPOINTED AGENCIES AND SOCIAL WATCHDOGS: THE MATANZA-RIACHUELO CASE IN ARGENTINA

The Matanza-Riachuelo case refers to one of the most significant environmental controversies in Argentina: the historic contamination of the basin of a river that runs through a densely populated metropolitan area.[39] The 64 km long Matanza-Riachuelo River runs through the industrial belt of the Metropolitan Area of Buenos Aires, across fourteen municipalities of the province of Buenos Aires and part of the

---

[38] Such cases include the preservation of forests in Tierra del Fuego, mining practices, and the placement of radar, to name a few.

[39] The reconstruction of the case study is based on interviews with different actors involved in the initiative, analysis of media coverage in national newspapers (mainly *Clarín*, *La Nación*, and *Pagina 12*), and examination of documents produced by the different actors and organizations involved in the case.

City of Buenos Aires (CABA). It is the most contaminated river basin in Argentina, and one of the thirty most contaminated sites in the world.[40] It is also one of the most socially and environmentally deprived urban areas in Argentina. Around 55 percent of its roughly five million inhabitants (13.5 percent of the total population of Argentina) lack sewage facilities, 35 percent lack drinkable water, and a large number live in shantytowns or otherwise precarious settlements.[41]

The current levels of pollution stem from the large volume of toxic waste that approximately 5,000 factories regularly release into the river, as well as liquid waste from clandestine sewage pipes and garbage from more than 100 open-air landfill sites on its banks.[42] Moreover, since the area is near water level and has poor drainage, severe floods are common. As a result of these conditions, an already vulnerable population suffers from many environment-related diseases, including typhoid fever, salmonella, hepatitis A and E, bubonic plague, lead poisoning, and cancer, among a long list of other conditions.[43]

Despite such a bleak situation, a highly fragmented governance structure within the basin area has made little progress in dealing with the problem. The large number of competing authorities at the national, provincial, municipal, and local levels, each with its own rules and procedures concerning regulation and control of pollution, flood prevention, and provision of essential services and health care, has made it difficult for state authorities to agree upon and implement solutions. The superposition and overlapping of jurisdictions has historically conspired against the establishment of effective laws and regulations. It has also worked against any effective exercise of horizontal accountability, with the presence of federal, provincial, and municipal accountability agencies conspiring against coherent and convergent monitoring activities. Similarly, the presence of such a complex and heterogeneous map of horizontal institutions has impaired citizens' ability to monitor the actions of public officials. The end result has been the perpetuation of a situation highly detrimental to the well-being of the inhabitants of the basin and a persistent and serious environmental hazard in the heart of Argentina's largest urban area.

In December 1992, then president Menem made an unexpected announcement to the public expressing his determination to clean up the Matanza-Riachuelo basin "in 1000 days." A few weeks later, Menem promised Argentines that by 1995 the basin would be converted into a recreational area where people would be able to fish, navigate, and bathe in the river's waters. The high hopes inspired by the president's

---

[40] See Fundación Ambiente y Recursos Naturales, "Problemática de la cuenca," April 3, 2009.

[41] C. Fairstein, "En busca de soluciones judiciales para mejorar la calidad de vida de los habitantes de la cuenca Matanza-Riachuelo," _CELSInforme Anual 2009_ (Centro de Estudios Legales y Sociales, 2009), 332–58.

[42] Ibid.

[43] See Defensor del Pueblo de la Nación, _Informe Matanza-Riachuelo, La Cuenca en Crisis_ (Buenos Aires: DPN, 2003).

words were nevertheless dashed by the administration's lack of action. Following the deadline, and with no significant change in the environmental situation of the area, a spokesperson for the administration dismissed criticism by claiming that the president's promise had been intended as a metaphor not as a literal undertaking.[44]

The most significant development of the period was the creation in 1995 of the Executive Committee for Environmental Control and Management of the Matanza-Riachuelo River (CEMR), an integrated committee with representatives of the federal, provincial and municipal levels of government, which would oversee the elaboration of an environmental management plan (EMP).[45] The plan's focus consisted of four main issues-areas: hydrologic regulation and drainage, prevention and control of pollution, citizen participation and environmental education, and institutional development and land use management. The CEMR was also mandated to examine the regeneration of rundown areas in the City of Buenos Aires.[46] In terms of process, the EMP entailed three phases: (1) identifying the issues that needed to be tackled; (2) establishing the goals of the plan with the CEMR presenting a preliminary plan to representatives from various levels of government; and (3) conducting a public presentation of the final version of the plan to the basin community and facilitating its dissemination in various national newspapers.[47]

In 1997, under the secretariat of Maria Julia Alsogaray, the Inter-American Development Bank approved a loan of $250 million to finance activities proposed by the EMP. The contract with the bank made the CEMR responsible for implementing the plan jointly with the government of the province and the City of Buenos Aires. Some initial action was subsequently carried out, including the partial cleaning of the river and work to control flooding.[48] However, these initiatives did not significantly alter the level of pollution and environmental degradation in the area

---

[44] Defensor del Pueblo, *Informe Matanza-Riachuelo*, 241.

[45] To the above entities we also need to add the presence of two further inter-jurisdictional bodies, Ecological Coordination for the Metropolitan Area and the Central Market Corporation, which represent between them the public utility companies, respective regulatory agencies, and private sector industries located in the basin. For a discussion of the problems posed for the implementation of environmental policies by such a complex map of different actors, see María Gabriela Merlinsky, "El Plan Integral de Saneamiento Ambiental de la Cuenca Matanza-Riachuelo: desafíos para la gestion integrada del agua en la región metropolitana de Buenos Aires," in María Gabriela Merlinsky, *Política y Gestión Hídrica en la Región Metropolitana de Buenos Aires* (Buenos Aires: Editorial Universidad Nacional de General Sarmiento, forthcoming).

[46] Defensor del Pueblo de la Nación, *Informe Especial de Seguimiento Cuenca Matanza-Riachuelo* (2003–2005), (Buenos Aires: DPN, 2005).

[47] Defensor del Pueblo, *Informe Matanza-Riachuelo*, 231.

[48] The Defensor viewed the CEMR's management plan as a mandate for hydrologic engineering rather than an environmental management plan. This was reflected in a proposal submitted to the Inter-American Development Bank by the CEMR to request an extension of the terms of the loan until the end of 2007. This proposal allocated 89.2 percent of the funds to hydrologic engineering and drainage, as well as sewage disposal, and only 5.1 percent to preventing and controlling pollution. Defensor, *Informe Especial de Seguimiento*, 58.

and a significant part of the Inter-American Development Bank funds was diverted to other areas of government.[49]

10.3.1. *Social Accountability Initiatives in the Matanza-Riachuelo Area*

Different types of civic action were initiated to confront the environmental and social issues affecting the basin's population. Daniel Ryan distinguishes between two forms of social intervention: mobilization of grassroots actors, such as community or associations, and mobilization by unemployed or *piqueteros* (protester) organizations in response to specific environmental emergencies, such as floods and hazardous spills. The latter group of actors is usually galvanized by a particular emergency affecting the community. Once the crisis has passed these organizations tend to return to their usual social and political activities.[50] As such, the activism of protester organizations on environmental issues is generally determined by the scale of the immediate crisis. Once the issue is resolved, or the sense of emergency dissipates, environmental claims recede to the background in favor of other type of demands.

The former group of grassroots actors is composed of neighborhood and community associations such as La Boca Neighborhood Association (AVLB) and others;[51] informal resident networks, such as the residents of Villa Inflamable ("City in Flames"), a town located in the Riachuelo basin opposite a Shell oil refinery; and NGOs including the national organization Foundation for the Environment and Natural Resources and Greenpeace that have made environmental issues the centerpiece of their advocacy agendas. At the outset, civil society lacked a shared view on the common problems and challenges affecting the basin community.[52] In the absence of area-wide organization, most early social initiatives were focused

---

[49] Daniel Ryan, "Ciudadanía y Control del Gobierno en la Cuenca Matanza-Riachuelo," Center for Latin American Social Policy, University of Texas, September 2004, 7. A report by the Defensor estimated that only 3 percent of the loan was used, of which 77 percent was spent on consultancies and other activities unrelated to the protection and improvement of the environment. Moreover, Argentina had to pay $6 million in fines for failing to use the loan. It is in this context that in 2002 approximately $150 million was reassigned to social plans in response to the dramatic socioeconomic crisis of 2001. In effect, EMP funding was diverted to finance welfare programs. Defensor, *Informe Especial de Seguimiento*, 10.

[50] Alfredo Alberti, president of the La Boca Neighborhood Association (AVLB), argues that while there are numerous neighborhood associations (at least one for every region within the basin) working on health-related, social, and environmental issues in the area, most focus on narrow local problems and do not engage in larger problems affecting the whole basin. Carolina Fairstein made a similar point regarding the political focus of territorially based associations. Interviews with Alfredo Alberti and Carolina Fairstein conducted by Silvie Varela.

[51] Other neighborhood associations include the Civil Association for the Environment in South Avellaneda (*Asociación Civil Ambiente Sur de Avellaneda*) and the Society for Public Works in Dock Sud (*Sociedad de Fomento del Dock Sud*).

[52] Ryan, "Ciudadanía y Control de Gobierno," 17.

narrowly on defined territorial demands targeting municipal authorities with little interaction or coordination within the wider community of organizations and movements that populate the basin.

10.3.2. *The Organization of a Mixed Network of Accountability*

The major breakthrough in the politics of social accountability can be traced to the decision by two different social actors to file complaints with the Defensor del Pueblo denouncing the severe pollution and flooding affecting the residents of the Matanza-Riachuelo basin. La Boca Neighborhood Association (AVLB) filed the first complaint in 2002.[53] This was followed shortly by an individual complaint by a resident of Villa Inflamable who denounced the serious health problems suffered by her three children as a result of the high levels of pollution. These initial claims were followed by a growing volume of complaints by various organizations and neighbors located in the basin. In response, the Defensor summoned together a group of organizations to coordinate and develop a unified strategy to address the issue.

After being approached by the AVLB, the Defensor del Pueblo Eduardo Mondino requested Mariana Garcia Torre, a lawyer within the Defensor and an expert on environmental issues, to evaluate the environmental situation in the basin. Among Garcia Torre's recommendations, particular emphasis was placed on an integral approach that involved social accountability actors in dealing with such a complex issue. The Defensor put this into operation by first establishing working relations with AVLB and subsequently reaching out to other interested civil society organizations capable of bringing additional mobilizing resources to the table.[54] For the AVLB, the Defensor played a crucial articulating role in the organization of a broad coalition of state officials and other relevant actors within civil society.[55] The result was the

---

[53] Among the neighborhood associations, the AVLB stands out because of its structural approach to the problems of the basin. This was not always the case. AVLB was set up in 2000 to deal with the various issues affecting the neighborhood such as education, health, broken pavements, and citizen insecurity. However, the organization eventually realized that tackling the problems of the Riachuelo effectively demanded a more holistic approach. While the AVLB does not have a mandate to represent other neighborhood associations, the president, Alfredo Alberti, notes that in an informal way, it serves as a source of information for them and "probably" represents their interests. Initially, AVLB's strategy consisted of talking to as many people as possible in the government to try to find someone who would take up the issue of the Riachuelo, as well as organizing rallies in the neighborhood. However, neither the government nor the opposition wanted to tackle the issue – it was a political "hot potato" associated with the spectacular failure of the Menem government's 1,000 days plan.

[54] Interview with Mariana Garcia Torres conducted by Silvie Varela.

[55] The coordinating role of the Defensor in this instance is particularly important given the absence of an "environmental justice" movement in Argentine civil society. Despite the large number of citizens, particularly those living in shantytowns directly affected by pollution, there is still no visible society-wide environmental movement. For an analysis of contemporary environmental conflicts in Argentina, see Maria Gabriela Merlinsky, "Legislating Environmental Rights in Argentina: A

creation of a working group comprised of local associations that had made the original complaint, four national NGOs, a national university,[56] and the Defensoría of the City of Buenos Aires (Defensoría de la Ciudad de Buenos Aires).[57]

The group produced a report in 2003 entitled "Matanza-Riachuelo, the River Basin in Crisis" documenting the environmental conditions in the area and identifying the institutional weaknesses that had led to the current situation.[58] The report contained a series of recommendations directed at the relevant authorities including the need to undertake studies to determine the impact of existing environmental conditions on the population's health, implement environmental audits of the factories based on the river banks, and devise a plan and timetable for their eventual decommissioning. Crucially, the report insisted on the need to create an independent Matanza-Riachuelo basin authority.

In December 2003 the Defensor and the organizations that co-authored the report held a joint press conference that received considerable press coverage.[59] The authorities' response was, however, disappointing. Expressions of broad agreement by public officials with much of the report did not translate into substantive action. A follow-up report produced by the Defensor in 2006, along with the coauthors of the earlier report and a host of new organizations, denounced the continuing inaction of government.[60]

In a separate initiative in 2004, a group composed of one hundred forty residents of the Matanza-Riachuelo basin, many of them from Villa Inflamable, along with twenty medical professionals from the local hospital filed a lawsuit before the Supreme Court of the Nation against the federal government, the province of Buenos Aires, the City of Buenos Aires, and forty-four firms for damage to health caused by the

Renewal of Citizenship?" in Alex Latta and Hannah Wittman (eds.), *Environment and Citizenship in Latin America: Sites of Struggle, Points of Departure* (Amsterdam: CEDLA Latin American Series, forthcoming).

56 This group included the NGOs Center for Legal and Social Studies (CELS), City Foundation, Foundation for the Environment and Natural Resources, Citizen Power/Transparency International, and the National Technical University.

57 The diverse nature of the network allowed for a more effective form of control of a complex problem requiring access to different types of knowledge and expertise. The combination of grassroots organizations such as the AVLB with access to reliable and updated on-the-ground knowledge of the affected area made a crucial contribution to the agenda of control and gave other actors access to information that would otherwise have been very difficult to obtain. Similarly, City Foundation contributed its ample experience in organizing neighborhood forums while the universities and specialized NGOs were crucial in evaluating and generating technical expert reports.

58 Defensor del Pueblo, *Informe Matanza-Riachuelo.*

59 See for example *Clarín*, "Un Informe Revela el Desastre Ambiental que Provoca el Riachuelo," December 3, 2003; *Clarín*, "En el Riachuelo hay mucho más plomo que los niveles permitidos," December 5, 2003; and the same newspaper's op-ed "Contaminación en el Riachuelo," December 13, 2003.

60 New organizations included the Popular Association La Matanza, the National University of La Matanza, and Greenpeace. See Defensor, *Informe Especial de Seguimiento.*

environmental pollution of the Matanza-Riachuelo River.[61] The Supreme Court dismissed the case for individual damages but admitted a class action for collective damages. The case received little publicity until 2006, when it became a priority for the Court after the president at the time, Néstor Kirchner, singled out "taking care of the environment as a state policy."[62]

In the face of government unresponsiveness to its recommendations, the Defensor decided to take part in the lawsuit as a plaintiff. The organizations that had co-authored the 2003 report also filed claims, but the Supreme Court denied most of them on a legal technicality admitting only the Center of Legal and Social Studies, FARN, Greenpeace, and La Boca Association.[63] This legal action bore results: on June 20, 2006, the Supreme Court ordered the national and local governments to develop a plan to clean up the Riachuelo.[64] The Secretariat for the Environment and Sustainable Development presented a first draft of the plan in August, which the Supreme Court returned with observations.

Under sustained pressure from the Supreme Court, the Defensor, and civil society organizations, the Argentine Congress passed a law in December that created the Matanza-Riachuelo Basin Authority (ACUMAR). This new body unites the various authorities with jurisdiction over the Riachuelo at the national, provincial, and municipal level. The objective of ACUMAR is to centralize government initiatives in the basin area and more effectively coordinate accountability agencies with a view to ensuring that polluters face sanctions. Among other responsibilities, ACUMAR is in charge of the implementation of the latest environmental cleanup plan, the "Integral Plan for the Environmental Sanitation of the Matanza-Riachuelo River" ("Integral Plan").[65]

---

[61] See Supreme Court of the Nation, *Mendoza, Beatriz Silvia et al. v. National Government et al.* (case no. 1569) for damages caused by environmental pollution of the Matanza-Riachuelo River. Sentence of July 8, 2008. Usually the Supreme Court of the Nation is a court of last appeal, that is, cases go to the Court after exhausting all other avenues at the lower level. In this case, however, the Supreme Court had "competencia originaria," that is, the case went directly to the Court, which was considered the court of first instance because the defendants were the national government and the provincial government.

[62] *Página 12*, "Un Fallo para Salvar el Riachuelo," June 21, 2006.

[63] Another NGO, the Civil Association for Civil Rights, filed a claim as an independent third-party plaintiff.

[64] The new composition of the Supreme Court after appointments made during Kirchner's first year in office gave the Court a more activist profile. Yet, if compared with other Supreme Courts in the region, like the ones in Costa Rica or Colombia, the Argentine Court represents a more moderate case of legal activism (personal communication by the author with Christian Courtis). The Argentine Court had in the past refused to grant judicial legitimation to the Defensor. That is why the latter decided to initiate the Mendoza case as a third-party plaintiff. Interview with Mariana Garcia Torres conducted by Silvie Varela. For further details on this episode see Thomas Pegram in this volume, "National Hman Rights Institutions in Latin America: Politics and Institutionalization."

[65] This plan is a modified version of the plan initially developed by the Secretariat for Environment and Sustainable Development which was approved by ACUMAR in December 2007.

ACUMAR is comprised of a board of directors headed by the Secretariat for the Environment and Sustainable Development and representatives from the three levels of government (representing federal, provincial, and city authorities),[66] a municipal council with representatives from the fourteen municipalities that make up the basin, and a social participation commission. The role of the commission is to coordinate the implementation of the Integral Plan alongside civil society. Any organization with an interest in the basin can join the commission. ACUMAR has also set up a "Forum of Universities" in the Matanza-Riachuelo Basin to facilitate interaction between university experts and the group of experts appointed to oversee the Integral Plan. The executive director's office and the General Secretariat oversee all the various actors involved in implementing the Integral Plan.[67]

In a further development, in July 2008 the Argentine Supreme Court ruled that the federal government, the province of Buenos Aires, and the government of the City of Buenos Aires have a legal duty to address the pollution in the river.[68] In the ruling, the Court set out specific requirements, including the repair of the environment, improving the quality of life of the population, and preventing future damage. The Court further ordered ACUMAR to fulfill these obligations within a specific timeline, leaving open the possibility of levying fines on this body if it failed to comply with the ruling. The Court designated the federal judge of Quilmes, Luis Armella, as the sole judicial authority with jurisdiction over ensuring that the deadlines are met. The Court also established a system for civil society to monitor the implementation process.

During the two years prior to this judgment, the Supreme Court organized a series of public hearings and information sessions, and generally worked to ensure the participation of all involved. The ruling itself also ordered the Defensor del Pueblo to consider and respond to citizens' suggestions and to coordinate a civil society body that includes representatives from NGOs involved in the case as third-party

---

[66] ACUMAR has been a frequent victim of political crises in the federal government with three different executive directors in 2008 and 2009. One previous director, Romina Picolotti, formerly head of the Secretariat for the Environment and Sustainable Development, was forced to resign after media exposés of corruption.

[67] ACUMAR includes a Social Participation Commission, the goal of which is to incorporate the perspective of civil society organizations in the management of ACUMAR – that is, to ensure that ACUMAR listens to civil society – and monitors the progress of the Integral Plan from a social perspective. Any organization that registers with ACUMAR may take part in it. According to Carolina Fairstein, the idea is for the Social Participation Commission to engage local neighborhoods in the development of solutions. However, while the Commission under the stewardship of Romina Picolotti held three meetings with social organizations working in the area before his departure in December 2008, it has held none since. Interview with Carolina Fairstein conducted by Silvie Varela (August 2009).

[68] Supreme Court of the Nation, *Mendoza, Beatriz Silvia et al. v. National Government et al.* (case no. 1569).

plaintiffs.[69] The Defensor thus plays a central role in articulating the voice of civil society within this process and conveying its message to the Supreme Court. In addition, the ruling further instructed the National General Auditing Office to control the budgetary implementation of the plan.

The role of the civil society body (CSB) is to monitor compliance with the obligations set out in the court sentence and to make the relevant recommendations to ACUMAR. Its role is not to make policy decisions. Despite some tensions, the body has complied fully with the ruling, duly answering all requirements from the judge. It has organized and taken part in the seminar, "Our Environment Is Precious," part of which focused on the Riachuelo, and actively sought to contact other organizations working in the area and to disseminate information about the ruling and its own work. In March 2009 the CSB presented a report in which it denounced ACUMAR's inaction.[70] The report argued that ACUMAR had made only a limited number of inspections of the industries that are located on the basin to determine which ones were contaminating the river. The report also argued that ACUMAR had not developed a comprehensive program of sewage installation in the basin and had not taken action to eradicate the numerous illegal garbage dump sites that exist in the area. As a result, the CSB requested that the judge make effective the sanctions that are contemplated in the Court's ruling.[71] In November 2009 the CSB produced another report in which it denounced ACUMAR for inspecting only 466 of the approximately 14,000 industrial sites in operation between April and October of 2009. The report demanded that a special body of inspectors be created to accelerate the pace of reform.[72]

In June 2009 the World Bank approved a loan to Argentina for $840 million specifically to finance the cleanup of the basin and develop basic infrastructure, such as the installation of sewage systems and waste-treatment plants.[73] The loan will finance cleanup, industrial conversion, land management (including the building of basic infrastructure such as sewage systems and proper housing), and the institutional strengthening of ACUMAR. Under its terms, the firm Water and Sanitation Argentina (AySA) is responsible for cleanup activities, including building sewage systems and waste-treatment plants, which will exhaust most of the loan

---

[69] These are Foundation for the Environment and Natural Resources, CELS, Greenpeace, AVLB, and the Association for Civil Rights.

[70] "El Riachuelo Todavía sin Avances," *Página* 12, March 24, 2009.

[71] Ibid.

[72] "Empresas que Contaminan el Riachuelo," *Página* 12, November 24, 2009.

[73] The World Bank loan adds to the previous one granted by the Inter-American Development Bank in 1997 to the then undersecretary of environment Maria Julia Alsogaray for $250 million. "El Banco Mundial Aprobó Créditos pero Critico la Política Económica," *Clarín*, June 10, 2009; "Dólares Frescos para Sanear el Riachuelo," *Pagina* 12, June 10, 2009.

($700 million). ACUMAR is in charge of industrial conversion toward environmentally friendly production systems, estimated to cost just over $60 million.[74] The initiation of the works was scheduled for September–October 2010 with the stipulation that it be completed within thirty-six months.[75]

On October 2009, Federal Judge Luis Armella ordered that the head of ACUMAR, Homero Biblioni, and the mayor of Lanus, Dario Diaz Perez, complete within five days the construction of a protective fence around an industrial complex in Lanus that had been stipulated in ACUMAR's original plan. If they did not meet the deadline, the mayor would be forced to return approximately $550,000 that had been previously transferred to the municipality to build the fence. Both Biblioni and Diaz Perez would also be personally fined if they failed to comply by the stipulated deadline. ACUMAR's request for an extension of the deadline was denied by the judge. When the deadline passed, the judge decided to personally inspect the sites in question to determine whether any work at all had taken place.[76] Upon finding that several of the construction sites were in progress, including the cleaning up of the river's margins and the building of a coastal road, he decided to suspend the fines.[77]

10.4. EVALUATING THE EFFECTIVENESS OF THE MATANZA-RIACHUELO INITIATIVE AND ITS CONTRIBUTION TO STATE ACCOUNTABILITY

A recurring theme in the different chapters of this volume is the contribution of NHRIs to state compliance with international and domestic law. To what extent does the creation of an NHRI have an effect on state compliance? Under what circumstances do NHRIs become effective compliance mechanisms? This chapter has focused on one possible path to greater effectiveness of NHRIs in achieving state compliance by analyzing a specific case that involves a significant degree of coordination between the Defensor del Pueblo de la Nación, National General Auditing Office, civil society organizations, and the judiciary. The Matanza-Riachuelo case provides a context-rich example of how increased levels of action and engagement among different actors in both society and the state can enhance governmental accountability and state compliance.

---

[74] *Página* 12, "Dólares frescos para sanear el Riachuelo," June 10, 2009.
[75] "Riachuelo. El gobierno chino, entre los once interesados en ganar la licitación para sanear el Riachuelo," *Clarín*, December 7, 2009.
[76] Judge Armella decided that he would personally monitor the progress of the works on site rather than relying on ACUMAR reports. "Demoras en obras en el Riachuelo," *Clarín*, November 2, 2009.
[77] "Riachuelo: multan al secretario de Ambiente y a un intendente," *Clarín*, October 28, 2009; *Clarín*, "Pese a las Sanciones, Continua Parada la Limpieza del Riachuelo," November 2, 2009; "Riachuelo: suspenden las multas," *Clarín*, November 4, 2009.

Social pressure → horizontal activation → greater effectiveness of horizontal agencies → greater incentives for social actors to resort to horizontal mechanisms

FIGURE 10.1. A reinforcing cycle of accountability.

What is the novel contribution of the Matanza-Riachuelo experience to the research agenda on political accountability? It sheds important light on an issue raised previously by Guillermo O'Donnell – the need to explore how different forms of interrelations between horizontal and social mechanisms (and between horizontal mechanisms) can help to advance the agenda of democracy, rights, and accountable government. Horizontal and social mechanisms of accountability, he argued, can reinforce each other in a virtuous cycle of "induction and stimulation" that in the end results in improved state compliance. It was O'Donnell's belief that civic pressure on horizontal agencies via mobilization and media exposés could trigger such a virtuous cycle of induction and stimulation. If civil society and the media were capable of sustaining social pressure through denouncing and exposing government wrongdoing they could eventually encourage a reinforcing cycle of accountability (see Figure 10.1).

The Matanza-Riachuelo experience, however, bears little resemblance to this confrontational model of societal activation – whereby largely hostile social pressure forces the activation of reluctant horizontal actors – that informs the initial wave of social accountability studies.[78] The experience analyzed in this chapter does not fit a confrontational pattern but rather a different form of action and engagement between horizontal and social mechanisms, one where social actors and state agencies act jointly in a coordinated manner to demand state compliance.[79] In this scheme, the Defensor has played a crucial role, acting as a broker between horizontal and social actors. Perhaps the fact that the Defensor (like some other NHRI) is not strictly a purely horizontal mechanism but an agency that combines both horizontal and vertical attributes has allowed it to play such a coordination and mediation role successfully.[80] For civil society actors, the Defensor provides an accessible entry point to the horizontal network of accountability agencies within the state,

---

[78] Typical examples of this pattern are the Cabezas, Maria Soledad Morales, and Carrasco cases that were mentioned in the first section. See the bibliography suggested in footnotes 4 to 7.

[79] I am not necessarily privileging cooperative over confrontational forms of accountability initiatives. Struggles for more accountable government in Argentina, as elsewhere, should rely on a variety of forms of intervention. What is positive is the pluralization of the repertoire of actions for those committed to an agenda of governmental accountability.

[80] Linda Reif defines an NHRI as a horizontal accountability mechanism with vertical accountability elements while Sonia Cardenas refers to them as "relatively new institutional actors situated uniquely between state and society." See Linda C. Reif, "The Shifting Boundaries of NHRI Definition in the International System" and Sonia Cardenas, "National Human Rights Institutions and State Compliance," both in this volume.

serving as a bridge between social accountability initiatives and the intrastate network of horizontal agencies.[81]

The combined and coordinated action of different actors has resulted in more effective intervention, with accountability actions benefiting from the specific and combined input of distinct accountability partners. By incorporating a heterogeneous group of civic stakeholders into their controlling activities, horizontal mechanisms profit from the specific input that actors as diverse as grassroots organizations, international environmental NGOs, and universities generate. Grassroots organizations, for example, have provided invaluable knowledge of the local terrain, monitoring on a daily basis the progress of construction and cleanup activities. They can also immediately report any incident or environmental emergency. Other organizations, such as environmental NGOs or universities, contribute with their professional and technical expertise, which is crucial in the evaluation of government reports. The backing that the Matanza-Riachuelo case has received from the Supreme Court of Justice and the fact that the Court now acts in concert with the Defensor del Pueblo de la Nación not only strengthens the legitimacy and political relevance of the initiative but gives proxy sanctioning powers to the Defensor. As such, the decisions of the Defensor in this particular case are no longer an expression of soft power but are now backed up by concrete legal sanction.[82]

But to what extent can we say that this innovative form of articulation between horizontal and vertical mechanisms actually generates a more effective tool with which to demand state compliance? Did the Matanza-Riachuelo initiative accomplish some degree of state compliance? State compliance is always difficult to evaluate, especially in such a complex case as the one that was the focus of this chapter. As Sonia Cardenas warns us in her contribution to this volume, we should avoid an "all or nothing" approach to compliance. Compliance, she argues "is accordingly a complex phenomenon that can occur to varying degrees and consist of diverse actions."[83] Thus it would be erroneous to assess an initiative "in a neat linear fashion." Rather, it might be more productive to analyze its "fits and starts" by focusing on a multiplicity of partial (yet relevant) accountability outcomes.[84] The balance of this chapter accordingly tries to identify some specific accountability outcomes of the

---

[81] Of course, for the Defensor to play such a role its political independence from government is crucial. This is why in the case of Argentina more than 100 civil society organizations engaged in a campaign to make the appointment of the Defensor a public, participatory, and transparent affair. See Asociación por los Derechos Civiles, "Campana Una Defensor del Pueblo, por el Pueblo y para el Pueblo," *Gacetilla de Prensa* 177, September 9, 2009.

[82] The Court intervention helped to convert the case from an instance of soft power into a new legal obligation for the Argentine state.

[83] See Sonia Cardenas in this volume, "National Human Rights Institutions and State Compliance."

[84] Ibid.

Matanza-Riachuelo initiative as well as elucidate the extent to which some of those outcomes are intrinsically tied to the specific accountability strategy of coordinated action between horizontal and vertical mechanisms.

What are the accountability outcomes of this case so far? It is impossible to pronounce a final dictum on the subject given that the Matanza-Riachuelo case is far from closed. While there have been significant advances, still to be seen is the extent to which all the measures, such as infrastructure work, cleanup activities, relocation or reorganization of industries, and relocation or proper urbanization of the population that is left in the basin are effectively accomplished. Yet, the initiative has already generated several significant accountability outcomes that should not be overlooked. To begin with, the Matanza-Riachuelo case contributes to the agenda of accountable government by generating an innovative form of articulation between horizontal and social mechanisms that expands the preexisting stock of accountability actions. This in itself is a valuable contribution to accountability politics in Argentina and in the region. The model that the Matanza-Riachuelo case introduced has already been replicated in other environmental cases. For instance, in 2004 the civic organization Pro-Tigre asked the Defensor to initiate a similar process to address a comparable environmental problem in the Reconquista river basin; and the Defensor has developed an approach modeled on the Matanza-Riachuelo experience.[85]

The Matanza-Riachuelo initiative has also generated accountability outcomes that concretely address its specific demands. First, the initiative had a major institutional impact: the creation of a public body (ACUMAR) that is responsible for the elaboration and coordination of the cleanup plan. This is no minor accomplishment, particularly given the complex web of state authorities and agencies that operate in the basin, highlighted by many actors as a principal obstacle to achieving concerted state action. The creation of ACUMAR can also serve as a positive model for other areas, such as public safety, police abuse, social services, or crime

---

[85] The Reconquista case refers to the contamination of the Lola stream (part of the Reconquista river basin in the province of Buenos Aires) due to the dumping of sewage and chemicals from industries located in the basin. In 2003, the neighbors of the locality of El Arco, contacted several local and national organizations for support. In 2004, they decided to bring the case to the Defensor. The Defensor followed the Matanza-Riachuelo methodology, integrating a collegial body that involved the universities of General Sarmiento, Lujan, La Plata, and Moron; several local civic organizations; environmental NGOs; and the Catholic church. The Defensor has produced a report denouncing the level of environmental degradation of the whole Reconquista basin. The Defensor has also demanded the intervention of the governor of the Province of Buenos Aires and of the National Chief of Staff. More specifically, the office has called for the authorities to elaborate a "Strategic Plan of Environmental Development for the Reconquista Basin." See Informe Digital Metropolitano, "Contaminacion en el Río Reconquista: La Situación del Otro Riachuelo,": http://www.metropolitana.org.ar/idm/idm_37/idm_37_nota_02.html.

prevention, especially in a country such as Argentina where there are few experiences of inter-jurisdictional cooperation among different authorities.

Second, the initiative successfully articulated a network of activated horizontal agencies (a federal judge, the Defensor and the Supreme Court of Justice) that act in coordinated fashion with a significant group of civic actors, making it more difficult for the responsible authorities to remain indifferent or evade responsibility for the specific social demands and legal obligations that have informed the case. The fact that coordination exists across horizontal agencies and between horizontal and social actors is particularly significant because, as O'Donnell rightly argues, the workings of accountability depend to a large extent on the ability of different agencies to act "in a convergent and coordinated matter."[86] The Matanza-Riachuelo is no longer a case that relies on the committed mobilization of civic actors alone or the solitary actions of a horizontal agency.[87] Instead, it is an initiative involving a dense and heterogeneous network of actors, from the justices of the Supreme Court to grassroots neighborhood organizations working together in a more or less articulated manner.

Third, such a mobilization of resources has helped to position the issue of the contamination of the Matanza-Riachuelo basin at the top of the public agenda. Sustained media attention to the case has ensured that the issue has become a politically sensitive one for public authorities at all levels of government. With the media watching, politicians and officials now find it difficult to dismiss the issue lightly knowing that media exposure and even legal sanctions might follow.

Fourth, social, media, and legal pressures have forced the initiation of part of the required works, such as the cleaning of some sectors of the basin and the building of a coastal road, albeit in a partial and disorderly fashion. Furthermore, the funds that are needed to finance the major infrastructure work that is stipulated in the Integral Plan have been secured and the bidding process to adjudicate the work is under way.

Accountable government rests on the proper workings of institutional and non-institutional mechanisms. The exercise of governmental accountability, O'Donnell warns us, cannot rest on the actions of a single actor within the state system but rather depends on the capacity of a very intricate web of agencies to act in a cooperative and synchronized manner. In those democracies where such horizontal coordination is far from consistent, as in many of the Latin American democratic regimes, civil society cooperation with horizontal agencies can help to address some of those

---

[86] O'Donnell, "Notes on Various Accountabilities," 336. See also the discussion above, n. 15.
[87] A single horizontal agency would likely encounter considerable resistance or indifference from other horizontal agencies.

accountability deficits with a view to eventually improving the monitoring capacity of controlling agencies. In brief, the experience analyzed in this chapter is a significant addition to the existing repertoire of accountability politics in the region. It is yet another attempt to find ways to strengthen the accountability of state actors and agencies that are still unaccustomed to this vital democratic exercise.

11

Through Pressure or Persuasion?

Explaining Compliance with the Resolutions of the Bolivian Defensor del Pueblo

Fredrik Uggla

11.1. INTRODUCTION

The human rights ombudsman is often held up as an important invention in the area of national human rights institutions (NHRIs). But it is a curious institution. While the ombudsman variant of the NHRI is in most cases endowed with a broad mandate and far-reaching powers to investigate and issue judgments as to whether state entities respect the legal and constitutional rights of the citizenry, it lacks coercive powers. Its resolutions are recommendations that other state actors may heed or disregard as they see fit.

The ability of the human rights ombudsman to protect citizens' rights is thus not a given, but rather varies across cases. While one national office may achieve compliance with most of its resolutions, another may find itself completely disregarded. This chapter addresses the reasons that underlie such variation, and how the human rights ombudsman may work to achieve compliance in the absence of formal enforcement powers.

The chapter focuses on one of several ombudsmen established over the last decade in Latin America: the Bolivian Defensor del Pueblo. Since its creation in 1998, this NHRI has managed to carve out an important position for itself in Bolivian politics.[1] Furthermore, it reports relatively high degrees of compliance with its resolutions. Given that it acts in one of the poorest and most politically turbulent countries in Latin America, this apparent effectiveness presents a puzzle for NHRI scholarship, one with the potential to generate significant insights into how a human rights ombudsman can overcome its formal limitations.

---

[1] Pilar Domingo, "Weak Courts, Rights and Legal Mobilisation in Bolivia," in R. Gargarella, P. Domingo, and T. Roux (eds.), *Courts and Social Transformation in New Democracies* (Burlington: Ashgate, 2006), 233–54.

The mandate of the Bolivian Defensor is intimately and explicitly tied to human rights. The constitutional articles establishing the institution express its mission as supervising the exercise of citizens' "rights and juridical guarantees ... in relation to the administrative activities of the entire public sector. Furthermore, it shall see to the defense, promotion and divulgation of human rights."[2] In practice, the institution has interpreted this statement as a mandate to undertake a range of activities, from public campaigns in favor of disadvantaged or vulnerable groups to legislative proposals concerning human rights in areas such as health care and compulsory military service.[3]

In the following, however, I primarily restrict discussion to the Defensor as a channel for complaints against the public bureaucracy regarding the violation of individual citizens' rights, which are the cases that give rise to the resolutions issued by the institution. As formulated in the law of the Defensor, it is tasked to investigate and denounce, by [the power of] its office or on receipt of a complaint, the actions or omissions which constitute violations of human rights, [and/or] of individual and collective guarantees and rights established in the Constitution, laws, treaties and international agreements signed by the Bolivian state.[4]

Even if the themes involved in actions against the public bureaucracy may sometimes seem relatively minor or mundane, the Bolivian Defensor treats and presents these cases as human rights issues with a view to advancing a human rights agenda in general. Furthermore, some observers argue that case handling and the possibility to access the institution and lodge different kinds of complaints is crucial to understanding the Defensor's popular appeal, as borne out in consistently high public approval ratings.[5]

The actual issues involved in these individual complaints vary considerably. While one case may involve the right to due process or a writ of habeas corpus, others may deal with the right to social security payments or health care. Thus, rather than being confined to a core set of civil and political rights, the resolutions of the Bolivian Defensor deal with a broad array of themes. In this respect, they reflect a current trend in Latin America (and globally) toward a thematic broadening of the rights conferred on the citizen by constitutions and international treaties.[6]

---

2   Bolivian Constitution of 1967 with its subsequent revisions, Art. 127 (1).
3   Defensor del Pueblo, *La Defensa de los Derechos Humanos: Un Compromiso con la Vida* (La Paz: DP, 2008).
4   Law 1818 of December 22, 1997 (*Ley del Defensor del Pueblo*), Chapter 3, Article 11 (2).
5   Mónica Bayá in interview with the author, technical secretary, Comunidad de Derechos Humanos, La Paz, Bolivia, October 26, 2009. Also, Susana Salinas in interview with the author, head of the Follow-up Unit at the Defensor del Pueblo, La Paz, Bolivia, January 13, 2009.
6   J. Foweraker, T. Landman, and N. Harvey, *Governing Latin America* (Cambridge: Polity, 2003).

In this chapter, I attempt to explain why public entities comply with the Defensor's resolutions even though they are not formally required to do so. In particular, I discuss three theoretical perspectives that present distinct views on how compliance can be achieved by an institution lacking in formal or coercive powers.

As I proceed to apply these three theories to the Bolivian Defensor del Pueblo, I draw primarily on material from the institution itself, either in the form of its publications or from interviews with key staff. In order to reduce the possible bias contained in the institution's own material, I have supplemented this evidence with interviews from external sources – representatives from human rights groups in civil society as well as from public institutions such as the police and Congress. Finally, I also make use of some of the very limited number of external studies regarding the Defensor.

11.2. THEORIES ABOUT COMPLIANCE

A defining feature of the human rights ombudsman is a lack of sanctioning power; the ombudsman generally lacks the ability to impose sanctions on the institutions it is mandated to control.[7] This lack of enforcement power has led some observers to dismiss the institution as irrelevant.[8] But the absence of such formal instruments of power should not be confused with political powerlessness. Nonstate entities such as the media and organizations in civil society similarly lack legal enforcement powers, but they may still have a political impact on the defense of human rights. Can the same also be true of the ombudsman?

Indeed, some observers have stressed the ability of the ombudsman to cooperate with third parties in order to ensure compliance with its resolutions. For instance, Scott Mainwaring has noted that agencies of oversight such as the ombudsman can pass on their findings to other state actors that do possess sanctioning power (such as the judicial system or parliament) and thereby achieve an "indirect sanctioning power."[9] In the particular case of the Bolivian Defensor, the institution is legally entitled to refer cases to Congress for follow-up.[10]

While Mainwaring points to how other state actors and agencies may act on behalf of an institution such as the ombudsman, other scholars have looked outside

---

[7] In contrast to other state organs that can compel obedience with their decisions, the ombudsman lacks such enforcement powers. True, it can issue resolutions and in several cases even bring cases before courts, but it cannot by itself enforce its will.

[8] See Erick Moreno et al., "The Accountability Deficit in Latin America," in S. Mainwaring and C. Welna (eds.), *Democratic Accountability in Latin America* (Oxford: Oxford University Press, 2003), 81.

[9] Scott Mainwaring, "Introduction: Democratic Accountability in Latin America," in Mainwaring and Welna, *Democratic Accountability in Latin America*, 12ff.

[10] Republic of Bolivia, Law 1818, Chapter 5: Art. 31.

the state. For instance, Enrique Peruzzotti and Catalina Smulovitz have advanced the concept of "social accountability."[11] They argue that by focusing exclusively on formal sanctions enforced by state organs we risk overlooking the contribution of actors within society to achieving compliance with the rule of law. Nonstate actors may lack the power to impose legal punishments, but this does not mean that they are unimportant. As Peruzzotti and Smulovitz argue, social accountability actors can activate state control mechanisms or impose electoral ("reputational") sanctions.[12]

Although Peruzzotti and Smulovitz focus on how society can pressure state organs to take certain actions despite the lack of institutional power (indeed, the authors mention that "legal mobilization has also been used to activate newly created oversight agencies such as defensorías and ombudsman agencies"), this relationship could also be reversed.[13] Through public proclamations, press releases, and the like, the human rights ombudsman may be able to generate public interest and support for its resolutions and advocacy positions. Such activities amount to a state entity accessing the resources of nonstate actors to pressure or sanction other state actors. A vivid example of this type of interaction can be found in the Guatemalan Ombudsman's response to the attempted "self-coup" (*auto-golpe*) by President Serrano in 1993. The ombudsman refused to accept the president's illegal actions, and promoted a popular mobilization against the attempted coup. Those developments, notes one observer, turned the ombudsman into "the leader of civil society's efforts to restore constitutional rule," which eventually met with success.[14]

These types of actions and relationships might be expected to have particular importance in Bolivia. During the last decade, Bolivian social movements have gained tremendous political clout vis-à-vis the political and bureaucratic establishment.[15] Through a policy of alliances and strategic communication, the Defensor could harness such societal levers to convince reluctant bureaucrats to comply with its resolutions.[16]

---

[11] Enrique Peruzzotti and Catalina Smulovitz, "Social Accountability: An Introduction," in E. Peruzzotti and C. Smulovitz (eds.), *Enforcing the Rule of Law: Social Accountability in the New Latin American Democracies* (Pittsburgh: University of Pittsburgh Press, 2006), 3–33.

[12] Catalina Smulovitz and Enrique Peruzzotti, "Societal and Horizontal Controls: Two Cases of a Fruitful Relationship," in Mainwaring and Welna (eds.), *Democratic Accountability in Latin America*, 311.

[13] Ibid., 314.

[14] Francisco Villagrán de León, "Thwarting the Guatemalan Coup," *Journal of Democracy* 4 (1993), 121.

[15] J. Crabtree, *Patterns of Protest: Politics and Social Movements in Bolivia* (London: Latin American Bureau, 2005).

[16] However, this strategy could also become a double-edged sword. The most powerful social movements are closely associated with partisan political forces in Bolivia – for the most part with the party that has been in government since 2006. While this has not prevented the Defensor from loudly criticizing individual ministers and policies, becoming too associated with such organizations might jeopardize the impartiality the Defensor seeks to project.

In light of this discussion, one might be led to believe that the ombudsman can be effective only if it manages to impose indirect sanctions either through other state organs (such as Congress and the courts) or through nonstate actors within civil society such as nongovernmental organizations (NGOs) and the media. But could it also be possible for the ombudsman to achieve compliance directly, in spite of its lack of formal sanctioning power?

Ideas of compliance even in the absence of direct threats or sanctions are not unknown to political science. Students of public administration have long recognized that the task of holding low-level bureaucrats formally accountable to higher levels of management is "virtually impossible."[17] In view of the difficulties inherent in creating formal mechanisms of oversight and control, various scholars have therefore come to stress the role of immaterial rewards, the importance of bureaucratic culture, and/or persuasive relations between state agents for ensuring compliance and adherence to the normative framework of the state.[18] As James Q. Wilson notes: "Bureaucrats have preferences. Among them is the desire to do the job. That desire may spring entirely out of a sense of duty, or it may arise out of a willingness to conform to the expectations of fellow workers and superiors even when there is no immediate financial advantage to do so."[19] Similarly, Judith Tendler has challenged the view of "mainstream development advice [that] pays little attention to the matter of worker commitment, except to argue that government workers are doomed by their self-interest to be uncommitted."[20] In her view, such commitment may well be an important part of explaining positive government performance.

According to this perspective, one could speculate that by drawing on feelings of duty, commitment, and desire for recognition and acceptance, the ombudsman could in certain cases exert direct leverage over the actions of individual bureaucrats through persuasion. Of course, such rewards and benefits are not awarded in a situation of institutional isolation in which only the accused institution and the ombudsman participate. Rather, recognition and feelings of obligation are embedded in social relationships that entail third parties in state or society. Recent studies of bureaucratic accountability have stressed how it is constructed in a multitude of relationships and interactions, some of which entail hierarchy and the threat of sanctions while others, such as peer pressure, do not.[21]

[17] M. Lipsky, *Street-Level Bureaucracy: Dilemmas of the Individual in Public Services* (New York: Russell Sage Foundation, 1980), 159.

[18] M. Hill and P. Hupe, *Implementing Public Policy: Governance in Theory and in Practice* (London: Sage, 2002).

[19] James Q. Wilson, *Bureaucracy: What Government Agencies Do and Why They Do It* (New York: Basic Books, 1989), 156.

[20] Judith Tendler, *Good Government in the Tropics* (Baltimore: Johns Hopkins University Press, 1997), 136.

[21] Hill and Hupe, *Street-Level Bureaucracy and Public Accountability.*

But even so, such a perspective differs from the theories of compliance described previously, with the active involvement by third parties in state or society not necessarily integral to the potential leverage or influence of the ombudsman. By drawing on immaterial rewards or sanctions as well as feelings of commitment and obligation, the ombudsman could, in spite of its formal lack of enforcement powers, exercise a persuasive power. As such, and in contrast to the hypotheses given, such a theory contends that the ombudsman can have a direct influence over other state actors.

Again, there are features of the political context in Bolivia that lend credence to such theories. As the consensus-oriented politics of the 1990s gave way to political turbulence and the rise of powerful protest movements during the following decade, Bolivia had five different presidents in as many years before Evo Morales ascended to the presidency in early 2006. But Morales represents an anti-establishment, strongly reformist political project, and he has embarked on large-scale constitutional and institutional transformations of the state. In such a context, public entities and individual bureaucrats may feel less secure and more predisposed to pay attention to a watchdog agency such as the Defensor, even in the absence of the direct involvement of third parties.

Following, these three hypotheses – compliance through indirect action by other state agents; through indirect action by social actors; or through a direct persuasive relationship – will be examined in relation to the resolutions of the Bolivian Defensor. Before doing so, however, I will provide some background to the institution and its work.

11.3. THE DEFENSOR DEL PUEBLO

After a protracted process of creation that began in the early 1990s, Ana María Romero took office as Bolivia's first Defensor in 1998. During her tenure (1998–2003) the institution rapidly assumed a position of political prominence. As Bolivian politics declined into a deinstitutionalized turmoil from 2000 onward, the Defensor took on an increasingly important role as mediator and guarantor of human rights in the country's political conflicts. Observers, such as Pilar Domingo, have described how "within a very short space of time it [the Defensor] established itself as a forceful, independent oversight agency."[22]

Such prominence was not always well received, however, and after Romero's term expired in 2003, the government of Sánchez de Losada (2002–2003) attempted to nominate a more pliant successor in the person of Iván Zegada.[23] After the fall

---

[22] Domingo, "Weak Courts, Rights and Legal Mobilisation in Bolivia," 246.
[23] Ibid.

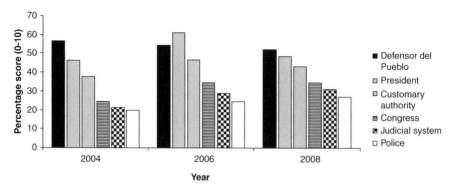

FIGURE 11.1. Above average confidence in certain Bolivian institutions (2004–2008). (Question asked: "To what extent do you have confidence in [NAME OF INSTITUTION]?" Scale from 1 (low) to 7 (high). Figure shows percentage of respondents giving values 5 to 7.)
Source: Data from the Latin American Public Opinion Project (LAPOP): www.vanderbilt.edu/lapop/.

of Sánchez de Losada in the same year, Zegada resigned, and the post was subsequently filled by long-term human rights activist Waldo Albarracín who would serve as Defensor until December 2008. Albarracín's term in office coincided with the reaffirmation of political authority under the government of Evo Morales, a factor in explaining the somewhat diminished political prominence of the Defensor during this period.

It should be noted, however, that the Defensor has remained a visible and present institution in Bolivian political life, especially through its high-profile media campaigns and involvement in the political and social conflicts that are a permanent feature of Bolivia. Figure 11.1 draws on aggregate data from the Latin American Public Opinion Project (LAPOP) to illustrate the degree of public confidence in different public institutions in Bolivian politics, shown as the percentage of respondents claiming to have above average confidence in each institution (i.e., positions 5 to 7 on a scale from 1 to 7). With the exception of 2006, the Defensor has consistently received the highest levels of popular confidence of those institutions sampled.[24]

High-profile interventions and public campaigns are one side of the Defensor's work. Another is the day-to-day handling of complaints from citizens. Figure 11.2

---

[24] It is of course possible that the high levels of public confidence in the Defensor owe more to the popular appeal of its name ("The Defender of the People") than to any intimate knowledge of its work. But that is not the view of the LAPOP researchers, at least. They explain the high public approval enjoyed by the Bolivian Defensor by pointing to its institutional activities, mediating efforts in a conflict-ridden polity, national geographic reach, and forceful public campaigns. See M. A. Seligson, D. Moreno, and V. Schwarz, *Auditoría de la Democracia: Informe Bolivia 2004* (La Paz: LAPOP, 2005), 118.

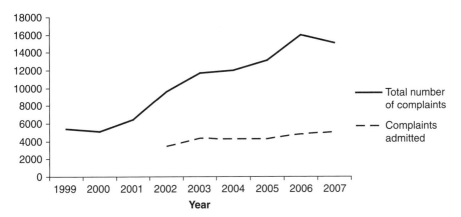

FIGURE 11.2. Number of complaints presented to the Defensor annually (1999–2007). *Source*: The Defensor del Pueblo's annual reports to Congress.

shows the number of cases brought before the Defensor by aggrieved citizens during its first eight years of existence.

The subjects of the complaints vary substantially, but a core set of themes dominate over the years. Typically, complaints focus on issues such as the right to a response from the public authorities, due process, and the right to work, salary, and social security.[25] Similarly, the authorities that feature most frequently as the targets of complaints are departmental service providers, including education authorities, municipal governments, and the national police force.[26]

Of the complaints, a substantial number are rejected as relating to issues that fall outside the institution's jurisdiction. In other instances, no evidence of wrongdoing is found, or the fault is rectified during the course of investigation. Of the remaining

[25] See, for instance, Defensor del Pueblo, *IX Informe Del Defensor del Pueblo al Congreso Nacional: Resumen Ejecutivo: Gestión 2006* (La Paz: DP, 2007), p. 36 [*hereafter* Defensor del Pueblo, *Annual Report 2006*]; Defensor del Pueblo, *Annual Report 2003*, 49. Note that these figures are based on the number of complaints admitted by the Defensor, that is, they exclude those grievances deemed to fall outside the institution's jurisdiction.

[26] Defensor del Pueblo, Executive Summary to Annual Report 2006, 33; Defensor del Pueblo, *Annual Report 2007*, 52. An independent review of complaints against the national police force received by the Defensor during the period 2005–2007 relates to a broad array of issues, including both violations of fundamental rights and other infractions that could be described as administrative complaints. The most common complaint related to "juridical guarantees," such as people being held without access to a lawyer or detained without due cause. This violation amounted to 25 percent of the total number of complaints. In second place were complaints related to "physical, psychic and moral integrity" such as physical or verbal abuse (19 percent). Complaints relating to the issuing of national identity cards by the police came in third place (18 percent). See Comunidad de Derechos Humanos, "Datos estadísticos sobre quejas contra la Policía Boliviana presentadas a la Defensoría del Pueblo" (Unpublished Manuscript: La Paz, 2009).

number, some are turned down for lack of a legal basis. In a small minority of cases, the Defensor finds that a rights violation has indeed occurred and that the situation persists. In such instances, a resolution is issued.[27]

In the following I focus on those resolutions issued by the Defensor and the extent to which the relevant public authority complies with them or not. I leave aside other aspects of the work of the Defensor, such as legislative proposals, provision of court orders, public campaigns, training of civil servants, and mediation work, among other actions. This is not because the latter are not as important as the handling of individual complaints. However, it is the complaints and resulting resolutions that speak most directly to the theoretical discussion of compliance outlined earlier. Among the instruments which the Defensor may deploy to address state violations of citizens' rights, resolutions are arguably one of the most important.[28] In turn, how resolutions are handled and resolved provides insight into the possible avenues that exist for the Defensor to protect the citizens' rights. As one of the Defensor's annual reports states:

> Without doubt, the investigation of complaints is one of the cornerstones of the institution. Not only because it constitutes the largest part of the Defensor's activities in the protection of human rights, but also because the persuasive power of the office resides primarily in the recommendations [of such investigations].[29]

11.4. THE DEFENSOR'S HANDLING OF COMPLAINTS

As shown in Figure 11.2, annual complaints have risen steadily since the creation of the Defensor; from less than 5,500 in 1999 (the first full year of its existence) to more than 15,000 less than a decade later. Equally striking is that a high and rising proportion of the complaints handled by the Defensor are apparently resolved in favor of the complainant during the course of investigation, as is shown in Figure 11.3. Defensor personnel claim that a substantial proportion of successful resolution of complaints is due to "direct action," the direct contact of Defensor personnel with the authority in question in follow-up on a complaint.[30] The fact that such initial

---

[27] For instance, of the 11,988 complaints presented in 2004, 7,742 were redirected to other institutions and mechanisms, 3,951 were resolved or dismissed following investigation, and 126 were found to lack legal basis.

[28] Alongside complaint-handling, the Bolivian Defensor also undertakes what is called "urgent actions," that is, direct and immediate interventions to end ongoing violations of citizens' rights. Such actions are usually undertaken ex officio in an informal manner and without going through the steps involved in elaborating a resolution. Defensor del Pueblo, *Annual Report 2007*, 60; Defensor del Pueblo, *La Defensa de los Derechos Humanos*, 189.

[29] Defensor del Pueblo, *Executive Summary to Annual Report 2006*, 27ff.

[30] Susana Salinas, January 13, 2009.

TABLE 11.1. *Yearly number of resolutions by the Defensor del Pueblo*

Year	Resolutions
2003	94
2004	88
2005	86
2006	121
2007	114
2008 (first six months)	63

Source: Defensor del Pueblo, "La Defensa de los Derechos Humanos: Un compromiso con la vida" (La Paz: DP, 2008).

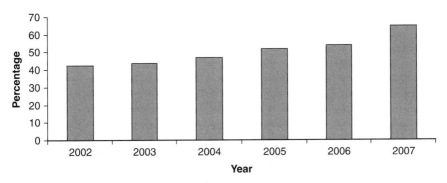

FIGURE 11.3. Percentage of accepted complaints that are rectified during the process of investigation.
Source: Defensor del Pueblo, "La Defensa de los Derechos Humanos: Un compromiso con la vida" (La Paz: DP, 2008).

contact often appears to be sufficient to produce results can be taken as an indicator of the effectiveness of the Defensor.[31]

In those cases where the response of the state actor or agency in question is deemed inadequate, the investigation may eventually lead to a resolution by the Defensor. Seen in relation to the total number of complaints brought before the office, the number of annual resolutions is minuscule – typically around 100, as shown in Table 11.1.

---

[31] Indeed, the Defensor itself chooses to interpret it that way, presenting it under the heading "the power of moral persuasion is already achieving results." Defensor del Pueblo, *La Defensa de los Derechos Humanos*, 23. For the case of the police force specifically, this fact is repeated by Mónica Bayá, October 26, 2009.

TABLE 11.2. *The three most common rights and thematic domains addressed annually in the resolutions of the Defensor del Pueblo*

2003	2004	2005	2006	2007
Social Security (28 percent)	Response from the Public Administration (25 percent)	Responses from the Public Administration (24 percent)	Responses from the Public Administration (43 percent)	Workplace-related rights (30 percent)
Due process (14 percent)	Paid vacation (13 percent).	Employment (12 percent)	Personal integrity (23 percent)	Access to public authorities (27 percent)
Vacation payment (12 percent)	Due process (12 percent)	Salary disputes (10 percent)	Salary disputes (15 percent)	Physical, intellectual, and moral integrity (21 percent)

Note: Comparisons between years should be made with caution as the categories appear to shift over time.
Source: Author's calculations based on the annual reports from the Defensor del Pueblo.

The text of a resolution contains some background information on the particulars of the complaint, the results of the Defensor's investigation, and the resolution arrived at by the Defensor. This final part recommends or instructs the relevant authority to immediately cease the violation of the claimant's rights, and in several cases also instructs the authority to implement additional internal measures to prevent a repetition of the violation, such as enhanced regulatory practices or education of personnel.[32]

As can be seen in Table 11.2, the issues that give rise to resolutions cover a variety of rights and thematic domains. In purely quantitative terms, the majority of resolutions address a lack of accessibility to and responsiveness of the public administration. In addition, a large number (perhaps a third of the total) relate to the violation of public servants' rights in the workplace.[33] With regard to the core set of civil and political rights, they account for a substantial minority of resolutions. During some of the years sampled, a quarter of all resolutions dealt with such fundamental rights violations, most commonly violations of the right to due process and to "personal integrity." Violations of the latter kind primarily relate to alleged physical mistreatment or abuse of citizens by police officers or other state agents. Also featured among the resolutions' subject matter are a broad array of socioeconomic rights such as the right to health care.

[32] See, for instance, the resolutions contained in Defensor del Pueblo, *Annual Report 2003*, chapter 9.
[33] This group of resolutions might more accurately be described as concerning internal administrative complaints rather than human rights violations per se, although the consequences for the concerned individual may of course be severe.

The issuing of a resolution by the Defensor further triggers an internal process of monitoring intended to achieve compliance. This process generally follows three steps, although it is not necessarily linear – Defensor personnel approach compliance in a flexible manner that often entails going back and forth between steps. A first step is to make contact with the concerned authority, notifying it of the resolution and encouraging swift action to rectify the situation. This step, for the most part, consists of meetings between the personnel of the Defensor and the target institution, the intention being to convince the state actors to mend their ways in light of sound factual arguments showing "that legally we [the Defensor] are right."[34]

The law of the Defensor stipulates that if the target actor or agency does not respond positively to the resolution within thirty days the matter may then be relayed to a more senior administrative level.[35] In practice, however, Defensor personnel often allow substantially more time to elapse, sometimes even waiting until a change of personnel has occurred within the public administration.[36] This practice appears to stem from the impression among Defensor staff that compliance is simplest to achieve in the first step of dialogue between parties; subsequent steps in seeking compliance carry the risk of provoking public officials to "stick to an obstinate position."[37]

If the superior administrative authority also fails to comply (the law allows only ten days for an adequate response), the third step is to bring the resolution to the attention of Congress. During its early years, relations between the Defensor and the parliament were very limited. In the 2003 annual report, the Defensor noted that of the substantial number of resolutions that had been submitted to Congress, few showed any signs of progress.[38]

Beginning in 2004, the Defensor began to establish closer working relations with Congress. High-level meetings were held with legislative commission presidents in each chamber alongside meetings at lower technical levels within the legislature.[39] With time, this cooperation has become more institutionalized. Apart from meetings at the presidential and technical level of parliamentary commissions, working breakfasts are also now a feature of relations and a yearly plan has been elaborated to guide cooperation around the enforcement of Defensor resolutions.[40] Most of the resolutions that end up in Congress appear to be tabled before the Commission of

---

[34] Susana Salinas, January 13, 2009.

[35] Republic of Bolivia, Law 1818, Chapter 5: Art. 31.

[36] Susana Salinas, January 13, 2009.

[37] Ibid.

[38] Defensor del Pueblo, *Annual Report 2003*, 54.

[39] Defensor del Pueblo, *Annual Report 2004*; Roberto Lazcano in interview with the author, technical secretary to the Parliamentary Labor Commission, La Paz, Bolivia, October 16, 2009.

[40] Susana Salinas, January 13, 2009.

Labor in the lower house, indicating that they primarily address workplace issues such as unfair dismissal and salary disputes. The increased involvement of Congress has brought with it some successes. In particular, Defensor personnel single out tripartite meetings – in which the offending authority is summoned before Congress – as having "produced very good results" in terms of compliance, a view supported by parliamentary sources.[41]

But interviewees from the Defensor also express some misgivings about working through congressional channels. They point to a range of challenges, including the very intensive workload involved in bringing cases before Congress. The parliamentary commissions responsible for follow-up to the Defensors' resolutions are subject to new appointments each year which, in practice, means that working relations have to be constantly reestablished and political considerations often affect the results. This state of affairs has led the Defensor to complain that "the National Congress still does not decidedly act in favor of the restitution of rights promoted by the Defensor."[42]

Furthermore, although the Constitution of 1967 gave parliament and its commissions in particular the authority to supervise the public bureaucracy, it did not establish any instruments through which those bodies could enforce their rulings, apart from the common attributions of Congress such as the interpellation of individual ministers. Therefore, a number of the Defensor's cases have been concluded with a standard explanation from Congress that "no further efforts can be made, and the case is closed."[43] Such communications are usually accompanied with a suggestion to take the matter to the courts instead.[44]

Available data on the different administrative levels at which the Defensor's resolutions are resolved reveal a highly unbalanced distribution. In 2003, sixty-two of eighty-four cases of successful compliance were resolved at the lowest administrative level (i.e., in direct contact with the targeted institution itself), with the remainder being resolved at the superior administrative level.[45] In that year Congress did not contribute to the solution of any of the Defensor's resolutions. This has begun to change during recent years. However, in 2006 and 2007 only seven of 88 and 10 of 108 cases of compliance, respectively, were generated after the case had been brought to Congress. Furthermore, attention by Congress does not guarantee a positive outcome. Of the ten resolutions that were closed following congressional

---

[41] Roberto Lazcano, October 16, 2009.
[42] Defensor del Pueblo, *Décimo Informe del Defensor del Pueblo al Congreso Nacional* (La Paz, 2008), 73.
[43] Susana Salinas, January 13, 2009; also Roberto Lazcano, October 16, 2009.
[44] Lazcano, Ibid.
[45] Defensor del Pueblo, *Annual Report 2003*, 53.

intervention in 2007, only four could claim full compliance.[46] Instead, the lowest rungs of the bureaucratic ladder remained the key to achieving compliance.[47]

These figures should be interpreted with some care. The cases that reach Congress are by definition often the hardest to solve, and the Bolivian Defensor does, as was shown above, try to secure compliance working through lower-level public officials before proceeding up the administrative hierarchy. Notwithstanding this caveat, these data demonstrate just how much compliance activity occurs at the lower levels of the public bureaucracy, and that the involvement of Congress is neither a necessary nor a sufficient condition to achieving a successful outcome.

11.5. EXPLAINING COMPLIANCE

In its annual reports to Congress, the Bolivian Defensor lists those institutions that have or have not complied with its resolutions. It should be noted that according to interviews at the unit responsible for follow-up on compliance within the Defensor, the definition of compliance is rather strict. It is not sufficient that an authority has responded favorably to the Defensor's requests. Rather, the actual fulfillment of the resolution through payment, restitution, or other action must have taken place.[48] Rates of compliance for different institutions and years can be found in Table 11.3.

According to these figures, the typical level of annual compliance is slightly under half of all resolutions issued. This does not, however, mean that successful compliance is achieved in only 50 percent of all resolutions. The strategy of persistent persuasion favored by the Defensor can take substantially more time than a year, with personnel reporting some cases of compliance taking up to seven years. Incorporating such time lags into the analysis, the true figure for compliance may be closer to 75 percent as estimated by the head of the Defensor's unit for follow-up.[49]

As can be seen in the table, there seems to be no significant difference in compliance levels between elected and non-elected public entities. Nor do election years

---

[46] Defensor del Pueblo, *Executive Summary to Annual Report 2007*, 56. According to Roberto Lazcano, the Parliamentary Labor Commission, which receives the majority of the Defensor's resolutions for follow-up, manages to secure a favorable result in only around half of its annual caseload. Roberto Lazcano, October 16, 2009.

[47] In 2006, engagement with low-level bureaucrats accounted for fifty-one of those cases being successfully resolved. In 2007 they accounted for sixty-four cases. Ibid. These figures document cases that are closed. At the lowest levels of follow-up, closure should amount to fulfillment, although some cases may have been closed for other reasons, such as a demand by the aggrieved claimant. However, the annual reports indicate that the number of cases closed for reasons other than compliance are minimal.

[48] Silvia Paz Soliz in an interview with the author, official in charge of follow-up of the Defensor's resolutions, La Paz, Bolivia. January 20, 2009.

[49] Susana Salinas, January 13, 2009.

TABLE 11.3. *Annual rate of compliance for different types of institutions*

	2003	2004	2005	2006	2007
Elected	0.44	0.57	0.48	0.41	0.53
Nonelected	0.40	0.72	0.49	0.47	0.49
Autonomous institutions	0.43	0.41	0.60	0.76	0.25
Nonautonomous institutions	0.40	0.73	0.47	0.41	0.53
Police and armed forces	0.71	0.83	0.67	0.67	0.55
Nonpolice and armed forces	0.37	0.67	0.46	0.40	0.50
Total	0.41	0.68	0.49	0.45	0.51

Source: Author's calculations based on the annual reports from the Defensor del Pueblo.

have any discernible effect, with municipal elections taking place in December 2004 and elections at the national and department level held in December 2005.

Moreover, state entities that can claim a degree of institutional autonomy, such as the judicial system and its component parts as well as public universities, do not present a clear pattern in comparison to other institutions. In some years, they comply more frequently than non-autonomous institutions and in other years less so. On the basis of these data, it is not possible to affirm that they exhibit a systematic difference in terms of compliance.

Equally striking are the results for those institutions that intuitively might be expected to be least compliant with regard to the Defensor's recommendations: the police and the armed forces. The data reveal a substantial and persistent difference, but it runs contrary to prior expectations with the police and armed forces appearing to be significantly more likely to respect the resolutions of the Defensor than the other public institutions surveyed.

This finding is puzzling, but it is supported by another external study.[50] It should be noted that the Defensor has devoted considerable effort to establishing close working relations with the police and armed forces, and that these institutions are themselves undergoing internal processes of reform intended to improve their performance with regard to human rights observance.[51] Indeed, one could speculate

[50] Indeed, this finding is supported by one of the few independent studies of compliance available. An investigation performed by a Bolivian NGO found that of over 3,200 cases brought before the Defensor which referred to alleged violations by the police, 52 percent were resolved during the course of investigation and the vast majority of resolutions sampled (over 95 percent) were complied with by the police. See Comunidad de Derechos Humanos, *Datos estadísticos.* The methodology and selection of cases for the study are, however, not clear.

[51] Defensor resolutions that concern violations committed by individual policemen are reportedly also sent to the internal affairs department within the police force, which gives the resolution additional authority. Major Rommel Raña in interview with the author, head of training in human rights, National Directorate of Human Rights, National Police, La Paz, Bolivia, October 19, 2009.

that recent political events have led to considerable pressure on the police and armed forces to improve their democratic credentials.

As the reader will have noted, these figures refer to the particular institution addressed in the resolution rather than the substance of the violation. Unfortunately, the latter aspect is not possible to discern from the available data, which is admittedly a distinct shortcoming of the analysis.[52] For instance, budgetary constraints are often cited as a reason for delayed or inadequate responses to Defensor resolutions.[53] Similarly, one might posit that cases involving the most serious violations of human rights will also exhibit lower levels of compliance. Unfortunately, available data do not allow such a proposition to be tested.

Ultimately, however, the most remarkable conclusion that can be drawn from the figures in Table 11.2, as well as from the multivariate logistic regression analysis presented in the Appendix to this chapter, is that neither proximity to election cycles nor the relative autonomy of the institution in the state apparatus appears to have any discernible effect on whether the Defensor's resolutions result in compliance. This is problematic for the two theories which suggest that the possibility of imposing electoral costs (sometimes called "social accountability") or pressures from other state organs (usually referred to as "horizontal accountability") are central to explaining why state institutions choose to cooperate with the resolutions of the Defensor. Furthermore, the statistical analysis presented in the Appendix shows that the involvement of superior authorities also fails to have a statistically significant effect on compliance.

Beyond these negative findings, the statistical analysis is unable to say anything more substantial about the reasons underlying the frequent compliance with the Defensor's resolutions. Testimony from key staff within the Defensor has provided some insights into this apparent puzzle. Above all, they have consistently claimed that compliance is, to a large extent, achieved through close direct contact between the Defensor and the responsible public servants.

11.6. COMPLIANCE AND BUREAUCRATIC RELATIONS

The prior description shows that compliance with Defensor resolutions has primarily been achieved at the lowest administrative levels and that a substantial number of cases have been resolved by "direct action," that is, preliminary contact between the Defensor and the offending institution. It appears that such direct action by the Defensor can have a significant impact on compliance outcomes independent of third-party engagement, whether by actors within the state or society.

---

[52] For an independent study of the cases involving the national police force, see note 26.
[53] Susana Salinas, January 13, 2009.

Indeed, such a view is firmly held among Defensor personnel, with staff expressing a number of misgivings regarding the involvement of administrative superiors or
Congress in the pursuit of compliance.[54] Several factors inform such a reluctance.
Chief among them seems to be the idea that approaching actors with enforcement
powers may trigger conflict with the targeted authority and make dialogue impossible. Instead, Defensor personnel voice a preference for maintaining pressure
through direct contact with the public officials involved in the case: "we insist, we
reiterate, we demand, we once more require that the [concerned] authority acknowledge [our resolution]."[55]

Similarly, the Defensor does not generally appear to cooperate with organized
social actors outside the state in seeking resolution of individual cases. For instance,
cooperation with the media is uncommon in the Defensor's handling of individual complaints. As noted elsewhere in this volume,[56] strategic engagement with
the media has been pursued by the Defensor as one significant instrument in its
overall activity. However, with regard to complaint-handling, seeking resolution
through exposure in the media has been used sparingly by the Defensor and its
personnel. This fact is somewhat surprising given the media and social mobilization backgrounds of key personnel within the Bolivian Defensor, in contrast with
the often lawyer-dominated NHRIs found elsewhere in the region. For instance,
Romero was a journalist before becoming Defensor and Albarracín came to the
Defensor after a long career as a prominent human rights activist within the NGO
community.

In interviews, Defensor representatives give three reasons for generally abstaining from working through public denunciations and the media. First, Waldo
Albarracín claims that publicizing a case in the media may violate the personal
integrity of the complainant, which would run counter to the discretion required
in handling individual complaints.[57] Second, one staff member contends that by
going to the media the institution may compromise its neutrality by appearing to
take sides in the dispute as well as risk its authority if the publicized action of the
Defensor is unsuccessful.[58] Third, and finally, other Defensor personnel argue that

---

[54] The Judiciary power is not even mentioned. Apparently, the Defensor has never involved the courts
     in follow-up to its resolutions. Susana Salinas, January 13, 2009.
[55] "Se insiste, se reitera, se solicita, se requiere nuevamente que la autoridad tome conciencia," Silvia
     Paz Soliz, January 20, 2009.
[56] See Thomas Pegram in this volume, "National Human Rights Institutions in Latin America: Politics
     and Institutionalization."
[57] Waldo Albarracín, former head of the Defensor del Pueblo (2003–2008), in an interview with the
     author, La Paz, Bolivia, January 19, 2009.
[58] Jorge Araoz, official in charge of follow-up of the Defensor's resolutions, in an interview with the
     author, January 20, 2009. Indeed, sources in civil society sometimes complain about what they see
     as the Defensor's excessive preoccupation with not taking sides and with its unwillingness to use the

taking a case to the media entails moving away from a strategy of persuasion to one of confrontation:

> If we would go public, well, then the dice would be thrown.... It is something that cannot be undone. It would mean to enter into a controversy with the authority, and that could have an effect on many other cases which are handled by the responsible Ministry. That is not a wise policy.[59]

This quote contains an important clue to how the Defensor conceives of its work in ensuring compliance with its resolutions in the absence of direct support from other state organs or nonstate actors such as the media. Rather than entering into confrontation, the Defensor first attempts to exhaust all possible avenues of working directly with the institution in question. Defensor personnel attest to this approach as characteristic of their work and consisting, to a large extent, in the persistent lobbying of low-level public officials:

> At times we have to proceed with kid gloves, with a lot of diplomacy, with a lot of gentleness. Even if they are very rude, we must keep smiling, be very friendly, start by talking about other things and only then tell them: "look, you have to comply with this resolution."[60]

This strategy of perseverance draws on a kind of relationship that differs from those identified in the dominant theories of compliance described in the first section. Rather than appealing directly to third parties for legal or reputational sanctions to be applied to the institution in question, the Defensor relies upon the self-interest of bureaucrats in safeguarding their image and reputation, as well as avoiding further meddling by the Defensor.[61] This provides the Defensor with the possibility of exerting leverage without relying on third-party involvement. Waldo Albarracín articulates this rationale in the following terms:

> To appear as an entity which disobeys the Defensor, is tantamount to appearing as an institution that violates human rights. I believe that this factor has a lot of influence.... They [officials] will always try to maintain a clean sheet. Being criticized by the Defensor for having not addressed a problem which has been presented to them is, I believe, a kind of pressure.[62]

media to further its objectives. Rolando Villena, president of the Permanent Assembly for Human Rights, in an interview with the author, La Paz, Bolivia, October 19, 2009. Rolando Villena was elected as the new Defensor del Pueblo on May 1, 2010.

[59] Silvia Paz Soliz, January 20, 2009.

[60] Ibid.

[61] The individual responsible for human rights training in the Bolivian police force when instructing high-ranking officers places particular importance on human rights observance for the sake of the police's institutional image. Mayor Rommel Raña, October 19, 2009.

[62] Albarracín, January 19, 2009.

And Albarracín continues:

> Basically, they do not want trouble. Nobody likes to have problems. And if they are
> questioned, they will try to resolve the matter. [Problems arise] only if they have
> a special interest in the case not being solved or if they are convinced that our
> demand is incorrect.... But such instances represent a minority; the majority of
> cases are resolved thus.[63]

It should be noted, of course, that this strategy does involve the presence of third
parties within society and the state as an audience in front of which the targeted bureaucrat may stand to lose face and reputation. Still, in contrast to theories that stress
the activation of third parties as a condition for compliance with the resolutions of
the Defensor, in the perspective elaborated here the role of such external actors is
more indirect or implicit, and they intervene only rarely. Furthermore, in contrast
to other theories of compliance, the experience of the Defensor suggests that some
of the most important third-party actors are located within the public bureaucracy
itself rather than in the judiciary or legislative powers, or within society.

As such, the importance individual bureaucrats attach to their own self-image
and broader institutional reputation is an important variable that will condition
the impact of compliance efforts through dialogue. This point is emphatically
supported by Defensor personnel who note that the successful follow-up of resolutions "depends a lot on the education, the training and the concept of justice as
understood by the [concerned] bureaucrat."[64] Therein may be a clue as to why the
statistical analysis in the Appendix uncovers so few systematic differences between
different types of institutions. Rather than differences across institutions, differences
within institutions and the role of individual bureaucrats in facilitating levels of
compliance may be more relevant.

In sum, the Defensor's strategy for achieving compliance with its resolutions is
primarily one of direct relations between bureaucrats and Defensor personnel as the
latter attempt to persuade, rather than force, the institution to change course and
take the appropriate action.[65]

11.7. CRITICISM OF THE DEFENSOR'S WORK

If the Defensor's preferred strategy of seeking compliance through direct contact
with the public institutions against which complaints have been directed has,

---

[63] Ibid.

[64] Silvia Paz Soliz, January 20, 2009.

[65] External sources confirm that this seems to be the preferred method of work of the Defensor. Víctor
Vacaflores, executive director of the Bolivian Chapter of Human Rights, in an interview with the
author, October 13, 2009; Mónica Bayá, October 26, 2009.

according to the evidence, yielded positive results, one should also be aware of the attendant criticisms.

Within the Bolivian human rights community there is a broad spectrum of views on the activity of the Defensor; while some observers are positive in their assessment, others express more mixed opinions, or are even decidedly negative in their appraisal.[66] Points of criticism include the political stance adopted by the Defensor, with Defensor personnel sometimes perceived as taking excessively conservative positions in fierce defense of the institution's autonomy,[67] even declining to cooperate fully with other entities,[68] as well as criticisms relating to differences in the background of human rights activists in civil society and the staff that populate the Defensor.[69] Criticism also falls on the tactical choices made by the Defensor and its personnel

While some observers in civil society express their approval for the Defensor's tactic of direct informal engagement with public bureaucrats over confrontation, others are more critical. In an almost direct challenge to the tenor of the earlier statements by Defensor personnel,[70] Rolando Villena, the president of the Permanent Assembly of Human Rights, argues that "it is more or less as if they [the staff of the Defensor] have put on kid gloves, right? They have got to take the gloves off."[71] Furthermore, this line of criticism typically emphasizes the limitations of the Defensor's focus on individual complaints when the underlying causes of human rights violations by state actors are fundamentally structural or cultural in nature. However, Defensor personnel counter with the claim that experience gathered from handling individual cases informs a range of institutional strategies intended to have a more general impact on public policy.[72]

Additionally, some representatives of the Bolivian human rights community are concerned that with a less credible and committed individual appointed as Defensor, the prevalent strategy at the institution could be used to "quietly disguise and underutilize the [authority of the office] through negotiations and conversations ... in order not to resolve things."[73] Indeed, given the tendency of the present Bolivian government to neutralize independent voices within the state and its efforts to weaken the division of powers across the different branches of government, fears are

---

[66] Mónica Bayá, October 26, 2006; Rolando Villena, October 19, 2009; and Víctor Vacaflores, October 26, 2009.

[67] Mónica Bayá, October 26, 2006.

[68] Jimena Fajardo, responsible for the area of fundamental rights, Ministry of Justice, in an interview with the author, La Paz, Bolivia, October 29, 2009.

[69] Rolando Villena, October 19, 2009.

[70] See supra note 61.

[71] Rolando Villena, October 19, 2009.

[72] Susana Salinas, January 13, 2009.

[73] Víctor Vacaflores, October 26, 2009.

sometimes expressed as to the ability of the Defensor to preserve its autonomy and political independence moving forward. As Victor Vacaflores of the NGO Bolivian Chapter of Human Rights poses a rhetorical question, "the future Defensor will not make problems with the [party in government], will he?"[74]

11.8. CONCLUSIONS

This chapter has argued that the Bolivian Defensor del Pueblo – in spite of its formal lack of enforcement powers – does appear to have had an impact on bureaucratic behavior and decision making. The rate of compliance with its resolutions is estimated to be relatively high, perhaps reaching as much as three-quarters of the total. As this figure does not take into account the actual issues at hand, it must be interpreted with caution. Moreover, the resolutions that never obtain compliance are obviously likely to include a number of particularly complicated and grave cases of violations of human rights. Even so, the evidence indicates that the Defensor's influence over other state organs is far from negligible.

Furthermore, the explanations for compliance with the Defensor's resolutions are not primarily those that the main theories on accountability developed with regard to Latin America would lead us to believe. The political prominence of different social movements notwithstanding and despite the Bolivian Defensor's legal capacity to refer cases to Congress, indirect pressure from nonstate entities or other state agencies does not figure prominently in the process of ensuring compliance. Rather, the main strategy employed by the Defensor relies on insisting on rectification through direct contact between the Defensor and the institutions concerned. This observation is based both on the statistical analysis, which detected almost no systematic differences in compliance that could be linked to pressure from third parties, and on the observations made by Defensor personnel and by human rights activists as expressed in interviews (even though the latter group are sometimes critical of this strategic choice). Although a national case study such as this does not allow us to assess with certainty whether this approach is the most effective strategy available to the Bolivian Defensor, it is nevertheless tempting to associate the relatively high level of compliance with the Defensor's preferred method of work.

---

[74] And indeed, after Albarracín's term ended in December 2008 no new Defensor was named until May 2010, which left the institution in a similar situation to several other independent or supervisory organs within the Bolivian state. During this time, the institution was run by an interim Defensor, and several observers claim that this severely weakened the public position of the Defensor. There were also attacks made on the institution by politicians from the government party. In May 2010 Rolando Villena, a critical voice from civil society quoted in this chapter, was elected as the new Defensor del Pueblo.

This observation does not deny the importance of potential pressure from other state entities or from social actors. The threat of such actions may be an important factor in prompting an institution to listen to the Defensor in the first place, and, in certain cases, the Defensor will eventually resort to handing the case over to Congress. But rather than being a necessary factor, in the absolute majority of cases the threat of involving other actors appears only as a remote, or tacit, possibility and it is seldom activated. In the end, Defensor personnel tend to stress aspects that are much more related to questions of personal disposition, bureaucratic culture, and normal administrative behavior as explanations for compliance or non-compliance. This view, obviously, is much more akin to the theoretical insights generated in public administration than to those theories that stress the need for third parties to give the Defensor's resolutions the force of legal or material sanctions.

But this way of working also entails some potential problems. Human rights organizations in Bolivia are divided in their views of the Defensor; but one criticism that is sometimes made of the office is that it works too cautiously, and that a preferred modus operandi of dialogue and persuasion may both lessen its larger impact at a structural level and make it politically vulnerable.

Finally, one should enquire as to whether the lessons of the Bolivian experience described here can be transferred to other countries. With reference to the theoretical discussion, one could argue that the last decade of political turbulence in Bolivia has affected the bureaucracy, with public officials less secure in their positions and consequently more susceptible to the demands and suggestions of a watchdog agency such as the Defensor. This is only speculation, of course, and the impact of contextual factors cannot be determined in a single-case study such as this one.[75] Turning the findings of this chapter into policy recipes would require further research to shed light on the extent to which its findings can be generalized.

Instead, I limit my conclusions to what I can state on the basis of the analysis: compliance does not always require sanctions to function; our ideas of how best to protect and promote human rights would do well to incorporate insights from public administration theory; and we need to pay more attention to the way factors such as bureaucratic culture, non-material rewards, and peer pressure contribute to the construction of a framework that may enhance the work of a human rights institution such as the Defensor. As we look beyond civil and political rights to consider the defense of economic, social, and cultural rights, such factors may assume even

---

[75] But it should be noted that relations between the Defensor and the present government, in power since January 2006, have often been far from cordial. Indeed, some observers claim that quarrels between the two actors may have lessened the degree of compliance with the Defensor's resolutions from central state organs (Mónica Bayá, October 26, 2006). Furthermore, the establishment of the Morales government in 2006 did not lead to any dramatic change in the overall level of compliance, as can be seen in Table 11.3 above.

greater importance. Ultimately, all human rights cases are different and require tailored solutions. But the tool box available to human rights defenders may contain more instruments than previously imagined.

11.9. APPENDIX: A STATISTICAL ANALYSIS OF COMPLIANCE

Despite the evidence generated by the descriptive analysis given earlier, any systematic patterns with regard to the degree of compliance would have to be detected by other methods such as a multivariate analysis. In order to perform such an analysis I have used the annual reports of the Defensor for the years 2003–2007 to build a database consisting of 984 cases that represent annual instances of compliance and non-compliance. Because the data were drawn from tables showing the number of times institutions of a certain kind (municipalities or the police, for instance) cooperated with the Defensor or failed to do so, the findings have a rather special character. Instead of resolutions that result in compliance or not, the units of analysis are discrete cases in which an institution complies with the Defensor during a specific year. In this database, a single resolution may actually generate multiple cases within a year (by being directed toward several institutions, for instance, although this is rare) or may generate a reiteration across years (as non-compliance during one year leads to another case in the following year). Even so, for the purpose of the present discussion on compliance these are not overwhelming limitations.

The information in the annual reports is sufficient to generate one dependent and five independent variables, which can in turn be connected to two of the theoretical perspectives outlined at the outset of the chapter.

The dependent variable is a dichotomy with values (0) for a case in which an institution has failed to comply with the Defensor's resolutions during the year and (1) where it has complied. As the dependent variable is a dichotomy, I use a binary logistic regression. With regard to the political context, the variable constructed involves dichotomous coding based on whether the year in question was an election year. Prefectural and national institutions are coded as (1) in 2005, and municipalities are coded as (1) for 2004. In 2004 and 2005 the elections were held in December.

Three variables relate to the character of the institution against which a resolution is directed. The first variable consists of a dichotomy between elected institutions that are coded as (1) and non-elected institutions coded as (0). The former class of institutions includes municipalities, ministries, the chambers of congress, and – beginning in 2006 (when the first elected prefects assumed power) – prefectures. Two additional variables consist of dichotomies for institutions that may lay claim to a position of independence within the state. One variable measures whether the institution in question forms part of the police or armed forces. Apart from the fact that these two institutions are commonly associated with the worst violations of human rights, they may also possess a position of de facto autonomy within the state (what in neighboring Chile has been referred to as "authoritarian enclaves").[76] Conversely, another dichotomous variable captures those public entities that are not directly subordinate to any government ministry and possess formal legal autonomy within the state bureaucracy. This group of entities includes the judicial system, the electoral courts, certain supervising agencies, and the universities.

The fifth and final variable refers to cases that are transferred to the central office of the Defensor for follow-up (a dichotomy coded as (1) when transferred). Transfer to the center occurs for two reasons: (i) because local attempts to generate compliance have failed, in which case the central office brings the case before a higher-level authority or Congress; or (ii) because the case is necessarily directed to a higher level within the public bureaucracy due to a lack of clear hierarchy (as is the case for government ministries and Congress). What is of interest here is whether rates of compliance increase when the resolution is brought before a more senior hierarchical level following failed attempts to persuade lower-level authorities. This variable is applied in a separate equation from which resolutions involving non-hierarchical institutions are removed in order to rule out the second of the two possibilities above. In practice, this means that all elected institutions are left out of the model.

Together these variables allow us to test some of the hypotheses on compliance that motivate this analysis. If the effectiveness of the Defensor was primarily dependent on social support entailing a "reputational" or electoral cost for the targeted institution, we should expect elected authorities to be particularly prone to compliance in election years. If, conversely, compliance is best explained by bureaucratic pressure brought to bear by the intervention of superiors or other state organs, we should expect lower rates of compliance among those institutions with autonomous standing and higher compliance rates when the resolution is brought to the attention of superiors or Congress.

The results of the statistical analysis are found in Table 11.4. This table presents the odds ratios – the increased odds for compliance caused by each factor. It is evident that the equations actually explain very little of the variation in the dependent variable (compliance) as the individual variables, with one exception, fail to show statistically significant effects.

As can be seen, the variables representing election years, whether the authority in question is elected or not; its degree of autonomy within the state structure; and whether the resolution was referred to superior levels fail to show any statistically significant effect on the dependent variable. The one variable that does appear to have a significant impact is whether the concerned institution forms part of the police or

[76] Manuel Antonio Garretón, "Revisando las Transiciones Democráticas en América Latina," *Nueva Sociedad* 148 (1997), 20–9.

TABLE 11.4. *Binary logistic regression results (odds ratios) for annual cases of compliance (2003–2007)*

	N=983	N=543
Brought before higher authority	–	.90 (.186)
Elected authority	1.06 (.156)	–
Police or Armed Forces	2.23 (.452)***	2.39 (.573)***
Autonomous entity	1.21 (.281)	1.32 (.390)
Election year	1.06 (.181)	.88 (.206)
Pseudo R-square	.013**	.021**

(**), Significant at the (.01) level (two-tailed)
(***), Significant at the (.001) level (two-tailed)
Note: Standard errors in parenthesis.

armed forces. In that case, the odds for compliance more than double, a point that seems to confirm the discussion in relation to Table 11.3.

Unfortunately, the available information does not allow us to control for another factor of potential importance: the subject matter of the resolution itself. The exclusion of this, in all probability, crucial factor is problematic for the equation.[77] But it should be noted that the prior theoretical perspectives do not take this thematic aspect into consideration either.

---

[77] Another problem is that the cases involved are not absolutely separate because the same resolution may generate several cases. Moreover, a likelihood ratio test shows that in the first equation the variables "Elected authority" and "Autonomous entity" could actually be left out as they do not make a statistically significant contribution to the model.

PART IV

Final Reflections

Tainted Origins and Uncertain Outcomes

Evaluating NHRIs

Peter Rosenblum

Interviewer: *What is the most frequent dilemma encountered in the establishment of a National Institution?*
Brian Burdekin: *The tendency of governments to establish the National Institution, but then to appoint inappropriate people to lead it and give it inadequate resources to fulfill its mandate.*[1]

12.1. INTRODUCTION

More than a decade has passed since the great proliferation of national human rights institutions (NHRIs) began in the early 1990s and they are now firmly implanted in the normative and institutional firmament. But despite a tendency to celebrate this phenomenon, the evidence suggests reasons for circumspection. Even the best reputed NHRIs perform inconsistently; political and economic contingencies drive major fluctuations. While many NHRIs have gained deserved fame for bold positions at critical times, these "heroic" moments are often followed by depressing, "post-heroic" periods when the NHRI bends more supinely to government interests.

It is not surprising that a relatively new institutional phenomenon that has spread so quickly around the world would be buffeted by competing forces, some pushing for real domestic human rights reform, others simply to profit from promotional opportunities. There are many reasons that countries adopt international models and no reason to assume that they share the goals of the promoters of those

[1] Brian Burdekin, Visiting Professor at the Raoul Wallenberg Institute, "Elaborates on Past and Present Experiences as the 'Founding Father' of National Human Rights Institutions": http://www.rwi.lu.se/news/pastact/interviews/burdekin.shtml.

Special thanks to Tseliso Thipanyane for his critical reflections on NHRIs and this chapter. JoAnn Kamuf Ward, Djemila Carron, and Risa Kaufman also made excellent recommendations that I have sought to incorporate. This chapter would not have been attempted and would certainly not have been completed without the unjustified encouragement and tested patience of Ryan Goodman and Tom Pegram, the editors, for which I am deeply appreciative.

models.[2] But the international advocates for NHRIs who played a major role in the proliferation of the past two decades have tended to understate the political strategizing that governments engage in and the attempted gaming of the system that goes on. What appears to commentators as a bureaucratic problem or a "dilemma" – like the appointment of "inappropriate" personnel or "inadequate" funds – will appear to others as the perfectly logical choice of a government that is seeking to satisfy international demands while frustrating local pressures and limiting real impact. Calling it a "dilemma" obscures its coherence. That government's "dilemma" is how long it can succeed in the ruse without exposing its motives or making meaningful changes. Because the international entities most involved with NHRIs, including the International Coordinating Committee of NHRIs (ICC) and the Office of the High Commissioner for Human Rights (OHCHR), do not focus on the effectiveness of NHRIs, there is little external pressure on them to show results

This chapter is an argument for an engaged, critical evaluation of NHRIs, one that assesses an NHRI in its local context, considers alternative institutional mechanisms, and directly confronts the tension between the promotional impetus and the local effectiveness. It is one that relies on process and an interrogation of relevance as much as conformity with Paris Principles or the tabulation of resolved complaints. It is one that looks at the changes in an NHRI over time in light of developments in the state, including evolving relationships with civil society. In other words, my purpose is to inject a dose of skepticism into a project that I perceive as resistant.

Underlying this chapter is an argument that the aspirational vision of NHRIs is a good one: the international community *should* support structures that can mobilize and leverage local institutions and laws in pursuit of the shared values represented by international human rights. International human rights mechanisms *should* be influenced by independent experts who draw on local experience. But our enthusiasm for the goals underlying the promotion of NHRIs should not blind us to the realities. We should not celebrate them before their time.

In the first section, I highlight the divorce between political reality and the international NHRI project, introducing the main international body responsible for both promoting and evaluating NHRIs, the ICC. The second section roots the problem in the history of the NHRI promotional project, describing, in particular, the role of the OHCHR in supporting the expansion of NHRIs in the 1990s. It is a personal story, in part, because I worked in technical cooperation at the predecessor to

---

[2] Ryan Goodman and Derek Jinks, "How to Influence States: Socialization and International Law," *Duke Law Journal* 54 (2004), 651–2. The authors note that "in general, the adoption of structural commitments or official policy goals in human rights does not necessarily entail concrete implementation," ibid., 651, and they describe various reasons for the "disjuncture."

the OHCHR for one year, and later worked with Human Rights Watch (HRW) on a report about NHRIs in Africa.[3]

The third section raises several challenges to NHRIs that often go unexamined. It describes countries in which NHRIs appear irrelevant to the development of human rights or even serve as shields for regimes that actively undermine local rights frameworks. It broadly explores other possible implications for countries that choose the path of NHRIs, particularly in terms of lost opportunities and spillover effects. These examples are not intended as empirical proof, but rather as elements in a blueprint for evaluation and as a further palliative to any overly optimistic assumptions about NHRIs. The section then examines an important counterargument that places NHRIs in the context of other human rights regimes that have sought to "ramp up" compliance over time. I devote particular attention to the role of the ICC, which is treated by many as a critical body in this process. In the final section, I lay out a few specific ideas for a process-based evaluation of NHRIs.

12.2. EYES WIDE SHUT: ASPIRATIONS THAT DISTORT REALITIES

The promotional project of expanding the number, resources, and access of NHRIs has colored the analysis of actual institutions and undermined any systematic evaluation. It is evident in the literature, which continues to make claims for NHRIs that are unsupported by – or, actually, at odds with – actual practice. It is also evidenced by the complete reliance on the ICC, an association of NHRI members, to evaluate their work.

Sometimes conflicting evidence is simply ignored. The issue of leadership is a characteristic example. The weakness of leadership is treated as a dilemma or a problem of capacity – as if political will were irrelevant and appropriate technical assistance could solve the problem. But from the short history of NHRIs, the opposite seems true: political circumstances go a long way toward explaining the quality of leadership.

The "heroic" moments, when NHRIs take bold action in the face of a reluctant regime, appear typically to come soon after their creation or a period of social upheaval when domestic and international pressure is strongest. Many of the "leaders" who emerge at that time, not surprisingly, are known human rights activists or academics – like Maina Kiai in Kenya, Victoria Velázquez de Avilés in El

---

[3] Human Rights Watch (hereafter cited HRW), *Protectors or Pretenders? Government Human Rights Commissions in Africa* (New York: HRW, 2001). Where I am making judgments based on my personal experience, it is indicated in the text or notes. At various times, I rely on unnamed sources. These sources are all professionals who are or were employed by an intergovernmental or nongovernmental human rights organization or who served as advisers, consultants, or rapporteurs for those organizations. They have asked not to be identified by name. Further details, including the names, have been provided to the editors.

Salvador, or Leo Valladares in Honduras, named precisely because of their legitimacy. Even in the exceptional cases where relative unknowns have demonstrated great leadership – for example, in countries like Togo or Indonesia, where allies of the regime led bold NHRI action – the political context explains more than any theory of leadership. In both of those cases, increased international and domestic pressures at the end of the Cold War opened up opportunities for change.

At times, the international advocates for NHRIs have engaged in near willful blindness to avoid the ramifications of actual practice. For example, the fact that the Cameroonian human rights commission was led, for years, by a befuddled ally of the president – a man who could not communicate in the government's principal language of French – was treated as an unfortunate problem of leadership, rather than a calculated act of cynicism.[4]

The tendency to argue on the basis of aspiration rather than actual practice carries into other areas as well. In the literature, NHRIs are presumed to bridge the international and domestic human rights worlds, bring international expertise to the local level, and convey local experience to the international community. But, in fact, we do not actually know very much about whether, or under what circumstances, NHRIs "bring independent expertise" and "transfer international standards" to the local level, as claimed in a recent report by the EU agency for Fundamental Rights.[5]

We do have some evidence about what NHRIs bring to the international level, and it should lead to skepticism. While they may sometimes bring an independent voice, they are more frequently cited for parroting government positions.[6] Moreover, we know, from Chris Sidoti, in this book, and the survey of the UN Office of the High Commissioner for Human Rights (OHCHR),[7] that despite the continued campaigns to bring NHRIs into international fora, they are doing a woeful job. They don't contribute their local knowledge to the activities of the treaty bodies, as their supporters claim, because they do not actually show up.[8] Even when meetings are scheduled to coincide, their substantive contributions are limited and self-interested.[9]

Despite progress, our tools for evaluating NHRIs are still deeply affected by the same promotional project. The ICC has improved its grading system for accrediting

---

[4] HRW, 112–31 (discussion of Cameroon).

[5] European Union Agency for Fundamental Rights, "National Human Rights Institutions in the EU Member States: Strengthening the Fundamental Rights Architecture in the EU" (2010), 8.

[6] See Chris Sidoti's discussion of NHRI engagement with international fora in this volume.

[7] United Nations, Office of the High Commissioner for Human Rights, *Survey on National Human Rights Institutions* (Geneva: UN, July 2009).

[8] European Union Agency for Fundamental Rights, supra note 5, 10.

[9] Chris Sidoti writes in this volume, "Having secured participation rights, however, few national institutions have played an especially active role in the Council." According to Sidoti, NHRIs tend to show up at the Human Rights Council – because ICC meetings are scheduled for the same time – and make statements about their work while missing the opportunity to "make a serious contribution."

NHRIs, but as a body whose stated purpose is to "promote and strengthen" NHRIs, it can only go so far. The ICC is effectively engaged in "brand protection," which does require some amount of quality control. But it would be unreasonable to expect such a body to vigorously assess the effectiveness of NHRIs. In practice, the ICC standards provide only tentative language opening the door to such a possibility. But nothing ensures systematic examination of whether NHRIs respond to critical local human rights issues in a country or whether they enhance (or detract from) the work of other state and nonstate agencies engaged in the protection of human rights.[10]

In the meantime, no other organization or process has risen to the challenge. The efforts of nongovernmental organizations (NGOs) like Human Rights Watch provide useful counterexamples, but are not suited to systematic monitoring over time. Any serious effort to do so would have to scrutinize NHRIs for their potential harm to human rights as much as their benefit. It would have to explore, for example, missed opportunities, the impact on NGOs and other human rights actors, and more sinister efforts to use NHRIs to deflect attention or distort reality.

Meanwhile, despite the tenuousness, the contingencies, and the political calculations, NHRIs have already been given a place at the adult table, and their advocates continue to fight for more. They have recognized status at the UN Human Rights Council and in a number of treaty mechanisms. Their role is also growing in Europe despite significant inconsistencies and misgivings among experts and has had a tangible impact on foreign policy. For example, the United Kingdom has incorporated the Ethiopian human rights commission – unaccredited by the ICC and widely suspect by NGOs – into its agreement to protect transferred detainees from torture.[11]

Even where the literature acknowledges the seriousness of problems with NHRIs, it has shockingly little impact on the global project of promotion. If the possibility of ineffectual NHRIs, motivated by political calculation, were taken seriously into account, the evaluation process would look quite different.

12.3. UNDERSTANDING THE ROOTS OF SKEPTICISM

The distortions in our understanding of NHRIs are rooted in a history dominated by the United Nations engagement to expand NHRIs at the end of the Cold War. This history is important for understanding both the particular form that NHRIs have taken and the ascendency of promotion at the expense of critical evaluation.

---

[10] Despite this, as discussed below, there have been some positive examples coming from the ICC. Particularly where local or regional movements engage with the accreditation process, the ICC appears able to make a meaningful contribution beyond its written procedures. But in many others, NHRIs emerge with high grades and continued international support despite serious problems and with no attention to whether such support provides a cover for other problems.

[11] See Human Rights Watch, "UK: Ethiopian 'Assurances' No Guarantee against Torture," September 17, 2009.

It is a history of the newly created Office of the High Commissioner for Human Rights finding a role during a period of dramatic change. It is also, more awkwardly, a history of individuals and international backers who came to play a preponderant role in moving the system in a particular direction.[12]

By the mid-1990s, as Sonia Cardenas and others have documented, human and financial resources were pouring into NHRIs, and the OHCHR was playing a central role in shaping the results.[13] The engagement was directed by Brian Burdekin, a charismatic, larger-than-life former commissioner from Australia, who tended to view his role in very personal terms.[14] Burdekin's 1991 paper is credited with playing a significant role in the formulation of the Paris Principles and the UN strategy for

[12] My own experience colors my perception of the phenomenon. From the late 1980s, I worked with international human rights NGOs, primarily on Africa, but also in transitional states in Eastern Europe (Romania) and Asia (Cambodia) where pressures to make institutions more democratic and accountable led to dramatic changes. Many states, like South Africa or countries in Central and Eastern Europe, were engaged enthusiastically in the process of transformation. Others were less committed to democratic change but equally active. Whether ambivalent (like Romania or Cambodia) or openly hostile (like Zaire), the states where I was working struggled to get the support of the international community while Cold War leaders sought to maintain their hold on power. For one year, 1995–1996, which coincided with the rising engagement of the UN in the promotion of NHRIs around the world, I worked in technical cooperation in what became the UN Office of the High Commissioner for Human Rights (OHCHR). Until 1997, the office was still known as the UN Centre for Human Rights. The name change under Mary Robinson was symbolic of the shift in accountability to the High Commissioner, whose control over the staff was not yet fully established. I refer to the OHCHR to include the period that immediately preceded the change.

[13] The critical role of the UN in the NHRI phenomenon is a central theme of Sonia Cardenas's leading article, "Emerging Global Actors: The United Nations and National Human Rights Institutions," *Global Governance* 9 (2003), 23–42 (*hereafter* "Global Actors"). See, in particular, her discussion of the UN's role in capacity building at 30–2 where, inter alia, she notes the increase of UN funding of human rights assistance into the mid-1990s. Anna-Elina Pohjolainen goes into more detail on the particular role of the OHCHR and the increases in funding that NHRI work invited. As she writes, NHRI work was popular with donors, and the OHCHR "had the monopoly of expertise." A. Pohjolainen, *The Evolution of National Human Rights Institutions – The Role of the United Nations* (Copenhagen: Danish Institute for Human Rights, 2006), fn. 266. The number of UN activities in the field of NHRI increased "fivefold" in five years, between 1995 and 2000; ibid., 245.

[14] See Pohjolainen, ibid., 67–8. With financing from the government of Australia, Burdekin was appointed Special Advisor to the High Commissioner in 1995, with a senior position outside the management structure of the OHCHR; ibid., 68. Among other things, this meant that "governments and other interested parties could request expert advice directly from the Special Adviser and, in this way, avoid many hurdles within the slow and inflexible technical cooperation procedure"; ibid. He remained in that position until 2003 at which point he was not replaced. The words "charismatic" and "larger than life" are based on my own observations and encounters. No one that I interviewed was willing to speak on record. However, even his supporters agreed with this characterization. For a taste of his tendency to characterize events in personal terms, see, Brian Burdekin, "National Human Rights Institutions: Giving Teeth to International Treaties," talk at Harvard Human Rights Program, November 11, 2007. See at http://www.law.harvard.edu/media/2007/11/12/hrp.rm.

promoting NHRIs that followed.[15] Funded initially by the Australian government, his role at the OHCHR was to promote the expansion of NHRIs, which he did with tremendous zeal.

The NHRI project was controversial within the OHCHR. Critics viewed it as disconnected from other aspects of what was known as "technical cooperation" – the assistance given to states to meet their international human rights obligations – because it failed to evaluate NHRIs in the context of other institutions or, eventually, in terms of their actual contribution to human rights.[16] Technical cooperation, itself, was still a disputed area of UN engagement because it relied so heavily on the good faith of governments. It is also significant that the OHCHR was a notoriously difficult bureaucratic environment in which to effect change. As a result, the internal challenges for the OHCHR were accompanied by the personal.

Even those who admire Burdekin and praise his role note that it was accompanied by tremendous ego. "Perhaps it takes that quality to move mountains," said one former colleague.[17] Among the turf conscious and easily discontented staff, Brian Burdekin's approach made him an extremely divisive figure. Both his manner and his single-mindedness were notable.

No one doubts the powerful influence that the OHCHR, under Burdekin's leadership, exercised over the development of NHRIs in those years. Without their engagement over the next years, it is unlikely that so many NHRIs would have been established or that they would have taken the form that they did.[18] Perhaps more countries would have chosen an ombudsman structure over the favored commission

[15] See Birgit Lindsnaes and Lone Lindhold, "National Human Rights Institutions – Standard Setting and Achievements," in B. Lindsnaes, L. Lindhold, and K. Yigen (eds.), *National Human Rights Institutions: Articles and Working Papers* (Copenhagen: Danish Institute for Human Rights, 2000), fn. 24. See also Burdekin, "Elaborates on Past and Present Experiences," supra note 1.

[16] The disconnect with other aspects of technical cooperation was controversial while I worked at the OCHCR and continued when Mary Robinson sought to bring NHRIs within the "mainstream" of the OHCHR after 1997. See Pohjolainen, *The Evolution of National Human Rights Institutions*, 69. The more explicit criticism of the detached focus on NHRIs came later. See C. Flinterman and M. Zwamborn, *From Development of Human Rights to Managing Human Rights Development* (Utrecht: Netherlands Institute of Human Rights, 2003), 54: "Since the adoption of the Paris Principles, there has been a tendency within the UN to take for granted the rationale for expanding NIs as a key area of support, based on positive experiences in different transitional situations. However, the weak documentation as regards positive impact renders it quite relevant to ask questions about the performance of national institutions in relation to the assumptions made about their promotional and protective roles. What is the value added of NI compared to other institutional initiatives? What core roles of NI are relevant under what circumstances?"

[17] Email exchange with former colleague on file with author.

[18] See, generally, Cardenas, "Emerging Global Actors," with regard to the UN role including her assessments that "in the absence of such UN assistance, it is unlikely that there would be as many NHRIs in the world today," at 35; see also Pohjolainen, supra note 16, with respect to the OHCHR in more detail.

model. Perhaps more attention would have gone to constitutional courts, civil society organizations, or hybrid bodies developed to respond to specific human rights issues. Perhaps, as Burdekin's supporters have argued, there would have been more splintering of NHRI functions into multiple bodies, encouraging them to focus on discrete popular issues and leave other important issues unaddressed. In other words, I am not suggesting that the outcome would necessarily have been positive, simply different.

Burdekin and the OHCHR were, of course, not solely responsible for the proliferation of commissions during those years, or for the form that they took. But they fed a trend which, then, channeled its support through them. The promotion of NHRIs became a very popular international project and one that, arguably, supported itself without diverting funds from other sources.[19] The enthusiasm of countries like Sweden, Norway, Denmark, Germany, New Zealand, and the UK which joined as funders after Australia was also notable. They too channeled assistance through the OHCHR and drew on its expertise.

Recent studies agree on the particular significance of UN technical assistance for the massive expansion of NHRIs in the 1990s, as well as the particular form that NHRIs developed. But they do not necessarily capture the contentiousness of the shift that was occurring internationally, or the extent to which international involvement may have distorted the emergence of domestic human rights institutions through the single-minded promotion of NHRIs.[20]

One element in this contentious shift was from critical engagement with states over human rights problems – as characterized by the "Special Procedures" of the Commission on Human Rights – to supportive engagement with state institutions, as characterized by "Technical Cooperation."[21] From the perspective of human rights advocates, the UN had become effective (or, at least, useful) in promoting human rights only because it had overcome the original barriers to exposing specific human rights violations by named states. At the UN Commission on Human Rights, NGOs and sympathetic governments were successfully expanding the critical functions of the UN system, focusing attention on individual country conditions through Special Procedures and Commission resolutions. The post–Cold War proliferation of civil society organizations around the world accelerated and expanded this process. Technical cooperation, on the other hand, had a problematic history that fueled

---

[19] Pohjolainen, *The Evolution of National Human Rights Institutions*.

[20] This is no criticism of any of the authors. Cardenas and Pohjolainen, in particular, identify all of the most significant moments in the UN's engagement on NHRIs, as well as the key actors and the potential problems, including inter alia the focus on quantity rather than quality, the willingness to provide support to any requesting government, and the absence of significant criteria for evaluating results.

[21] The reference to "technical cooperation" includes "advisory services" which was a more commonly used term in prior years.

concerns about its expansion in the 1990s. When the precursor to the OHCHR, expanded technical cooperation in the late 1980s – primarily increasing document distribution and training seminars – it was fiercely criticized as a sop to governments that, in fact, opposed the UN's critical role.[22] It was particularly troublesome that every country that requested advisory services or technical cooperation received it without regard to the genuineness of its commitment.

With the end of the Cold War, perceptions were changing, and there was increasing recognition that states needed assistance to fulfill the obligations of the human rights treaties. More advocates recognized technical cooperation as a reasonable response to the increasing number of states that did, in fact, demonstrate good faith in seeking to fulfill those obligations. But progress varied across the world and even supporters agreed on the need to maintain the UN's role as a forum for criticism.

A. African Checkerboard

Changes on the African continent illustrated the full range of variation from most earnest to most insincere proponents of institutionalizing human rights.

Many states had gone through major constitutional reform, expanding freedom of speech, instituting presidential term limits and ending de jure single party rule. Full-fledged democratic transfers of power came early to countries like Benin (1991), Zambia (1991), Mali (1992), Mozambique (1993), and eventually South Africa (1994). But they were still a minority in the late 1990s. More common were countries like Togo, Uganda, Kenya, Zimbabwe, or Cameroon, where Cold War leaders were successfully clinging to power in the face of reforms. In another significant group of countries, including Ethiopia, Eritrea, and Rwanda, recently victorious rebel leaders were building new regimes with a stated but uncertain commitment to democracy. All kinds were receiving technical cooperation support from the OHCHR, and many of them were dangling their interest in NHRIs.[23] The fact that so many of these leaders resisted or eventually reversed reforms demonstrates in retrospect how tenuous the changes were and how risky it was to take them at their word.[24]

---

[22] See Pohjolainen, *The Evolution of National Human Rights Institutions*, note 264; Lawyers Committee for Human Rights, "Abandoning the Victims: The UN Advisory Services Program in Guatemala" (February 1990). In discussions at the Lawyers Committee for Human Rights and in the Delegates Lounge in Geneva, where I visited, it was privately attacked as a campaign tactic by Martenson to position himself for nomination as secretary general.

[23] The OHCHR was providing advice or support to nineteen out of twenty-four NHRIs in Africa in 2000. Pohjolainen, ibid., 68.

[24] Despite constitutional changes, transitions were halted or reversed in Zimbabwe, Uganda, Cameroon, Togo, Chad, and Equatorial Guinea, inter alia, where term limits were overcome and Cold War leaders maintained power. In other countries, like Liberia, Kenya, or Sierra Leone, change came, but significantly later.

The shift to technical cooperation, in general, and support for NHRIs, in particular, also reflected a broader shift away from promoting civil society and toward building state institutions.[25] As a practical matter, it was difficult for the UN – an intergovernmental body – to support NGOs directly. But for some, technical cooperation was nevertheless perceived as a return to discredited notions of sovereignty and a betrayal of the forces pressuring for change.[26] Even in South Africa, where there was a predictable shift in international funding from NGOs to the government at the end of Apartheid, there were profound concerns about the shift. Some of those most concerned were NGO leaders who, themselves, joined the government.[27]

Fueling these concerns was the fact that the OHCHR was not only supporting governments but it was also putting its imprimatur on a very particular institutional structure for promoting human rights, an NHRI model most familiar to common law countries and not necessarily reflective of disparate domestic dynamics. As Cardenas and others (see also Reif in this volume) have pointed out, the ombudsman model from Latin America was specifically disfavored. Hybrids of other kinds did not come into consideration.

In this context, the OHCHR project to support NHRIs was always at risk of being implemented (1) in opposition to NGO concerns, (2) in tension with UN staff members who were pressing to allocate more funds to NGOs, and (3) with a proprietary zeal for a particular product. As a practical matter, doubts were laid aside and the OHCHR supported NHRIs with little regard to specific human rights issues in a country or to the role of other important actors, particularly NGOs, in addressing them.

With political capital to be gained and actual funding to be provided, it was perfectly reasonable for a government to create an NHRI in these circumstances. At

[25] The immediate post–Cold War period coincided with major growth in the power and legitimacy of international civil society as embodied in nongovernmental organizations (NGOs). The UN World Conferences, particularly the World Conference on Human Rights in 1993 and the Women's Conference of 1995, were triumphs of NGO human rights networks across the world. The Landmines Convention of 1997, which resulted in a Nobel Prize for the coalition of NGOs that promoted it, and later, the treaty establishing the International Criminal Court, were celebrated (and also savaged) for the fact that NGOs played a critical role in drafting the norms of the international system. This followed a period in which NGOs had battled – often successfully – against reluctant states in order to bolster the UN's critical capacity. In human rights circles, "sovereignty" became a dirty word, brandished by states to block interference in their "internal affairs."

[26] I have argued, elsewhere, that many NGOs viewed themselves as "anti-sovereignty" in reaction to this phenomenon and the particular opposition of human rights and Chapter 2(7) of the UN Charter. This spirit was captured in Louis Henkin's line, "Away with the S Word, where S stands for sovereignty." See Peter Rosenblum, "Teaching Human Rights: Ambivalent Activism, Multiple Discourses, and Lingering Dilemmas," *Harvard Human Rights Journal* 15 (2002), 301–16.

[27] United Nations High Commissioner for Human Rights, *Report of the Needs Assessment Mission to South Africa* (Program of Technical Cooperation in the Field of Human Rights, 1996), on file with author.

best, governments used international funding and support to reinforce a national commitment to human rights ("transition states" referred to by Cardenas).[28] At worst, they played to the international audience without any intention of expanding domestic protection of rights ("hypocritical states" in Cardenas's characterization).[29] The UN appeared largely indifferent to the distinction.

Again, the extremes were played out in Africa. By 1998, at the same time that South Africa was implementing a robust, constitutionally mandated human rights commission, a calcified dictatorship in the small west African country of Togo was celebrating the tenth anniversary of its commission, Africa's oldest NHRI. The Togolese Commission shocked the region with its "heroic" and unanticipated boldness at the outset, but was subsequently crushed into embarrassing boosterism for the government. Still, the Togolese Commission continued to benefit from the UN machinery; the chair of the Togolese Commission never failed to participate in the UN meetings and to vaunt the commission's compliance with the Paris Principles.

In less obvious cases, like Ethiopia and Rwanda, the UN continued to support the development of NHRIs even as the governments engaged in sustained repression of independent human rights activism and democratic reform. In between were many countries where NHRIs were playing an ambiguous role in the face of ongoing struggles.[30]

The title of the Human Rights Watch report, "African Commissions: Protectors or Pretenders," published in 2001 captured the extreme perspectives on the NHRIs that were emerging on the continent with the support of the UN. Using country case studies, the report sought to demonstrate how some states used commissions to respond to local and international interests, and then worked over time to undermine them. It noted, as well, the peculiar fact that some commissions could work well without really having an impact on human rights.

By itself, however, the HRW report had little effect on the promotional effort in full throttle. As if to drive the point home, after publication of the report, African NHRIs chose to hold their regional meeting in Togo with the support of the OHCHR. It was a very public endorsement of the Togolese Commission by, among others, the South African Commission that had hosted the prior meeting. Those who made the decision had no illusions about the state of human rights in Togo or the role of the commission. But, as we were told at the time, regional harmony and balance between Francophone and Anglophone nations was so much more important that the issue hardly arose.[31]

---

[28] See Sonia Cardenas in this volume, "National Human Rights Institutions and State Compliance."

[29] Ibid.

[30] Much of this account is contained in the Human Rights Watch report, in which I was a coauthor. See supra note 3.

[31] The HRW report was not going to be repeated. As is typical for an organization like Human Rights Watch, the allocation of resources was for a report and advocacy, not for a sustained iterative process.

12.4. NHRIS = RESPECT FOR HUMAN RIGHTS?

History provides reasons to approach NHRIs with skepticism, but it does not negate the possibility that NHRIs will still contribute to human rights even when such an outcome is unintended. The current tools of evaluation, however, will not resolve that question. They tend to focus on the structure, financing, and the operation of the NHRI itself, with less attention to questions of its effectiveness or its relationship to larger issues of human rights compliance in the country. Such a methodology would only make sense if NHRIs were presumptively contributing to human rights in a country.

This section queries that presumption. It explores, first, a few examples in Africa where NHRIs appear to have no correlation with improvements in respect for human rights and, then, other examples where NHRIs are compatible with the denigration of such rights. It also touches on the missed opportunities and diversion of resources that accompany the choice to create an NHRI. The second part explores, but treats skeptically, the possibility that early promotion followed by increased scrutiny and pressure are, in fact, working to "ramp up" the effectiveness of NHRIs.

12.4.1. *Irrelevant or Worse?*

From a broad glance at human rights in a number of African states, there is no obvious reason to believe that NHRIs correlate with improvements. There are countries that appear to be improving human rights without NHRIs and others that are systematically suppressing traditional human rights mechanisms while building NHRIs. In this section, I consider the example of one country, Benin, where the NHRI appears irrelevant to the institutionalization of human rights, and a number of other African countries that have institutionalized NHRIs in "creative" ways without appearing to affect their generally ambivalent, or openly negative, attitude to human rights. For those who follow Africa, closely, it will not be surprising to read criticism of human rights behavior by the governments of Ethiopia and Rwanda, discussed in this section. But one of the most disturbing examples is that of Uganda, whose Human Rights Commission has been celebrated internationally even while losing legitimacy at home. The Ugandan case demonstrates the difficulty of devising any fixed measure to assess whether NHRIs are contributing to human rights in a country. Most clearly, however, the determining factor is *not* how well the NHRI appears to function or whether it has been accredited by the ICC.

The director, Ken Roth, expressed great appreciation for the report, but subsequently questioned whether it was the right kind of effort for HRW in light of the effort expended. The director of the Africa Division supported further work on NHRIs, in principle, but couldn't afford the appropriation of staff time.

A. Benin, Rwanda, Ethiopia, and Uganda

The small west African state of Benin is a country where an NHRI played a passing role. Benin led the way toward democratization in Africa at the end of the Cold War and its democracy has largely thrived since then. There was a human rights commission in the early phase of the Benin's transition, before the UN became involved in promoting NHRIs. It played a dynamic role during the transition to democracy in 1990, and was one of the few African organizations to participate in the drafting of the Paris Principles. Afterward, the state focused attention on developing other institutional safeguards, and left the commission to flounder.

The Benin experience gives a hint of other opportunities that might have been overlooked in the promotion of NHRIs. While the commission ceased functioning, Benin "reconstituted" itself, establishing a hybrid Constitutional Court that achieves many of the same goals with enhanced powers.[32] The Court has a pluralistic membership and a mandate that includes (1) broad access for human rights complaints – including standing for any individual or NGO – (2) rulings on legislation, and (3) implementation of international human rights norms. It also has *sua sponte* powers to raise and investigate human rights issues. But since the Constitutional Court doesn't fit the NHRI mold, it is largely ignored, while the floundering commission gets a "C" grade from the ICC.

Benin is not alone for having pursued human rights without NHRIs. Among Africa's relatively thriving democracies, Mali and Botswana have also done well by any measure, without NHRIs. They may have lost out on international support, but it has not noticeably affected their commitment to human rights.

At the other end of the spectrum are countries where the NHRI promotion has gone hand-in-hand with the systematic repression of civil society and democratic pluralism. Togo, Rwanda, Ethiopia, and, more controversially, Uganda are all examples in Africa. Togo, which was discussed in Section 12.2 – and which borders Benin to the east – is one of the most obvious. It vaunted its status of having the first NHRI in Africa long after it had become an organ of propaganda for the state. In private conversation, few denied the cravenness of the commission and its chair.[33] While the commission has reportedly improved – and was reaccredited

---

[32] See, generally, Anna Rotman, "Benin's Constitutional Court: An Institutional Model for Protecting Human Rights," *Harvard Human Rights Journal* 17 (2004), 285. ("Benin's Constitutional Court can be considered a hybrid institution that encompasses the competencies typically associated with constitutional courts *and* a human rights mandate generally advanced by state sponsored human rights institutions.")

[33] As the author of the HRW chapter on Togo, I had discussed the situation widely, both during and after the writing. Most disturbing was my meeting with the French Consultative Body on Human Rights, whose overall view of African human rights NGOs was so patronizing that some seemed to believe that the Togolese Commission was truly the best that could be hoped for.

in 2007 – leadership of the country has passed from father to son with few signs of improvement in the overall human rights situation.

The cases of Rwanda and Ethiopia are slightly more complicated, but only because the NHRIs are not as obviously compromised as the case of Togo. On the other hand, few deny the extent to which the two governments have cracked down on traditional civil and political rights.[34] Both countries established NHRIs with the support of the UN and bilateral donors during a time of concern about government commitments to human rights. In both countries, the concern has grown stronger. Elections have been accompanied by arrest and intimidation of opposition candidates. Both countries have enacted laws that effectively undermine independent NGO activity and have clamped down further on domestic and international human rights activists operating in the country.

In Rwanda, before the genocide of 1994, there was a vibrant domestic human rights community; its members were targets during the violence unleashed with the slaughter of Tutsis. In the immediate aftermath, the government of Paul Kagame maintained, at least, the appearance of pluralism in government and openness to NGOs. Since that time, there has been a progressive crackdown that has affected most of the local human rights activists and increasingly extended to international human rights organizations like Human Rights Watch, which were previously allowed to function freely.[35]

In the face of open hostility between the government and the human rights community, no one expected a dynamic, independent commission, and none emerged. But in the view of some observers, low expectations have assisted a modest – even mediocre – commission to play a beneficial role. The existing commission has reportedly brought meaningful attention to problems in the justice system, without joining the anti-NGO frenzy that has periodically gripped the government.[36] The

---

[34] Characteristic is this comment by HRW, "The government has publicly proclaimed that the country is moving toward democracy – albeit slowly given the many challenges it faces – but the evidence shows that civil and political rights have been deteriorating in Ethiopia, not improving. Ethiopia's democratic transition is not merely stalled, it is regressing." See HRW, "One Hundred Ways of Putting Pressure," *Violations of Freedom of Expression and Association in Ethiopia*, 2010, 10.

[35] In the year before her death in 2009, Alison Des Forges, one of the leading authorities on the genocide and a researcher for Human Rights Watch, was denied access to the country by the government. They subsequently expelled Human Rights Watch's resident researchers, ending a presence that dated from soon after the genocide in 1994.

[36] According to one researcher who was, until recently, based in Rwanda, the commission played a positive role in prison visits and denouncing abuses of the Gacaca courts system, a traditional justice system found at the community level in Rwanda. It has conducted useful and inclusive trainings for local organizations and even faced attacks from parliament for failing to criticize Human Rights Watch. Nevertheless, another researcher who had been based in Rwanda dismissed the commission: "The first President, Gasana Ndoba, was at least a former HR defender (albeit coopted)," the researcher wrote. His successor has been more thoroughly detached from human rights issues.

Rwandan human rights commission was accredited by the ICC in 2001 and reaccredited in 2007.

In Ethiopia, the forces that overthrew the repressive government of Mengistu Haile Mariam in 1991 have maintained and consolidated power since then. Local human rights and democracy activism has been severely constrained throughout this time, though conditions have gotten significantly worse since a brief political opening before elections in 2005. In 2009 the country adopted an extremely repressive law governing civil society that effectively criminalized human rights work by any group that received more than 10 percent of its funding from foreign sources.

In contrast to its relationship with civil society generally, the government has been investing considerable resources in promoting the human rights commission that was set up in 2000, gaining international support, including technical support from the OHCHR. The commission was scheduled to undergo accreditation by the ICC in April 2010, but the date passed without action.[37] Nevertheless, the United Kingdom named the commission as its monitor under the Memorandum of Understanding with Ethiopia to prevent torture in the case of detainee transfers.[38]

One of the complexities in evaluating the net contribution of the Rwandan and Ethiopian NHRIs is that, according to at least some observers, the commissions do periodically perform useful functions, particularly in the absence of human rights NGOs or government bodies willing to stand up for human rights. In the case of Rwanda, the commission has regularized its operations and, reportedly, intervened in a number of individual complaints. In the case of Ethiopia, the commission has surprised observers, recently, by issuing reports critical of the government's human rights record, particularly on prison conditions.

But there is an acknowledged irony to the relative success of the commissions. Even those who describe their positive contributions suspect that while "better than nothing," their existence may be providing cover to a broader repression of human rights. In the case of Ethiopia, in particular, the recent strength of the commission's action corresponds with discredited national elections and government plans to submit the commission for accreditation to the ICC.

For anyone struggling to understand the connection between NHRIs and human rights, the case of Uganda is perhaps the most complicated. The Ugandan Human Rights Commission has been celebrated widely for reasons that are arguably, entirely legitimate. Its willingness to confront serious violations of rights by the state, including torture and disappearance, marked it out from an early date. Such action would constitute a major breakthrough in many other countries. The complexity stems

---

[37] Chart of the Status of National Institutions Accredited by the ICC, status as of June 2010, at www.nhri.net.

[38] Supra note 11.

from assessing the commission over time, in light of local struggles. Uganda is a relatively open society in terms of free speech, active NGOs, and functioning courts, but it has a strikingly closed political system that shields the state from actual accountability for increasingly serious human rights violations.

The Ugandan Human Rights Commission (UHRC) has been operating for ten years with the benefit of substantial international support and tremendous optimism based on its first years of operation. With some concern as to whether the commission's dynamism would survive its first director, Margaret Sekaggya, Human Rights Watch characterized it as a "strong example for other human rights commissions in the region."[39] "If it continues to build on the gains it has made to date, the UHRC has the potential to contribute an important role in making long-term gains for human rights in Uganda."[40]

But in a relatively open country like Uganda, a well-functioning commission does not necessarily meet local expectations. In 1999, one observer already noted the tendency of the commissioners to avoid what appeared to be the most serious human rights issues for the country, including multiparty democracy and the death penalty.[41] Even before the first director left in 2008, criticisms of the commission grew in intensity. According to the critics, the commission continued to investigate and award damages in cases of torture – something that had impressed initial observers – and to inspect places of detention. But after several years, the commission's activities were having little effect. This is not uncommon in Uganda, whose government is well known for launching significant investigations without acting on the results. But as with responses to other major disclosures, the government was frequently refusing to pay damages with no consequences for it or for individual violators.[42]

Then, as hopes for peaceful democratic reform began to recede after 2005,[43] the commission seemed increasingly irrelevant to some, complicit to others. Rather than focusing on the abuses of state officials, it invested more resources in private

---

[39]   HRW, *Protectors or Pretenders?* 371.

[40]   Ibid., 366. Margaret Sekaggya even includes HRW's praise on her official resumé posted by the OHCHR; see http://www2.ohchr.org/english/issues/defenders/docs/MARGARETSEKAGGYA_CV.doc.

[41]   Markus Topp, "Human Rights Protection by the State in Uganda," in B. Lindsnae et al., *National Human Rights Institutions: Articles and Working Papers* (Copenhagen: Danish Institute for Human Rights, 2000), 169–98. The chapter is based on research undertaken in 1999.

[42]   The commission decides only on the "vicarious" liability of the state. In 2009 the UHRC reported that the government owed torture and detention victims US$ 1,030,000. U.S. Department of State Human Rights Report for 2009, see http://www.state.gov/g/drl/rls/hrrpt/2009/af/135982.htm.

[43]   While respect for human rights has been inconsistent throughout recent times, what has perhaps changed most significantly since 2006 is public perception. The constitution was amended to eliminate term limits in 2005, permitting President Museveni to stand for a third term in 2006 (and almost certainly a fourth in 2011), at which point many were shocked with the extent that state power was used to stop the opposition. This frustrated the hopes of many that Museveni would yield peaceably to multiparty democracy and a strengthened rule of law.

disputes, particularly mediating child maintenance cases, and reporting on private violations.[44] Since Ms. Sekaggya's departure, the situation has apparently gotten even worse, with commissioners joining in more overt support of the government.[45]

No one denies that issues of child maintenance are important to the country; the same may be true of other categories of the Ugandan Commission's work, including "road carnage," "human sacrifice," and "school fires." But the commission is starting to look like a bystander to a decay of rights – maybe even an enabler, by virtue of the strong international cover that it provides – rather than a promoter of "longer-term gains" as hoped.

In trying to assess whether NHRIs make a net contribution to human rights, it muddies the waters further that cause and effect are so hard to gauge in human rights.[46] In response to the widespread disjuncture between rhetoric and practice in human rights, Louis Henkin was fond of quoting the adage that "hypocrisy is the tribute that vice pays to virtue."[47] There is certainly anecdotal evidence that even bad events and institutions can be formative in the struggle for human rights.[48] No

---

[44] See, e.g., Uganda Human Rights Commission, Annual Report 2008, xxi.

[45] Work in the commission was suspended between November 2008 and May 2009, when Museveni appointed five new commissioners. According to one researcher in Uganda, all the independent members were replaced with people more loyal to the government. One of the few who could have remained left quickly afterward. This researcher described the situation as having moved from a "holding pattern" at the end of 2008 to a "disaster" by the end of the year of 2009. As one extreme example, the researcher notes that at a December 18, 2009, meeting on the criminalization of homosexuality, organized by the OHCHR and moderated by a member of the UHRC, the commission did not respond after openly gay participants fled in fear and the meeting was "hijacked" by Pastor Sempa, one of the leading figures in the campaign against gays and lesbians. The event was described in a Wikileaks cable that characterized it as a one-sided debate that exposed the gay rights activist, David Kato, who was later murdered. See http://www.guardian.co.uk/world/us-embassy-cables-documents/241596 (last accessed March 10, 2011.)

[46] Goodman and Jinks have explored in rich detail the question of cause and effect in the spread of international human rights norms. See Goodman and Jinks, "How to Influence States," and, in particular, "Measuring the Effects of Human Rights Treaties," *European Journal of International Law* 14 (2003), 171–83, where they confront Professor Oona Hathaway's claim that ratification of international human rights treaties is associated with poor human rights records; ibid., 172 et seq. Historians have struggled to explain the rise of a particular normative posture in national contexts. See, e.g., C. L. Brown, *Moral Capital: Foundations of British Abolitionism* (Chapel Hill: University of North Carolina Press, 2006) for a profound exploration of the emergence and rise to dominance of abolitionism in Britain.

[47] Goodman and Jinks also celebrate "defections" and "decoupling" that often characterize the relationship between an international model and the state that has endorsed it for the contribution that this can make to the global diffusion of the model. See Goodman and Jinks, "How to Influence States," 669 ("Specifically, [our theory] predicts that pressure to conform will produce a particular form of defection: decoupling, in which structural adherence to globally institutionalized models does not correspond to actual state practices on the ground.... [T]his form of decoupling, in important respects, makes possible the diffusion of global models and the resultant convergence of policies and organizational structures.")

[48] There seems little doubt about how important historical experiences of apartheid, slavery, or dictatorship have been in shaping the rights regimes that have emerged in countries like South Africa,

one would deny the extent to which apartheid shaped the South African transformation or slavery shaped the American civil rights movement. The early heroism of
the Togolese Commission followed by its obvious hypocrisy may have helped to fix
a high standard for human rights in the thinking of the population. The impressive efforts by the succeeding chair of the Nigerian Human Rights Commission,
Kehinde Ajoni, to prove her independence after the previous chair's termination by
the executive, as described by Okafor in this volume, may do more for human rights
than a functioning commission.[49] On the other hand, the Ugandan Commission
might undermine aspirations by conveying international support for a low standard
of human rights when the population is struggling for more.

These are subtle, and perhaps unanswerable, questions that should render one
extremely modest in making judgments about what contributes to the long-term
improvement of human rights. But they should not drive us, in turn, to ignore the
big picture when interrogating the place of institutions like NHRIs. The promotional project of NHRIs has been consistent with a general decay in human rights
conditions in some states, while improvements in human rights have occurred without NHRIs in others. Any assessment must account for these variables and interro-
gate the relationship among an NHRI, the government that created it, and the civil
society it should be working with. Using these elements to inform evaluations and
the broader promotion of NHRIs will temper the unguarded enthusiasm for these
institutions and ultimately lead to a more nuanced understanding of when and how
these institutions can be most effective.

12.4.2. *Ratcheting Up Compliance?*

Historical disconnects and anecdotal evidence of failure should not obscure the possibility that NHRIs would contribute to eventual improvements, even in states that
adopt them without the best of intentions.[50] In this regard, one possible response
to my criticism of NHRIs is that it is too static, and possibly outdated. It fails to
place the promotional effort in its proper context as a valuable phase in creating the

---

the United States, or Chile, for example. Poor human rights institutions have also presented a foil
for advocates. In the United States, the Reagan administration's Human Rights Bureau, in the
Department of State, was an important adversary in the struggle to secure the place of human rights
NGOs and human rights policies.

[49] See Obiora Okafor in this volume, "National Human Rights Institutions in Anglophone Africa."

[50] I take very seriously the argument of Goodman and Jinks that "conditions favorable to acculturation are amenable to manipulation to promote change through institutions"; see "How to Influence
States," 654. This section is largely framed in response to the question of whether NHRIs are such an
institution. The authors suggest, albeit tentatively, that NHRIs might serve as "receptor sites" to facilitate the diffusion of international norms; ibid., 673. My answer, not surprisingly, is not necessarily, not
predictably, and if we rely on the ICC, not likely.

conditions for effective diffusion of norms and compliance with higher standards of human rights over time. Moreover, it does not recognize important regional and international developments, particularly in the accreditation process of the ICC, that are intended to move in this direction. This section seeks to address this possibility, situating NHRIs in the context of related initiatives that set a low bar for access and seek to ratchet up compliance over time. It is true that there are positive indications in this regard, but the limitations of the ICC are profound and it is not clear that it can do more as an organization of NHRIs.[51]

There have been numerous important initiatives in the recent past that seek to create a regime through broad, inclusive membership at the outset, followed by efforts to "ratchet up" compliance through coercion, persuasion, and/or measures to induce acculturation.[52] The human rights treaty regimes have elements of this, as do more recent efforts to implement human rights in business practice. In many of those regimes, it is characteristic to reward those who sign on, without placing stringent conditions on full compliance from the outset.[53] It also seems characteristic that some members will try to obtain benefits while seeking to avoid compliance. Promotion raises the stature of the enterprise, which, in turn creates a disincentive for withdrawing, if and when more stringent conditions are demanded.

[51] With regard to the accreditation process of the ICC, the following documents are relied on: (1) ICC Working Group on Accreditation, *Decision Paper on the Review of ICC* (2008) (*hereafter* "Decision paper on the Review of ICC,"); (2) Rules of Procedure for the ICC Sub-Committee on Accreditation. Adopted by the members of the International Coordinating Committee at its 15th session, held on September 14, 2004, Seoul, Republic of Korea. Amended by the members of the ICC at its 20th session, held on April 15, 2008, Geneva, Switzerland (*hereafter* "Amended Rules of Procedure,"); (3) Guidelines for Accreditation & Re-Accreditation of National Human Rights Institutions to the International Coordinating Committee of National Human Rights Institutions, Version 4, June 2009 (*hereafter* "Guidelines,"); (4) General Observations of the SCA (*hereafter* "General Observations,"); and (5) Report and Recommendations of the Session of the Sub-Committee on Accreditation (*hereafter* "Report of the SCA"). With regard to the ICC, more generally, this chapter draws from the reports of the annual sessions of the ICC. All documents are available at www.nhri.net.

[52] See Goodman and Jinks, "How to Influence States," 657–9 (noting the inclusive membership of UN mechanisms for human rights), and ibid., 701–2 ("These insights suggest that a human rights regime might also enhance its effectiveness by demanding modest initial commitments and ratcheting up obligations over time.... This strategy of delayed onset coercion reflects, in many respects, the evolutionary path of the European Convention on Human Rights").

[53] Goodman and Jinks discuss this phenomenon in regard to human rights treaty mechanisms. See Goodman and Jinks, "How to Influence States," 702. Of particular significance (and controversy), the Council of Europe allowed the entry of some Central and Eastern European states before they had achieved full compliance with the European Convention on Human Rights. In regard to business and human rights, there have been a number of significant initiatives in the past decade. This chapter is informed primarily by a number of multi-stakeholder initiatives (MSIs) whose members include some combination of business, civil society, labor unions, and governments, including the Fair Labor Association (FLA), Social Accountability International, the Extractive Industry Transparency Initiative (EITI), and the Voluntary Principles for Security and Human Rights. All of them use elements of "sequencing and delayed onset coercion" (Goodman and Jinks, ibid.). The EITI, for example,

From the chapters in this book, it might be argued that regional mechanisms, local pressures, and ICC accreditation are creating the conditions for ratcheting up compliance. It might also be argued that expanding the role of NHRIs – for example, to include more active participation in international fora and designated functions in international agreements like the Optional Protocol for the Convention against Torture – increases both the incentives and the scrutiny that contribute to improvements.

A number of good examples throughout this book support the argument, including, in particular, the cases of Nigeria, Malaysia, and Fiji, where challenges to the integrity of the NHRI met strong responses from some combination of domestic, regional, and international actors. The chapters on Asia Pacific, Latin America, and Eastern Europe point to significant sharing of experience among NHRIs in each region, which doubtless exerts some pressure. The studies from the Asia Pacific are strongest in this regard, and the case study of Malaysia gives a particularly strong indication of possibilities when NGOs and regional actors bring their concerns to the ICC. On the other hand, the ICC continues to deal out "A" accreditation scores disproportionately to any other rating.[54]

The ICC is in fact a very curious organization to rely on for the critical evaluation of NHRIs. As an association composed of NHRIs – whose purpose is to "promote and strengthen" them – its critical engagement is necessarily limited. It takes for granted the positive contribution of Paris Principle-compliant NHRIs and actively promotes their participation in the international sector, without particular regard for the actual, substantive contribution they make.[55]

As an association of NHRIs, it is more like a trade association than an intergovernmental organization or multi-stakeholder initiative (MSI), albeit one that operates to promote a public good rather than private profit. This contrasts markedly with organizations like the UN, the International Labor Organization, or many of the emerging organizations involved in issues of business and human

has created a process for obtaining "candidate status" on the road to full verification. The Fair Labor Association (FLA) was launched with a number of businesses participating before the full extent of obligations was known or applied. Another example from outside the MSIs is the UN's Global Compact, which has sought to enforce and increase obligations after initial membership, though with mixed results.

54 Chart of the Status of National Institutions Accredited by the ICC, status as of June 2, 2009, at www. nhri.net.

55 In reviewing the documentation of the ICC, this is particularly true of any discussion of the role of the NHRIs in international fora. See discussion of these issues in the Report of the 22nd Session of the ICC, Geneva, March 23–27, 2009. In contrast, the ICC has played a more active role in developing shared principles and practices in relation to some of the domestic practices of the NHRIs. The Nairobi Declaration stands out in this regard as the most significant effort. Nairobi Declaration, Ninth International Conference of National Institutions for the Promotion and Protection of Human Rights, Nairobi, Kenya, October 21–24, 2008. Available at www.nhri.net.

rights.[56] Unlike the ICC, the others recognize diversity of interests among different constituencies and build these into organizational structures.

In recent years, MSIs and intergovernmental bodies have developed a broad range of tools to ensure compliance. They typically rely on some combination of transparency and disclosure, independent monitoring, and processes to challenge violations.[57] Strikingly, the ICC has almost none of this. Like a bar association or an association of doctors, the ICC may have a genuine interest in maintaining and improving quality, but it will be constrained by the interests of its members. At times they may support higher standards and more restrictive gatekeeping, and at times, not. They do not offer to subject themselves easily to external processes of review or verification, and in the case of the ICC that is clear from the rules for accreditation. In 2006, the ICC initiated a process that led to a revision of the rules for accreditation and required re-accreditation every five years. There is much that is good in the revised process and, particularly in the rhetoric that accompanied it. But the reform of accreditation has been full of mixed messages about how independent it should be and how seriously it should assess the actual work of the NHRIs in terms of human rights.

The end result of the ICC reform is a narrowly structured process carried out in-house, among NHRIs. It is deeply deferential to the NHRI under review and its regional association. With a limited exception for the OHCHR, it makes no requirement for seeking external opinion in the process of accreditation. Moreover, at least on paper, there is hardly any substantive requirement that would measure whether the NHRI commitment to human rights or the effectiveness of the NHRI within the state is genuine.[58] The practice appears to reach beyond the narrow requirements and hint at important substantive discussions. But the record is limited.

The mixed messages come across in the reports documenting the reform of the accreditation process and the various meetings of the ICC and the Sub-Commission

---

[56] The ILO is tripartite, with members coming from governments, and organizations of employers and workers. The MSIs typically have some combination of representatives from business, civil society, labor unions, and governments.

[57] Though somewhat dated, a good survey of MSIs in business and human rights was produced by the OHCHR for the review of the Draft Norms on Business and Human Rights. See "Draft Norms on the Responsibilities of Transnational Corporations and Other Business Enterprises with Regard to Human Rights," UN Doc. E/CN.4/Sub.2/2003/12 (2003).

[58] I would note two General Observations of the ICC Sub-Committee, in particular – one of which requires the government to consider recommendations of the NHRI (Observation 1.6) and another which stresses the NHRI's interaction with "other human rights institutions" (Observation 1.5), including those of the state and civil society. There are also three general observations that reference the role of the NHRI in periods of volatility or emergency (Observation 5.3), which call for heightened vigilance but acknowledge the possibility of not being able to meet all the requirements of the Paris Principles. See ICC Sub-Committee on Accreditation General Observations, Geneva, June 2009, http://www.nhri.net/2009/General%20observations%20June%202009%20(English).pdf.

on Accreditation. At its 2006 annual meeting, where the ICC initiated the process to reform its accreditation procedures, it did note the "need to ensure that [NHRIs] were truly legitimate," but only as one among several motivations.[59] The 2008 Sub-Committee Discussion Paper that served as the basis for the reform affirms the goal but ultimately appears more concerned with internally determined standards of legitimacy. It defines critical terms by reference to its members rather than to any external standards. For example, it stresses that the accreditation process needs to be improved with a view "to strengthening the credibility and efficiency of the process, as well as that of its inherent fairness." It might be suspected that "credibility" relates to a community beyond NHRIs, but this is never clearly explained. On the other hand, "inherent fairness" is explained only in term of the fairness to the NHRI under review.

The "guiding principles" of the reform, "transparency, rigor and independence," further accentuate what might be viewed as, at best, ambivalence. Only the definition of "rigor" clearly relates to external criteria for accreditation:

> A more rigorous process would mean that only applicant Institutions which conform to both the letter and the spirit of the Paris Principles, and demonstrate this through their actions, will be accredited, and that the methodology used to arrive at this decision is defined, supported by sound policy decisions and applied consistently and precisely.[60]

But the other principles highlight how hermetic the process is intended to be. "Transparency" is defined in terms of the NHRI under review[61] and "independence" does not suggest any process or participation that is separate from the ICC and its membership drawn from NHRIs.[62]

The written rules confirm the narrow intentions. Besides the OHCHR, there is no mandatory participation or consultation with any individual or organization outside the community of NHRIs. The OHCHR is a permanent observer and serves as secretariat to the ICC. As a practice noted in the Guidelines, the Sub-Committee has invited the relevant desk officer from the OHCHR to attend the accreditation sessions. That is hardly any assurance of profound vetting, particularly given the OHCHR's role in promoting and supporting NHRIs. Beyond this, any other

---

[59] And, strangely, there is one motivation that is not independently justified but framed as a need that "corresponds" to the "growing role of [NHRIs] in the international arena." ICC, "Decision paper on the Review of ICC," supra note 51.

[60] Ibid.

[61] The NHRI under review should understand the process and criteria being applied. When at risk of losing accreditation, it should have an opportunity to "provide written evidence" contesting the decision. Finally, transparency requires the ICC to demonstrate that it applies a consistent standard "in accordance with shared, accepted definitions and understandings"; ibid.

[62] Independence is defined as "a clear definition of roles" and an absence of "bias"; ibid.

outreach is left to chance and discretion: the chair of the Sub-Committee "may invite a person or institution as an observer" (rule 4.2) and civil society groups may submit comments in writing at least four months before the session.[63]

As regards the substantive grounds on which NHRIs are assessed, it is very hard to find the basis for the "rigor" that was supposedly implemented. The Guidelines for Accreditation claim that the process "now considers the effectiveness of NHRIs," but there is actually nothing in the Guidelines, the Rules of Procedure, or the General Observations issued thus far that provides any serious requirements in this regard, or even a description what a measure of "effectiveness" might be.[64] There are two General Observations that open the door to a more significant inquiry, one that would allow the Sub-Committee to review the NHRI's operations with respect to other government institutions and NGOs,[65] and one that states that NHRI recommendations "should normally be discussed within a reasonable amount of time, not to exceed six months by the relevant government ministries as well as the competent parliamentary committees."[66]

These are extremely limited. In practice, the Sub-Committee may be going further than the rules require and may be focusing more attention on the substantive work of the NHRI. In recent accreditation of Sri Lanka, for example, the Sub-Committee maintained a "B" rating, noting the NHRI's failure to release "regular and detailed reports or statements in relation to killings, abductions and disappearances stemming from the human rights crisis in Sri Lanka," and its "selective" engagement with NGOs.[67]

The Sri Lanka case is exceptional, even for the length of the public comments – four short paragraphs. In the case of Uganda, the Sub-Committee maintained the "A" rating of the commission and stated in one sentence: "it encourages the

---

[63] The main concerns of the procedure appear to be deference to the NHRI under review and its regional grouping. Regional balance is required in the sub-committee and, since November 2008, the sub-committee has invited the relevant regional coordinating member to attend sessions as an observer. The OHCHR is a permanent observer and secretariat of the ICC. The summary is also shared with relevant OHCHR desk officers and United Nations field presences. See ICC, "Guidelines and Rules of Procedure."

[64] ICC, "Guidelines and Rules of Procedure." The most significant possibilities are offered by the "General Observations" that enable the sub-committee to elucidate and, potentially, expand on the Paris Principles in light of practice. But thus far they tend also to focus on structural issues rather than substantive ones. Observation 1.6 states: "NHRI recommendations contained in annual, special or thematic human rights reports should normally be discussed within a reasonable amount of time, not to exceed six months, by the relevant government ministries as well as the competent parliamentary committees. These discussions should be held especially in order to determine the necessary follow up action, as appropriate in any given situation. NHRIs as part of their mandate to promote and protect human rights should ensure follow up action to recommendations contained in their reports."

[65] General Observation 1.5, Cooperation with other human rights institutions.

[66] General Observation 1.6.

[67] ICC, "Report of SCA" for March 26–30, 2009.

Commission to issue public reports on *all* delicate and critical human rights incidents within the country."[68] In other cases, there has been far less.

The ICC embodies the perception that the shared interests of all NHRIs will result in standards that are best for each. If we assume the best view of NHRIs – that they are independent, committed to improving human rights in the state, and willing to impose those standards on themselves and others – then that might be true. It is telling, however, that they did not implement such high standards in their written rules of accreditation. In any event, the combination of the promotional and the gatekeeper functions in an association composed exclusively of NHRIs is likely to impose limits on the ICC in the future. It may be able to "ramp up" compliance, particularly where local NGOs and regional groupings support the process. But it will have to do so with far fewer tools than have been deemed necessary or advisable in other settings.

12.4.3. *Refocusing Priorities for Evaluation*

Much of what has preceded is selective, based on intermittent research that should not stand in for systematic investigations. But if, in answer to the question of whether an NHRI contributes to the promotion and protection of human rights in the country, a substantial number of informed observers would respond with doubt or uncertainty, that should be relevant. If the insertion of NHRIs in a state has had an uncertain influence on other state and nonstate actors involved in the protection of human rights, that is significant. If the state can nurture an "A" status NHRI while systematically undermining human rights in the country, that should be a cause for major concern. Until now, these have not been critical areas for evaluation. The process of accreditation does not even ensure that such concerns will be seriously explored. Independent international NGOs like Human Rights Watch do not have the incentives or means to provide the necessary analysis and local NGOs may not desire or be in a position to do so.

I would propose three threshold elements to a meaningful evaluation: (1) focus on process, (2) identify and assess the most critical national human rights issues, and (3) locate the NHRI in terms of time and place.

Process

A meaningful evaluation process should draw lessons from other initiatives to raise standards in human rights and corporate social responsibility. "Independence" and "transparency" in the process should be defined in terms of the constituent groups

---

[68] ICC, "Report of SCA" for April 21–23, 2008 (emphasis in original).

that have an interest in the work of the NHRI, and not the NHRI itself. If the ICC is to remain central to the process, it should consider creating an affiliated body that is truly independent in order to conduct the accreditation process.

What is important is how the evaluation is conducted and who conducts it. The evaluators should be independent of those national and international actors who are a part of the system in place. The process should require evaluators to seek and convey the voices of others, including those most harshly critical. In that way, the process would not leave the input of critical regional and local actors to chance.

The process must also be iterative or ongoing. The ICC made an important advance by requiring re-accreditation every five years, but it also limited the opportunities for interim review based on changed circumstances.[69] As the HRW report shows, a single one-off report has severe limitations. The critical reporting on an NHRI should be collected continuously.[70]

Critical National Human Rights Issues

The evaluation should seek to identify the critical human rights issues in the country and determine how the NHRI addresses them. As obvious as this may appear, it would throw the evaluation into the center of contention. A long rhetorical commitment to the "indivisibility" of human rights has made human rights professionals allergic to prioritizing rights in any given context. But NHRIs make choices and respond to demands, or else they avoid them. If domestic (and international) resources are being devoted to child support and road carnage, but not suppression of political pluralism, that should be explained.

Locate the NHRI in Time and Place

The contribution of an NHRI depends on local circumstances that vary over time. A dynamic NHRI may set the standard for the future, influencing the society more profoundly and rendering the work of successors more difficult. On the other hand,

---

[69] See Report 22nd Session of the International Coordinating Committee of National Institutions for the Promotion and Protection of Human Rights (ICC), Palais des Nations, Geneva, March 23–27, 2009, p. 10. ("4. Article 16.2 – initiation of a review: proposed amendment seeks to allow any voting member to request that the ICC Bureau begin an investigation: 'when, in the opinion of the member of the ICC, it would appear that the status of an NHRI with status A may have changed such that it may affect its compliance with the Paris Principles, it will request to the Bureau that the SCA initiate a review of that NHRIs accreditation status.' GWG: the current initiation power lies with the ICC Chairperson or the SCA and that this constitutes an important filter, because an accreditation review is an onerous process that should only be undertaken if necessary. Vote: rejected, by majority.")

[70] This might take the form of a "Wiki model" that would provide a constant source of updated information on ICC-accredited organizations.

a modest NHRI operating in a space of low expectations may still be performing a useful function. The ups and downs of an NHRI might be part of the healthy give and take of institutional development. Or, they could be evidence of a government's effort to resist encroachment and assert control.

Moreover, NHRIs do not exist in a vacuum. A host of other state institutions may play overlapping roles, including ombudsmen, courts, inspectors general, and specialized commissions. It would be difficult to make any general assessment of the significance of the NHRI without understanding the role of other institutions and the interactions among them.

12.5. CONCLUSION

The promotional intensity and transitional ferment of the 1990s resulted in the widespread diffusion of the NHRIs that we see today. Their creation was celebrated; criticisms were stated in parentheses, if at all. In that light, it is no "dilemma" that some states created institutions with "inappropriate people" and "inadequate resources" to function, as Brian Burdekin suggests. It is completely unsurprising, even reasonable. What is surprising is that many of them have functioned, nonetheless. NHRIs are playing a significant role in many states around the world. It is worthwhile to engage with them, study them, and critically evaluate their contribution to human rights.

But while tainted origins do not necessarily determine outcomes, neither can they be overlooked in a critical evaluation of the institutions. There are too many reasons for skepticism about the good faith and genuineness of both NHRIs and the international actors who have promoted them to overlook the impacts of conflicting motivations. A serious evaluation has to elicit critical reactions and seek to understand the NHRI in local context.

What we do know from the short history of NHRIs also suggests that there are phases in their operations. If there are "heroic periods" where NHRIs take exceptional and courageous stands, there are likely to be "post-heroic" periods when the leadership takes cover. This might be part of the normal cycles of building and maintaining legitimacy, or responding to changes in the state. But it might be evidence of an effort by a state to undermine the NHRI when the spotlight is removed after a first generation of leaders. There may also be different kinds of legitimate NHRIs, corresponding to the struggles faced by the state – institutions of resistance, institutions of transition, and, perhaps, institutions of long-term integration that may serve as receptors for international norms, at least in some areas.

The variety of operations among NHRIs in different states and within a single state over time highlights the further complexity of evaluation. We do not really know what contributes to the sustained promotion and protection of human rights in a state, but our collective experience suggests that one size does not fit all. The demonstration effect of courageous but futile actions of an NHRI – or an NGO or an individual – might be more important in some settings than the consistent efforts of a well-ordered bureaucracy in others. We cannot know without scrutinizing the relationship of the NHRI to the critical issues of human rights in a particular country.

Finally, we should be careful to avoid presumptions about where we are headed. We should critically examine, for example, the arguments for giving a privileged place to NHRIs in the international arena. Is this based on their proven contribution or an aspirational vision? Perhaps, we have passed through the phase of promotion into a period of critical consolidation and refinement. According to that argument, the promotional period was an important one for gaining adherence to a shared set of principles. The cost of entry was low since credit was gained simply by adherence and no verification was immediately likely. Now, the combined solidarity, bureaucracy, and vested interest in remaining might sustain continued adhesion in the face of critical evaluations. The institution that results would have coherence across national boundaries and might merit a place at the international table.

It is not a far-fetched argument. It parallels the strategy for building treaty regimes and voluntary processes for corporate social responsibility. But if so, the process has still not evolved far. The examples from this volume suggest that only local activism (Malaysia), egregiously *ultra vires* behavior (Fiji), or offenses against the vested interests of the NHRI community (Nigeria) trigger a critical reaction at the international level. On the other hand, a well-churning bureaucracy can win accolades (Uganda) or, at least, a good grade (Togo) without ever addressing the question of whether the NHRI plays a meaningful role in the most important human rights issues in the country.

But we might also be in a different phase altogether, one of dissipation and differentiation in the face of international disinterest rather than consolidation. The transitional ferment of the 1990s is largely over. The interest in new institutional structures for enhancing good governance and human rights, whether NHRIs, constitutional courts, truth commissions, or anti-corruption bodies, may have passed. Other issues, including global warming and international security have seized the agenda. In that case, NHRIs will remain the quirky, but interesting institutions that they are today, contributing to the long-term gains in human rights in some cases, and frustrating it in others.

13

National Human Rights Institutions, Opportunities, and Activism

David S. Meyer

13.1. INTRODUCTION

Protecting and promoting human rights has been a historical give and take. Activists at the grass roots have worked courageously to expose violations of human rights, attempting to enlist more powerful authorities to pressure or punish violators. They have used the tools of social movements, including protests and demonstrations, in attempts to mobilize an audience into action. A wide range of institutions, including national institutions, as well as supranational bodies and transnational organizations, have articulated universalistic standards of human rights and publicized the work of activists, calling for states to protect human rights. Nothing happens easily, as effective enforcement of human rights generally involves more powerful actors intervening to alter the balance of power within a state. Both activists and authorities seek to move beyond ad hoc enforcement of human rights, establishing a permanent presence to keep human rights in view. What are we to make of the establishment of new institutions at the national level specifically charged with the protection of human rights? How do these national human rights institutions (NHRIs) influence the ongoing campaigns to advance the cause?

The chapters in this volume emphasize the limitations of NHRIs. It is difficult to get states to create institutions that are independent enough and sufficiently powerful to provide meaningful redress, particularly when the national bodies that create human rights institutions are often also culpable in the violation of human rights. Even institutions that comply with ideal organizational structures (in theory)[1] suffer from political interference, inadequate funding, and leadership failures. Indeed, the intense attention to the need for exceptional leadership undermines the notion that establishing NHRIs can, in itself, address ongoing concerns about human rights.

---

[1] For example, the "Paris Principles," as discussed by Julie Mertus in this volume, "Evaluating the NHRIs: Considering Structure, Mandate, and Impact."

But institutions outlive the circumstances of their creation, and particularly today's leaders, and can be consequential over a long period of time. In these comments, I want to suggest the potential importance of NHRIs over this long period, particularly in providing a venue for activists to lodge claims. I begin by discussing the nature of institutions, drawing from Max Weber's classic formulation, and I note the severe structural constraints inherent in establishing a venue for human rights nested at the national level. I then consider NHRIs as a component in the structure of political opportunities human rights activists face, operating as both agents and venues for independent action.

13.2. INSTITUTIONS

Institutions, by nature, promise more than they can deliver, and virtually always disappoint. This is likely to be more, rather than less, true of institutions devoted to human rights, particularly when situated at the national level. From Weber, we learn that institution-building is a critical component in the creation of a rational-legal system of legitimation of authority.[2] This means that rather than accepting the practices of authorities by virtue of tradition or the extraordinary claims of circumstance or personality, laws and routines come to dominate citizen practices. Alliteratively, we can think about Weber's ideal-type institutions as organized around a series of "R's": rules, responsibilities, routines, and records. Advocates for new institutions seek to create a system of relationships and actors that systematize and standardize the processing of claims and the delivery of services. (And thinking about dispensing justice as a service requires something of a conceptual stretch as well.) Hiring and advancement are based on formal meritocratic criteria, authority is based on the office, not the person, and bureaucrats enjoy little discretion in responding to claims. Each claim receives consideration based on explicit standards, with officials bound by both laws and clearly established procedures. The mandate of the institution is clearly delineated by political authorities, with formal criteria determining what are legitimate concerns and responses. The promise of institutionalization is permanence and consistency in ensuring the protection of human rights, beyond the political contingencies or leadership talents of the moment. When a state creates an institution, it legitimates its mission publicly, and effectively creates public expectations for its performance.

Rights, a fourth "R," are not explicitly delineated in Weber's ideal type, but are implicit in the notion that all claimants with standing for redress receive equal treatment based on their claim, not their beliefs, appearance, heritage, status, or wealth.

[2] M. Weber, *The Theory of Social and Economic Organization*, ed. by T. Parsons, trans. by A. M. Henderson and Talcott Parsons (New York: Free Press, 1964).

This is a powerful promise, but one that can appear mundane and woefully inadequate in the face of great injustice. The ideal-type NHRI takes testimony and produces reports but lacks the formal power to rectify oppression or to punish oppressors.[3] For redress, NHRIs depend upon other authorities, often those who have perpetrated – or ignored – violations of human rights. When their leaders recognize their limitations and tailor their efforts to what they are likely to achieve, they disappoint advocates of human rights with their weak leadership. When those leaders do not do so, articulating principals clearly and documenting violations without regard to political power, they produce powerful rhetoric and, alas, demonstrate the limits of their institutions.

And for NHRIs, there are additional inherent difficulties. The notion of human rights implies universal standards that transcend national boundaries. Situating a human rights institution at the national level may provide a body that is more proximate, and thus potentially more responsive, to violations and victims. Yet it is also likely to be more responsive to local standards and pressures – indeed, this is one definition of democracy. But whenever the execution of human rights is circumscribed by the established custom or powerful constituencies, the promise of universal standards is compromised. There is an inherent tension between responsiveness to local domestic conditions and international human rights norms that floats through all of this discussion. While we want to have powerful NHRIs on the ground, power usually comes with the acceptance of local, rather than universal, standards of justice. (This is the tension between dualism and monism that Richard Carver articulates so clearly in his chapter.)

The Weberian notion of an institution executing, but not establishing, its mission, which comes from political authorities, summons images of bureaucrats who ignore gross violations of human rights because they fall outside explicit mandates or, worse, perpetrate violations themselves, following the directives of political authorities in what was long ago described as the "banality of evil."[4] The effectiveness of an NHRI clearly begins with the directions forged *outside* that institution, and somehow, outside the vision of the state that created it. Indeed, the notion that a state would have the vision to create an institution that could offer more than what Linda Reif describes as a "soft" counterweight to its own initiatives can inspire admiration and/or strain credulity.[5] There is, of course, a paradox here, one with inherent limitations, but also possibilities.

---

[3]   In fact, NHRIs operate in cooperation and conflict with other institutions that effectively serve as checks and balances, and constraints on meaningful initiative. This issue is discussed in further detail in Enrique Peruzzotti, "The Societalization of Horizontal Accountability: Rights Advocacy and the Defensor del Pueblo de la Nación in Argentina," and in Fredrik Uggla, "Through Pressure or Persuasion? Explaining Compliance with the Resolutions of the Bolivian Defensor del Pueblo," both in this volume.

[4]   The phrase is from H. Arendt, *Eichmann in Jerusalem* (New York: Penguin, 1965).

[5]   For this reason, attention to the features of each institution that promote autonomy and responsiveness to local, national, or supranational pressures is critical. The number and tenure of

The global recognition of human rights has encouraged the development of NHRIs. Creating an institution is a visible step toward addressing a serious problem and responding to political pressures about that problem, effectively recognizing and legitimating those pressures.[6] What is more, the creation of NHRIs leads to the creation of more NHRIs, as nations develop patterned solutions to recognized problems. Mimetic pressures led to the creation of similarly structured institutions in general[7]; in the case of human rights, a template structure for NHRIs has been codified in the Paris Principles. Each new NHRI comes into existence nested in a set of supranational bodies pursuing human rights, transnational NGOs pressuring for action, and an increasing number of ostensibly similar institutions in other nations. All of this should lead to continual pressures on these organizations to develop similar structures and missions, and the impact of this isomorphism is unclear: even as NHRIs have proliferated, their actual impact on the conduct of state policy poses questions and concerns. Most notably, is the creation of NHRIs a step toward protecting and promoting human rights or a way of containing and insulating the pressure to provide such protection?[8]

And the pressures for action are significant, and often countervailing. While supranational bodies press for action – or more visibly, institutions that codify and report on human rights – domestic constituencies press for individual redress. Even the most well-funded NHRIs face a stream of claims that outstrip their capacity to manage expeditiously, and many of those claims are focused not on egregious violations of fundamental civil or political rights so much as inadequate administrative competence in handling the provision of basic services. Thus, NHRIs must balance the constant claims of citizens to investigate and process claims about past abuses with more proactive (inherently political) action to promote human rights domestically by identifying patterns, exposing the sources of abuse, and pressing for substantive reforms.[9] The processing of individual claims, once begun, becomes generally endless; NHRIs immediately fall behind any reasonable schedule and come up against inevitable shortfalls in staffing and budgets.

commissioners, the sufficiency and stability of funding, and the formal extent of powers are all likely to be consequential.

6 Lisa L. Martin and Beth A. Simmons, "Theories and Empirical Studies of International Institutions," *International Organization* 52 (1998), 729–57.

7 Paul J. DiMaggio and Walter W. Powell, "The Iron Cage Revisited: Institutional Isomorphism and Collective Rationality in Organizational Fields," *American Sociological Review* 48 (1983), 147–60.

8 The evaluation of the impact of NHRIs is complicated; their effectiveness is constrained not only by institutional charters but also by domestic political pressures, and changes over time. See S. Cardenas, *Conflict and Compliance: State Responses to International Human Rights Pressure* (Philadelphia: University of Pennsylvania Press, 2007).

9 The tension between service and advocacy is not peculiar to NHRIs (see, e.g., Debra C. Minkoff, "Bending with the Wind: Organizational Change in American Women's and Minority Organizations," *American Journal of Sociology* 104 (1999), 1666–1703), although it may be particularly painful and difficult.

NHRIs thus face the challenge of developing a politically strategic triage, as leaders recognize that maximizing their influence on the climate of the nation necessitates focusing on the most consequential cases, even as they realize that each delayed case is of critical importance to the claimant, and that each disappointed petitioner is, effectively, testimony that the institution is falling short of expectations.[10] Whereas international pressures push for the promotion of human rights, domestic constituencies demand justice at an individual level. And domestic pressures are likely to be more consequential in ensuring stable support for the NHRI's continued functioning, particularly in difficult budget environments. And the availability of individual remedies and redress for human rights violations (in the past!) may undermine activists' framing human rights as a larger, political problem requiring collective action. This is particularly important in new democracies that bear the responsibility for responding to the violations of the regimes they replaced, even as they seek to look forward to creating a more just and responsive government.

It is not that NHRIs cannot aid in the pursuit and protection of human rights, but rather, that their effectiveness in doing so is a function of their relationship to other actors, including both grassroots activists, transnational NGOs, and supranational governance bodies, which operate both regionally and globally. It is important to consider how the establishment of an NHRI can affect the prospects for those other actors of operating effectively. For the most part, the NHRIs themselves depend upon the commitment of other institutions to act on their findings, and the studies presented here document a broad range of commitments and capacity to do so. In each state, the efforts of an NHRI are amplified or dampened by both governmental, business, and civil society actors.

13.3. HUMAN RIGHTS ACTIVISM AND SOCIAL MOVEMENTS

Grassroots activism has been critical to the pursuit of human rights. Activists often knowingly challenge strictures on speech, dress, religious practice, and assembly, recognizing that they risk punishment. Others have drawn attention to the plight of the persecuted, often bearing great personal costs in the process. I am particularly concerned with the constellation of factors that lead people to mobilize. To be sure, there are always some people willing to take great risks in the service of a deeply held belief, but most people are not saints or lunatics. Rather, most people respond to the environment around them; they engage in activism when they believe that it is necessary – and at least potentially effective – in helping them get

---

[10] Richard Carver, "National Human Rights Institutions in Central and Eastern Europe: The Ombudsman as Agent of International Law," in this volume describes the critical importance, and exceptional difficulty, of setting strategic priorities that prioritize some cases at the expense of others.

what they want.[11] If they can get what they want in some less costly or risky way, they will do so, writing letters, voting, or contributing money. If people believe that their efforts will be futile, few are likely to dedicate much attention or embrace serious risks. And when larger numbers of people are active, they will respond to the openings and constraints that the larger political environment offers. For example, dissidents in countries with low threshold proportional representation systems may choose to form political parties, while that is an extremely unattractive strategy for their counterparts operating in systems with single member district systems or no elections at all. Judicial review can make litigation attractive; the presence of allies in government can encourage moderation, and so forth. Students of social movements refer to the world outside a movement, which offers signals about the most promising issues and routes to influence, the "structure of political opportunities."[12]

Political opportunity structure is the world outside of social movements that affects the prospects for mobilization and their influence and thereby what activists think they can or should do. It provides resources, constraints, claims, and routes of rules for getting things done. Changes in the constellation of institutions and actors around activists can encourage particular influence strategies and also affect when their efforts will gain outside attention. If we begin by thinking about human rights, we can sort out a range of factors that influence the mobilization and potential influence of activism. First, it is critical to realize that human rights politics necessarily address multiple levels of governance. The very notion of human rights recognizes transcendent values of individual worth that are not contingent upon recognition by a local government, whether democratic or not. In this regard, we can think about opportunities as "nested," in which a supranational regime (more or less) constrains what is possible at the national or subnational level.[13] Activists at the local level may try to get around the oppressive local or national government to mobilize supranational attention and pressure, thereby effecting what Margaret Keck and Kathryn Sikkink have termed the "boomerang" effect.[14] The strength of supranational regimes – as well as the extent of autonomy enjoyed by institutions

[11] D. S. Meyer, *The Politics of Protest: Social Movements in America* (New York: Oxford University Press, 2007).

[12] Peter K. Eisinger, "Conditions of Protest Behavior in American Cities," *American Political Science Review* 67 (1973), 11–28; C. Tilly, *From Mobilization to Revolution*, (Wellesley, MA: Addison-Wesley, 1977); D. McAdam, *Political Process and the Origins of Black Insurgency* (Chicago: University of Chicago Press, 1982); S. Tarrow, *Power in Movement* (New York: Cambridge University Press, 1998). For review, see David S. Meyer, "Protest and Political Opportunity," *Annual Review of Sociology* 30 (2004), 125–40.

[13] Franklin Daniel Rothman and Pamela E. Oliver, "From Local to Global: The Anti-Dam Movement in Southern Brazil, 1979–1992," *Mobilization* 4 (1999), 41–57; David S. Meyer, "Political Opportunity and Nested Institutions," *Social Movement Studies* 2 (2003), 17–35.

[14] M. E. Keck and K. Sikkink, *Activists beyond Borders* (Ithaca: Cornell University Press, 1998).

operating at national and subnational levels – affect how likely activists are to try to throw such a boomerang, and that claim's odds of getting out – and returning.

New institutions affect the terrain, that is, the world outside of movements, by their very existence, and of course, by what they do. Of course, how they affect will vary across settings and over time – a critical reason that the empirical treatments in this volume are so important. The NHRI is particularly important, because it provides a venue for activists, even as it is constituted as an actor in itself. It also provides an outlet for professional employment and status for activists, which means that some individuals acquire the resources to become stable advocates for human rights, even as they must accommodate to intrinsically limiting institutional means of doing so.[15]

In professionalizing the protection of human rights, we risk off-loading the responsibility of political vigilance from citizens to government employees. At once, the establishment of an NHRI offers an official statement about the importance of human rights. It also offers a site, or venue, for action on behalf of human rights, as well as a prescribed set of procedures for making claims. At face value, this can legitimate and channel human rights activism. This can encourage citizens and states to pay more attention to human rights, and alert potential violators to an official set of norms. To return to the political opportunity formulation, the existence of an NHRI can encourage activism by leading potential activists to think their efforts are more likely to matter; alternatively, it can depress activism by leading would-be activists to think their mobilization is unnecessary.

Even while an NHRI is a venue, it can also become an actor, making – as well as responding – to claims. It can group disparate cases and claims to advocate larger reforms, thus turning cases into causes. The ideal-type NHRI does not have to wait for claims to be brought to it but can investigate and make its own reports and statements. Advocates for human rights can have an official position and whatever legitimacy comes with it, as well as some resources for pursuing their work. The impact of these institutions is, as sharply demonstrated in this book, virtually always less than advocates would want.[16]

Over the longer haul, the question that will haunt analysts and activists alike is the developing utility of these institutions. Will the NHRIs encourage activists to make more claims for human rights, and to make them more aggressively? Will it provide a platform for that claims-making, amplifying those claims and the pursuit of human rights? Or, alternatively, will NHRIs serve to insulate activist claims from

---

[15] Note that Chris Sidoti, author of one chapter in this volume, is a significant actor (as activist, then as human rights commissioner) in another chapter, "National Human Rights Institutions in the Asia Pacific Region" by Catherine Renshaw and Kieren Fitzpatrick.

[16] Because NHRIs ostensibly serve the populace but are chartered and funded by the state, they inevitably face cross-pressures in charting a course of effective action.

meaningful redress or politics? Will the institution become a place to segregate human rights from the actual practice of real politics? Simply, it is clear that NHRIs provide human rights activists an additional lever to pound upon; it is less clear that those levers are routinely connected to any meaningful political influence. Even as the emergence of NHRIs reflects the purposive efforts of activists, NHRIs, in turn, affect the structure of political opportunities human rights claimants face, but not necessarily by creating meaningful openings; we have to ask whether these institutions might develop as barriers to – or diversions from – more effective advocacy. The case studies in this book give both answers, which underscore the necessity of continued scholarly attention.

But the establishment of permanent structures concerned with human rights at the national level will surely have long-term effects, far beyond the current achievements and limitations of those institutions.

13.4. THE VIRTUES OF HYPOCRISY

Statecraft, and politics more generally, includes some degree of dissembling. In seeking attention, in trying to mobilize action from citizens or legislators, and in forging agreements, political figures must become accustomed to seeing a gap between their words and actual occurrences. Optimism leads to overstatement and hyperbole, as partisans oversell the importance of an election or a prospective reform in efforts to generate passionate support. Efforts at courtesy and civility can lead to obfuscation, as political opponents receive honorifics and credulity that may not be earned. And, of course, it is far easier to craft inspiring rhetoric than effective moral and political policies. The speaker can control his words but not the efforts of others inspired or annoyed by them. Nonetheless, the gap can provoke and inspire activists, and provide critical rhetorical support.

For example, the distance between rhetoric and reality may be nowhere greater than in the area of human rights. Americans point to founder Thomas Jefferson's inspiring words (adapted from John Locke) in the Declaration of Independence, asserting that "all men are created equal." Jefferson, of course, owned African men (and women) who received decidedly less equal treatment from the United States Constitution and from Jefferson himself. More than fourscore years later, Abraham Lincoln appropriated the Declaration as a goal for America, using it to justify his efforts to maintain the Union and to end slavery. Another fourscore years forward, civil rights activists used Jefferson's words to frame their cause as fundamentally consistent with American values. The civil rights activists who approached a segregated library and asked for a copy of the Declaration knew that they would not be served, but also knew that they were creating a visible demonstration of systematic injustice, which might translate into powerful political action – by themselves, and by the mobilization of others. Would a Jefferson whose words were constrained by the reality of his life have been a more effective resource for equality and justice? Would a more honest writer have been as influential?

I do not mean to excuse hypocrisy and distortion but rather to suggest that aspirational words can inspire others, animating and legitimating meaningful action. In some ways, it is better to say the right things even when not living up to them.

Ryan Goodman and Derek Jinks argue that a state's expression of a commitment to human rights, no matter how insincere or superficial, is likely to deepen through what they describe as "the civilizing force of hypocrisy."[17] They argue that the articulation of a human rights standard creates expectations in both international and domestic audiences that translate, over time, into political pressure for compliance. Internationally, formal commitments as expressed in an institution or treaty, create a rationale for monitoring, and the distance between those commitments and performance forces leaders to explain, justify, or work to obfuscate, their shortfall. In any case, the norm is reinforced.

Domestically, the impact of new standards can work to undermine the legitimacy of long-term practices that violate international norms.[18] Elizabeth Boyle and Sharon Preves, for example, examine the establishment of laws forbidding female genital mutilation in states where the practice is common and find that the new laws push for changes in culture and norms. These cultural changes are enforced both through articulating new values from the international community, while also sometimes providing sanctions against those who would continue traditional practices in violation of the new law.

Moreover, articulating norms for human rights more generally encourages activists to mobilize to secure those rights. In essence, when citizens are confronted with a promised right, they will seek to find or create a remedy. Beth Simmons has investigated the impact of international human rights treaties on state compliance with human rights and finds that a state that signs such an agreement is more likely to encounter *domestic* political activism to honor those commitments.[19] Through this process, over time, even undemocratic states will increase their compliance with international norms on human rights.

When the leaders of a state announce their approval of international norms on human rights and their commitment to them, they signal to their populations that they consider human rights important and implicitly suggest that claims based on

---

[17] Ryan Goodman and Derek Jinks, "Incomplete Internalization and Compliance with Human Rights Law," *European Journal of International Law* 19 (2008), 725–48.

[18] Elizabeth Heger Boyle and Sharon E. Preves, "National Policies as International Process: The Case of Anti-Female-Genital-Cutting Laws," *Law and Society Review* 34 (2000), 703–37.

[19] B. Simmons, *Mobilizing for Human Rights: International Law in Domestic Politics* (New York: Cambridge University Press, 2009).

those norms may meet with success. The articulated standard can provide a resource to sympathetic figures in government, who then can try to use new laws against their political opponents, mobilizing support from the larger population. Even if the signal of responsiveness is a clear misdirection, the signal itself becomes significant. Over time, activists following bad directions carve out new roads that were only previously imagined. As waves of activists try to tread a nonexistent route to influence, by their efforts, they can create that route.

The onset of activism demonstrates the gap between articulated standards and actual performance, underscoring hypocrisy. It may spur repression, and thus invite international pressure, or it may be followed by reform, thus generating new incentives for greater activism. We have seen this process unfold in China, strangely following the massacre at Tiananmen Square. Rationalizing repression led Chinese leaders to offer rhetorical commitments to some sorts of citizen participation – in sharp contrast to that offered to the activists in the Square in 1989. Activists in the provinces took those commitments perhaps more seriously than the leaders who made them, leading to cycles of activism and challenge.[20]

When U.S. President Ford negotiated the Helsinki Accords with Soviet General Secretary Brezhnev, he was widely derided for dishonesty and/or naïveté. The agreements codified universal standards for human rights, standards that the Eastern bloc did not come close to honoring. At the same time, the Helsinki agreement provided powerful political leverage for dissidents within the Soviet bloc. Activists in Eastern Europe founded Charter 77, which called for their states to live up to the agreements.[21] Helsinki, endorsed by the Soviet Union, provided rhetorical leverage for the activists, who sought to embarrass their governments by calling upon them to live up to the agreements they had made. In effect, constantly pointing to Helsinki became part of a larger moral and political strategy, articulated by dissident and future Czech president, Vaclav Havel, as "living in truth."[22] The Charter 77 heroes spent time in jail or exile, as their claims provoked repression. At the same time, their efforts established networks of activists that proved to be critical in the revolutions of 1989.[23] Rhetoric and symbols matter, but often not immediately or even soon.

The NHRI can work both domestically and internationally in the same ways as laws and treaties, providing a state-sponsored place where international norms about

[20] See particularly K. J. O'Brien (ed.), *Popular Protest in China* (Cambridge: Harvard University Press, 2008); K. O'Brien and L. Li, *Rightful Resistance in Rural China* (New York: Cambridge University Press, 2006).

[21] D. C. Thomas, *The Helsinki Effect: International Norms, Human Rights, and the Demise of Communism* (Princeton, NJ: Princeton University Press, 2001).

[22] Vaclav Havel et al., *The Power of the Powerless: Citizens against the State in Central and Eastern Europe* (Armonk, NY: M. E. Sharpe, 1985).

[23] See, for example, Mary Kaldor, "Who Killed the Cold War," *Bulletin of the Atomic Scientists* July/August (1995), 57–61.

human rights are given attention and an institutional constituency. By giving official credence to the universal standards of human rights, an NHRI can establish a symbolic and rhetorical foundation for collective action. It creates a platform for professionals to reaffirm those standards and assess the state's progress in meeting them. By failing to deliver on those promises, NHRIs can, paradoxically, encourage others to do more.

13.5. CONCLUSION

The focus in this book on national human rights institutions and human rights is an important step toward solving a set of puzzles. The first analytical problem is to make progress in understanding a set of institutions that are meant to respond to very great expectations, and that function in diverse ways. NHRIs are at once a site for discourse and a place for purposive action on human rights. They also operate as organizations nested within both domestic and global environments which offer different, and sometimes countervailing, constraints and pressures. NHRIs can also operate as actors, both domestically and globally, creating incentives and pressures for others to act on human rights. As a site, NHRIs can be a conduit for transmission of international norms and information, a locus for making human rights claims, like an arena where people can make claims and redress grievances. As an actor, NHRIs can function as a watchdog, an editor, a promoter, and an administrative overseer. As organizations, NHRIs confront all the questions of bureaucracy, mission, maintenance, operations, and interests that bedevil all other organizations. Perhaps most consequential is the role NHRIs play in getting others, including governments, nongovernmental organizations, and citizen activists, to take up their cause.

The challenge of this book is to focus on NHRIs without fetishizing them. When we expect NHRIs to solve the problems of human rights that have occupied both NGOs and the international system for a much longer period of time, we set ourselves up for disappointment and cynicism. Rather, we need to think about NHRIs as a relatively new and potentially important factor embedded in a larger web of institutions and relationships working to protect and promote human rights. As such, they provide scholars with a useful window through which to view complicated political processes. For activists, they provide another tool, with specific capabilities and limitations, for continuing what will surely be a long-term struggle.

Annex 1

Principles Relating to the Status of National Institutions
(The Paris Principles)

Adopted by General Assembly Resolution 48/134 of December 20, 1993

COMPETENCE AND RESPONSIBILITIES

1. A national institution shall be vested with competence to promote and protect human rights.
2. A national institution shall be given as broad a mandate as possible, which shall be clearly set forth in a constitutional or legislative text, specifying its composition and its sphere of competence.
3. A national institution shall, inter alia, have the following responsibilities:
   a. To submit to the Government, Parliament and any other competent body, on an advisory basis either at the request of the authorities concerned or through the exercise of its power to hear a matter without higher referral, opinions, recommendations, proposals and reports on any matters concerning the promotion and protection of human rights; the national institution may decide to publicize them; these opinions, recommendations, proposals and reports, as well as any prerogative of the national institution, shall relate to the following areas:
      i. Any legislative or administrative provisions, as well as provisions relating to judicial organizations, intended to preserve and extend the protection of human rights; in that connection, the national institution shall examine the legislation and administrative provisions in force, as well as bills and proposals, and shall make such recommendations as it deems appropriate in order to ensure that these provisions conform to the fundamental principles of human rights; it shall, if necessary, recommend the adoption of new legislation, the amendment of legislation in force and the adoption or amendment of administrative measures;
      ii. Any situation of violation of human rights which it decides to take up;

iii. The preparation of reports on the national situation with regard to human rights in general, and on more specific matters;

iv. Drawing the attention of the Government to situations in any part of the country where human rights are violated and making proposals to it for initiatives to put an end to such situations and, where necessary, expressing an opinion on the positions and reactions of the Government;

b. To promote and ensure the harmonization of national legislation, regulations and practices with the international human rights instruments to which the State is a party, and their effective implementation;

c. To encourage ratification of the above-mentioned instruments or accession to those instruments, and to ensure their implementation;

d. To contribute to the reports which States are required to submit to United Nations bodies and committees, and to regional institutions, pursuant to their treaty obligations and, where necessary, to express an opinion on the subject, with due respect for their independence;

e. To cooperate with the United Nations and any other organization in the United Nations system, the regional institutions and the national institutions of other countries that are competent in the areas of the protection and promotion of human rights;

f. To assist in the formulation of programs for the teaching of, and research into, human rights and to take part in their execution in schools, universities, and professional circles;

g. To publicize human rights and efforts to combat all forms of discrimination, in particular racial discrimination, by increasing public awareness, especially through information and education and by making use of all press organs.

COMPOSITION AND GUARANTEES OF INDEPENDENCE AND PLURALISM

1. The composition of the national institution and the appointment of its members, whether by means of an election or otherwise, shall be established in accordance with a procedure which affords all necessary guarantees to ensure the pluralist representation of the social forces (of civilian society) involved in the protection and promotion of human rights, particularly by powers which will enable effective cooperation to be established with, or through the presence of, representatives of:

a. Non-governmental organizations responsible for human rights and efforts to combat racial discrimination, trade unions, concerned social and professional organizations, for example, associations of lawyers, doctors, journalists and eminent scientists;

b. Trends in philosophical or religious thought;

c. Universities and qualified experts;

d. Parliament;

e. Government departments (if these are included, their representatives should participate in the deliberations only in an advisory capacity).

2. The national institution shall have an infrastructure which is suited to the smooth conduct of its activities, in particular adequate funding. The purpose of this funding should be to enable it to have its own staff and premises, in order to be independent of the Government and not be subject to financial control which might affect its independence.

3. In order to ensure a stable mandate for the members of the national institution, without which there can be no real independence, their appointment shall be effected by an official act which shall establish the specific duration of the mandate. This mandate may be renewable, provided that the pluralism of the institution's membership is ensured.

METHODS OF OPERATION

Within the framework of its operation, the national institution shall:

a. Freely consider any questions falling within its competence, whether they are submitted by the Government or taken up by it without referral to a higher authority, on the proposal of its members or of any petitioner,

b. Hear any person and obtain any information and any documents necessary for assessing situations falling within its competence;

c. Address public opinion directly or through any press organ, particularly in order to publicize its opinions and recommendations;

d. Meet on a regular basis and whenever necessary in the presence of all its members after they have been duly concerned;

e. Establish working groups from among its members as necessary, and set up local or regional sections to assist it in discharging its functions;

f. Maintain consultation with the other bodies, whether jurisdictional or otherwise, responsible for the promotion and protection of human rights (in particular, ombudsmen, mediators and similar institutions);

g. In view of the fundamental role played by the non-governmental organizations in expanding the work of the national institutions, develop relations with the non-governmental organizations devoted to promoting and protecting human rights, to economic and social development, to combating racism, to protecting particularly vulnerable groups (especially children, migrant workers, refugees, physically and mentally disabled persons) or to specialized areas.

ADDITIONAL PRINCIPLES CONCERNING THE STATUS OF
COMMISSIONS WITH QUASI-JURISDICTIONAL COMPETENCE

A national institution may be authorized to hear and consider complaints and petitions concerning individual situations. Cases may be brought before it by individuals, their representatives, third parties, non-governmental organizations, associations of trade unions or any other representative organizations. In such circumstances, and without prejudice to the principles stated above concerning the other powers of the commissions, the functions entrusted to them may be based on the following principles:

a. Seeking an amicable settlement through conciliation or, within the limits prescribed by the law, through binding decisions or, where necessary, on the basis of confidentiality;

b. Informing the party who filed the petition of his rights, in particular the remedies available to him, and promoting his access to them;

c. Hearing any complaints or petitions or transmitting them to any other competent authority within the limits prescribed by the law;

d. Making recommendations to the competent authorities, especially by proposing amendments or reforms of the laws, regulations and administrative practices, especially if they have created the difficulties encountered by the persons filing the petitions in order to assert their rights.

Index

DATE DUE

MAR 0 7 2012	
FEB 1 0 2014	